Secret War in the Middle East

Andrew Rathmell
Secret War in the Middle East
The Covert Struggle for Syria, 1949-1961

New paperback edition published in 2014 by I.B.Tauris & Co Ltd
6 Salem Road, London W2 4BU
175 Fifth Avenue, New York NY 10010
www.ibtauris.com

First published in hardback in 1995 by Tauris Academic Studies, an imprint of I.B.Tauris & Co. Ltd

Copyright © Andrew Rathmell, 1995, 2014

The right of Andrew Rathmell to be identified as the author of this work has been asserted by him in accordance with the Copyright, Designs and Patent Act 1988.

All rights reserved. Except for brief quotations in a review, this book, or any part thereof, may not be reproduced, stored in or introduced into a retrieval system, or transmitted, in any form or by any means, electronic, mechanical, photocopying, recording or otherwise, without the prior written permission of the publisher.

ISBN: 978 1 78076 495 5

A full CIP record for this book is available from the British Library
A full CIP record is available from the Library of Congress

Library of Congress Catalog Card Number: available

Contents

Acknowledgements	vii
A note on transliteration	viii
Abbreviations	ix
Preface to paperback edition	xi

Introduction ... 1

CONSPIRACIES, COVERT ACTION AND TERRORISM/2
SYRIA: COVERT BATTLEGROUND/4   VICTIM AND
PERPETRATOR/5

1 Syria in its environment ... 7

HISTORY/7   DOMESTIC POLITICS/9
SYRIA'S GEOPOLITICAL POSITION/11
SUMMARY/20

2 Coups and covert action, 1949 ... 22

PROLOGUE/23   ZA'IM'S COUP/25
THE SA'ADAH AFFAIR/44   HINNAWI'S COUP/50
SHISHAKLI MAKES HIS MOVE/58

3 The Shishakli era, 1949–54 ... 62

'AZM'S GOVERNMENT/63   TRANSJORDANIAN
PLOTTING, SA'UDI AND EGYPTIAN TERRORISM/65
THE MIDDLE EAST COMMAND AND SHISHAKLI'S
COUP/73   SHISHAKLI'S DICTATORSHIP/78

4 Syria between Nasser and the West, 1954–56 ... 91

THE STRUGGLE COMMENCES/92   THE MALKI
ASSASSINATION/97   THE PRESIDENTIAL
ELECTIONS/103   THE IRAQI PLOT/111

CONTENTS

5 Battling the Eisenhower Doctrine, 1957–58   125
TERRORISM AND THE SSNP/126   SUBVERTING LEBANON/128   SUBVERTING JORDAN/131   THE AMERICAN PLOT/136   FORMATION OF THE UNITED ARAB REPUBLIC/143

6 The United Arab Republic, 1958–61   145
REACTIONS TO THE UNION/147   ISOLATING JORDAN/149   NASSER VS QASIM/153   DISCONTENT IN THE NORTHERN PROVINCE /158   THE END OF THE UNITED ARAB REPUBLIC/159

Conclusion   160
REWRITING SYRIAN HISTORY/163   PAST, PRESENT AND FUTURE/166

Notes   169

Appendix 1   Key dates   222

Appendix 2   Key personalities   223

Bibliography   227

Index   238

Acknowledgements

Many people helped me in the course of preparing this book. My thanks to all of them, especially those who agreed to be interviewed. In particular, I would like to record my debt to Dr Efraim Karsh whose supervision during my research for my doctoral thesis kept me on track. My thanks also to Patrick Seale whose introductions helped me to find my feet in Damascus. My fieldwork in the Middle East could not have been accomplished without the assistance of numerous friends. In Damascus, Beirut and Amman the staffs of the British Council offices were invariably helpful, as were the staff at the Institut Français pour les Etudes Arabes à Damas, the American University of Beirut and Jordan University. In Damascus Dr Muhammad Harb Farzat and Dr Georges Jabbour gave generously of their time. On my visits to Beirut I enjoyed the hospitality of Georges Charabati and his family and the assistance of Farid el-Khazen and Hisham Abu Jaoude. Itai Yemeni and Ronnie Bregman provided invaluable help in locating and translating Israeli sources. Needless to say, I take full responsibility for any errors of fact or judgement in the pages that follow.

My most profound debt is to my parents and my Oma, who have supported me every step of the way. It is to them that I dedicate this work.

Andrew Rathmell

A note on transliteration

In this book I have tried to adhere to a relatively simple form of transliteration and not use a proliferation of diacritical marks. The only ones used are *ayns* and *hamzas*. On the whole commonly accepted English forms are used, especially for Arabic place names.

For personal names, I have tried to strike a balance between forms well known to the Western reader and accuracy. Where the individuals themselves use a certain form in English or French then this has been retained, even where the transliteration may seem strange to the purist. For instance, Chamoun is used instead of Sham'un and Kobecsy instead of Qubaysi. King Hussein's spelling of his name has been retained, though Husayn has been used elsewhere. Commonly used Western renderings of names of certain well-known individuals have been retained. For instance, Malki instead of Maliki and Tlass instead of Talas. Where names of individuals have appeared only in third-party sources then these have either been transliterated by the author (if from an Arabic source) or kept as in the source material (if from a Western source).

Abbreviations

ABSP	Arab Ba'th Socialist Party
AIOC	Anglo-Iranian Oil Company
ALM	Arab Liberation Movement
ARAMCO	Arab-American Oil Company
ASP	Arab Socialist Party
CIA	Central Intelligence Agency
CIG	Central Intelligence Group
DGI	Directorate of General Intelligence
DMI	Directorate of Military Intelligence
DZ	Demilitarised Zone
ESS	Egypt-Syria-Sa'udi pact
IAF	Israeli Air Force
IBRD	International Bank for Reconstruction and Development
IDF	Israeli Defence Forces
IPC	Iraq Petroleum Company
JCS	Joint Chiefs of Staff
MEC	Middle East Command
MEDO	Middle East Defence Organisation
MEPL	Middle East Pipeline Ltd
NATO	North Atlantic Treaty Organisation
NSC	National Security Council
OCB	Operations Coordinating Board
RAF	Royal Air Force
RJAF	Royal Jordanian Air Force
SDECE	Service de Documentation Extérieure et de Contre-Espionage
SIS	Secret Intelligence Service
SSNP	Syrian Social Nationalist Party
Tapline	Trans-Arabian Pipeline Company
UAR	United Arab Republic
UN	United Nations

ABBREVIATIONS

UNF	United National Front
UNOGIL	United Nations Observer Group in Lebanon
UNRWA	United Nations Relief and Works Agency
UNSC	United Nations Security Council
UNTSO	United Nations Truce Supervision Organisation
USIS	United States Information Service

Sources

ANA	Arab News Agency
AUB	American University of Beirut
CF	Confidential File
CLS	Centre for Lebanese Studies, Oxford
DDEWHCF	Dwight D. Eisenhower White House Central Files
DDRS	Declassified Documents Reference System
DoS	Department of State
FO	Foreign Office
FOIA	Freedom of Information Act
FRUS	*Foreign Relations of the United States*
JFD	John Foster Dulles Papers
NARG	National Archives Record Group
PRO	Public Records Office
SCOR	*Security Council Official Records*
SS	Secretary of State
SWB	Summary of World Broadcasts
TC	Telephone Calls Series
WDDE	Dwight D. Eisenhower Diaries Series
WDH	Dulles-Herter Series
WHCF	White House Central Files
WHM	White House Memoranda Series
WHO	White House Office
WNSC	NSC Series

Currencies

LL	Lebanese Pounds
LS	Syrian Pounds
$	US Dollars
£	Pounds Sterling

Preface

This book tells the story of Syria, newly emerged from centuries of foreign rule, struggling to emerge as an independent actor in the Middle East. *Secret War* recounts how local, regional and global rivalries were played out inside Syria through political manoeuvrings, covert action, terrorism, and diplomatic and military intervention. Today, nearly two decades after the book was first published, Syria is once again at the centre of a high-stakes geopolitical struggle, albeit one waged with far more brutality than that recounted in these pages.

Today's conflict is very different from the one played out between 1949 and 1961. Syria's society, domestic politics and international environment have been transformed in the interim. The ideological fashions motivating participants inside Syria, and their foreign allies, have moved on; there are few serious partisans of socialism, communism or Ba'athism in the current struggle. Since 1961, Syria has been through urbanisation, land reform, nationalisation, the rise to power of a sectarian-based security elite and, more recently, the emergence of crony capitalism. Regionally, Saudi Arabia, Qatar and Iran now compete to impose their stamp on the country, with Egypt relegated to observer status.

Nonetheless, the current conflict has many echoes with that recounted in these pages. Many of today's news headlines would have been familiar to readers in the 1950s. Smuggling of arms and fighters across the Syrian-Lebanese border or plots and counterplots between Syrian, Turkish, Saudi and Jordanian intelligence are the stuff of the current conflict as much as they were half a century ago. While the old family elites who dominated Syria were largely swept away after the 1960s, the emergence of Shishaklis and Attasis in the front ranks of the opposition is a reminder that old symbols of authority still resonate. Meanwhile, though the wilder fringes of twenty- first -century Islamism such as Jabhat al-Nusra may bear little resemblance to their mid- twentieth-century forebears, Western concerns over rising Muslim Brotherhood influence in Syria's opposition sound very familiar. At the global level, a weakened Russia may not be looking to Syria as part of its Cold War rampart against the US, but the line-up of the US, UK and France behind their proxies, and Russia behind its, is all too familiar.

Bringing the story up to date

The narrative in this book stops in 1961 for two reasons. First, the end of the United Arab Republic marked a clear break in Syria's modern history, with the next chapter being of the gradual emergence of an ever narrower cabal within the Ba'ath party and the military, leading eventually to the consolidation of the Asad regime.

The second reason for stopping the story in 1961 was more pragmatic. At the time when this research was conducted, in the early-1990s, the Asad faction of the Ba'ath party was at the height of its powers. It was therefore impossible to do serious academic research that covered the period of its emergence – too many of the players were still active and had too many skeletons to hide. Indeed, during fieldwork for this book, even when interviewing then "retired" Ba'athists and other political actors, I had to deal with thinly veiled warnings from the ubiquitous Syrian *mukhabarat*.

Fortunately, distinguished scholars have filled in the story of the construction of the Ba'athist state.[1] From the 1960s to the 1970s, an already small political-military faction mutated into an even narrower military, sectarian and family elite. It was this consolidation, allied with nimble international footwork, that enabled Asad père to make Syria a regional force to be reckoned with. Taking a ruthless but astute approach to realpolitik, the regime obtained political, financial and materiel backing from Russia and the Gulf; brutally manipulated the conflict in Lebanon; and staved off US pressures with strategies that varied from cooperation, during the 1991 Gulf War, to covert conflict, in Lebanon in the mid-1980s and again in Iraq after 2003. In short, Syria became an arch manipulator and intervener.[2]

---

[1] Patrick Seale, *Asad: The Struggle for the Middle* East (London: I.B. Tauris, 1988); Nikolaos van Dam, *The Struggle for Power in Syria* (London: I.B. Tauris, 1979); Steven Heydemann, *Authoritarianism in Syria* (Ithaca, NY: Cornell University, 1999).

[2] Itamar Rabinovich, *The View from Damascus* (London: Valentine Mitchell, 2011).

Domestically, the construction of an authoritarian regime in the name of nationalism and socialism, but increasingly in the interests of a narrow, neo-patrimonial elite, led eventually to stasis.[3] Having brutally crushed any serious political opposition in the 1980s the regime morphed into one run by and on behalf of an intelligence apparatus – an archetypal "*mukhabarat* state".[4]

However, Hafez al-Asad's very success in building a coup-proof autocracy with a vast security apparatus stored up trouble for his son. Particularly after the turn of the century, the regime struggled to find ways of maintaining the combination of repressive capability and economic redistribution that had ensured domestic peace.[5] An abortive "Damascus spring", economic liberalisation which favoured crony capitalism and exacerbated socio-economic divides, and declining strategic rents, seriously weakened the regime.[6] By 2011, when the first winds of the wider "Arab spring" blew into Daraa, the "fierce" but weak Syrian state was rotting away. Against the backdrop of the Saudi-Iranian covert war, which escalated after the US invasion of Iraq, the growing disaffection of Syria's economic and political losers meant that Syrian rebels were able to make relatively rapid gains even against Syria's once unchallenged security apparatus.[7]

At the time of writing, it is hard to see how the Syrian regime can continue in the long term in its present form, but its resilience has surprised some observers who had hoped for a rapid Egypt or Libya style resolution. Whatever the course of the conflict in the coming months and years, it is sadly safe to say that there will be no peaceful transition. Syria's violent history, as well as bloody present, suggests that the

---

[3] Steven Heydemann & Reinoud Leenders, eds, *Middle East Authoritarianisms* (Stanford, CA: Stanford University Press, 2013).

[4] Radwan Ziadeh, *Power and Policy in Syria: Intelligence Services, Foreign Relations and Democracy in the Modern Middle East* (London: I.B. Tauris, 2012); Andrew Rathmell, "Syria's Intelligence Services: Origins and Development," *The Journal of Conflict Studies* (Vol. XVI, No. 2) Fall 1996, pp. 75-96.

[5] Raymond Hinnebusch and Soren Schmidt, *The State and the Political Economy of Reform in Syria* (St Andrews: St Andrews University, 2009); Raymond Hinnebusch, *Syria: Revolution from Above* (London: Routledge, 2002).

[6] Alan George, *Syria: neither Bread nor Freedom* (London: Zed Books, 2003); Volker Perthes, *Syria under Bashar al-Asad: Modernisation and the Limits of Change* (London: IISS, 2004).

[7] Stephen Starr, *Revolt in Syria* (London: Hurst, 2012); David W. Lesch, *Syria: The Fall of the House of Assad* (New Haven; Yale University Press, 2012).

process of trying to build a more civil polity at peace with its neighbours will be a very long haul indeed.

Why this new edition ?

The fact that Syria's current crisis contains echoes of the past recounted in this book proves the maxim that, given its location on several geopolitical faultlines, Syria will either be troubled or will be trouble. For its first three decades after independence, Syria's weakness, which enabled its neighbours to play out their rivalries, destabilised the region. For the following three decades, as Hafez al-Asad consolidated his rule, Syria was able to throw its weight around in the region, acting as a thorn in the side of the dominant powers. Now, with the slow-motion collapse of the Asad regime, Syria once again finds itself acting as a regional maelstrom, sucking in regional and international powers and exporting instability.

As a new Syria struggles to emerge from the ruins of the old, and as Syria's neighbours and the great powers compete over the carcass of the state, it is critical for everyone involved to have a clear picture of how modern Syria emerged. Given the many continuities with the past, contemporary policy-makers, and Syrian actors themselves, need an unvarnished picture of their past in order to build a better future.

This book is not an update on the story of the period 1949-1961. Having left academia over a decade ago, I will leave it to others to mine the archives and add further texture to the story told in these pages. Since the original publication, there has been some excellent work which has added nuance and detail to the story. Rather, my intention in re-publishing is to ensure that those who will be making decisions on the future of Syria are equipped with a detailed understanding of the history that has shaped this magnificent yet troubled land.

Since my departure from academia at the start of the so-called "9/11"wars, I have worked on the frontline of attempts to transform fractured and conflict-ridden states into stable and peaceable societies. A key lesson from this experience is the danger of seeking solutions which are ahistorical and not fit for the local context.[8] There always

---

[8] Andrew Rathmell, "Planning post-conflict reconstruction in Iraq: what can we learn?," *International Affairs*, Vol. 81, No. 4 (2005), pp. 1015-1040; Andrew Rathmell, *Reframing Security Sector Reform for Counterinsurgency - Getting the Politics Right* (NATO Defence College, 14th Forum Paper 'Complex Operations: NATO at War and on the Margins of War') July 2010.

seems to be too little knowledge of the context. Having had the privilege of working with a range of Syrian activists and international officials involved in the Syrian conflict over the past year, it is striking how little knowledge there is about Syria's history, society or politics. My hope is that this re-publication will help to fill this gap.

A dedication

Since 2012, I have had the honour and privilege of working with courageous and principled Syrian men and women who are risking their all to build a better society. This edition is dedicated to those Syrians of all political persuasions who are working towards a resolution of the current conflict and who cling to a vision of a more positive future.

Andrew Rathmell
Oxford
August 2013

Introduction

'For all Middle Eastern players dirty tricks were an accepted extension of diplomacy. ... Politics were often reduced to struggles between rival intelligence agencies.'

Patrick Seale, *Asad*[1]

'In the Near East, the language of terrorism doubled the usual diplomatic channels.'

Michel Seurat, *L'État de Barbarie*[2]

The shadow world of the secret agent and the terrorist looms large in popular perceptions of the Middle East. In Arab countries the conspiracy theory has been elevated to an art form. In the West the spectre of terrorism often dominates coverage of the region. Political violence and covert intrigue have long played major roles in the politics of the modern Middle East and they continue to do so. A cursory reading of a typical day's headlines in either the Western or the Arabic press will confirm this. What published contemporary accounts cannot however document are the scope and range of the covert activities that underlie visible events. Observers are all too often wrong-footed when the results of machinations in the secret world come to light. Behind the overt comings and goings of diplomats shelter the shadowy activities of secret agents.

And yet scholars have been reluctant to focus on these issues. Citing the lack of reliable source material, they have left the field to journalists and writers of popular fiction. This reluctance has meant that our understanding of politics in the Middle East is only partial. No diplomatic or political history can explain events if it omits the roles played by covert action and political violence. Admittedly, academics are in a poor position to write authoritatively on such issues in a contemporary context. However, recent historical work on British and US intelligence activities has shown that it is possible to use archival material to shed light on this twilight world.

This study explores these themes by taking an in-depth look at Syrian politics and foreign relations from 1949 to 1961. This was a period of great fluidity in Syrian political life. The newly independent country was riven by internal strife as the nationalist coalition that had led Syria to independence succumbed to internal disunity and to the onslaught of a variety of more ideological and disciplined parties. At the same time, Syria was intimately involved in the conflicts that racked the region – the Arab-Israeli struggle, the inter-Arab competition between dynasties and states and the East–West Cold War.

The combination of these cross-cutting rivalries and conflicts provided both the motive and the opportunity for extensive use of 'dirty tricks'. The struggle for power in Syria was of concern to a far wider circle than the Syrian politicians and officers directly involved. The fate of Syria aroused the interest of the great powers as well as of its neighbours. All of these governments actively pursued their interests in the country, often launching covert operations or sponsoring terrorism when they deemed it necessary.

Conspiracies, covert action and terrorism

Any student of the Middle East soon realises that, in Arab countries, the 'conspiracy theory' explanation for events holds pride of place.[3] Political actors and observers alike, and also public opinion, tend to believe that major political developments are orchestrated by external powers. Political opponents commonly accuse each other of being agents of a foreign power.

This tendency is perhaps understandable in societies which were for centuries controlled from foreign capitals and in countries which owe their very existence to the secret diplomacy of external powers. Outside observers should nonetheless not dismiss this trait as merely a curious cultural anomaly. Although the cruder conspiracy theories may do more to illuminate the state of mind of the theorist than they do political events, it is clear that intelligence agencies have had a role in shaping events in the Middle East, just as they have elsewhere in the world.

Scholarly literature on the activities of intelligence services in the Middle East is sparse. Numerous works have been produced dealing with Israel's intelligence services but most are poorly documented and lack objectivity.[4] Some of the more significant activities of Western intelligence services, such as the removal of the Mossadeq government in Iran in 1953 by the American Central Intelligence Agency (CIA) and the British Secret Intelligence Service (SIS) or the assassinations of Algerian nationalist leaders by France's Service de Documentation Extériure et de Contre-Espionage (SDECE) in the 1950s have been researched.[5] On the whole, though, scholars have had to depend on memoirs of former intelligence officers, which are of dubious reliability.[6] The activities of Arab intelligence services remain almost wholly unstudied.[7]

This book deals with conspiracies initiated or abetted by intelligence services in pursuit of foreign policy goals. In modern intelligence terminology such activity comes under the rubric of 'covert action'.[8] This can be defined as 'any operation or activity designed to influence foreign governments, persons or events in support of the sponsoring government's foreign policy objectives while keeping the sponsoring government's *support* of the operation secret'.[9] Covert operations can be grouped into three categories: *propaganda, political action* and *paramilitary*. Propaganda is often overt but in its covert forms it may be grey, 'in which true sponsorship is not acknowledged', or black, purporting to come 'from a source other than the true one'.[10] Political action involves 'attempts to change the balance of political forces in a country, most often by providing money to particular groups'.[11] Paramilitary operations may involve secret military aid or training, or actual participation in acts of subversive violence.[12]

Terrorism is one type of paramilitary operation. Essentially it is just another tool in the covert operator's armoury. The approach taken here is in line with Professor Paul Wilkinson's observation that terrorism 'is *not* a philosophy or a political movement. Terrorism is a weapon or method which has been used throughout history by both states and sub-state organizations for a whole variety of political causes and purposes.'[13] The key problem with employing the term is that, to date, governments and scholars alike have found it impossible to agree on what precisely the term means.

For the purposes of this study the definition proposed by American academic Thomas Thornton will be adopted. Thornton defined terrorism as: 'a symbolic act designed to influence political behaviour by extranormal means, entailing the use or threat of violence'.[14]

This book is concerned partly with the activities of sub-state groups but primarily with clandestine state agents. In the terminology of contemporary terrorism studies, the focus is 'state-sponsored' and 'state-supported' terrorism.[15] American lawyer John Murphy has defined these terms. Sponsorship indicates that a state 'contributes active planning, direction and control to terrorist operations' whereas support signifies a lesser degree of direct state control and will cover a variety of relationships.[16]

Syria: covert battleground

Syria in the 1950s provides an excellent case study of the covert dimension of international politics since during this period international conflicts in the Middle East often centred on the country. Powerful interests were at stake and numerous states and factions were engaged in the no-holds barred free-for-all that was the 'Struggle for Syria'. As Patrick Seale wrote in 1965 in his book of that title:

> Syria ... held so central a position ... that for a state to have an 'Arab policy' in the post-war years came primarily to mean for it to have a plan concerning Syria: to seek to extend its influence there ... or ... to prevent a rival from entrenching itself there. ... When reduced to terms of power politics, the story of the struggle for Arab unity in the past two decades has been little else than that of rival bids to control Syria. ...
>
> [Syria] was also the hinge on which more grandiose setpieces of diplomacy attempted by both the West and the Soviet Union turned. It was to a very large extent on the plane of internal Syrian politics that were fought the decisive battles over the Baghdad Pact, the Eisenhower Doctrine, and Russia's bid to bring Syria within the Soviet sphere of influence in 1957.[17]

The Syrian case is made even more interesting by the fact that it provides a link with contemporary debates over terrorism. At the time of writing Syria is labelled by the US government as a sponsor of international terrorism. In recent years much concern has been expressed by both governments and observers in the West at the role of Syria's intelligence agencies in supporting subversion and terrorism.[18] Syrians, however, often portray themselves as being victims of terrorism rather than perpetrators.[19] By examining the 1950s one can gain some historical perspective and better appreciate the Syrian state's dual role as both perpetrator and victim.

Academic studies on Syria during the 1950s are relatively sparse. Syrian historians have paid little attention to the period. History in contemporary Syria is largely the domain of the ruling Ba'th party and its ideologists, leaving little room for independent scholarship.[20] Western research has made surprisingly little progress since Patrick Seale's *The Struggle for Syria* was first published. Although an excellent account of Syrian politics during the period from independence to the formation of the United Arab Republic, Seale wrote his book without the benefit of the archival material now available. Other standard works include Gordon H. Torrey's *Syrian Politics and the Military 1945–1958* and Nikolas Van Dam's *The Struggle for Power in Syria* but these focus primarily on internal politics and the rise to power of the Ba'th party, rather than on foreign relations.[21] More general surveys of modern Syrian history such as Tabitha Petran's *Syria*, Derek Hopwood's *Syria 1945–1986: Politics and Society* and Volker Perthes' *Staat und Gesellschaft in Syrien: 1970–1989* provide little fresh material on the 1950s.[22]

Four recent studies have used archival material to look specifically at Syria's foreign relations. Itamar Rabinovich's *The Road Not Taken: Early Arab-Israeli Negotiations* examined Syrian-Israeli relations in the immediate aftermath of the first Arab-Israeli War. Anthony Gorst and W. Scott Lucas' article, 'The Other Collusion: Operation Straggle and Anglo-American Intervention in Syria, 1955–56', focused on British and American covert action in Syria at the time of Suez. Douglas Little's article, 'Cold War and Covert Action: the United States and Syria 1945–1958', dealt with US covert operations in Syria until 1958. David Lesch's thesis, *The United States and Syria, 1953–1957: The Cold War in the Middle East*, covered US-Syrian relations in the same period more comprehensively.[23] These works formed a useful basis for this study but they all have their limitations. First, they only cover part of the period and some of the actors. This book, in contrast, covers the period from 1949 to 1961 as a whole. It also looks in detail at the roles of Jordan, Iraq, Lebanon and groups such as the Syrian Social Nationalist Party, rather than just focusing on Israel, the United States or Britain as the other studies have done. Second, all previous studies share the weakness of an almost exclusive reliance on US and British official documents. Such documents must form the core of any account but they need to be supplemented by Middle Eastern sources, specifically press, memoirs and interviews.

Victim and perpetrator

Commenting on the Syrian regime in the early 1980s, French sociologist Michel Seurat argued that 'they export their state terrorism to establish it as a new code of international relations'. The intention of this study is to demonstrate that such a 'diplomacy of "pistoleros"' is nothing new.[24] During the 1950s covert action and state-sponsored terrorism were the common currency of international relations in the Middle East. Syria was both the victim and the perpetrator of 'dirty tricks'. In the early 1950s Syria was largely a battleground on which rival intelligence services competed. By the late 1950s, Syria's intelligence agencies had become aggressively active abroad. For many Syrians, the history of the 1950s is one of foreign conspiracies. Many Lebanese and Jordanians, meanwhile, recall the late 1950s as a time of Syrian subversion and terrorism.

It is hoped that the story told in the pages that follow will provide the fullest account yet available of the shadow world underlying the politics of these turbulent years. At the very least this account will enable outsiders to better comprehend the forces which have shaped Syria. If it also helps Syrians to better understand their recent past then the author's labours will not have been in vain.

I

Syria in its environment

The aim of this chapter is to set the context of the story, to introduce the actors and to outline their interests in the 'struggle for Syria'. This will be done by presenting a synopsis of Syrian history up to independence and then outlining the political forces in the country and the interests and activities of external parties. The discussion of Syrian political parties will be brief since there is no need to duplicate already published work. The discussion of Syria's foreign relations will be lengthier. This is necessary since in subsequent chapters much attention will be paid to the intrigues occasioned by the conflicting interests and philosophies outlined here. In this chapter, I have attempted to reduce these issues to their bare essentials. The description of inter-Arab and Great Power rivalries given here applies primarily to the late 1940s and early 1950s. In the mid-1950s patterns shifted with the rise of Nasserism, the decline in British influence and the rise of Soviet influence. Later, in 1958, the Iraqi revolt upset the pattern of politics in the Mashreq by removing one of the two remaining Hashimite kingdoms. These changes will be discussed at the appropriate point in the story. Nonetheless, the background below provides a framework in which these changes can be seen in context.

History

During the Ottoman occupation of geographical Syria, which began in 1516, administrative control was divided up between *vilayets* (provinces) centred on the region's major towns.[1] The collapse of Ottoman rule in the wake of Turkey's defeat in World War I led to a re-organisation of the region's political structures.[2] In October 1918, Amir Faysal, son of Sharif Husayn of the Hijaz, entered Damascus with his troops. He hoped to replace Turkish suzerainty with the sovereignty of his family, the Hashimites. In agreements between his father and the British, known as the Husayn-McMahon correspondence, the Hashimites had been promised the opportunity to establish an Arab state in return for their role in leading the Arab revolt against the Ottomans.[3] However, under the terms of the Sykes-Picot agreement, signed between Britain and France in 1916, the Ottoman territories were to be divided up between the European powers.[4] The Paris Peace Conference and an American commission of enquiry failed to settle the conflicting claims but at the Conference of San Remo in April 1920 France was awarded Mandatory authority over the territory of Syria and Lebanon.[5] French troops enforced their claims and, after defeating his army at Maysalun, evicted Faysal from Damascus on 25 July 1920. The League of Nations formally ratified the French Mandate on 24 July 1922.[6]

The French Mandated territory was divided into several political units, known as 'The Levantine States'.[7] These were the states of Aleppo and Damascus (in 1924 combined into a single Syrian state), Greater Lebanon and the governments of Latakia (the 'Alawi State') and the Jabal Druze. Between 1925 and 1927 opposition to French rule boiled over into a rebellion which temporarily removed French forces from the Jabal Druze and southern Syria, before being crushed by French-led forces.[8] In December 1936 a 'Treaty of Friendship and Alliance between France and Syria' was signed which set out the residual rights that France would have in Syria upon her entry to the League of Nations as an independent state, which was to take place after three years.[9] However, when Leon Blum's Popular Front government fell, the French Senate refused to ratify the treaty. At the same time the Jabal Druze and Latakia were annexed to the Syrian state. The Sanjak of Alexandretta had become part of the French Mandate in 1920 but Turkish claims to it persisted. They were resolved in 1939 when France, seeking Turkey's favour in the looming war, ceded control over the territory. This move was a bitter blow to Syrian nationalists, who were further disappointed when the Vichy regime, established after France's capitulation in July 1940, declared the continuation of the Mandate.

In the summer of 1941 British and Free French forces invaded Syria and Lebanon and on 27 September 1941 France formally proclaimed the independence of Syria. In July 1943 constitutional government was restored and elections took place. Shukri al-Quwatli became President and National Bloc politicians dominated the cabinet. The Bloc were nationalist politicians who had negotiated independence between the wars and represented the traditional ruling classes.[10] The government which took over liberated France in 1944, however, proved unwilling to give up Syria and Lebanon so easily. During 1944 and 1945, France refused to hand over control of the locally raised Troupes

Spéciales and insisted on negotiating binding treaties. In May 1945 fighting broke out when the French tried to impose their will on an increasingly recalcitrant population. After French-led forces bombarded Damascus, Britain, which regarded a stable Levant as in its interest, intervened militarily and pressured France into fulfilling its commitments. On 15 April 1946 the last French troops withdrew from Damascus.[11]

Domestic politics

Traditionally, Syrian politics were dominated by Sunni landowning and merchant families who operated a semi-feudal system which changed little with the advent of democratic elections. While the National Bloc had been the unifying national movement during the struggle for independence, within the Bloc there were centrifugal rivalries between towns and dynasties. By the time of the 1947 elections, the Bloc was splitting apart and was also coming under pressure from more modern, ideologically motivated parties.[12]

In early 1947 the dominant wing of the Bloc transformed itself into the National Party. This was led by Damascene notables who derived their position from their record of nationalist struggle against the French and their control of patronage networks among the city's lower middle class. Shukri Quwatli, who had led the Bloc since 1940 and held the Presidency since 1943, was the most prominent figure in the National Party. His family had long had good connections with the House of Sa'ud, a relationship that guided his foreign orientation. Other Damascene notables, notably Jamil Mardam Bey, Faris al-Khuri, Lutfi al-Haffar and Sabri al-'Asali, worked with him in the new party.[13]

In August 1948, Quwatli's opponents in the Bloc organised themselves into the People's Party. This was led by Aleppo notables Rushdi al-Kikhia, Nazim al-Qudsi and Mustafa Barmada. The origins of the split could be traced to rivalry between Quwatli's Damascene backers and the business community in Aleppo, a city which had lost its traditional role as trading station for the Fertile Crescent as a result of the creation of the Syrian state. Although most of the People's Party leaders did not want to risk Syria's republicanism, they tended to favour close ties, even federation, with Iraq so as to regain Aleppo's traditional economic status. The party also gained the support of the powerful Atasi family, which controlled the Homs region.[14]

The National and People's parties had little interest in ideologies or doctrines. They were loose alliances of community leaders concerned with taking and holding power in order to further the interests of their clients and clans. They attempted to smother controversy with consensus and would compromise in the face of serious opposition, whether in parliament or on the streets. The other four major parties, in contrast, were more 'modern' in terms of their organised party structures and dedication to formal ideologies.[15]

The Syrian Social Nationalist Party (SSNP), formed in 1932 in Beirut by Antun Sa'adah, advocated the creation of a Greater Syrian state which would include Syria, Lebanon, Jordan, Palestine and Cyprus.[16] Its ideology was divided into two sets of principles, national (or basic) and reform. The eight national principles defined Syrian nationalism and stressed the dissociation of the Syrian nation from the Arab nation. The five reform principles concerned secularising and modernising measures to be applied in a future Greater Syrian state.[17] The SSNP has often been labelled as fascistic due to its ideology, the dictatorial style of Sa'adah's leadership and its espousal of violence.[18] While this label is rejected by party adherents, it is clear that Sa'adah accepted the necessity for armed struggle. His fifth reform principle stated 'force is the decisive factor in the assertion ... of national right'.[19] Always an elitist, rather than mass, party it gained large numbers of influential supporters in the region but its strongholds were Lebanon and Syria. Although it was never able to seize power, the SSNP was to play a leading role in political conflicts in both countries.

The Ba'th Party, led by Syrian school teachers Michel 'Aflaq and Salah al-Din Bitar, was formally inaugurated at its first congress in 1947. Its ideological trinity was reflected in the slogan 'unity, liberation and socialism'. Its primary goal was the resurrection of what it believed was the one Arab nation. This involved reuniting the Arab world which had been divided, according to the Ba'th, by foreign imperialism. This unity would enable the Arabs to achieve the second goal, of freeing the Arab world of foreign imperialism and colonialism. Socialism was the least important of the party's goals but was seen to be the natural concomitant of Arab nationalism. In practice the Ba'th focused its attacks on the traditional parties, which it labelled agents of the 'imperialists', serving only their own class interests.[20]

During the late 1940s and the 1950s, the fledgling Ba'th Party was closely associated with Akram al-Hawrani. Hawrani was a populist socialist leader from Hama who had significant support among the peasantry and in the army. Backed by his Arab Socialist Party, he emerged as a leading radical force opposing the traditional parties and 'imperialist' powers. Between 1948 and 1953 the two groups worked closely together and in 1953 the parties merged.

The Communist Party, led since 1932 by Khalid Baqdash, had maintained good relations with Quwatli during the war and had established itself as a leading political force. In early 1944 it had split from the Syrian-Lebanese Communist Party to form an independent Syrian Party. It maintained close relations with the French Communist Party and strongly opposed Hashimite schemes for unity as these would involve the expansion of British influence. However, the USSR's favourable attitude to the establishment of a Jewish state, evinced by its vote in favour of the Palestine Partition Plan at the United Nations in November 1947, discredited the party and it was dissolved in December 1947.[21] None the less, as Walter Laqueur noted, 'there seems to have existed some tacit understanding between the Syrian police and the Communist Party, and the communists could, in fact, do as they liked, within certain ... limits. They were persecuted only when their publications printed particularly violent anti-government material or when their demonstrations got out of hand.'[22] The relative strength of the Syrian Communist Party and its activity through front organisations, such as the 'Partisans of Peace', was to be a major source of concern for Western governments and their Arab allies as the Cold War evolved.[23]

The remaining significant party was the Muslim Brotherhood. Founded in Egypt in 1928 by Hasan al-Banna, the Brethren agitated for the adoption of strict Islamic social practices and the institution of an Islamic government. The Syrian Brotherhood had been put on a formal footing after its first congress in September 1946.[24] As was to be the case with future generations of Brethren, its modest successes in Syrian electoral politics aroused a great deal of alarm among its secular opponents and in the West.[25] Although first banned during Za'im's rule, the Brotherhood re-emerged in the November 1949 elections following his overthrow as one of four groups which constituted Shaykh Mustafa al-Siba'i's Islamic Socialist Front.[26] This Front was described by one of its leaders as a 'Marxist drink in a Moslem cup', and advocated reformist social measures and an anti-Western stance in addition to the extension of Islamic laws.[27]

Syria's geopolitical position

After the withdrawal of French forces, Syria found itself at the conjunction of three circles of international conflict. The first, the competition between the Hashimite dynasty and their Arab rivals, had been in progress since the end of World War I but took on a different form after the granting of independence to the Levantine Mandates. The second, the Arab-Zionist struggle for control of Palestine, entered a new stage with British withdrawal and the establishment of the state of Israel. The third, the rivalry between the Great Powers, also changed its nature with the collapse of French influence and the onset of the Cold War.

Inter-Arab

Since being thwarted in their attempts to construct a unitary Arab state ruled from Damascus, the Hashimites had sought redress for their grievances. After his ejection from Damascus, Faysal had gained the support of Britain to become king of newly created Iraq in 1921. His older brother, 'Abdallah, angry both at Faysal's usurpation (the throne of Iraq had been promised to him) and the Anglo-French carve up of Arab lands, marched north from the family home in the Hijaz ostensibly intent on re-taking Damascus. In the event, he halted in Amman, capital of the British mandate of Transjordan. In July 1922 Britain recognised his rule over the territory east of the river Jordan, in return for his pledge to respect the French Mandate to his north.

As Seale put it, 'the Hashimite failure to carry out their family plan resulted in two powerful currents of thwarted ambition'.[28] Faysal I died in 1933 but his successors developed the concept of a union of countries in the so-called 'Fertile Crescent'. Faysal's grandson, Faysal II, did not reach the age of majority until May 1953 and in the meantime Iraq was ruled by the Regent 'Abd ul-Ilah and the general-turned-politician Nuri al-Sa'id.[29] It was Nuri al-Sa'id who, in December 1942, put forward detailed proposals for a Fertile Crescent union, declaring that 'in my view the only fair solution, and indeed the only hope of securing permanent peace, contentment and progress in these Arab areas is for the United Nations to declare *now* ... that Syria, Lebanon, Palestine and Trans-Jordan shall be reunited into one state'.[30] The plan involved the union of the component parts of a Greater Syria, which encompassed the same area as that envisaged by Antun Sa'adah, with the exception of Cyprus, and the new state's subsequent accession to an Arab League with Iraq which would have a single ruler.

'Abdallah's ambition, meanwhile, envisaged only the creation of a Greater Syria.[31] Syria and Transjordan were to form a federal or confederal unit, to which Lebanon and Palestine would subsequently affiliate. Notwithstanding the coincidence of interests, the Hashimite monarchies proved unable to cooperate fully. Discussions on unity took place during World War II and gathered pace after Transjordan's independence in March 1946. In the event these talks resulted only in the signing of an insignificant Treaty of Alliance and Brotherhood, on 15 April 1947.

Apart from family disagreements, Hashimite schemes were thwarted by their regional rivals, Egypt and Sa'udi Arabia.

Egypt came to adopt the slogans of Arab nationalism in the early 1940s, partly as a result of domestic political rivalries.[32] In reaction to Nuri al-Sa'id's Fertile Crescent proposals, Egyptian Prime Minister Mustafa al-Nahhas initiated discussions with other Arab leaders on the formation of an alternative form of Arab grouping. In October 1944 the leaders of Iraq, Syria, Lebanon, Yemen, Sa'udi Arabia and Transjordan agreed to the Alexandria Protocol, which in March 1945 became the Arab League Charter. Backed by Britain, which saw the scheme as a way of preserving its dominant role, Cairo took on the leadership of the League.[33] The Charter was a framework which recognised the post-Mandate system of sovereign and independent states. Although the Hashimites were mollified by the inclusion of article nine, which read: 'states of the League which desire to establish closer cooperation and stronger bonds than are provided by this Pact may conclude agreements to that end', the Charter was essentially at odds with both of the Hashimite schemes.[34]

In this respect the pact reflected Egypt's traditional desire to prevent the emergence of a united Mashreq which would rival its position. As P.J. Vatikiotis put it, 'short of imposing its own hegemony over the western Fertile Crescent ... it has been a foremost Egyptian national interest [from the early times of its history] to deprive others ... from doing so'.[35] Specifically, in the late 1940s and early 1950s, Egypt sought to prevent Syria falling under the sway of Amman or Baghdad.

Sa'udi Arabian policy likewise opposed the Hashimites but for dynastic as well as geopolitical reasons. Ibn Sa'ud's troops had forced the elder Hashimite, Husayn, to abdicate the throne of the Hijaz in 1924 and in 1925 had forced his son 'Ali out of Jeddah. Having thus conquered the Hashimites' ancestral homelands, the Sa'udis were concerned at the prospects for Hashimite irredentism. A union of Syria with either Iraq or Jordan would give Husayn's descendants the resources to recapture the territories they had lost to the House of Sa'ud. Sa'udi leaders thus sought to prevent the extension of Hashimite influence by taking any opportunities that arose to thwart pro-Hashimite elements in Syria.[36]

Palestine and Israel

The second arena of conflict was the struggle over Palestine. The Arab Revolt of 1936–39 had galvanised Arab public opinion and the wave of Jewish immigration after World War II intensified Arab fears and opposition to the establishment of a Jewish state. The struggle for Palestine was instrumental in shaping Arab politics, especially after the defeat of the Arab armies in 1948. Syria was intimately involved in the struggle, by virtue of its geographical proximity and strongly held beliefs that Palestine was part of the Syrian homeland, 'southern Syria'.

In the years following the first Arab-Israeli war, the Palestine question played a crucial role in Syrian politics in two respects. First, the cause of Palestine, or more specifically avenging the shame of the Zionist victory, became one of the central issues on which any political leader was judged. Although some Syrian rulers were privately willing to accept Israel and to establish a *modus vivendi*, public opinion, as mobilised by opposition parties, would not accept this.[37] Governments thus had limited room for manoeuvre and had to toe a fierce anti-Zionist line in public.

The other major impact was that Syrian leaders were haunted by a sense of insecurity and what they feared were Israel's expansionist tendencies. The country's primary national security objective became to resist the Israeli military threat. Damascus was constantly reminded of this threat by frequent border clashes in which Israeli arms usually prevailed. These disputes centred around three Demilitarised Zones (DZs), two in the Hula Valley marshes and one south of the Sea of Galilee, and upon fishing rights on the Sea of Galilee. During the 1949 armistice negotiations Syria withdrew from its forward positions, which were then declared demilitarised under the supervision of the United Nations Truce Supervision Organisation (UNTSO).[38] Sovereignty over these areas was left undecided, pending peace negotiations. Since these never took place and Syria rejected Israeli proposals to divide the territories, they remained the subject of dispute. In early 1951 Israel began work on draining the marshes, preparatory to building an irrigation canal. Viewing this activity as an Israeli attempt to establish *de facto* control over the DZs, Syrian forces harassed the Israelis with sniper and artillery fire. Over the following years the dispute escalated as Israel continued its encroachments (introducing armed frontier police into the zones, evicting Arab villagers and beginning work on the canal itself in September 1953) while Syrian forces continued to fire on Israeli workers and settlers. However, Syria was unable to stop the Israeli advances, often being outgunned by the Israeli Defence Forces (IDF).[39]

Writing in 1967, Israeli commentator Ze'ev Schiff described succinctly the character of the border dispute:

> These incidents generally took on the following form: Israelis desired

to cultivate a piece of land which they claimed to be in Israeli possession, while the Syrians interfered by gunfire from their positions on the heights, arguing that the land was theirs. Israel would persist in cultivating the land and returned fire. ... Israel was generally the more successful in these battles. She was able to mobilize greater means and her development plans were more thorough.[40]

Meanwhile, on the Sea of Galilee there were disputes over the exercise of fishing rights enjoyed since the 1920s by fishermen on the Syrian side of the now Israeli-controlled lake and over Syria's attempts to prevent Israeli boats coming close to its shores. There were numerous engagements between Israeli police boats and Syrian shore positions as well as instances of Syrian troops firing on Israeli fishing boats.[41]

Apart from inflaming Syrian public opinion in general, the effect of this chronic tension was described by an American Chargé d'Affaires in Damascus. Writing in 1951, he argued that the:

> record of [the] last two years proves Syria will procure arms with whatever cost to constitutional ideals and development possibilities and that it will accord internal leadership to whoever can procure them and friendship to [the] country which supplies them. ... [The] Syrian conception of [the] purpose of [these] arms is ... primarily security against [a] feared Israeli attack and only secondarily security against Communist aggression.[42]

Great Powers

The third arena of conflict was Great Power rivalry. During the Mandatory period Anglo-French competition had shaped the region's politics. After World War II French influence receded and Britain enjoyed a predominant position. British influence, however, soon went into decline as the country struggled through the process of decolonisation and the evolving Cold War saw an extension of American influence into the region.

Britain As had been the case between the wars, Britain's main interests in the Middle East after World War II were to protect its communication routes to east of Suez and its oil supplies. Along with these interests British military planners began to focus on the possibility of general war with the Soviet Union. This possibility reinforced the central position of the Middle East in British strategy and Clement Attlee's Labour government made strenuous efforts after 1945 to preserve Britain's strategic position.[43]

In pressuring France to leave the Levant, Britain had emerged as the dominant power in the Eastern Mediterranean. In the immediate aftermath of World War II London helped the Greek government to resist assaults from communist insurgents and encouraged Turkey to oppose the Soviet Union's territorial claims. Iraq, although independent since 1932, was linked to Britain by the 1930 'Preferential Alliance' which gave Britain the right to station forces in Iraq and use the airbases at Habbaniyya and Shu'aiba. Transjordan was dependent on British aid and British officers controlled its Arab Legion. The 1936 Anglo-Egyptian treaty had given Britain basing rights in the Suez Canal Zone and during the war the British Middle East Command had transformed the Zone into a huge military depot.[44]

By the late 1940s, however, Britain's position was under threat from its own economic weakness and from rising indigenous nationalisms. Attlee's government responded to these pressures by seeking to draw the United States into supporting Britain's position in the region, while concluding revised bilateral treaties with Arab leaders which would preserve Britain's military basing rights at a lower profile.

In early 1947 the British government informed Washington that it would no longer be able to support the Greek and Turkish governments. President Harry S. Truman responded by formulating the doctrine that came to bear his name and talks were initiated on coordinating American and British policies in the region. On the whole, London succeeded in persuading the United States to provide the backing which enabled Britain to maintain its leading role in the region.

Britain's handling of local nationalist pressures was not so successful. This was most marked in Palestine where the Arab-Zionist rivalries led Britain to hand over the problem to the United Nations in February 1947 and carry out a hasty withdrawal the following year. In April 1946 discussions with Egypt began on revising the 1936 treaty and a draft treaty was prepared calling for the evacuation of British troops by September 1949.[45] However, disagreements over the future of Sudan, which Egypt wanted united with itself and Britain wanted independent, led to the collapse of the talks. Although British troops withdrew from Egypt's cities to the Suez Canal Zone by March 1947, the presence of these troops embittered Anglo-Egyptian relations and provoked escalating banditry and guerrilla attacks. In Iraq, Salih Jabr became Prime Minister in March 1947 and talks began on revising the 1930 treaty. A treaty was signed at Portsmouth on 15 January 1948, giving Iraq peacetime control of the bases. Publication of the treaty, however, provoked nationalist riots in Iraq and it was repudiated after the collapse of Jabr's government later the same month.[46] The only country in which a British military role was welcomed was Transjordan. In March 1948 King 'Abdallah responded to nationalist pressures by concluding a new 'Treaty of Alliance' to replace the 'Preferential Alliance' which had been signed on independence. Like the aborted Anglo-Iraqi treaty, this gave Transjordan peacetime control over its military bases (apart from two airbases) but granted Britain extensive wartime rights.[47]

As Britain's position deteriorated, it reconsidered its strategy in the region. By 1950 the old method of using bilateral treaties to ensure basing rights was being replaced by attempts to bring host countries into multilateral alliances which would include the weight of the United States and make it easier for Arab governments to accept a British presence.

The United States Between the wars, the United States had been only marginally concerned with the Middle East but the perceived growth of communist influence in the late 1940s led to a greater US role in the region. When asking Congress to authorise aid to Turkey and Greece in March 1947, Truman argued that: 'it must be the policy of the United States to support free peoples who are resisting attempted subjugation by armed minorities or by outside pressures'.[48]

During October 1947 the United States and Britain held talks to coordinate their roles in the Middle East. The State Department outlined its approach to the region, stating:

> we now take full cognizance of the tremendous value of this area as a highway ... between the East and the West; of its possession of great mineral wealth; of its potentially rich agricultural resources. We also realize the serious consequences which would result if the rising nationalism of the peoples of the Middle East should harden in a mould of hostility to the West. Our main objective is therefore to prevent great power ambitions and rivalries and local discontents and jealousies from developing into open conflict which might eventually lead to a third world war.[49]

In November President Truman confirmed the American position when he approved a paper stating that 'the security of the Eastern Mediterranean and of the Middle East is vital to the security of the United States'.[50] The US administration decided that Britain should take the lead in the region, due to its long experience, but that the United States would provide the necessary support. American policy would move on two tracks; first, seeking to organise the Middle East for defence against Soviet military aggression in the case of a world war and, second, providing economic and technical aid to bolster 'moderate' governments and political movements.[51]

Anglo-American rivalry Despite the strategic reasons for Anglo-American cooperation, the relationship between the countries was also marked by rivalry.[32] One source of tension was the resentment by many in the United States at Britain's imperialist ways and the desire not to be closely associated with these for fear of alienating former colonial peoples. Likewise, American attempts to undermine British imperialism provoked hostility in London. Discussions between Prime Minister Winston Churchill and President Franklin D. Roosevelt in August 1941 had produced the Atlantic Charter, which stated that the two leaders 'respect the right of all peoples to choose the form of government under which they will live'.[33] Although the United States did not actively try to dismantle the British empire during the war, America's anti-imperialist sentiments did generate friction.[54]

The other source of tension was over access to Middle Eastern markets and oil reserves. Control of oil became more important in the late 1940s because Middle Eastern oil was a vital component in the Marshall Plan for Western European recovery and because of the perceived Soviet threat to the region's oil fields.[55] Tension rose in the post-war years because British dominance of the oil industry was squeezed between growing nationalist pressures to revoke oil concessions on the one side and the expansion of American companies on the other.[56]

Between the wars Britain had dominated the oil trade and Anglo-American rivalries were restrained by agreements within the industry. The main British company was the Anglo-Persian Oil Company, subsequently renamed Anglo-Iranian (AIOC), while US interests were represented by the Arab-American Oil Company (ARAMCO) and the Near East Development Corporation, a consortium of five US companies. In 1928 an Anglo-American clash over control of the growing oil industry in Mesopotamia was averted by the formation of the Iraq Petroleum Company (IPC).[57]

During the war ARAMCO had increased its production levels and sought US government support for the construction of a pipeline from Dhahran to the Mediterranean coast. Realising that this would undercut IPC's position, the British government protested and the US administration shelved the project. Nonetheless, American oil firms went ahead with the scheme and in July 1945 established the Trans-Arabian Pipeline Company (Tapline). At first the Mediterranean terminal was planned for Palestine but US government intervention led to the agreement of Lebanon and, eventually, Syria for the pipeline to pass across their territories. Subsequently, Tapline was to be a significant factor in both US-Syrian and Anglo-American relations. Its direct competitor was Middle East Pipeline Ltd (MEPL), which was established to manage the construction of a pipeline from AIOC's fields to the Mediterranean.[58]

France Although France emerged from the war as the junior partner in the Western alliance and lost much of its influence in the Eastern Mediterranean, Paris continued to perceive Syria and Lebanon as its special preserve. Under the terms of the Anglo-French agreement which regulated the evacuation of British and French forces from the Levant, signed in December 1945, 'each Government affirm[ed] its intention of doing nothing to supplant the interests or responsibilities of the other in the Middle East'.[59] During Anglo-French talks in January 1948, France accepted that for the time being Western security would be better served if Britain took the lead in seeking to preserve a military position in the Levant. However, after British efforts during 1948 to conclude defence agreements came to nothing, Paris took the opportunity to regain some of its former influence by supplying arms to Syria.[60] France's perception of this special role was evident in January 1950 when the US Minister in Damascus reported that '[the] French Minister has repeatedly indicated ... that France is [the] natural source [of] arms supply for [the] Syrian army'.[61]

France's attempts to restore its position in the Levant meant that relations with Britain were often characterised by suspicion. Officials based in the region, smarting at their removal from power by the British in 1945–46, were especially sensitive to what they perceived as British intrigue. At the inter-governmental level there were attempts to pursue cooperative policies in the region but London often found it necessary to proceed cautiously so as not to offend French sensitivities. These sensitivities were most acute over the question of Fertile Crescent and Greater Syria. Like many Syrians, French officials were convinced that Britain and Iraq were constantly scheming to incorporate Syria into the Hashimite kingdom. These fears were largely exaggerated but, until the mid-1950s, they led France to throw its support behind pro-Egyptian and leftist elements in Syria who shared their distrust of 'perfidious Albion'. This approach angered the British and the Americans who were taking an increasingly active role against the leftists. It was only in 1956 that French fears of Nasser and communism led Paris to cooperate with London. This had little effect as, in the wake of Suez, French influence finally collapsed and the United States moved to centre stage in the region.[62]

USSR Under Stalin, the Soviet Union acknowledged the existence of only two camps, the socialist and the imperialist, and so was slow to capitalise on indigenous anti-imperialist sentiments in the Middle

East. Furthermore, until the mid-1950s Moscow's attention was focused on the northern tier of Middle Eastern states with which it shared borders. For these reasons, the Arab states were of marginal interest to the USSR in the late 1940s and early 1950s.

Partly as a result of US and British pressure, Soviet claims on Turkish territory and for joint control of the Turkish Straits were rebuffed and Soviet troops withdrawn from northern Iran.[63] In 1947 Moscow sought to capitalise on Zionist opposition to Britain by reversing its anti-Zionist stance and accepting the UN Partition plan. This earned it Arab hostility and over the following years the USSR gradually distanced itself from Israel, labelling it a 'tool of Wall Street'. Egypt's anti-British struggle was applauded but credited to popular organisations rather than the Wafdist government. Iraq and Transjordan were the subject of hostile propaganda for their status as 'feudal monarchies'. Although Syrian military dictators were criticised as Western agents, the Soviet Union retained some influence there through the relatively strong Communist Party.

It was only after Stalin's death in 1953 that Soviet policy-makers began to recognise the existence of a neutralist camp in international politics which could be an arena of competition between East and West. Under Stalin's successors the Soviet Union began to pursue a dual strategy of supporting local communist parties and courting Arab rulers. By offering arms and diplomatic support to nationalist anti-Israeli leaders the USSR was able to counter the West's attempts to 'contain' it by forging a chain of pro-Western regimes around its borders. This struggle became more intense in the mid-1950s as the USSR responded to the formation of the Baghdad Pact by breaking the Western monopoly on arms supplies and beginning to arm Egypt and Syria.[64]

Summary

The combination of internal and external conflicts outlined here meant that the fledgling Syrian polity was not destined to have a peaceful childhood. The personal, clan and regional rivalries which had split the National Bloc prevented the National and People's parties from cooperating against the radical Syrian Nationalists, Ba'thists and communists. The result was to be that the radical parties, working largely through the army, expanded their influence at the expense of the old-guard politicians. The Palestine conflict meanwhile helped to propel the army to the centre of the political stage, while inter-Arab and Cold War rivalries led foreign states to exploit Syria's internal divisions. This process both exacerbated domestic differences and linked Syria's domestic politics inextricably to regional politics. These factors were all evident during 1949, when the Palestine débâcle shook Syrian society and the army moved for the first time to take political power into its hands.

2

Coups and covert action, 1949

The withdrawal of French troops had left the fledgling Syrian state at the mercy of its Arab brothers. The rival Arab leaders competed for influence over Syria but, by 1948, the conflict in Palestine overshadowed all other issues. The humiliating performance of Syrian forces in the war led to disenchantment in the military and frustration among the populace. These pressures contributed to the destabilisation of the country and, in 1949, plunged Syria into a cycle of military coups and counter-coups.

This chapter examines four political upheavals in Syria during the tumultuous year when Syria's officers took matters into their own hands. In all cases both contemporaries and historians have argued that foreign agents and covert action played important roles. The intention here is to examine the evidence now available to assess what degree of truth there may be in these conspiracy theories, as well as to highlight aspects of Syrian politics during the year which have remained opaque.

The events of interest include: Husni Za'im's coup of 30 March, Sami Hinnawi's coup of 14 August and Adib al-Shishakli's pseudocoup of 19 December. Za'im's coup receives the most attention since it is possible, by a detailed analysis of the evidence, to cast doubt on the widely held assumption that the CIA sponsored the coup. The evidence concerning foreign backing for Hinnawi and Shishakli is not so extensive but there is nonetheless enough new material concerning secret diplomacy and covert action to warrant discussion of their activities. The fourth topic is the Sa'adah affair. Syria's role in backing and then betraying Antun Sa'adah's rebellion against the Lebanese government is of interest as a case study of covert action. Furthermore, many questions remain unanswered in published accounts of the affair. It is hoped that the account presented below will help to answer these questions.

Prologue

The formation of the Arab League had been a setback to Hashimite plans to incorporate Syria into their territories. Nonetheless, as soon as he got his independence from Britain in March 1946, Transjordan's King 'Abdallah intensified his efforts to create a Greater Syria.[1] In January 1947 he signed a treaty of friendship with Turkey and in February the Arab Legion held manoeuvres on the Syrian border. Fearing Hashimite encirclement, some Syrians responded forcefully. Three bombs that exploded in Amman were attributed by the Transjordanian authorities to a dissident group backed by Syrian anti-Hashimites.[2] In May 'Abdallah issued his *White Book*, reiterating Hashimite claims to Syria, while during the summer there were persistent rumours that Transjordan was encouraging tribal leaders in the Jabal Druze to rise up against Damascus.[3] The Druze needed little encouragement, being traditionally hostile to the rule of Damascus and enjoying close ties with the Hashimites. As *La Bourse Egyptienne* remarked, 'it is among his ['Abdallah's] loyalists in the Jabal Druze that the project of a Greater Syria finds great support'.[4] In August 'Abdallah raised the stakes by calling for the convening of a conference to draw up plans for unity.[5]

These moves were interpreted by both Arabs and the French as a British-inspired plot to extend their control over the Levant. In March a British journalist had been expelled from Syria, accused of agitating in favour of Greater Syria. The Foreign Office did its best to dispel such suspicions. In July, Hector McNeil, Minister of State, stated in Parliament that His Majesty's Government's attitude 'on the subject is ... one of strict neutrality'. After 'Abdallah's call for a conference it was reported that British representatives were 'conferring' with the king and were as surprised as other observers by the move.[6] Egypt and Sa'udi Arabia reacted strongly to 'Abdallah's campaign. Egypt re-emphasised the pre-eminent role of the Arab League and King Ibn Sa'ud threatened to revive his claims to the Jordanian territories of Aqaba and Ma'an if 'Abdallah did not stop causing 'discord' among the Arabs.[7]

Towards the end of the year, however, the Palestine question moved to the forefront of the agenda and the struggle over Greater Syria was eclipsed by the Arab-Israeli war and 'Abdallah's attempts to absorb the West Bank.

In domestic politics, Shukri al-Quwatli's National Party had entrenched itself in power after the 1947 parliamentary elections. The party had won only 24 seats in the 135-seat chamber but the co-operation of most of the 51 independents had enabled Jamil Mardam to form a government. Quwatli subsequently persuaded the Chamber to amend the constitution to allow him to stand for re-election and he was elected for a second five-year term on 18 April 1948.[8] During that year the Palestine conflict dominated Syrian politics. Despite the best efforts of government propagandists and censors, the scale of the defeat being inflicted on the Arabs gradually became clear. The defence minister, Ahmad al-Sharabati, was forced to resign soon after the entry of Syrian forces into combat and dissatisfaction with Mardam's cabinet became widespread among both the public and the army.

On the anniversary of the passage of the UN Partition Resolution (29 November) demonstrations and riots broke out in Syrian cities. Led by Ba'thist and Muslim Brotherhood students, the demonstrators attacked the government's failures in Palestine and called for an intensification of the war effort. On 1 December King 'Abdallah's assumption of the title of 'King of All Palestine', provoked further outbursts. The People's Party appears to have orchestrated many of the disturbances with the aim of removing Mardam's cabinet and succeeded when the cabinet resigned on 2 December 1948.[9] Reluctant to allow the People's Party into power, President Quwatli accepted a fortnight's interregnum until an independent millionaire, Khalid al-'Azm, was able to form a cabinet.[10]

'Azm's cabinet proceeded immediately to tackle several controversial issues that Mardam had blocked. In June 1947, Syria and Lebanon had signed agreements on the division of revenues from the Tapline project, which was expected to begin shortly. Three months later Mardam signed an agreement with Tapline regarding the construction of their pipeline across Syrian territory. The Palestine war had, however, disrupted these plans and neither had been ratified by the Syrian parliament. 'Azm's government addressed itself to the issue. In January the Syro-Lebanese accord was ratified and the Tapline 'Convention Regulating the Transit of Mineral Oils by Trans-Arabian Pipe Line Company Through the Republic of Syria' was put before the Chamber on 16 February. The government also restarted negotiations with the rival MEPL.

The second issue was the question of Syria's financial situation and its ties with France. In January 1948, Lebanon had signed a currency agreement with France but Mardam had refused to go along.[11] Instead, he had tried to seek financial backing for an independent Syrian currency. This policy had failed and in the course of 1948 the Syrian pound had collapsed and taxes had quintupled.[12] Despite popular suspicions of a return of French influence, 'Azm's government sought to rectify the situation and on 7 February signed a financial agreement with France. The pressures under which these moves put the government were described by the British Legation:

> Franco-Syrian and Tap Line Agreements have given an excuse for criticism of the Government's policy by the Popular Party and various opposition groups. One of the causes of this criticism has been the payment by Tap Line and the French of various sums to newspapers; there have also been rumours of money offered to Deputies. As a result those who have not been paid are out to make trouble.[13]

In a third departure from Mardam's legacy, the Syrian government announced on 20 March 1949 that it would take part in armistice talks with Israel. Syria was the last Arab state to become involved in this process, Egypt, Lebanon and Jordan having been involved in the Rhodes armistice talks since January.[14]

Za'im's *coup*

On 30 March 1949 the Army Chief of Staff, Colonel Husni al-Za'im, led a *coup d'état*. The only casualties appear to have been three of a minister's bodyguards. The President, the Prime Minister and several senior officers were arrested.[15] In the judgement of the British Minister, Philip Mainwaring Broadmead, 'there seems to be little doubt that Husni Zaim has carried out his ... coup without any assistance from any group outside the army, his primary aim being to get rid of Shukri Quwatli. ... There is ... no indication that anyone had been sounded in advance.'[16] Probably as a result of this lack of preparation, Za'im was unable to persuade any politicians to form a government and the next day invested himself with the powers of head of state and formed a temporary cabinet made up of the Secretaries General of the government ministries. On 1 April he dissolved the Chamber of Deputies, declaring that there had been 'irregularities' in its election.[17]

At the time, Za'im's coup provoked a storm of speculation concerning his possible foreign backers. To this date it is a common assumption, among both Syrians and foreign observers, that Za'im was backed by an external power. The most common supposed culprit is the United States but Britain and France have also been accused.[18] Since these assumptions are so commonly accepted, it is worth looking at the Za'im episode in some detail to see whether these conspiracy theories can really be justified.

The primary motives for the coup appear to have been a combination of Za'im's personal ambitions and the dissatisfaction felt by many army officers with the civilian government. The coup's initial communiqué expressed the feelings of many army officers towards Quwatli's rule:

> The amendment of the Constitution [in 1947] ... was the greater evil from which all the other evils flowed, namely the falsification of the Elections and then the connivance of the ruling clique with the profiteering and falsely elected majority of the Chamber against the Treasury of the State ... connivance which led to the squandering of public money, violation of the Laws, and a useless waste of the nation's interests.[19]

Several of the army officers who mounted the coup had been angered by their experiences during the war for Palestine in which they had been poorly equipped and supplied. They returned from the front disillusioned with Quwatli and 'Azm's management of affairs.[20]

It is likely that the idea of leading a coup had occurred to Za'im, who had been appointed Chief of Staff in June 1948, the previous autumn when the army had been called in to restore public order. Alfred Carleton, then President of Aleppo College, described how Za'im's public profile had been boosted in December when, 'during the period of near anarchy following the fall of the Mardam cabinet ..., it was the intervention of the army and the personal tour of the country by ... Za'im ... that restored order ...'.[21] Although this public exposure may have fed his ambition, it appears that the timing of the coup was due largely to the personal hostility between 'Azm and Za'im. Relations between the two were poor, with 'Azm labelling Za'im a 'dumb and irresponsible man' and treating him in a high-handed manner.[22] Immediately prior to the coup 'Azm accused Za'im of corruption in purchasing faulty weapons and impure cooking oil for the army.[23] Za'im's personal position was threatened and so he encouraged his colleagues to undertake the coup, of which he then proclaimed himself the leader.[24]

However, the presence of domestic motivations does not rule out foreign interference. There have been few, if any, accusations of covert action by any of the Arab states in backing Za'im's coup. All conspiracy theories have centred round one of the Great Powers. The roles played by London, Paris and Washington will be examined in turn but first an account of Za'im's place in inter-Arab politics will be given in order to contextualise his relations with the Great Powers. This will make it easier to assess allegations of covert meddling, both before and after the coup.

Inter-Arab manoeuvrings

Za'im's coup put Syria back into play in the tug-of-war between the Hashimites and their rivals. Egypt and Sa'udi Arabia were stunned by the loss of 'their man' in Damascus. Their only reactions in the days following were to ask the Great Powers to ensure that Za'im did not have Quwatli executed, as it was rumoured he was planning to do.[25] King 'Abdallah and Nuri Sa'id, on the other hand, seized on the chance to further their schemes.[26]

For King 'Abdallah the signs were at first favourable. It is unclear what ties he had had with Za'im earlier but, in December 1948, British diplomats noted that 'Zaim is known to have been in touch with King Abdullah in the past'.[27] Nonetheless, after a conversation with the Syrian Druze leader, Amir Hasan al-Atrash, who had traditionally good ties with 'Abdallah, the British Minister in Beirut, William Evelyn Houstoun-Boswell, reported: 'it is perhaps not unreasonable to suppose as the Atrash were not involved [in the coup] King Abdullah too had no part in it'.[28] Whether or not he had prior knowledge, 'Abdallah was quick to notify Za'im and Ibn Sa'ud that he took a neutral attitude and would not interfere in Syrian politics.[29] His real hope, however, was that Za'im would react against Quwatli's Sa'udi connections by turning to the Hashimites. As *La Bourse Egyptienne* put it, 'Abdallah hoped that the coup would be 'a springboard towards a Greater Syria'.[30]

In Iraq, the policy towards Za'im appears to have gone through a rapid evolution and to have been hamstrung by differences between the Prime Minister and the Regent.[31] At first Nuri saw the opportunity to intervene and install a union government by force. On 9 April the British Minister reported that Nuri 'was clearly elated and itching to take action. ... It would not be necessary to send in much force. Zaim was a poor creature and Nuri [P]asha was sure that the threat of action would be sufficient to make him retire.'[32] The Regent was more cautious than Nuri and was hopeful that Syrian domestic opposition would oust Za'im, but he did agree that attacking Syria would be a good safety-valve for the restless Iraqi army.[33] Within a few days, however, Nuri changed his approach and saw the opportunity to work with Za'im. This change took place as Za'im, concerned at Israeli military pressures during the forthcoming armistice talks, asked Iraq for military assistance. On 14 April a Syrian delegation arrived in Baghdad with a draft military agreement and on the 16th Nuri himself visited Za'im. Za'im wanted Iraq to station two brigades on the Syrian-Israeli border for the duration of the negotiations to deter any Israeli actions.[34] The following day Iraq announced its recognition of Za'im's government.

By now, however, Egypt and Sa'udi Arabia were working hard to foil these plans. On 9 April Ibn Sa'ud contacted 'Abdallah, calling the coup 'disastrous for the Arabs', and stating that he would 'not tolerate intervention in Syria by anyone'.[35] On the 17th 'Azzam Pasha, the Secretary General of the Arab League, visited Damascus.[36] Za'im was invited to visit King Faruq, which he did on 21 April. This visit, which his propagandists labelled 'historically momentous', convinced him to throw his lot in with Egypt and Saʻudi Arabia.[37] The communiqué issued on his departure stated: 'His Excellency the General wanted to demonstrate by this visit the close brotherly sentiments and the deep respect which the government and the people of Syria hold for Egypt.'[38] On the 23rd Egypt, Saʻudi Arabia and Lebanon extended their recognition to the new regime.[39]

Subsequently, relations between Zaʻim and the Hashimites deteriorated rapidly. When Transjordan's Prime Minister visited Baghdad on 26 April, Zaʻim perceived this as the preliminary to an invasion. He reacted aggressively declaring: 'It must be understood that Transjordan is a small part of Syria and should she wish to yield to her motherland she will be welcome.'[40] Damascus Radio added to the insults when it asked rhetorically: 'whether those supporting the present monarchy [in Transjordan] consisted of more than two or three percent of mercenaries, relatives and opportunists'.[41] Zaʻim also mobilised Syrian troops and closed the border with Transjordan.[42]

Zaʻim appeared to be obsessed with the threat from ʻAbdallah. In a conversation with a British diplomat at the end of April he declared: 'If I ever lay my hands on him I shall hang him. But his days are numbered. ... I am stronger than Abdullah.'[43] The Foreign Office desk officer, L.G. Thirkell, noted that: 'Zaʻim ... is ... really frightened, [and] is in a dangerously anti-Hashemite mood.'[44] In response to a suggestion that ʻAbdallah be persuaded to tone down his criticisms of Zaʻim, Thirkell minuted: 'I think it is on Col Zaʻim rather than on King Abdullah that the brake needs applying hardest ... his policy of stirring up Hashemite antagonism is a very dangerous one.'[45] It was, however, not just Zaʻim who was aggressively taking on ʻAbdallah. In the last week of April a team of four would-be assassins were arrested in Transjordan after they had placed bombs by the side of a road the king was due to use. One of the two Syrian members was Colonel Muhammad Hindi, formerly Inspector General of the Syrian police under Quwatli's regime. He had been arrested along with Quwatli after the coup but had been released or escaped soon after. At the trial charges were brought *in absentia* against Quwatli, then still confined in Syria, and ʻAbdallah's longtime Palestinian rival, Hajj Amin al-Husayni. These were dismissed for lack of evidence but the four saboteurs were convicted. No clear evidence of foreign involvement in the plot emerged but given Quwatli's close ties with Egypt, where he was received when he was eventually allowed to leave Syria, it is possible that Egyptian intelligence played a role.[46]

Syrian-Iraqi relations in the fortnight following recognition by

Egypt and Sa'udi Arabia were not so overtly hostile. After Sir Alec Kirkbride, British Minister in Amman, accompanied Transjordan's Prime Minister to Baghdad he reported that

> Nuri Said ... [is] now unfavourably disposed towards the new régime in Syria which had first asked for closer relations ... and then re-buffed them. [However he] did not propose ... to interfere in the internal affairs of Syria unless that country fell into disorder, in which case Iraq would have in self defence to restore order.[47]

In early May the Iraqi Foreign Minister asserted that 'we seek unity ... but we do not want to impose that on any country. ... We have no scheme which we wish to impose on any Arab country.'[48] Syrian Foreign Minister Amir 'Adil Arslan subsequently visited Baghdad and agreements were concluded on economic issues and the attachment of 31 Syrian officers to the Iraqi army. Arslan's requests for artillery ammunition, though, were turned down.[49]

By the end of May, however, Nuri appears to have decided that he had to remove Za'im, by intrigue or force. In late May he proposed a plan to Britain in which his troops would install a friendly government in Damascus. This, he argued, could be achieved if Britain would ensure that neither Israel nor Turkey took advantage of the situation to intervene. When Britain refused to cooperate he began working with Syrian politician Husni al-Barazi, who had recently fallen out with Za'im and Lebanese Prime Minister Riyad al-Sulh, to bring about Za'im's removal.[50] In the second week of June, Nuri began discussions with both the National and People's parties who wanted to establish a provisional government. They had been alienated from Za'im since his decree dissolving all political parties issued at the end of May.[51] The plan was to install the government on the back of Iraqi tanks. Britain again opposed this plan, arguing that if Iraq invaded Syria, 'Egyptian intervention ... would follow and Nuri would have caused a final split in the Arab world which could only be of advantage to Israel and Russia'.[52]

This dissuaded Nuri but he turned up the heat in the run-up to the Syrian referendum, scheduled for 25 June. This referendum was crucial for Za'im whose initial popularity had been eroded by his dictatorial and personal rule.[53] The referendum was an attempt to put his rule on a firmer footing by approving a new constitution and electing him President. On 16 June Za'im accused Iraq of massing 5,000 troops on his frontier and stirring dissension among border tribes. Despite Iraqi denials, he moved troops to the border.[54] Nuri tried to persuade Britain, France and the United States not to recognise the legality of the plebiscite and so nullify the legitimacy it was designed to provide. Sa'udi Arabia and Egypt protested strongly at this move and no one took Nuri up on his suggestion.[55] In an interview on the 22nd, Za'im called for 'a consolidated union between Syria, Egypt and Sa'udi Arabia [that] will create a strong front against the Greater Syria plan'.[56] The same day it was announced that Sa'udi Arabia would make a $6 million loan to Za'im, most of the funds being earmarked for military spending.[57] Bolstered by this support, the plebiscite went ahead as planned and Za'im, as the only candidate, was elected President. He took on the title of Marshal and tasked Muhsin al-Barazi to form a new government.[58]

The day after the poll a massive explosion rocked an ammunition dump in Mezze, Damascus, killing three people. The timing naturally aroused suspicions and Israeli radio reported rumours that British and Iraqi agents were behind it.[59] The British Minister, however, reported that the 'explosions [were] apparently caused by careless regard for regulations in ammunition shed whilst shells and cartridges were being prepared for following day's ceremonies'.[60]

Despite having consolidated his hold on power, Za'im continued to be nervous of Hashimite plots. The First Secretary of the British Legation in Damascus, C.G. Man, reported a conversation on 20 July: Za'im 'is utterly convinced that Nuri Pasha is plotting his downfall. He said that the Iraqis were barbarians living in a barbaric country; how could Syria, which was hundreds of years ahead of Iraq ... ever consent to live under Iraqi domination.'[61] Concerned to protect himself, Za'im constantly reaffirmed his loyalty to King Faruq and Ibn Sa'ud. In a 7 July interview he stated: 'My relations with Egypt and King Faruq have been more than excellent since the first day. ... King Ibn Sa'ud has also acted towards me like a true gentleman.'[62] Egyptian enthusiasm for his rule was demonstrated, *inter alia*, by press articles extolling his social policy and his desire to help the poor.[63]

This pattern of relations continued until Za'im's overthrow by Hinnawi on 14 August.

Britain's role

Soviet propagandists at the time stressed the alleged role played by British and American oil and strategic interests in backing the coup. *Pravda* argued that Za'im's 'dictatorship' was related to plans for a Near-Eastern bloc backed by the United States and that the coup had been organised 'by the Anglo-American rivals for the oil resources and strategic bases in that area'.[64] The Paris-based *Combat* suggested that "Azm's favourable attitude to Tapline had provoked Britain to remove him.[65] The other motive frequently attributed to Britain was its supposed support for the formation of a Hashimite-dominated Greater Syria or Fertile Crescent. Although British diplomats reiterated the argument that they did not control the actions of the Iraqis or the Jordanians, they were unable to convince the majority of Arab or French opinion of this. As a French reviewer of King 'Abdallah's memoirs commented in April 1949, 'strange thing, his ['Abdallah's] dreams always match Great Britain's plans'.[66]

In fact, Britain appears to have been taken by surprise by Za'im's move. Furthermore, after the coup, Britain did not push very strongly on any of the issues from which it was accused of seeking to benefit. Iraq's and Jordan's attempts to subvert Za'im's régime were restrained, the MEPL agreement was only ratified after complicated negotiations over arms supplies and financial aid and policy was in general coordinated with the French, rather than being at odds.

Although Britain had been interested in discussing defence arrangements with Syria in early 1948, Syria had rebuffed all approaches. In July 1948 Muhsin Barazi, then acting Minister of Foreign Affairs and described by the Foreign Office as 'well disposed towards the British', tentatively proposed to Britain some form of military cooperation.[67] Although the Foreign Office was interested in the idea, it believed that the proposal could not be followed through for three reasons. First, Britain could not guarantee Syria's borders while the Palestine war was still in progress. Second, there was no desire to upset the French. Third, Britain could not supply arms in any significant quantities.[68] 'Azm's government renewed these requests, arguing for a British military role in protecting MEPL's pipelines when they were built. These requests caused alarm in Egypt, provoking *Minbar as Sharq* to comment 'we never expected to see [Syria] ... stab the Arab League in the back'.[69]

Egypt need not have worried as the Foreign Office procrastinated on these requests and so fulfilled the promise made by Foreign Secretary Ernest Bevin to the French that Britain would support France's military primacy in the Levant.[70] The lack of a strong policy-line led Minister Broadmead to plead with Bernard A.B. Burrows, Head of the Foreign Office's Eastern Department, in December 1949 that: 'the only conclusion I can draw is that our policy towards Syria is completely negative. ... Perhaps we should get somewhere with these people ... if we could have a more positive policy.'[71]

London's only forewarnings of the coup appear to have come from Lieutenant Colonel V. D'Oyly Harmar, the Military Attaché accredited to Beirut and Damascus. In mid-March 1949 he reported: '[Za'im] hinted at coming disturbances involving downfall of regime. C. in C. known to be disgruntled with President and politicians generally but no rpt no firm evidence he contemplated military coup.'[72] Two days before the coup, Broadmead reported that Za'im had told Harmar that 'he would take action in the near future' and that the forthcoming demonstrations opposing the Tapline were being organised to give the army cover for its coup.[73] Concerned that Harmar's comments to Za'im during this conversation not be misconstrued, the Foreign Office cabled Damascus on the day of the coup, 'it is important that no grounds should be given for any allegations that His Majesty's Government or His Majesty's representatives in Damascus are involved in a plan to overthrow the government or the régime by unconstitutional means'.[74]

After the coup, Britain remained wary of giving its opponents any grounds for their chronic suspicions that it was working to create a Greater Syria. In April, Sir William Strang, Permanent Undersecretary of State, approved a minute which argued:

> closer relations between the Arab states in the Fertile Crescent is [sic] on the whole to our advantage but we must be very careful on account of French and American susceptibilities not to suggest that we are sponsoring the scheme. ... The French are strongly against this but we cannot possibly afford to be tied by their peculiar views on Middle East policy. We must however be extremely careful not to re-awaken long-standing suspicions of our 'Greater Syria' plans i.e. that we favour the conquest of Syria by Transjordan.[75]

In the days following the coup, as the Hashimites manoeuvred for influence, the Foreign Office advised Ambassador Mack in Baghdad that 'we must be careful how we approach the subject. Whatever happens the world will accuse us of being responsible'.[76] Mack was instructed to advise the Regent to proceed cautiously. When Nuri appeared ready to intervene to remove Za'im in early April, the Foreign Office advised that it would oppose any such move due to the 'possibility of a state of chaos developing in Syria with the consequent chance of Communist penetration'.[77]

This policy, of cautious support for a negotiated union but rejection of any covert or military action, continued as the inter-Arab struggle for Za'im's allegiance heated up. Britain's responses to some of Nuri al-Sa'id's requests for support in his moves against Za'im have been mentioned above. It did not prove easy to keep Britain's hands clean as there was a stream of anti-Za'im plotters seeking British assistance. In June, after discussions with the Lebanese Prime Minister, Houstoun-Boswell reported that 'it looks to me ... as if both [Riyad al-Sulh and Nuri al-Sa'id] were trying to involve His Majesty's Government in a plot' against Za'im.[78] In July Sir John Bagot Glubb, British Commander of the Arab Legion, reported that he had been approached by an informant seeking British assistance for a Druze-led uprising in Syria. Thirkell responded: 'a singularly futile opposition. Whatever Za'im's fault, we sh[oul]d have nothing to do with it.'[79]

Za'im's relations with Britain were characterised by his paranoia concerning Hashimite plots and the belief that Britain was behind them. This led him to fear and chastise Britain, even while he was offering military cooperation. In August, for instance, he carpeted the British First Secretary on the grounds that a consular clerk had made seditious remarks. The Eastern Department commented:

> It is going to be very difficult to maintain friendly relations with Col. Zaim if he is ... constantly subject to fits of childish rage. ... We may desire friendly relations with [Za'im], but not ... at the expense of our ... more valuable friendship with the Hashemites. ... It should not appear that we can be cajoled into giving up our long-standing friendships simply by such empty bribes as the use of airfields in time of war (when if we wanted them we should take them whatever the Syrians might say).[80]

Za'im's outbursts were, however, not as 'childish' as the Foreign Office portrayed them. While British diplomats viewed this incident as an instance of Za'im's paranoia, the US Embassy reported that their sources had uncovered an Iraqi plot to assassinate Za'im and that Za'im was 'convinced [that] Brit[ain] [was] implicated in ... [these] plots against his life'.[81] While US diplomats attributed the plots to Nuri alone, Za'im's suspicions of a British hand were understandable. Subsequently, he directed his security forces to extend their surveillance activities from Iraqi citizens to cover British as well.

Britain's attempts to have the MEPL agreement ratified were dogged by these suspicions. 'Azm's Finance Minister, Hasan Jabara, was kept on by Za'im as his economic advisor and the new government showed the same positive attitude towards signing foreign economic deals as 'Azm's had. Jabbara promised MEPL that the agreement would be ratified quickly but Za'im disavowed this commitment and stalled on ratification in an attempt to persuade Britain to supply him with aid and arms.[82] In mid-May he put forward a request for the supply of £2 million worth of hardware, including 26 Meteor jet fighters and 63 Sherman tanks.[83] Even if it had wanted to, Britain was not able to supply this quantity of heavy equipment.[84] In any case, Britain had no desire to break the UN arms embargo that had been imposed during the Palestine war. Za'im tried to persuade the AIOC to give him a loan for the purchase of arms prior to ratification of the agreement but this was rejected by the company as well as the Treasury.

On the eve of a visit by Sir William Strang on 13 June, Za'im sought to show goodwill by signing the relevant agreements. He stated his position clearly: 'I have now done my part in authorising the signature; it is up to you to do yours and see I get the arms I want.'[85] The Foreign Office responded by arranging a deal whereby MEPL would give Za'im a £100,000 advance on their royalties to be used to purchase British arms. Za'im ratified the agreements on 20 June.[86]

Negotiations over the details of the arms supply, however, bedevilled Anglo-Syrian relations for the remainder of Za'im's rule. As First Secretary Man reported in August, 'in Zaim's view ... as long as we do not furnish him with what he considers an adequate supply of arms, we are ... deliberately keeping him weak so that he will be unable to resist an eventual threat from Iraq or TransJordan'.[87]

Britain thus seems to have resisted intrigue in relation both to Fertile Crescent/Greater Syria schemes and in relation to the MEPL agreement. With respect to relations with France, the suspicions of conspiracy theorists seem to have been only partially justified.

British diplomats certainly took a supercilious attitude to France's attempts to re-establish its influence in the Levant. Houstoun-Boswell remarked that 'it is most unfortunate that the French are so sensative [sic] about their position in the Levant which they seem to regard as affecting their prestige and which they have used as a sort of barometer of their "great powerdom" since they established themselves here after the first world war'.[88] On the whole, though, Britain was sensitive to French concerns and was careful to coordinate policy with Paris. In the course of the Hashimite plots in April, the Quai d'Orsay was kept informed of the general line of British policy, although not of the details of Nuri Pasha's intrigues.[89]

Foreign Office officials did not share the concerns of the British press at the revival of French cultural influence in Syria under Za'im.[90] The views of the Eastern Department's officers were expressed in a minute written in July. Desk Officer Thirkell noted that: 'the French have recently come back on a large scale in the Levant States. There has been considerable French economic penetration and also a considerable French come-back in the cultural field. But presumably, in view of our working arrangements with the French, both of these have our approval.' First Secretary T.E. Evans, just returned from Beirut, concurred, writing that 'the French "come-back" should not result in a British "set-back." My view ... is that there is room for us both and that our interests do not conflict fundamentally. Our interests are, I take it, mainly politico-strategic; those of France economic and cultural.'[91]

The differences between Britain and France appear to have been more pronounced at local than at the inter-governmental level. In particular the French Minister in Damascus, Serre, appears to have been chronically suspicious of 'perfidious Albion' and worked to undermine Britain's influence. In January 1949 the American Minister reported that the 'French Minister loses no opportunity to try [to] arouse in [the] Middle East distrust [of] Britain'.[92] Thirkell commented in May that 'relations are good between the French and ourselves as regards the Middle East both in London and Paris. Not so however in the Levant, where, to judge from recent confidential reports, the French still remain supremely suspicious of our intentions and anxious to oust us.'[93] In July he directed his criticisms more specifically. 'It is ... I think true that the French Minister at Damascus ... is very anti-British. There have been indications that the French hope to run Colonel Zaim as their man and that they have been distributing large quantities of money for political and propaganda purposes.'[94] The Americans recognised that this was so, reporting that 'local French representatives lose no opportunity to pour oil on the fire of Za'im's Anglophobia. Whether or not this goes further than inflammable (encouraging) words, it is difficult to judge.'[95]

In spite of these concerns, Britain appears to have been content for France to re-assert its influence in Syria and refused to be drawn into any anti-French plots. When Riyad al-Sulh sought British assistance in July, Thirkell noted 'it has ... been made apparent to the Lebanese P.M. that we will not be drawn into any intrigues against the French'.[96]

France

Another conspiracy theory holds that France backed Za'im's coup. This theory has some plausibility in view of the close relations that developed between Za'im and France during his rule. On 16 April Za'im ratified the monetary agreement that 'Azm had signed on 7 February. This took Syria out of the Franc area and reportedly brought Za'im £5 million in credits.[97] France became his primary arms supplier and trained several Syrian officers. In May it arranged to supply 10,000 rifles and 250 machine-guns, as well as mortars and ammunition.[98] His hostility to the Hashimites was also welcomed by the Quai d'Orsay.[99] 'Adil Arslan, Za'im's Foreign Minister, even claimed that Za'im sent an assistant daily to get advice from the French Minister.[100] In July Za'im declared a propos France that 'our present relations are perfect'.[101]

There is, however, no evidence that the French encouraged his coup in the first place. It may be the case, as Shawkat Shuqayr, the head of Za'im's *cabinet militaire*, told Seale, that 'Za'im's ratification of the ... [financial agreement] should be taken to reflect his conscious need to win friends after the coup, rather than ... French backing *before* it.'[102] Two pieces of evidence validate this view. First, the fact that Paris, despite its suspicions of the Hashimites, coordinated its policy towards Za'im closely with Britain. This indicates that France was unlikely to take drastic measures, such as staging a coup, which would threaten Anglo-French relations. Coordination was most evident in regard to arms supplies as Britain and France kept each other informed of the levels of arms supply. French officials even suggested a formal divison of responsibility in which Britain would supply and train Syria's air force, while they looked after its army.[103]

The other piece of evidence is the fact that the French position had already been improving under 'Azm's government. Formerly Syrian Minister in Paris, 'Azm had not only signed the monetary agreement but had arranged the supply of small arms for 'internal security' purposes.[104] It is true that Za'im, who had had close relations with France during his service with their Troupes Spéciales, brought Syria closer to France than 'Azm's weak government could have done. It remains open to question, though, whether the SDECE would have removed an already friendly government.

The United States and Za'im

The most popular candidate in the conspiracy theories surrounding the coup is the United States. This suspicion was voiced by 'Azm:

> The United States believed ... that there was little chance of securing parliamentary ratification [of the Tapline agreement]. They may therefore have looked with favour on anyone who promised to remove this obstacle. The facts speak for themselves: shortly after Husni al-Za'im came to power he ratified [the convention].[105]

Not surprisingly Moscow Radio took the same line.[106] More convincingly these claims were also made by Miles Copeland, then CIA station chief in Damascus.[107] According to Copeland,

> it was clear ... [that] Quwwatli [sic] and his establishment ... would remain blind to the ... fact: that a political explosion was looming. 'We have before us only two alternatives,' said Keeley [the new Minister], 'both of them undesirable' – by which he meant that either political opportunists, with covert Soviet support, would shortly stage a bloody uprising, or that the Syrian army, with *our* covert support, would take over the government ... [Keeley thought the second option] would at least ... give the responsible elements in the society a fair chance. ... A 'political action team' under Major Meade [the Assistant Military

Attaché] systematically developed a friendship with Za'im, ... suggested to him the idea of a coup d'état, advised him how to go about it, and guided him through the intricate preparation in laying the groundwork for it.[108]

In his recent study of declassified US documents, American academic Douglas Little has supported Copeland's account. Little argued that US frustrations with Quwatli in autumn 1948 due to his refusal to accept a UN truce proposal, the prospects for renewed agitation over Alexandretta, growing anti-Americanism and the stalled Tapline negotiations, led Meade to open discussions with Za'im in November. In these talks Meade encouraged Za'im to mount a coup and planning proceeded during the winter. At the end of March Assistant Secretary of State George McGhee visited Damascus. Little speculates that final approval was given at this stage.[109]

Since much of the US material remains classified, a definitive account of the American role cannot yet be given. None the less, it is worth reconsidering the evidence as it is far from conclusive. From the available evidence, it appears that US officials had foreknowledge of Za'im's plans. Locally based officials may also have given him some encouragement. There is, however, no solid evidence of a coup plotted in Washington.

Syrian-US relations Syrian-US relations had begun well after World War I when Syrian opinion supported the idea of becoming an American Mandate.[110] After World War II Washington facilitated the French withdrawal, winning further sympathy. Truman's pro-Zionist stance, however, aroused popular resentment. Truman's support for the UN Partition Resolution provoked an outburst of anti-American sentiment and on 30 November 1947 a mob attacked the US Legation burning several cars and the American flag.[111] Resentment at American policy intensified with the escalation of fighting between Jewish and Arab paramilitaries. During 1948, remarked the British Legation in Damascus, 'American views on Palestine were held in contempt as the plaything of domestic politics'.[112]

Against this backdrop of rising anti-Americanism the US had four major concerns – Tapline, communists, Turkey and Israel. The failure of the Mardam government to ratify the Tapline convention has been discussed above, so it is only necessary to discuss the other three issues here.

During Mardam's government there was concern that the Soviet Union could make gains either by exploiting the domestic turmoil through Khalid Baqdash's banned, but active, Communist Party, or by extending military aid to the government. After the fall of Mardam's government, the US Legation reported that Soviet Minister Solod had returned to Damascus to prepare the Communist Party for 'more effective participation [in] public disorders after [the] failure [of the] present government which Communists expect in two–three months'. The Military Attaché also believed that party members were being trained in 'military intelligence and sabotage duties'.[113]

Syria's claims on Turkey for the return of the Sanjak of Alexandretta (Hatay) further disturbed the Truman administration.[114] Turkey and Syria had established diplomatic relations in 1946 but neither country was willing to compromise on sovereignty over the territory. Since 1947 the United States had been concerned at Syrian threats to take its claim to the United Nations or the International Court of Justice. This would present the United States with a dilemma. If it supported Turkey it would alienate Arab opinion but support for Syria would 'weaken Turkish morale and resistance to the USSR'.[115] Turkish officials also made the point that Syria's claim would encourage the Soviet Union's territorial demands on northern Turkey.[116] Although attention was distracted from the dispute by the situation in Palestine, the Mardam government's attitude was similar to that expressed by a parliamentary deputy who declared in October 1947: 'we will never abandon our rights to the territories'.[117]

The Mardam government's refusal to enter the UN-sponsored armistice talks with Israel or to contemplate the resettlement of refugees was also frustrating to the United States.[118] Copeland argues that it was this issue which persuaded the State Department to remove the civilian government. According to him, it was Za'im's promise to '"do something constructive" about the Arab-Israel problem ... [that] neutralised any inclination the Department might have had to give us explicit instructions to lay off'.[119]

If one compares Za'im's actions once in power with this list of concerns it is certainly tempting to conclude that he had some understanding with the United States. He moved rapidly to address all of these issues. On 2 April he announced his intention to ratify the Tapline agreement and did so on 16 May.[120] The State Department noted that Tapline was 'keen on' Za'im as he was 'the first high official of the Syrian Government who had kept his word on the matter of ratification'.[121]

Days after coming to power he pledged to destroy any 'destructive Communistic propaganda'.[122] A fortnight later he declared, 'I will unleash a war to the death against communism in Syria'.[123] This was not merely rhetoric. On the 6th the gendarmerie began rounding up suspected communists and by the 8th the Sûreté claimed to have arrested 150. A week later the US Legation reported that around 400 alleged party members had been arrested. The party had to move its printing press to Haifa and began to operate from across the Israeli-Lebanese border.[124]

Turkey was initially concerned that the coup would destabilise its southern border but moved quickly to recognise the government when Za'im's intention to improve relations became apparent.[125] By the middle of April Turkey was confident enough to declare that it considered the question of Alexandretta closed.[126] By mid-July there was press speculation that Za'im would take Syria into an alliance with Turkey and the United States.[127] This speculation was given substance in August when, in an interview with the Associated Press, Za'im declared his willingness to take on the leadership of a pro-Western military bloc in return for military aid.[128]

On the Israeli front, Za'im proved willing to move ahead on the armistice talks. Indeed, according to 'Adil Arslan, Za'im's erstwhile Foreign Minister, the Syrian leader was even willing to meet Israeli Prime Minister Ben Gurion at one stage.[129] When Za'im offered to resettle 250,000 refugees in Syria, the State Department was ecstatic, arguing that 'if this opportunity can be exploited [the] back of [the] refugee problem can be broken'.[130]

However, the fact that Za'im's policies coincided with US interests does not prove that his coup was backed by the CIA. If one examines events more closely, there are four pieces of evidence which cast doubt on the picture of an American protégé ousting a troublesome régime. The areas which need to be considered in more detail are: the 'Azm government; the State Department's attitude to Za'im; the Tapline negotiations; and Za'im's anti-communist record.

The fact that 'Azm's government took a markedly more pro-Western stance than Mardam's has been mentioned above. What is striking, though, is that 'Azm's administration made positive moves on most of the issues of concern to the United States.

Although it did not act as ruthlessly as Za'im was to, the 'Azm government took steps to crack down on the Communist Party. In February 1949, the US Embassy reported that the newly appointed Sûreté chief, Hindi, was the 'most capable ... to date', that he was reforming the Sûreté's anti-communist branch and establishing links with the Lebanese security services.[131] A fortnight later Hindi had centralised anti-subversive activities by incorporating the army's counter-espionage branch into his department. He also agreed on joint anti-communist measures with Iraq and Egypt and was negotiating agreements with Turkish police chiefs.[132] In March, the police ruthlessly put down communist-inspired demonstrations.[133]

'Azm and his ministers were very keen to ratify the Tapline

convention. In mid-February Syrian leaders were confident that the convention would be ratified, even though there were up to forty deputies demanding cash payments in return for their vote.[134] In late February negotiations stalled when the Tapline board unilaterally repudiated two minor annexes to the agreement. Afraid of the reaction from the parliamentary opposition, 'Azm refused to accept this but proposed a compromise formula. The US Legation recommended that Tapline accept the deal fearing that 'growing opposition to convention and other problems ... may well cause [the] fall [of the] government'.[135] British officials were more optimistic, arguing that 'there can be little doubt that ... [the convention] will be accepted in the coming session, since munificent largesse has influenced even the newspapers in its favour'.[136]

As far as Israel was concerned, as early as January 1949, the US Legation concluded that, if they were given some face-saving formula, 'the Syrians are prepared ... to acquiesce in some form of *modus vivendi*'.[137] In March the government entered the Rhodes armistice talks.

In general, it appeared to Damascus-based Foreign Service officers that there were good prospects for aligning the 'Azm government with the West. In February, the Embassy reported: 'in past two weeks many responsible Syrian officials including President Quwatli and Pri[me]min[ister] Azm have so emphasized Syrian desire for active cooperation with U.S. and U.K. as to leave little doubt but that soundings represent agreed Syrian policy line'.[138] Keeley concluded that 'it would seem worthwhile, at least, to endeavor to consolidate Syrian friendship by some tangible evidence of our appreciation of its strategic position, of its fears and of its willingness to play more than a passive role in any future test of strength between the democratic and totalitarian ways of life'.[139]

The picture that emerges from a detailed look at the 'Azm government is one of improving Syrian-US relations. It is not true, as has sometimes been portrayed, that Za'im overthrew an anti-American régime. However, 'Azm's government was weaker than Za'im's dictatorship. Whether this in itself was enough of a motivation for the CIA is another question.

The second piece of evidence which casts doubt on the conspiracy theory is the State Department's ambivalent attitude towards Za'im. Its coolness was most clearly demonstrated over the question of recognition. Britain and France decided within days of his coup that they should recognise Za'im's government.[140] While the Foreign Office was uncomfortable with giving legitimacy to an unconstitutional government, it argued that 'delay ... will pre-dispose that regime against ourselves and against Western influence in general'.[141]

Despite the urgings of Paris and London, however, the State Department waited over three weeks before extending recognition. The State Department argued that 'we do not want by too speedy recognition of Zaim [to] inspire or encourage similar movements in other Arab armies'. The Department also hoped that 'neighboring Arab states might well take lead in granting recognition' and 'thought it desirable that Zaim should form some type of constituted Govt other than his purely personal rule'.[142] Za'im's conclusion of a ceasefire with Israel on 13 April, his formation of a cabinet on the 16th and the recognition of his government by Egypt, Lebanon and Sa'udi Arabia on the 23rd finally convinced Dean Acheson who recommended to Truman on the 25th that recognition should be extended as 'Zaim has ... affirmed ... his intention to honour Syria's international obligations. He has given ... evidence of his sincerity ... in undertaking armistice negotiations with Israel.'[143] The US Minister, in conjunction with the British and French, presented his credentials on 26 April. This delay seems rather a strange reaction if Za'im had coordinated his moves with the United States.

The third element which throws doubt on the conspiracy theory is a comparison of the Tapline and MEPL negotiations. Za'im did not initially give preference to Tapline over MEPL, as would have been expected if he had been a CIA protégé. Indeed, the day after the coup, the US Legation reported that 'Tapline chances appear lessened because [of the] probability [that the] new gov[ernmen]t will contain some of its outspoken critics'.[144] In the event, of course, Za'im ratified Tapline before MEPL.[145] The reason for this, however, may have been AIOC's refusal to give him a loan prior to signing, whereas, according to Hasan Jabbara, Tapline promised to come up with a loan of between $5 million and $10 million.[146]

Finally, a closer analysis of US documents reveals that Za'im's anti-communist drive was not the success he liked to portray it as. In fact, on the day of the coup a source in the Syrian Communist Party informed a US official that the party was 'overjoyed' as they believed that his regime would be vulnerable to a programme of dissension and violence. Soviet 'strongarm' teams were reported to have congregated in Damascus to exploit the situation. Despite Za'im's anti-communist pronouncements, from the start Meade felt that 'Zaim not adverse strike deal with commies'.[147] Za'im's initial anti-communist sweep did disrupt the party's operations but his security agencies were unable or unwilling to carry through their efforts. By late April half of the 500 suspects arrested had been released for lack of evidence and soon the party began major efforts to infiltrate the labour movement. The US Legation 'reached [the] conclusion [that the] Zaim gov[ernmen]t's announced anti-communist drive [is] impossible ... [to implement effectively] under [the] present police system'.[148] By mid-May, it was clear that the 'mass arrest program ... [had] practically petered out'.[149] The failure of these efforts was confirmed in August, when Baqdash spent several days in Damascus without any interference from the police. By then Za'im's security forces were more concerned with the activities (real and imagined) of Iraqi and British agents than with communists.[150] On the whole, US officials appear to have recognised that Za'im's anti-communist pronouncements and demonstrations were staged primarily for their benefit.[151]

Copeland and Meade Ultimately the best way to determine the degree of CIA or State Department support for Za'im before his coup is not to infer from US interests and Za'im's actions but to consider the evidence of the US personnel actually involved. Unfortunately, this evidence is inconclusive. Copeland's version of events in *The Game of Nations*, quoted above, suggests that he and Meade masterminded the coup. However, in his subsequent autobiography, *The Game Player*, he denies that he and Meade masterminded the coup, stating that 'it was Husni's show all the way'.[152] He claims only that he gave Za'im advice on planning the operation and promised him that the United States would recognise the new regime after the coup. It is probable that Copeland's claims in *The Game of Nations* owed more to his well-known tendency to exaggerate his own role than to the facts.[153] Indeed, in an internal Agency publication a CIA reviewer labelled the book 'complicated nonsense' which was 'confused, and ultimately incomprehensible'.[154] In a personal communication to this writer, a former director of the CIA remarked that 'if you can sort out fact from fiction in "The Game of Nations", you are a clairvoyant'.[155]

An independent source is the accounts of Assistant Military Attaché Stephen Meade's conversations with Za'im before the coup. There is no doubt that Meade was close to Za'im. The British Legation labelled Meade 'one of Zaim's cronies' and in July Za'im decorated Meade, ostensibly for his liaison services in the weeks before recognition permitted official diplomatic contact to resume.[156]

Starting in late 1948, Meade had a series of confidential conversations with Za'im in which the Syrian officer outlined his ambitions and, as they crystallised, his plans to seize power. In themselves the record of these conversations demonstrates only that the US Legation, unlike the British, made little effort to steer clear of involvement in Za'im's plots. They provide no evidence of direct assistance.[157]

Meade talked to Za'im at least six times before the coup, beginning on 30 November 1948. Their initial conversations indicated to Meade that Za'im's 'strongman characteristics give rise to [the] possibility [of] army supported dictatorship'.[158] Za'im's expressions of a desire for closer relations with the United States were, however, not seen as marking him out from others in 'Azm's government. According to the Military Attaché, 'Zaim's statements apparently stem from [a] new Syrian policy [for] better relations with [the] U.S. as [the] same line being followed in [the] remarks of high-level Syrian officials to U.S. representatives'.[159] It was only in March that Za'im's plans crystallised and he pushed for the United States to ally itself with him rather than the civilian leadership. On 3 March, Za'im's comments 'clearly indicated [his] personal ambitions [to] control [the] country'.[160] He requested that the United States should conduct aid negotiations directly with him, arguing that he would ensure the stability of the country. He claimed to have drawn up plans for the construction of concentration camps in the desert to intern communists and 'weak' politicians.[161]

During these discussions, he apprised Meade of an alleged Soviet-backed plot to throw the Middle East into turmoil in late March. He claimed that Soviet hit-squads would assassinate the Egyptian Prime Minister on the 27th, that a hit-list of Syrian leaders had been drawn up and that these attacks would be the signal for mass disturbances. At the same time, the Soviets were allegedly arming the Kurds in preparation for an uprising. Za'im planned to use these disturbances as an excuse to seize power. However, US officials judged that the alleged hit-list may have been 'fabricated by Zaim to provide [an] excuse [to] alert [his] troops for "internal security"'.[162] That this judgement was close to the truth is indicated by the fact that Za'im also 'requested U.S. agents [to] provoke and abet internal disturbances which [would be] "essential for [his] coup d'etat", or that U.S. funds be given him this purpose'.[163] Quwatli, who was 'long aware [of] Zaim's ambitions', however took firm action and, by threatening to close the schools, prevented student demonstrations from taking place on the 19th. Za'im 'indicated [a] certain disappointment' at this turn of events and pleaded again for US assistance.[164] There is no indication that he received any and 11 days later launched his coup anyway.

Meade clearly had an unusual degree of access to Za'im prior to his coup.[165] It is possible that he encouraged or advised Za'im informally, perhaps without the knowledge of the State Department. This is plausible as relations between Foggy Bottom and the Damascus Legation were characterised by serious estrangement and lack of communication during 1949.[166] At the end of the year, Keeley wrote to Washington bitterly attacking the State Department's handling of Syria: 'I had Za'im and Barazi eating out of our hand and begging for

U.S. leadership in telling them what to do to reach a settlement with Israel'. However, when Za'im had agreed to resettle refugees, Keeley had been instructed in a circular telegram to berate the government for its failure to move on improving relations with Israel. Then,

> a few weeks before his assassination [see below] Barazi said to me, when he agreed to go along with the Department's urgent recommendation that Syria sign an armistice with Israel, 'I'm probably committing political suicide and I'm even taking a calculated risk of assassination in the hope thus of getting American assistance to put my country on its feet; your country must not let me down.' It did just that.[167]

This extraordinary tirade indicates the close relations which developed between the US Legation and Za'im. More significantly, it demonstrates that the State Department did not appreciate this relationship.

Without access to CIA archives it is not possible to determine precisely what role the Agency played before the coup. Nonetheless, from the evidence available, it appears that the United States' role was far more limited than is often believed. The State Department had little reason to be enthusiastic about the coup. Copeland and Meade, as far as one can tell, did no more than discuss Za'im's plans with him shortly before he moved. Even the minimal encouragement they may have offered was not necessarily authorised by the CIA, given Copeland's tendency to report 'out of the chain of command'.[168] Unless further evidence comes to light, the notion of Za'im as having been put in place by the United States, or France, or Britain, must be assigned to the class of conspiracy theories which contain more fiction than fact.

The Sa'adah affair

On 8 July 1949 the Lebanese government executed Antun Sa'adah, the charismatic leader of the SSNP, after a summary military trial. The affair had major political repercussions in both Syria and Lebanon as the SSNP took its bloody revenge. In Syria, Husni Za'im's alleged betrayal of Sa'adah led to his overthrow and execution a month later. Riyad al-Sulh, Lebanon's Prime Minister, survived longer but was gunned down by SSNP assassins two years later.[169] The affair left the SSNP with a martyred leader and probably also encouraged its propensity to violence which was to be evident in the following years. For these reasons, and because the details of the affair remain murky, it is worth unravelling the events that led to Sa'adah's death.[170]

Under the French Mandate, the SSNP had been suppressed and in 1938 Sa'adah had left Lebanon. In his absence the party re-oriented itself towards participation in Lebanese politics and diluted its commitment to pan-Syrian ideals. In 1944 it dropped the word 'Syrian' from its title and Lebanese Interior Minister Camille Chamoun gave it permission to operate legally. However, when Saʻadah returned from his self-imposed exile in Brazil on 2 March 1947, he reimposed his autocratic control and purged the party moderates. The speech he made at Beirut airport on his return was a call to action: 'my word to you, National Socialists, is to return to the field of struggle'.[171] Although Chamoun and Druze leader Kamal Junblatt had facilitated Saʻadah's return, in the hope of gaining his party's support in the forthcoming elections, this speech provoked the government into issuing an arrest warrant for him. He fled into the mountains and issued a conciliatory statement, after which the gendarmerie made little effort to apprehend him.[172]

At the time the Lebanese government was in the hands of President Bechara al-Khuri and President of the Council of Ministers (Prime Minister) Riyad al-Sulh. Khuri had been elected to the Presidency in 1943 and was widely regarded as 'Britain's man' as the United Kingdom had backed him against his pro-French rival Emile Eddé. Saʻadah clashed with Khuri soon after his return as he opposed Khuri's plans to amend the constitution to enable him to serve a second term as President when his mandate expired in 1949. The antagonism between Sulh and Saʻadah was more deep-rooted. In 1937 Saʻadah had backed Khayr al-Din al-Ahdab's government against Sulh's challenge.[173] More fundamentally, the SSNP's ideology was in total contradiction to the terms of the National Pact which Sulh had been instrumental in negotiating in 1943. Under this informal arrangement, the Lebanese Sunni elite had agreed to accept the existence of a Greater Lebanon separate from Syria in return for Christian acceptance of the country's position in the Arab world.[174]

During 1948 tensions between the SSNP and the government increased as Saʻadah intensified his criticism of Sulh's government for its failure to deal with Israel, the existence of which Saʻadah intransigently opposed. These tensions often spilled over into violence as gendarmes broke up SSNP rallies. By early 1949 Saʻadah was convinced that Sulh was out to destroy his party and had come to believe that co-existence between the SSNP and the government with its 'feudal allies' was impossible and that it was 'them or us'.[175]

Husni Zaʻim's unexpected coup suddenly shifted the balance of forces, providing Saʻadah with an opportunity and posing a threat to Sulh.

Since Sulh was close to Shukri al-Quwatli, it was inevitable that relations between Zaʻim and the Lebanese government would be strained. In fact, they rapidly became hostile. Immediately after his coup, Za'im declared to Major Meade that 'eventually Lebanon should be part of Syria' and argued that 'with one hundred additional armored cars he could take Lebanon'.[176] In April he received opposition leaders Camille Chamoun and 'Abd al-Hamid Karamah, encouraged them to oppose President Khuri and offered them arms.[177] In May a crisis blew up when Lebanese gendarmes arrested a Syrian Deuxième Bureau officer, Captain Tabbarah, and three soldiers who had assassinated a suspected Israeli spy on Lebanese territory. There were rumours that other Syrian hit-squads were at large in Lebanon, seeking out political opponents such as ex-Defence Minister Sharabati. Za'im reacted to the arrests by closing the border, calling for the overthrow of Sulh and making aggressive troop movements. The incident was eventually smoothed over and Syrian military pride assuaged with the return of the men but it indicated Za'im's 'fierce, bullying attitude towards his neighbours'.[178] Za'im's hostility towards Sulh was heartily reciprocated. Sulh gave Za'im justified grounds for his attitude by his plottings with the Hashimites and attempts to inveigle Britain into these plots. The relationship between the two men was summed up by the Foreign Office in July: 'there is no love lost between Riadh Solh and Za'im, the former being convinced that Za'im is a dangerous madman ... while the latter continues to suspect Riadh of intriguing against him'.[179]

Sa'adah and Za'im thus shared a common enemy and Sa'adah was quick to seek his assistance. In late April an SSNP delegation went to Damascus but Sulh himself had chosen the same day to make an official visit to Za'im and the SSNP delegation was unable to gain admission.[180] During the row that followed the arrest of Captain Tabbarah the SSNP resolutely backed Syria's position, thus coming to Za'im's attention.[181] In late May Sa'adah was granted a meeting with Za'im. In this meeting Za'im fulminated against Sulh and Khuri, talked about using force to remove them and promised the SSNP 'unlimited' cooperation in any moves they made against the Lebanese government.[182]

Whether or not he knew of this meeting, Sulh must have been concerned at the prospects of Syrian help for the SSNP and he moved to pre-empt the possibility. In early June he brokered a reconciliation between the Maronite paramilitary organisation of Pierre Gemayel, the Phalange (more commonly know by its Arabic name, *Kata'ib*) and the Sunni *Najjada* party under 'Adnan al-Hakim. This provided him with the means to move against Sa'adah. On 9 June clashes between the *Kata'ib* and the SSNP occurred at the SSNP's printing press in the *Jamayzah* district of Beirut, in which a handful of SSNP members were injured. The Lebanese government claimed that the *Kata'ib* had aborted a planned coup by the SSNP, stating that the SSNP 'plotted a seditious movement'.[183] The British-backed *Sharq al-Adna* radio station supported this line, reporting that SSNP men had attacked a *Kata'ib* rally.[184]

However, American diplomats judged that the 'incident ... [was a] deliberate government provocation'.[185] SSNP members, for their part, were convinced that the attack was organised by Sulh, noting that the Juge d'Instruction who investigated the incident was Rashid al-Sulh, Riyad's brother, and that when party members went to lodge a protest at the gendarmerie, they found Phalangist leaders there in discussion with the Internal Security Forces.[186] In any case, the government dissolved the party and launched a crackdown, arresting around 700 alleged supporters.[187]

Despite a national manhunt, Sa'adah evaded the Lebanese authorities. SSNP members in Damascus approached Za'im and asked him to offer Sa'adah asylum. He agreed and Sa'adah crossed the border, was received by Syrian officials and brought to Damascus.[188] Sa'adah subsequently had a meeting with Za'im in which the latter promised Sa'adah support for an armed insurrection. He promised to supply arms and 2,000–3,000 Syrian soldiers in SSNP uniforms. As a pledge of honour he handed Sa'adah his personal revolver.[189]

Although they did not fully trust Za'im's extravagant offers of help, the SSNP leadership finalised their plans for a revolt. Sa'adah realised the party was too weak to launch a full-scale revolution, instead he intended the uprising to signal to the Lebanese government that they should cease their harassment of the party.[190] Preparations for an armed confrontation had been in progress for a while and now the operation was scheduled to begin at dawn on 4 July.[191] The plan was for SSNP militiamen to attack gendarmerie posts in Beirut, the Shuf and the Matn to seize arms. Other groups would then launch attacks in the Biqa' and Harmal. Za'im had arranged for fighters from the Dandash tribe in the Biqa' to launch simultaneous attacks. Although some of the party's men supplied their own arms, shortage of small arms was the SSNP's main problem. After the *Jamayzah* incident 'Isam al-Mahaiyri, the party's representative in Damascus, had collected money and sent four men to purchase weapons in Jordan. These had then been smuggled into Lebanon.[192] On the whole, though, the SSNP was relying on Za'im's promised munificence.

In the last days before 4 July, however, SSNP leaders began to doubt Za'im's word. They were concerned at the appointment of Muhsin Barazi, a former ambassador to Egypt and friend of Riyad al-Sulh, as Prime Minister after the 25 June referendum. The SSNP's friends in the government were unable to arrange any more meetings with Za'im. Nonetheless, the party could not turn back. On 3 July three Syrian army trucks delivered small arms and ammunition to SSNP members at an unofficial crossing point on the Lebanese border, from where they were smuggled across and added to the existing stockpiles.[193]

Before dawn on the 4th Sa'adah delivered a speech to the assembled fighters who had gathered from across Syria and Lebanon.[194] The fighters then moved out but the 'revolution' was a disaster from the start. One group walked straight into a gendarmerie ambush and retreated back into Syria. Another group, led by the militia's commander 'Assaf Karam, was surrounded and its survivors captured after a seven-hour firefight. A third group inexplicably delayed their attack until the next day. The Syrian weapons proved useless, many malfunctioning and the machine guns having been supplied with the wrong calibre ammunition. Dandash's fighters never appeared on the battlefield.[195]

On hearing news of the disaster Sa'adah, who was in Damascus, sent his wife into safekeeping in Sayyidana Convent and tried to arrange a meeting with the Syrian President. Ibrahim Husayni, Za'im's Chief of Military Police, came to see Sa'adah on the 6th and passed on Za'im's offer to supply 300 armed soldiers. Sa'adah replied that he wanted arms, not men. Husayni subsequently returned with an invitation to meet Za'im and that evening collected Sa'adah in his own car. The suspicions of SSNP leaders had deepened during the day as they had observed a number of unmarked cars belonging to the Lebanese security services in Damascus. Their suspicions were confirmed when military policemen arrested one of Sa'adah's bodyguards. The leaders asked Adib Shishakli, an SSNP sympathiser who had been Za'im's Sûreté chief until two days before, to find out what was going on. When he informed them that Sa'adah had been handed over to the Lebanese, they fled to Jordan.[196]

Although the official Syrian line was that Sa'adah was arrested inside Lebanon, the true story soon emerged.[197] Although he did drive Sa'adah to the Presidential Palace, Husayni there handed the party leader over to Lebanese Sûreté Commander Farid Chehab and Gendarmerie Chief Nur al-Din Rifa'i. Although they had been ordered to kill Sa'adah on their return to Lebanon, as Za'im was afraid that if Sa'adah went on trial he would expose Za'im's double-dealing, the two officers refused to do so and delivered Sa'adah to their superiors in Beirut.[198] Embarrassed with their controversial captive, the Lebanese authorities hastily convened a military tribunal and had Sa'adah executed the following morning, 8 July.[199]

The main unresolved question about this sordid affair is why did

Za'im renege on his promises to Sa'adah? He must have had very good reasons for doing so as it discredited him among a wide circle of opinion who did not necessarily support Sa'adah but which objected to the breach of trust. As the British Legation put it, 'many sections of public opinion ... regard his conduct as a flagrant act of betrayal'.[200] It is not the case, as the British Military Attaché suggested, that Za'im dropped Sa'adah when he realised he was a lost cause and decided that it would be better to concentrate his support on the more effective opposition leaders, Chamoun and Karamah.[201] The fact that Za'im personally ordered the delivery of ineffective weapons to the SSNP, cancelled his arrangement with the Dandash and, probably, passed on information to the Lebanese that allowed them to ambush the SSNP units indicates that Za'im was involved in a plot to set up the SSNP which would provide Riyad al-Sulh the excuse to have Sa'adah killed.[202]

There have been suggestions that Britain or the United States persuaded Za'im to betray Sa'adah as he was destabilising a friendly government. It is clear that both countries backed Sulh's government. The US Legation in Beirut even recommended the Lebanese government be supplied with military equipment to fight the insurrection.[203] However, they do not appear to have treated the issue as of great importance.

The SSNP has always claimed that Egypt's King Faruq first encouraged Sulh to move against the SSNP and then pressured Za'im to hand him over. The reason, the party argues, was Sa'adah's opposition to the armistice accords with Israel.[204] In this view, Sa'adah 'paid ... the price of the Israeli-Arab armistice accords'.[205] Although Sa'adah's opposition to the armistice talks may not have been the motive, it does appear that the SSNP's accusations are accurate. The Egyptian establishment's hostility to Sa'adah is shown by the fact that even two years after Sa'adah's execution, the Egyptian commentator Muhammad Heikal sought to blacken the party's name by claiming that Sa'adah had agreed with Israel in 1948 to mount a coup in Lebanon.[206]

Muhsin Barazi, who may have been appointed Prime Minister as a result of Egyptian pressure, was the leader of the pro-Egypt and pro-Sulh faction in Za'im's government.[207] Since his appointment he had been working to improve Syrian-Lebanese relations and must have seen Za'im's impetuous support of Sa'adah as a blow to his hopes. Rather than confront the President directly, he exploited Za'im's reliance on Egypt to force a change in policy. At the end of June Barazi met King Faruq in Cairo and persuaded him that Za'im's support for Sa'adah posed a real threat to Sulh's position.[208] Al-Sulh and al-Khuri had already asked Faruq to persuade Za'im to extradite Sa'adah and

Barazi's visit seems to have convinced the Egyptian king. It is not known exactly what pressure Faruq applied to Za'im but it proved irresistible. Nadhir Fansah, Za'im's brother-in-law, recalls that when he subsequently castigated Za'im for the betrayal, the Syrian President broke down, crying 'what could I do?'[209] Za'im may also have been persuaded by the prospect of increased aid which Egypt offered.[210] Whatever the details, the consequences were clear. The pro-SSNP Shishakli was dismissed, giving Husayni time to orchestrate the trap into which the party fell. On the day of Sa'adah's execution Syria and Lebanon signed an economic agreement which had been under discussion for several weeks.[211] Barazi's politicking had succeeded.

Hinnawi's coup

On 14 August 1949 Za'im was overthrown in a coup led by Colonel Sami al-Hinnawi, commander of the First Brigade. Za'im and Prime Minister Muhsin Barazi were executed. The exact reason for the executions remains controversial. The second and third communiqués issued after the coup stated that a 'Supreme Council of War' had been established and that Za'im and Barazi were executed by firing squad after they had been tried by a military court.[212] Fadlallah Abu Mansur, one of the officers who executed Za'im and Barazi, supported this account. He wrote that Air Force Captain 'Isam Mraywad arrived at the location where Za'im and Barazi were being held, informed the conspirators that the High Command had sentenced Za'im and Barazi to death and ordered them to carry out the sentence.[213]

The British Military Attaché, however, gave a different account. His source was Colonel Hrant, the head of the gendarmerie who was retired after the coup. Hrant's story was that he had been summoned to the Ministry of Defence by Hinnawi early in the morning:

> A little later Major Amin Abu Assaf (commander of the First Brigade's Cavalry Group) came in and told Hinawi that Zaim had been shot. Hinawi made a wry face at this and gave Hrant the impression that he had not intended that Zaim should be killed. It was only *after that* that they composed the 'Supreme War Council' and made up the story about the trial by a military tribunal, the sentence and execution. ...
> Hrant says that Abu Assaf, two Circassian Captains, Abdul Rauf Hajmat and Khaled Issa, and a Bedouin Control Officer (believed to be a Druse, named Captain Abu Mansur) took Zaim to Mezze, and that Mrewed took Muhsin Barazi there, but he does not know who actually did the shooting. Probably they all did.[214]

The American Military Attaché also discounted the official version of events. According to him, the leaders of the coup had not planned any bloodshed. They were surprised to hear of the deaths and reacted quickly to legitimise their followers' actions retroactively. In this account, Hinnawi's brother-in-law As'ad Tallas was brought in to write the communiqués and dignify the putschists' motives with nobler aims.[215]

It appears, then, that the executions were decided upon by Mraywad and Abu Mansur for their own reasons. Both were members of the SSNP and had ample motivation to carry out the killings in revenge for Sa'adah's death. In his conversation with Za'im before the latter's death Abu Mansur berated Za'im for the insult to military honour which the betrayal of Sa'adah had entailed.[216] 'Abdallah Kobescy, then chairman of the SSNP's political committee, recalled that in Abu Mansur's report to the committee after the coup he emphasised that vengeance was the primary motive for the killings.[217]

Seale's suggestion that the plotters were spurred into action by Za'im's proposal to move an armoured unit to the Jabal Druze appears to have been accurate but the British Legation was wrong in its assessment that the coup 'appears to have been planned for not more than a week'.[218] According to Abu Mansur, he had been involved in discussions with Hinnawi and Assaf concerning a coup since early July. The Sa'adah affair may have pushed them to make concrete plans but Za'im's election to the Presidency in June and subsequent assumption of the title of Marshal had alienated a wider circle of officers. More significant was his appointment of Muhsin Barazi as Prime Minister. Barazi was 'regarded by most Syrians as Zaim's evil genius' and was 'really hated and feared'.[219] He was held responsible for the betrayal of Sa'adah and, more importantly, had increased the gap between Za'im and his fellow officers. This was because his 'policy was gradually to isolate Zaim from his officers in order to establish his own control over' him.[220] This policy resulted in Za'im sidelining some of his leading supporters. Colonel Adib al-Shishakli was designated as the Military Attaché to Sa'udi Arabia while 'Adnan Malki was despatched to France on a training course.[221] The dismissal of Lieutenant Colonel Hamad Atrash and fifteen other officers in the wake of the Sa'adah affair increased dissatisfaction. During July and August the atmosphere in the army became 'frantic' as Za'im put his spies to work.[222] There were reports that in the weeks preceding Hinnawi's move Shishakli was involved in an abortive plot to assassinate Za'im while he attended the Red Crescent Ball.[223] Za'im certainly sensed some danger and strengthened his bodyguard in early August.[224]

The alleged grievances of Hinnawi and his co-conspirators were summed up in their first communiqué:

no sooner had ... [Za'im] been established in power than he and his clique began to abuse the wealth of the nation and squander it illegitimately in complete disregard for the prestige of the country, the sacred sanctity of the laws and the freedom of its individuals. Furthermore, the administration was characterised by abuse and deterioration to such an extent that people began to disparage the Army and resent the conditions in the State. What seems worse is that a chaotic internal policy was accompanied by an unsuitable foreign policy.[225]

Hinnawi's internal backers included a variety of individuals whom Za'im had alienated. While vengeful SSNP officers, such as Shishakli and Abu Mansur, spearheaded the revolt, the conspirators included populist socialist leader Akram al-Hawrani. He had originally backed Za'im but had been alienated by the latter's cooperation with the Barazi clan who were his traditional rivals. The pro-Hashimite Druze leader Hasan al-Atrash had also been an early supporter of Za'im but had been aliented by Za'im's hostility to King 'Abdallah. This circle of conspirators received backing from a wider group of officers who resented Za'im's authoritarian rule and his failure to carry through promised reforms in the army.[226]

Support for the coup appears to have been fairly widespread. The British Legation reported that 'there was satisfaction at the passing of the dark cloud of oppression which had weighed on the country since Zaim came to power', and the Syrian press switched overnight from sycophancy to the castigation of Za'im.[227]

Despite its roots in domestic disputes, the coup provoked speculation regarding foreign involvement. It was a sharp setback for Za'im's former friends. King Faruq proclaimed a three-day mourning period and the Egyptian press compared the bloodshed unfavourably with Za'im's bloodless coup.[228] The American press also mourned Za'im, whom they had depicted as Syria's Ataturk. The *Christian Science Monitor* lamented that 'Middle East reform may once more revert to a snail-pace progress'.[229] *Le Monde* reminded its readers of the progressive legislation Za'im had passed and his agricultural reforms which had 'revitalised' Syria.[230] Inevitably, fingers were pointed at Britain and the Hashimites.

Communist propaganda blamed Britain, arguing that Britain's interest in Middle Eastern oil led it to remove Za'im who had favoured US oil companies and French arms interests.[231] The French and Francophone press also took this line. *Combat* ran the headline 'Great Britain reconquers its positions in the Middle East'.[232] The prevalence of this belief, among junior French officials as well as the public, makes it worth quoting at length from an article in *Franc-Tireur* which summed up these suspicions. The newspaper wrote:

The Quai d'Orsay welcomed ... [Za'im's] accession with secret but real joy. ... Great Britain, on the contrary, watched anxiously as a regime hostile to all its projects consolidated itself in Syria. The new coup therefore broke out in time. Defeated in Israel, in Egypt, and in Iraq, trying by all means to bring the United States into their strategic and oil game rather than allowing her to take sole control of the Middle East, the Foreign Office, the Colonial Office and the Intelligence Service will be relieved tomorrow, whereas the event will no doubt disturb Paris and Washington.[233]

However much these theories were believed in the region, there is actually little evidence to support them. It would be going too far to adopt the outraged tone of the *Yorkshire Post*, which called French suspicions 'astonishing'.[234] Given the background, French suspicions were quite understandable. Nonetheless, it appears that the *Neue Züricher Zeitung* was correct in its report that the British were as surprised as the French about the coup.[235] Although the Foreign Office did not have especially good relations with Za'im, there is no indication that it was willing to risk cordial relations with France in order to remove him. British officials may not have agreed precisely with the comments of the British Minister in Baghdad that 'no Frenchman is quite sane on the subject of Syria', but they understood French concerns and trod carefully.[236] This was recognised by *Le Monde*, a newspaper which, according to the Foreign Office, was 'connected with' the Quai d'Orsay.[237] *Le Monde* reported that 'nothing would be more disastrous, they believe in London, than to see revived in the Middle East the old Franco-English quarrels which appeared to have been eliminated'.[238] Even if they had wanted to oust Za'im, it is unlikely that Hinnawi would have been Britain's choice. In his first meeting with Hinnawi, the British First Secretary was not impressed: 'he is a fat, slug-like creature without much brain'.[239]

Allegations of Anglo-American rivalry as a motive were also overblown. The two countries' oil interests were to some extent in competition in Syria and in the summer of 1949 Britain's oil situation was in crisis. The IPC was in the midst of renegotiating its concession with Baghdad and was suffering from the closing of its Kirkuk-Haifa pipeline, while the Iranian Majlis was refusing to ratify AIOC's renegotiated concession.[240] As a result, Britain was importing $129 million of oil per annum from the United States. This was the second largest import and a tremendous drain on Sterling.[241] Nonetheless, it is hard to see what Britain could have gained by ousting Za'im as the MEPL Convention had already been ratified. Indeed, one of the Foreign Office's concerns after the coup was whether the new government would abide by the agreement. In any case, the fact that MEPL was 40 per cent owned by Standard Oil of New Jersey indicates that Anglo-American interests were more closely entwined than was commonly realised.[242]

A more fruitful line of enquiry for those seeking Hinnawi's external backers is the Hashimite connection. Seale suggests that 'Hinnawi was Iraq's choice to overthrow Za'im'.[243] Contemporary speculation inevitably saw Britain behind the Hashimites. *La Bourse Egyptienne*, for instance, warned, 'London had more than a finger in this affair and ... the project of a Greater Syria and that of the Fertile Cescent will soon be ... leading issues'.[244] From Foreign Office archives it appears that, although there was some degree of Iraqi involvement, this was not directed from London. The nature of Iraq's role is unclear. In talks with the Foreign Office, Nuri Sa'id, who was 'very pleased at the change of régime', claimed that he had known of the planned date of the coup in advance and had helped Hinnawi to produce propaganda leaflets. The Foreign Office replied to this news with a hint of alarm. 'He was ... told that we strongly disapprove of judicial assassination ... and that we hope that ... [he] will not boast of his prior knowledge of the coup or of his relations with those who planned it.'[245] Two days later Iraqi Foreign Minister Fadil al-Jamali gave a contradictory account. He claimed that the Iraqi Minister in Damascus had been approached by As'ad Tallas who had asked for the loan of an Iraqi aircraft so that the plotters could escape if their coup failed. Five months earlier it had been Tallas who had misled Nuri into believing that Za'im wanted union but this time the Iraqis did not listen to him and so were surprised by the coup.[246]

It is hard to judge which account, if either, is correct. It would be natural for Nuri to lie and boast of foreknowledge of an event which benefited him. It would be equally sensible of Jamali to deny knowledge when it was clear that Nuri had incurred Britain's displeasure. For what it is worth, the US Secretary of State reported to President Truman that there was 'no evidence to indicate that any outside power participated in the coup in any way'.[247] It seems probable that Nuri had had contacts with disgruntled Syrian army officers. To what extent he sponsored Hinnawi's move, however, remains unclear.

Fertile Crescent and its opponents

The role of external covert activity preceding the coup may remain unclear but such activity was rife afterwards as the coup tore Syria out of the Egypt-Sa'udi axis and pushed it in the direction of Iraq. Over the next few months a renewed struggle for political control erupted, fought largely through political action. Bribery was the prevalent technique.

Nuri's pleasure at the coup was echoed by 'Abdallah. He crowed that Za'im's régime 'had met the natural death of every "baseless" revolution' and proclaimed 'that Greater Syria will unite and will be ruled by Hashemites'.[248] 'Abdallah, however, was to be disappointed as it was to Iraq rather than Transjordan that Syria turned.

The day after the coup Hinnawi fulfilled his pledge to restore constitutional government. The veteran independent politician Hashim al-Atasi formed a coalition cabinet in which the People's Party took the leading posts. An electoral law was passed and elections to a new Constituent Assembly were planned for November.[249] The new government was keen to move closer to Iraq. Nazim al-Qudsi, who became Foreign Minister, suggested that the government had popular support in this attitude as Syrians no longer wanted to be 'pawns' of Egypt. The British Minister explained the pro-Iraqi mood that swept the country by arguing that after Za'im's death there was a feeling that stability could only be achieved with the assistance of a strong neighbour and 'Abdallah was widely despised.[230] Whatever the reason, Qudsi immediately turned to the British for assistance in negotiating closer ties with Iraq. He insisted that the talks be kept secret from France and the United States, afraid that the news would immediately leak to Egypt and Sa'udi Arabia. Unwilling to risk annoying its allies, Britain declined to help. The British Legation was instructed, 'you should make it clear to the Syrian Minister ... that you cannot continue to discuss this subject with him any further ... as it is too embarrassing for us in relation to the Americans and the French'.[251]

Undaunted, Atasi's government continued its efforts. As'ad Tallas, now Secretary General of the Ministry of Foreign Affairs, led the negotiations with Iraq which began in earnest in mid-September.[252] Despite the Foreign Office's efforts not to be implicated in the talks, both Syria and Iraq consulted it at regular intervals. London reiterated the line that it would not oppose a voluntary union but that any form of union which eroded British military rights under the Anglo-Iraqi treaty was unacceptable. By adopting this line, Britain did, if unintentionally, hinder the negotiations. A large section of Syrian opinion believed that any form of union which preserved Britain's rights would extend British 'imperialism' into Syria as well.[253] Nonetheless, by the end of September an agreement in principle had been reached and the Iraqi Regent 'Abd ul-Ilah visited Damascus on 5 October.[254]

The talks were not, however, allowed to proceed unhindered. Thrown into consternation by the sudden reversal of their gains, the Hashimites' opponents fought back. With Shukri al-Quwatli and Jamil Mardam still in Egypt, the National Party was led by Sabri al-'Asali.[255] In a dramatic reversal of its former anti-Hashimite stance, the party sought to capitalise on the pro-Iraqi mood by issuing a manifesto calling for complete union. These demands went further than those of the People's Party but may merely have been a cynical ploy to win the elections by outbidding the People's Party. Nazim Qudsi's explanation was that it was a trick orchestrated by Egypt and that once the party was in power it would revert to its previous policy.[256]

Whatever game 'Asali was playing, the government's external opponents were not so subtle. Allegations of dirty tricks flew in all directions. Sa'udi Arabia was accused of stirring up Syrian tribes, who were due to lose seats under the new electoral law. Sa'udi agents also increased their efforts to bribe sympathetic politicians. Egypt sought to discredit its opponents by claiming that Israel supported the union proposals.[257] Egypt was also, according to a British intelligence source, financing Quwatli's long-distance attempts to forge a bloc of anti-union army officers.[258] After studying the various allegations, the Foreign Office concluded 'that action and bribery by Sa'udi agents has been on a considerable scale, and, combined with that of Egyptian agents, has contributed substantially to the present unrest'.[259]

The British also received numerous reports of French covert activity. There was evidence that France was using its influence with Circassian and Moroccan army officers to encourage them to resist the government.[260] There were reports of attempts by French officials, based in Beirut and Damascus, to bribe candidates in the elections. Although many of these reports can be discounted as deriving from anti-French sources, the number of reports indicates that, at least at the local level, the French mounted a major covert effort to forestall the emergence of a pro-union parliament. Apart from their traditional opposition to the Hashimites, the specific French concern at this stage appeared to be that an Iraqi-Syrian federation would threaten the independence of Lebanon.[261]

Washington became concerned at the turmoil. While there is no evidence to support Qudsi's allegation that the United States and France were working together, Dean Acheson decided that the unionists should not be encouraged as the 'ultimate popular reaction may not be sufficiently favorable to ensure the orderly formation of a federated Hashimite monarchy without prejudice to the stability of ... the Near Eastern area'.[262]

The most surprising opponent of the Iraqi-Syrian *rapprochement* was King 'Abdallah. Excluded from the talks, he saw his hopes for a Greater Syria vanishing. At the beginning of October he fired off a threatening note to Damascus: 'the King warns that he will assert all his power ... to ward off these dangers, and states that if need be he will immediately intervene to prevent the destruction of Syria in the interest of any party or foreign power'.[263]

With tension rising in the run-up to the 15 November elections, an act of terrorism occurred which reverberated round the region. On the night of 6 November, three gunmen shot and wounded Colonel W.F. Stirling at his Damascus residence, wounding his servant (mortally) and a policeman as they made their getaway. Colonel Stirling was a retired British officer who had spent his career as a political officer in the Arab world and had been closely involved with T.E. Lawrence's activities during World War I. In his retirement he acted as Damascus correspondent for *The Times*.[264] Both his newspaper and the Foreign Office claimed that he no longer had any official status. At a December 1949 meeting, British Foreign Secretary Bevin sought to assure French Foreign Minister Schuman that Stirling was not a British agent. Bevin begged Schuman 'not to confuse the British Government's policy with that of "irresponsible individuals such as General Spears [another retired British officer] or Colonel Stirling"'.[265] In the conspiracy-prone Arab world, however, Stirling's guilt was popularly assumed. Za'im had believed that Stirling had been working against him and just prior to the assassination attempt the Arabic press had portrayed Stirling as a British intelligence agent engaged in 'sabotaging' the elections.[266]

In its hunt for the assailants, the Syrian authorities took the opportunity to lay the blame on various opponents. Some sources saw a French hand at work, others speculated about the role of Kurdish Communists. Two more plausible theories were presented to British officials by their contacts. The Deuxième Bureau claimed to have arrested two of the assailants, one in the pay of Egypt, the other 'linked' to the Sa'udi Legation. Several days later, the investigating magistrate pointed the finger at the ex-Grand Mufti, who was then working with Egypt. The magistrate argued that, on a recent visit to Damascus, the Mufti had arrived with an entourage of eight men but left with only four.[267] The US Minister, however, favoured the view that the attack 'may be [the] first in [a] series of attempts [to] create such disorders in [the] country that [the] Army ... will be forced take over gov[ernmen]t under [the] pretense [that] it [is] "obviously incapable [of] coping with internal disturbances"'.[268] He may well have taken this view in light of his intimate knowledge of Za'im's attempts to do just that nine months before. As it turned out at the trial of those subsequently indicted for the crime, both the American and British assessments contained an element of the truth. This story will be told in the next chapter.

In any case the Stirling attack had little effect on the elections, which were conducted fairly peacefully. Most members of the National

Party, however, boycotted them, claiming unfair government practices. The People's Party emerged as the strongest bloc and on 13 December al-Atasi resigned from the premiership to become acting Head of State while a new constitution was agreed upon and a government formed.[269]

Shishakli makes his move

The entrenchment of the pro-unionists in power brought the conflict between them and their opponents to a head. The Constituent Assembly began debating the proposed new constitution immediately. Initial disagreements centred round the accountability of the executive to the legislature but the most serious opposition derived from concerns that an unaccountable government could take Syria into a union over the heads of legislators.[270]

With the National Party having excluded itself from the Assembly, the most significant opposition to the unionists came from certain factions within the army. Their motives were mixed. Some wanted to protect Syria's republican constitution and independence from Great Power domination. Others were afraid that the army's influence would be reduced in a union. There were also many who had been persuaded by offers of Sa'udi gold. In the week following the election there had already been rumours of a coup which would re-install Quwatli in office.[271]

On 19 December the anti-unionists moved. Colonel Adib al-Shishakli, who had been given command of the First Brigade, arrested Hinnawi and several other officers after a short fight in which one soldier died and six were wounded.[272] His communiqué stated:

> It has been proved to the Army that ... General Sami Al-Hennawi [sic], ... As'ad Talas, and some professional politicians in the country were plotting with certain foreign circles against the security of the Army, the integrity of the country, and its republican regime. Army officers knew about this plot from the very beginning; they tried by various means ... to persuade the conspirators to abandon their plans, but ... in vain. The Army was then forced to remove the conspirators in order to safeguard its security as well as the security of the country and its republican regime.[273]

Morale in the army had been low since Za'im's overthrow. In October two senior officers complained to the American Military Attaché that there was a feeling of guilt over the deaths of Za'im and Barazi, that discipline was poor, the officer corps split into factions and resentment at the shortage of equipment widespread.[274]

Shishakli and his compatriots were, however, spurred into action by the previous day's parliamentary debate over the oath of office to be taken by the President and Deputies. As it stood it stated that the office-holder undertook to work for 'the realisation of the unity of Arab countries', but made no mention of the duty to preserve a republican regime. This was perceived as opening the door to a federation under King Faysal. The mention of Tallas in the communiqué was also significant. He had taken the lead in talks with the Iraqis and was widely regarded as Hinnawi's 'evil genius'. It is likely that Shishakli was aiming as much at him as at Hinnawi but the Iraqi Minister managed to smuggle Tallas out of the country before he could be arrested.[275]

In fact, Shishakli's move did not really constitute a *coup d'état* since the head of state remained in place and the process of forming a new government continued. It did, however, serve notice that the army would 'pounce on anyone who flirted with the idea of union with Iraq'.[276] Nazim Qudsi remained in office, free to bemoan the end of his hopes. He blamed the Iraqis, whose impatience, he argued, had provoked the army.[277] The Iraqis in turn accused the Sa'udis, whom it was believed had outbid Iraqi offers of bribes.[278]

Accusations of foreign meddling followed predictable lines. Moscow, which labelled Hinnawi 'a British Intelligence Agent', quoted *Ce Soir*:

> in the struggle for hegemony in the Middle East the upper hand has again been won by the Americans, whose interests are in constant collision with the British. In view of the fact that Iraq is fully controlled by the British, it is not surprising that the plan to merge Syria with Iraq should arouse resistance from the Americans. Neither the US oil-producers nor the State Department ... will allow themselves to be pushed out of Syria.[279]

The French newspaper *L'Humanité*, however, unwittingly demonstrated the tangles which conspiracy theorists could get themselves into when it argued that, either Shishakli was backed by London, as Hinnawi had become an American agent, or that Washington backed the coup to prevent the union going ahead.[280]

It is possible that the United States encouraged Shishakli as the State Department had been concerned at the attitude of the civilian government with regard to Tapline and the Communist Party.

Progress on the Tapline project had been hampered by disagreements on terms with Syrian contractors and the government. A major reason for these delays appears to have been obstructionism by Akram Hawrani and Michel 'Aflaq. These radical politicians held ministerial posts in the government and were able to disrupt Tapline operations, which they opposed in principle as an imperialist enterprise.[281]

US officials were more concerned at the government's lack of action in the face of the communist 'threat'. Days after Hinnawi's coup Major Salah al-Bizri, the new director of the Deuxième Bureau, had told the US Military Attaché that the 'commies [are] your problem not ours' and made it clear that Syrian security forces would take no action unless the United States paid the bill.[282] By late September, 'communist political activity on [a] semiovert level ... [was] at [its] highest point since [the] end [of the] war'.[283] It became clear to the United States that the Interior Minister, Rushdi al-Kikhia, was not concerned with countering the communists and only ordered his men into action in the event of major communist demonstrations which risked embarrassing him in the West. In the run up to the elections, the Communist Party intensified its activities but the government's 'activity against commies [had come to a virtual] ... standstill'.[284] Bizri was removed from the Deuxième Bureau on charges of engaging in unauthorised political activity, while the head of the Sûreté's Political Section was dismissed for allegedly passing information to a foreign government. Bizri's replacement, Major Mahmud Rifa'i, argued that his efforts were hampered by Tapline's refusal to advance part of the payments it had agreed to make.

Although the anti-subversive picture was bleak for US officials, they showed a marked preference for the army's handling of the situation. The Legation noted 'the Syrian army (through its Deuxieme Bureau) is conducting enthusiastic, though somewhat maladroit, anti-Communist activities, Kikhya's Ministry of Interior ... continues to stumble along in an almost completely ineffectual manner'.[285]

In light of the problems over Tapline and the civilians' failure to crack down on the communists, it is clear that the United States would have had an interest in backing a military coup. However, even Copeland, who claims he was close to Shishakli, suggests that Shishakli acted alone and without US assistance.[286] It is nonetheless probable that Shishakli realised that the United States would look favourably on his move and was encouraged by this.

French influence was another obvious suspect in the search for a foreign hand. Salah al-Bizri, for instance, argued that France must have had a hand in the army's move, pointing out that two of Shishakli's senior compatriots had had close links with the French Mandatory authorities.[287] For its part, the British Foreign Office, however, accepted the Quai d'Orsay's blunt denial. The French Foreign Ministry said that it disapproved of Egypt's and Sa'udi Arabia's methods as the unrest which these stirred up threatened the region's stability. France did, however, appreciate the results of these methods and so would not condemn them.[288] The American Legation reported its 'impression ... that Sa'udi Arabian influence may have been more specific than French, although local representatives [were] both clearly delighted over move'.[289]

Sa'udi Arabia and Egypt were pleased by Shishakli's coup and Cairo warned Amman and Baghdad not to interfere in Syria.[290] This was a timely warning as, on hearing of the coup, 'Abdallah had ordered the Arab Legion mobilised and made ready to move.[291] Nonetheless it is unclear what prior connection Egypt and Sa'udi Arabia had with Shishakli. It seems likely that they gave the conspirators some encouragement.

3

The Shishakli era, 1949–54

For two years after he had ousted Hinnawi, Shishakli allowed the parliamentarians to continue running the country. The army's General Staff nonetheless constituted an 'inner government' which closely supervised the civilians. Shishakli took the post of Deputy Chief of Staff, preferring to remain in the background, while Anwar Bannud fronted the army as Chief of Staff.

Internal power struggles in these years continued to make Syria easy game for foreign intervention. The National Party, now excluded from the legislature, tried to remove the People's Party. Civilian governments wrestled with the General Staff for the leading institutional and political role, while rivalries within the General Staff led to bloodshed. At the same time, the radical parties, notably the Ba'th, the SSNP, the communists and the Arab Socialist Party, made inroads into the monopoly of the traditional parties.

In foreign policy, the primary issue continued to be Syria's alignment along the Hashimite/anti-Hashimite divide. The efforts of Jordan on one side and the Sa'udis and Egyptians on the other to bring Syria into their respective camps led to intrigues and acts of terrorism during the first year after Shishakli's coup. At the same time, the Cold War began to intrude more forcefully on the Arab world. In 1950 and 1951 America and Britain initiated attempts to marshal the Arab states into the struggle against the USSR. US interests in an authoritarian, anti-communist ruler in Syria coincided with Shishakli's coup in November 1951, leading to accusations of foreign support for the Syrian strongman.[1]

Shishakli's subsequent dictatorship aroused hopes in the United states that Syria could be incorporated into American strategic plans for the region but these hopes were not to be fulfilled. In any case, the fate of Shishakli's regime was eventually decided at the level of domestic and inter-Arab politics, rather than at the level of superpower geostrategy. Shishakli alienated his domestic supporters and aligned the country with the anti-Hashimites, so laying the basis for his own dethronement. In early 1954 Iraq launched a major covert effort to undermine him but it was Shishakli's opponents in the army who finally toppled him.

'Azm's government

After the departure of Hinnawi, political manoeuvrings over the formation of a new government continued for almost a fortnight. Hinnawi's removal had not totally vanquished the pro-unionists. Major Salah al-Bizri, working with Rushdi Kikhia, tried to persuade the United States to pressure Britain into allowing Iraqi troops to enter the country in order to oust Shishakli and Bannud. Baghdad backed its sympathisers with 'a good deal of ... money'.[2] Major Ibrahim al-Husayni, the new head of the Deuxième Bureau, countered by requesting that the United States persuade Britain to restrain its 'puppets' in Amman and Baghdad.[3] Sa'udi Arabia did its best to buy a friendly government, offering loans of up to $36 million to an anti-unionist cabinet.[4]

By the end of the year, Khalid al-'Azm had managed to put together an acceptable line-up. Although the government was explicitly an interim one, in place only until a new constitution could be agreed upon, the anti-unionists had clearly won this round. Despite its majority in the Constituent Assembly, the People's Party was not formally represented in the cabinet. The four People's Party members who held posts did so on personal rather than party grounds.[5] Although not directly involved in political affairs, the army institutionalised its supervisory role and the pro-unionist press came under military censorship. Iraq was warned not to interfere in Syria's internal affairs and Major Bizri was arrested by his former colleagues on charges of working for a foreign power.[6]

With the army's encouragement the government consolidated ties with Egypt and Sa'udi Arabia and brought Syria's foreign policy into line with the Arab League. In January 1950 Shishakli led a military delegation to Cairo to discuss the terms of an Arab League collective security pact which would enable Egypt to ward off moves for Syrian-Iraqi union. In February Sa'udi Arabia welcomed the new order by agreeing on the terms of a $6 million loan.[7] Riyadh and Cairo's positive attitude indicated that they had come round to accepting the new order in Damascus and had at least shelved their attempts to reinstate Quwatli in power. In January, Quwatli had approached British representatives to gauge their reaction if he did return to seize power and a National Party delegation had visited him in his Alexandrian exile. By March, though, it appeared that his erstwhile backers were content to keep him in reserve for future contingencies.[8]

Iraq, going through its own governmental crisis, made little effort to restore its position. King 'Abdallah continued to work assiduously, if cautiously, on behalf of Greater Syria. His plottings, however, had few overt ramifications in the first half of 1950.

Nonetheless, the relative quiescence on the inter-Arab front did not give much cause for satisfaction in Washington and London. True, the Syrian *rapprochement* with Sa'udi Arabia had meant that it was amenable to Riyadh's pro-American advice. Damascus thus entered into quiet discussions with the United States on the possibility of gaining military and economic aid. During February talks with the US Minister, the People's Party Minister of National Economy, Ma'ruf al-Dawilibi, pointed out that 'any Syrian statesman who seeks cooperation with [the] US in political or economic sphere will be plagued by criticism and opposition because of US connection with Palestine tragedy'. Nonetheless, he wished to explore the possibility of US economic assistance, even though 'Azm's request for fighter aircraft had been turned down the month before.[9]

These approaches, however, rapidly came under strain. On 29 March a bomb exploded outside the British Legation in Damascus, injuring a policeman.[10] In April Dawilibi made a speech attacking the West's record on Palestine. He threatened that, if the United States continued to pressure the Arabs, then he would call for a plebiscite to demonstrate that the Arab people would prefer domination by the Soviets than by the Jews.[11] This sparked off an anti-American campaign in the press and on 18 April a bomb exploded in the grounds of the US Legation, injuring a Marine guard.[12] As with the bomb at the British Legation, it was at the time believed to have been the work either of followers of the ex-Great Mufti, or of the Muslim Brotherhood.[13]

On 25 May the United States, United Kingdom and France issued their Tripartite Declaration in an attempt to reduce regional tensions. They declared 'their opposition to the development of an arms race between the Arab states and Israel ..., their unalterable opposition to the use of force ... between any of the states in that area' and pledged to prevent the violation of any of the frontiers in the region.[14] The Syrian press reacted suspiciously to this, seeing in it a plot to protect Israel and divide the Middle East into spheres of influence. The outbreak of the Korean war in June 1950 provided an opportunity for the Syrian press to demonstrate their desire for neutrality in world affairs, an attitude which inevitably angered the Western powers.[15]

In fact, Syrian-Soviet relations made little progress. Negotiations over a commercial treaty got nowhere and rumours of an arms deal proved unfounded.[16] Nonetheless, the United States and Britain were concerned at the prospects for Soviet inroads. An exasperated Dean Acheson responded to the anti-American campaign by ordering the Legation to reiterate America's desire for good relations and deny rumours that the United States had 'concealed political or economic motives' in the region.[17] The head of the Foreign Office's Eastern Department proposed that overt and covert anti-communist propaganda efforts be intensified.[18]

Transjordanian plotting, Sa'udi and Egyptian terrorism

On 29 May 1950 'Azm's cabinet resigned. The underlying reason was its inability to handle the economic chaos into which Syria was falling. Syria's problems had been exacerbated by the collapse of the Syro-Lebanese Customs Union in March.[19] A week later, Nazim al-Qudsi, Secretary-General of the People's Party, formed a new government.[20] Although the cabinet was dominated by the People's Party, the army's oversight ensured that it charted a cautious course.

Internally, Qudsi's main task was to steer the new constitution through the Assembly. It was due to be passed later in the summer and would pave the way for the introduction of a new parliament. Externally, he remained committed to the Arab League umbrella, signing the collective security treaty in June, but simultaneously he sought to chart an independent course in inter-Arab affairs. Western governments regarded him as favourable to them and were pleased that he was amenable to 'advice'.[21]

As the time for the approval of the constitution neared, the domestic political struggle intensified. On the one hand Shishakli fought to consolidate his position in the army. At the same time the General Staff as a whole struggled to keep the civilians in their place, especially by maintaining control over the gendarmerie. Meanwhile, conflicts between civilian political factions followed traditional lines.

The bitterness of the intra-military struggle for power was highlighted by the assassination of Air Force Commander, Colonel Muhammad Nasir. Nasir had been head of the Operations Branch but had been moved to the Air Force after Shishakli's coup. According to the British Military Attaché, Nasir regarded this as a demotion and was 'fed up with being pushed out of the centre of the picture'.[22] According to the US Chargé d'Affaires, Nasir was part of a clique in the General Staff which, in opposition to Shishakli, argued for the army's withdrawal from politics.²³ There were also suggestions that Nasir was sympathetic to 'Abdallah's Greater Syria plans.²⁴ Whatever the exact motives, Nasir was shot dead in Damascus on 31 July. Before he died he named the Director and Deputy Director of the Deuxième Bureau, Ibrahim al-Husayni and 'Abd al-Ghani Qannut, as his assailants. They were arrested along with a sergeant and charged with murder by the Minister of Defence. Both men were protégés of Shishakli and he fought hard to protect them after they were committed for trial in October. There seems little doubt that the two were guilty. Chief of Staff Colonel Bannud told the British Minister that 'there was no doubt whatever that Major Hussaini was the murderer'.²⁵ On 7 December, however, they were acquitted and Shishakli honoured them with a celebratory dinner.²⁶

Although he saved his protégés, Shishakli's action weakened the army's political position. In the wake of the murder, the civilian government capitalised on the scandal by striking a deal with the army. On 10 August the Chief of Staff declared that the army would not intervene in politics and on the 24th the Assembly approved an amnesty for all political crimes committed since Za'im's coup. Although the army continued to assert its self-declared role as defender of the nation, for instance by arraigning alleged subversives before military rather than civilian tribunals, this represented a temporary shift in the balance of power.²⁷

In the civilian political arena, the National Party, denied a parliamentary platform, turned to the streets. Sabri al-'Asali forged ties with the Socialist Cooperative Party. This had been formed by Faysal al-'Asali in December 1948. It called for pan-Arab and pan-Islamic federation and the nationalisation of capital. It was a populist party, whose main asset was its ability to attract young men and to provide gangs of toughs to intimidate political opponents.²⁸ On 26 June a bomb exploded near the parliament building. Although no one was prosecuted, this was taken as a National Party-inspired challenge to the legality of the Assembly.²⁹ More overt signs of the National Party's tactics emerged in August when Quwatli openly backed their calls for the restoration of the pre-Za'im parliament. On the 24th the party staged demonstrations in Damascus, in the course of which grenades were thrown.³⁰

Despite the efforts of the National Party, the Assembly approved the constitution on 5 September and voted to transform itself into a parliament without holding new elections. Atasi was elected President and Qudsi formed a cabinet. It was dominated by the People's Party and the pro-Hashimite but independent Hasan al-Hakim was also brought in.³¹

Although the approval of the constitution gave the Qudsi government a greater degree of internal stability, it had to fight to ward off the machinations of its neighbours. The trials of two sets of plotters who were arrested in September and October provided a good insight into state-sponsored subversive and terrorist activities, as well as into the murky nature of the role played by Syrian military intelligence.

The Kallas-'Ajlani plot

On 27 September a military communiqué announced the arrest of parliamentary deputy and former Minister of Education, Munir al-'Ajlani. The communiqué stated that investigations into the activities of military officers accused of plotting against the state had been in progress over the preceding month. These enquiries had identified certain civilians who were also implicated in the plot. The trial of ten alleged conspirators began on 17 December but was adjourned until the 23rd. It eventually concluded on 28 January 1951. 'Ajlani and six officers were acquitted but an army officer and two civilians were convicted on the charge of 'instigating the commission of armed resistance and [the] annexation of Syria to a foreign state'.[32]

Although the court forbade the press from naming states or foreign persons implicated during the trial, it was obvious to most observers that King 'Abdallah was the guilty party. In October Israel Radio broadcast an account of the plot. This stated that Jordanian Education Minister Shaykh Muhammad Amin al-Shanqiti had employed 'Ajlani, Lieutenant-Colonel Bahij al-Kallas, Vice-Chief of the General Staff, and Hasan al-Hakim to work for the imposition of a Greater Syrian state. This had been discovered by Egyptian intelligence who had cooperated with the governments in Damascus and Baghdad to thwart the plot.[33] It is not possible to comment on the alleged role of Egypt in uncovering the plot but from Foreign Office records a fuller picture of the affair arises.

In February 1950 the Foreign Office had got wind of two pro-Jordanian plots. One was led by Kallas. Already in December 1949 he had proposed executing a pro-Jordanian coup but King 'Abdallah had been unwilling to finance him and the plot had gone no further. In February 'Abdallah sent Shaykh Amin al-Shanqiti to meet him. Kallas informed Shanqiti that he was planning a coup which would install a pro-union government. He requested that the Arab Legion be sent to Damascus after the coup to 'keep order', and that the king provide asylum for him if the attempt failed, or a pension for his family if he died.[34]

The other alleged band of plotters were an improbable group. Information reaching the Foreign Office stated that Colonel Anwar Bannud, the Chief of Staff, Lieutenant Colonel Ibrahim Husayni, Director of the Deuxième Bureau and Major Sa'id al-Hubbi, a former Military Attaché in Washington, were cooperating with the outspoken pro-Hashimite Hasan al-Hakim and his son Nuri to bring off a pro-Jordanian coup. The three officers met 'Abdallah in May and Nuri al-Hakim did so in June. They asked for assistance but 'Abdallah did not like their conditions and gave them some funds but little encouragement. He was probably right to do so, since it is safe to assume that the officers were acting as agent provocateurs. Bannud had become Chief of Staff with Shishakli's agreement, while Husayni had been Director of the Deuxième Bureau during Za'im's aggressively anti-Hashimite phase. As the Nasir case proved, Husayni had close relations with Shishakli and was mixed up in his dirty work. Hubbi, as we shall see, played a dubious role in Kallas's subsequent plot.[35]

It appears that the second group took their efforts no further but Kallas proved more persistent. In July, he asked Britain to facilitate a clandestine visit to Amman. The Foreign Office refused but he made the trip anyway. According to Hasan al-Hakim, who was not implicated in the trial, Kallas finally decided in August to begin planning a coup. This time he was encouraged by 'Abdallah. As Sir Alec Kirkbride, the British Minister in Amman, put it, 'I have no doubt that ...['Abdallah] was aware of the conspiracy ... and gave them what encouragement he could'.[36] Indeed, the event which precipitated the arrests of the plotters was the apprehension of a driver entering the country from Jordan, carrying cheques made out to the plotters signed by Shanqiti.[37] One of the officers approached by Kallas was Hubbi, recently promoted to Lieutenant-Colonel and appointed Commander of the Air Force. He informed Shishakli of the plot and was told to play along. Thereafter, it appears that the 'Deuxieme Bureau ... overplayed its role of agent provocateur to such an extent that the case became ... hopelessly confused'.[38] The British Minister in Damascus suggested that:

> Hubbi, an arch intriguer who works very closely with ... Shishakli, was prepared to play with both sides and would have joined the conspiracy if he had been convinced that it was likely to succeed. But the risks of siding with Jordan were far greater than were those of double-crossing the conspirators, seeing that there were other officers like ... [Husayni], ... Shawkat Shuqair, Administrative Assistant to the Minister of Defence, and ... Nas[i]r who were in the know. ... There is no concrete evidence to show how far Nas[i]r was involved, but ... the fact that ... [he] was suspect may well have provided an additional motive for his murder.[39]

Strangely enough, despite his evident guilt, Kallas was vouched for during the trial by Husayni himself who 'maintained that ... [Kallas] would never work against the Syrian Republic'.[40] This may perhaps be explained by the fact that Kallas's brother was a friend of Akram Hawrani, who had been closely associated with Shishakli since his coup. It was also fairly clear that 'Ajlani had been implicated in the scheme, though perhaps less deeply than Kallas.

Both Kallas and 'Ajlani denied the charges and claimed that they were victims of a Deuxième Bureau entrapment operation. Some of the Syrian press accepted their claims and suggestions that Hawrani had sought to frame 'Ajlani as a result of the latter's pro-British views further discredited the prosecution's case.[41] Furthermore, 'as the tortuous pattern of the case unfolded and the sordid role played by the Deuxieme Bureau became clear, ... Shishakli ... [probably] decided that it would be best to terminate the trial quickly and obtain 'Ajlani's acquittal' in order to avoid further damage to the army's credibility.[42]

The discovery of this plot worsened relations with Jordan but on 29 November the two countries exchanged diplomatic relations for the first time. Prime Minister Qudsi hoped that this would force 'Abdallah to recognise the independent existence of Syria and reduce his propensity for intrigue.[43]

Tawfiq's terrorists

The other trial which occurred at the same time concerned a more violent group, which would qualify as the Syrian Republic's first state-sponsored terrorist organisation. The group came to light in the wake of an attempt to assassinate Shishakli. On 12 October four gunmen ambushed his car on the road between Dumar and Damascus. An officer travelling with him was injured but he escaped unharmed. The military responded with a wave of arrests which led to the smashing of an underground terrorist gang, allegedly active since the previous autumn.[44] The group called itself the 'Arab Suicide Redemption Phalange'.[45] In the course of their investigations, the authorities alleged that the group had additionally been responsible for a grenade attack on a Damascus synagogue in August 1949 which had killed six and injured 27, bombing the Damascus UN Relief and Works Agency (UNRWA) office in September, the shooting of Colonel Stirling in November 1949, and the bombings of the US Legation in April 1950 and the British Legation in March 1950.[46] Furthermore, it was alleged that the group had sent agents to Baghdad to assassinate the Regent and Nuri al-Sa'id and to Amman to kill King 'Abdallah. In both cases the would-be assassins had been unable to carry out their tasks.[47]

The Redemption Phalange had originally been formed as an Arab nationalist political party. Guéhad al-Dahi had founded the Damascus branch, while Georges Habash and Hani al-Hindi, later of the Arab Nationalist Movement, founded a branch in Beirut. The organisation's operational unit was headed by Husayn Tawfiq, an Egyptian fugitive wanted for the 1946 murder of Egyptian Finance Minister Amin Osman. According to al-Dahi, Tawfiq and a countryman of his, 'Abd al-Kadir Amir, soon took over the leadership of the group and encouraged its members to turn to terrorism.[48] According to the Syrian Military Investigator's report,

> at first the Society seems to have confined itself to so-called patriotic acts such as the attacks on the Jewish synagogue and on Colonel Stirling, and the British and American ... incidents. ... Later on Dr. Ruwaiha suggested that the Society should assassinate 'Jordanian traitors' like King Abdullah ... who wanted to come to terms with the Jews. ... [After the failure of these efforts] the gang turned to terrorist acts inside Syria [such as the attack on Shishakli].[49]

Dr Amin Ruwayha, Dean of Syria's Syndicate of Doctors, had helped Rashid Ali in his efforts against the Hashimite monarchy in Iraq in 1941. He had a reputation as a protagonist of Sa'udi interests in Syria. According to the prosecution, Ruwayha received money from his Sa'udi contacts and supplied Tawfiq with arms and cash, as well as suggesting targets to him. After the murder of Colonel Nasir he was afraid that Shishakli would target him next and persuaded the group to carry out the attack on Shishakli by 'promises of endless streams of gold'.[50] Ahmad Sharabati, the ex-Defence Minister, was allegedly the group's link with Quwatli, with whom he retained close ties. Other Quwatli loyalists who were implicated included Bahjat Alabi, the Secretary-General of the Muhafazah of Damascus under Quwatli. Arms and ammunition were discovered stored in his house.[51]

Initially, the Sa'udi connection was thought to run through Amir Fawwaz Sha'lan, Chief of the Ruwalla tribe.[52] Sha'lan was King Ibn Sa'ud's brother-in-law and, earlier in October, Shishakli had publicly insulted him.[53] Sha'lan's private secretary was among those arrested but, when the prosecution brought their charges in November, the finger was pointed instead at Nasha't Shaykh al-Ard, manager of the Sa'udi Airways office in Damascus. He was the brother both of Ibn Sa'ud's personal physician and the Sa'udi Minister in Damascus, Dr Midhat Shaydah al-Ard. The military prosecutor charged him with passing Sa'udi funds to Ruwayha. The military prosecutor's blunt accusation, made while Qudsi was on a visit to Riyadh, provoked Sa'udi ire and Riyadh declared that it 'categorically rejected this malicious accusation'.⁵⁴ Damascus sought to avoid a rift in relations by banning any mention of the source of external funds during the trial and Qudsi despatched a gift to Ibn Sa'ud to mollify him.⁵⁵

Despite this diplomatic reticence on the part of the authorities, the Egyptian and Sa'udi role was clear to foreign observers. The British Legation reported that there was 'little doubt that the criminals were acting at the instigation of Egyptian and Sa'udi Arabian agents'.⁵⁶ The US Legation noted that 'both Sa'udi and Egyptian subversive activity seems to be indicated', and that Quwatli had backed the assassination attempt.⁵⁷

The court passed sentence in March 1951. Tawfiq, Amir and two others were condemned to death. Al-Ard was sentenced to five years, while al-Dahi and al-Hindi got three years each. Sharabati received 18 months and five others got one year each. By the end of the year, however, most of the prison sentences had been rescinded and the death sentences commuted to terms of imprisonment.⁵⁸ This leniency appears to have been as a result of Sa'udi and Egyptian pressure. Dr Ruwayha, for instance, claimed that his release in June had come about after Sa'udi Arabia threatened to close its Legation in Damascus and Egypt threatened to withhold military equipment Syria had purchased in Egypt.⁵⁹

Although the Tawfiq affair appeared at first to be an open and shut case of Sa'udi- and Egyptian-sponsored terrorism, which aimed to remove Shishakli and pave the way for the return of Quwatli, the trial left questions unanswered. In examining the Stirling case, British diplomats queried the official line. It was clear that confessions had been coerced and 'there can be little doubt that Hussein Tawfiq's confession was extracted from him by third degree'.⁶⁰ Nonetheless, observers did not dispute that the Military Prosecutor was correct in his portrayal of the group's decision to target Stirling. As his report stated: 'the ... Society contemplated an attack on one of the British spies in the country and decided that ... Stirling was suitable, especially as they believed that he had played an important role in the assassination of ... Zaim and that he carried out espionage activities among the tribes.'⁶¹ Suspicions, however, arose over the role of the Deuxième Bureau in backing the group. British diplomats concluded that Tawfiq and Amir were working for the Bureau when they attacked Stirling. American diplomats suggested that they may have been still employed when they attacked Shishakli.⁶² Intriguingly, the British Minister reported that the two men had been recruited by Sharabati when he was Defence Minister but that they had been recommended to him by King Faruq. This would fit with the other evidence concerning the group's links with Egypt. Perhaps Faruq sought to provide a haven for two individuals whom he knew could later be of use, even though they were then sought by Egyptian police.

There is insufficient evidence to come to precise conclusions on the extent of Syrian military intelligence involvement in sponsoring the Redemption Phalange.[63] It is possible that elements in the Deuxième Bureau loyal to Sharabati and/or Quwatli were working with Sa'udi or Egyptian intelligence to assist the group. Whether any of the Bureau's directors were involved is a more problematic question. Husayni, who was director under Za'im and again under Shishakli may well have worked with the Egyptians but he was hostile to Quwatli and Sharabati. The two directors under Qudsi's government in late 1949, Bizri and Rifa'i, had more pro-Hashimite sympathies. While it is possible that Husayni would have approved the bombing of the synagogue, it is not clear that he would have sanctioned the attack on the US Legation, and at the time of the attack on Shishakli he was on trial for Nasir's murder.[64] It is possible that Rifa'i authorised an attack on Stirling, either to counter perceived British espionage or to promote instability. However, to say anything further would be mere speculation.

The news of the discovery of these two plots was accompanied by news of further bloodshed. On 30 October, Sami Hinnawi was shot dead in Beirut. He had been released from prison in August under the terms of the amnesty passed by the Constituent Assembly. As soon as he arrived in Lebanon from Syria, a relative of Muhsin Barazi, whose clan had sworn a blood feud against their relative's murderers, had tried to kill him. Hinnawi's assassin was also a cousin of Muhsin Barazi. Although the motive for the killing may have been purely personal, there is little doubt that it was a boon for Egypt and Sa'udi Arabia and their Syrian sympathisers. Since his exile, Hinnawi had worked assiduously to promote the Hashimite cause in Syria.[65]

This turmoil led Qudsi to intensify his efforts to persuade the Arab states to stop their meddling. In November he visited Riyadh, Baghdad, Beirut and Cairo but does not appear to have made much of an impact.[66] Contrary to British advice, Washington decided to back this diplomatic offensive in an effort to bring a modicum of stability to the area. In December Acheson instructed US missions in the Arab world to 'stress ... [the US Government's] strong view that [the] Syrian Republic should have [a] fair chance [to] set [its own] house in order and decide [its] own destiny unhindered by [its] neighbors'.[67] Such overt displays of US support, however, probably did the Syrian government more harm than good. At the time, the US administration, concerned that 'the hard core of ... [Palestinian] refugees ... constitutes a serious threat to stability, and an important impediment to peace between the Arab states and Israel' was pushing for the 'reintegration' of refugees in the Arab countries.[68] Even more provocatively, in January 1951 the Export-Import Bank made a $35 million loan to Israel. These moves sparked off anti-American demonstrations in Damascus the same month.[69]

The Middle East Command and Shishakli's coup

While inter-Arab and domestic rivalries were escalating into violence on the streets of Damascus, London and Washington had been galvanised by the invasion of Korea and convinced of the imperative need to construct a chain of military alliances to contain communist 'expansionism'. During 1951 the attempts of Western military planners to fit the Middle East into their scheme of containment were to lead them to place greater emphasis on the need for stable and pro-Western local regimes. The chaos in Syria did not fit into their plans but at the end of the year Shishakli emerged from the shadows and established a firm grip on the country. The convenient timing of his move, from the Western point of view, and his subsequent good relations with the United States raise the question of a Western role in encouraging his coup. To assess whether this was the case, a brief review of Western concerns is in order.

Western security concerns

American concerns over the security of the Middle East were made clear by Assistant Secretary of State for Near Eastern Affairs, George C. McGhee, in May 1951 after he returned from a tour of the region:

> The United States is concerned about several things in the Near East. The trend toward neutrality had been clearly indicated recently. Egypt and Syria by their voting in the United Nations on Far Eastern issues, had demonstrated an international attitude which was highly unsatisfactory to the West. In addition ... the economic structures of the states in the Near East are basically unsound. A feeling of insecurity was clearly developing in the Near Eastern states.[70]

The Foreign Office concurred with this view. In October it defined Western objectives in the region as:

> (a) To organise the defence of the area against Russian aggression.
> (b) To promote stable political and economic conditions in the individual countries, and so to enhance their resistance to Communism.
> (c) To preserve our economic interests, particularly oil.[71]

Anglo-American policy evolved along two tracks. First, it sought to construct a regional military structure for use in time of war. Second, it sought to stave off the threat of communist subversion by offering economic aid.

Anglo-American discussions over how the Eastern Mediterranean could be organised for defence went on throughout the year. They were hampered by the problem of Britain's bases in the Suez Canal Zone. Britain sought to retain these bases, granted under the 1936 Anglo-Egyptian treaty, in order to protect its imperial lines of communication.[72] Egypt regarded them as a colonial legacy and sought to remove the British presence. Consequently, any defence proposals would have to take account of Egyptian opposition to the permanent stationing of British troops. In the autumn, the Western powers decided to propose the formation of a Middle East Command (MEC), which would include the United States, United Kingdom, France, Turkey and Egypt.[73] The Suez bases would be handed over to the MEC and excess British forces withdrawn. Other Middle Eastern states would be invited to join subsequently. Britain and the United States hoped that this would enable British forces to remain in the region without being seen as colonial occupiers.[74]

On 13 October the proposal was formally put to the Egyptian government. Five days earlier, however, the government had unilaterally abrogated the 1936 Anglo-Egyptian treaty, as well as the 1899 Condominium Agreement Regarding the Sudan. This move had been met with great popular acclaim in Egypt and the government's rejection of the MEC proposals on the 15th was inevitable.[75] Since no Arab government was willing to break ranks publicly with Cairo, Egypt's rejection made it impossible for any other Arab state to accept the proposals.[76]

The United States encouraged Britain to take the lead in multilateral defence issues but economic aid was the main American tool of bilateral diplomacy. This came in various forms – direct grants, International Bank for Reconstruction and Development (IBRD) credits and Point IV assistance. Point IV was the most prominent element in this arsenal. It was a programme of American technical assistance to Third World countries that had been proposed by President Truman in his January 1949 inaugural address.[77] The attitude of the Syrian government toward US aid became a barometer of US-Syrian political relations.

Syrian political developments

On 7 February 1951 the commander of British land forces in the Middle East, General Sir Brian Robertson, visited Damascus. His visit was the result of a reformulation of British strategy for the defence of the region. Previously, Britain had envisaged holding a Soviet thrust on the Ramallah line, believing it did not have the resources to defend east of this line. During 1950, the Chiefs of Staff had adopted 'Plan Celery' which envisaged a forward defence on the 'Lebanon–Jordan line'. This line included much of Syria, so the Chiefs of Staff were keen to arrange logistic facilities for British use in time of war.[78]

Two days after the visit, Prime Minister Qudsi told US Minister Cannon that the West 'need have no fear about where Syria will stand against Commie aggression. ... But I cannot ask Syrian people to defend their misery. We must fulfill our promises for economic balance.'[79] This desire for Western assistance among some Syrian politicians was counter-balanced by vociferous opposition among others who perceived Western military and economic blandishments as neo-colonial bullying. Both Robertson's visit and McGhee's in March were met by demonstrations organised by the Communist Party, the Ba'th, the Islamic Socialist Front and Hawrani's Arab Socialist Party.[80] Before Robertson's visit the British Consulate in Aleppo and, after McGhee's, the US Ambassador's Residence, were bombed by unknown assailants.[81]

Qudsi's government fell on 9 March, unable to balance its conflicting desires for closer ties with Iraq and its wish to avoid appearing pro-Western. Khalid al-'Azm formed a new cabinet on the 27th, dominated by independents.[82] This government formally rejected Point IV aid on 7 June. In the judgement of the US Chargé d'Affaires, Harlan Clark, the rejection was primarily due to 'the Syrian suspicion of the United States because of its attitudes towards Israel'.[83] Syrian opinion had been inflamed as a result of clashes which had broken out in the Hula Valley in March and which led to the introduction of Iraqi fighter aircraft and anti-aircraft units into Syria.[84]

On 1 August 'Azm's government fell after a series of public sector strikes and was replaced by one under Hasan al-Hakim.[85] Although Hakim was pro-Hashimite and pro-Western, Shishakli appears to have accepted him as he was able to convince Shishakli that he had no intention of pushing for a union.[86] His ministry was welcomed by the United States. Cannon reported 'new cabinet [may be?] means of bettering US–Syrian relations. ...We anticipate that Hakim Government will show more realistic attitude toward Point IV and [Mutual Security Programme].'[87] Despite Hakim's orientation, the United

States was still unwilling to supply Syria with the arms that it sought, as it feared their use against Israel.[88] This was despite Clark's plea that US military aid would prevent the tendency for 'the present nihilism to drift towards a culmination which will be pro-communist as well as anti-Israel'.[89]

Hakim did not emphasise his pro-Western orientation but the storm that erupted after the MEC proposals were presented proved too much for his government. The army showed interest in studying the proposals but Egypt's unilateral rejection forestalled any such move. The Egyptian Minister distributed money to leftist groups and Hawrani led demonstrations against the 'imperialist' proposals.[90] On 10 November the cabinet resigned after Foreign Minister Faydi al-Atasi, who strongly opposed the MEC, publicly split from Hakim.[91] After several candidates had tried, People's Party deputy Ma'ruf Dawilibi managed to form a cabinet on 28 November. The domination of his proposed cabinet by People's Party members and their outspoken opposition to the army's role in politics were, however, unacceptable to Shishakli. The same night Shishakli staged a coup and had the leaders of the People's Party arrested. On 2 December President Hashim al-Atasi resigned and Shishakli made Colonel Fawzi Selu Head of State and granted him executive powers.[92]

The causes and consequences of Shishakli's coup

The immediate cause of the coup was the power struggle between the army and the People's Party. Control of the gendarmerie had continued to be a matter of contention and Dawilibi's assumption of the post of Minister of Defence worried the army.[93] As Shishakli put it, the People's Party ignored 'the opinion of the military men' and so the army was 'compelled to rectify the behaviour of the Party'.[94] Shishakli summed up his concerns in a statement issued on 2 December. Speaking to the Syrian public, he attacked a 'conspiring group' of leaders which

> as soon as it had acquired influential positions, ... started making preparations and drawing up plans to drag you into jeopardy, and to surrender to and cooperate with foreign quarters ... in order to tie you to the cart of the foreigner. ... This conspiring group is responsible for the country's remaining without a Budget for a whole year. It aims at withholding the necessary allocations for strengthening your Army and its means of defence. ... We saw them transfer the Gendarmerie to the Ministry of the Interior and appoint a civilian in the Ministry of Defence, with the object of putting on the Army the responsibility for their shortcomings, confusion, and the (?subjugation) of the supreme

interests of the country to their personal ambitions. ... The era of swindlers, professional politicians and jugglers must end.[95]

Paris and Washington welcomed Shishakli's coup but London was less keen. As a result of its intimate involvement with the Syrian army, France appears to have been involved in backing the army's political role over the preceding year. Rushdi Kikhia, for instance, argued that French influence had encouraged the army to provoke the government crisis in March which had removed Qudsi. The motive was his perceived sympathy to partisans of Greater Syria and his criticism of French policy in Morocco.[96] After Shishakli's coup, France moved quickly to recognise his regime and extended its hand. The Iraqis were convinced that Paris had backed the coup but exactly what role the French Minister played remains unclear.[97]

Washington greeted the coup with relief, seeing in it an opportunity to stem what it perceived to be the rising tide of leftism. The *Christian Science Monitor* headlined its report: 'Syria Coup Held Victory for Pro-Western Policy'.[98] Dawilibi had been of especial concern since his April 1950 call for a non-aggression pact with the USSR. The *New York Times* described him as 'the most outspoken anti-American leader in the Arab world'.[99] Shishakli was viewed favourably as his desire for arms had led him to forge ties with the United States. In July Major Ghassan Jadid, Shishakli's representative on the Mixed Armistice Commission, had asked the US Military Attaché 'what do you want us to do' in order to be eligible for arms supply?[100]

The State Department immediately sought to strengthen ties with the new regime, believing that a strong ruler would stabilise the country. In December Acheson instructed the US Legation: 'it is in [the] interest [of the] West [to] aid Shishakli in [any] efforts he may make to establish [a] pro-West stable and progressive gov[ernmen]t in Syria'.[101] A few days later Syria became only the second country in the Middle East, after Sa'udi Arabia, to be eligible for military aid under the Mutual Defence Act.[102]

The Foreign Office was not so enthusiastic. Relations with Shishakli had been strained due to Britain's continued reluctance to supply arms in the quantities he requested. In addition, Nuri al-Sa'id's hostility to Shishakli meant that Britain was wary of alienating him by backing Shishakli strongly.[103] The Foreign Office's attitude towards the Syrian Chief of Staff was summed up by the Head of the Eastern Department, who described him as 'a sinister, ruthless and unscrupulous figure'.[104]

On the inter-Arab scene, it was only Iraq which reacted strongly to the coup. The Fertile Crescent/Greater Syria debate had lost some of its vigour over the preceding year. In July King 'Abdallah had been assassinated. His death had been followed by a certain amount of agitation in Greater Syrian circles. Groups of exiled Jordanians in Syria, for instance, had called for the annexation of Jordan by Syria.[105] Shishakli had, however, ensured that these plans remained still-born, travelling to Riyadh a fortnight after the assassination to claim the $4 million outstanding on the promised Sa'udi loan.[106] After 'Abdallah's son, Talal, acceded to the throne on 5 September, he showed little interest in pursuing his father's quest. By the end of 1951, Sir Alec Kirkbride could report that Jordanians regarded events in Syria as none of their business.[107]

Nuri Sa'id, however, regarded Shishakli as 'a dangerous and unfriendly adventurer'.[108] He was also motivated by the need to divert domestic nationalist opinion, which was criticising his support for the RAF bases and the IPC pipeline and so threatened to intervene. He warned the British Ambassador that, since he regarded Dawilibi and President Atasi as the legitimate government, he would respond to any call for assistance by intervening militarily if necessary. The Foreign Office felt it necessary to warn him that, under the Tripartite Declaration, Britain was committed to opposing any such move. This dissuaded him.[109]

Shishakli's dictatorship

After his coup Shishakli took a firm grip on the country. He imposed order by building a police state. Foreign visitors and residents were put under strict control, most political parties were banned, the civil service and educational establishments were purged and the autonomy of the Druze region was restricted.[110]

Repression was exercised primarily through the military security services, whose position was greatly strengthened.[111] Syria's intelligence services had been established by the French Mandatory authority. External intelligence had been handled by the services of Metropolitan France, while the French-officered Syrian services had been responsible for internal security and counter-espionage. This 'Service des Renseignements' 'was the cornerstone of French administration in Syria', and its 100 officers had learnt to manipulate the levers of political power in the Levant.[112]

After independence, the Deuxième Bureau, the intelligence branch of the army General Staff, was responsible for ensuring the loyalty of the military, while the Interior Ministry's Sûreté Générale maintained surveillance over the civil population and foreigners. Za'im's coup had, however, inaugurated a tradition of military involvement in politics, which was reflected in the gradual expansion of the role of the Deuxième Bureau at the expense of the Sûreté. Although the latter was nominally controlled by the Interior Minister, under Shishakli it came to be staffed largely by soldiers. The traditional gendarmerie-army rivalry was also resolved in favour of the latter.[113]

Shishakli and the West

Over the next two years, especially after John Foster Dulles became Secretary of State in President Dwight Eisenhower's administration in January 1953, American concerns over Third World neutralism and communist subversion intensified.[114] However, by April 1952, the National Security Council (NSC) recognised that 'the danger in [the Near East] ... arises not so much from the threat of direct military attack as from acute instability, anti-Western nationalism and Arab-Israeli antagonism which could lead to disorder and ... to a situation in which regimes oriented towards the Soviet Union could come to power'.[115] Thus, although Anglo-American efforts to promote regional defence structures continued, the primary effort turned to bolstering the domestic positions of friendly regimes and reducing sources of regional tension. In May 1953 Dulles visited the region to sell new Anglo-American proposals for a Middle East Defence Organisation (MEDO).[116] He encountered widespread opposition to the concept and, on his return to Washington, ordered that the proposal be put 'on the shelf' for the time being.[117]

Instead, the United States concentrated on encouraging the Shishakli regime's privately expressed desire to reduce friction with Israel. In public, Shishakli's government took a robustly anti-Israeli stance. The Syrian Foreign Minister, for instance, declared that Israel 'depends ... on ... terror, threats ... and subversive opinions, and ...directs its foreign policy towards the destruction of the existing international system'.[118] However, in a January 1953 conversation with Ambassador James S. Moose, President Fawzi Selu 'recognised the fact of Israel's continued existence and ... predicted peace ... provided Israel can be persuaded to abandon its provocative tactics'.[119] Shishakli was keen to pursue a dialogue with Israel in order to reduce the incidence of border clashes but was unwilling to take the risk of negotiating a peace treaty.[120] The United States accepted this argument as 'to expect relatively temperate Arab leaders to add Israel peace issue ... is asking them to court downfall'.[121]

At the same time, Shishakli's government resisted US pressure to disavow publicly the principle of repatriation of Palestinian refugees. Nonetheless, although the government complained that the settlement of refugees would pose an impossible burden on the Syrian economy, it did authorise the discreet resettlement of 80,000.[122] Shishakli's primary concern, as with his predecessors, continued to be to get access to US military aid. In this he was supported by the US Embassy, who argued that this would strengthen the government and enable it to move further ahead of public opinion in its dealings with the West and Israel.[123] As ever, these requests were opposed by Israel and turned down by the United States as Shishakli refused to give the public assurances called for under the terms of the Tripartite Declaration that the weapons would not be used aggressively.[124]

During his May 1953 visit Dulles concluded that: 'Syria was a state that offered real possibilities, thanks to Shishakli. ... He was a man of much broader vision [than Egypt's President Neguib] and deeper understanding of the relation of his country to world problems.'[125] Efforts to woo Syria were subsequently increased. In September grants and technical assistance for three Syrian infrastructure projects were approved.[126]

The main thrust of US policy in late 1953 was to reduce Arab-Israeli tensions by securing agreement on the division of the river Jordan's waters and on the internationalisation of Jerusalem. Washington feared that if these issues were not addressed, the evolving Israeli policy of military 'retaliations' would destabilise the region.[127] The State Department's concerns were expressed in a November paper:

> Israeli policy has served to counter United States endeavours to stabilize conditions in the area. Israel's unpredictable and uncontrollable dynamism, rather than the static negativism of the Arab states, [is] the major present source of danger in the Near East.[128]

These concerns led Eisenhower to appoint Eric Johnston as his Personal Representative and during November he visited Middle Eastern capitals, seeking to gain agreement on a scheme, which had been formulated by the Tennessee Valley Authority for UNRWA, for the development of the Jordan Valley through use of its waters.[129] Dulles recognised the importance of military aid to Shishakli and authorised Johnston to offer him such if it would help gain Syrian agreement to the scheme, but this aid 'would be conditional on Syrian assurances that the arms would ... not [be] used to wage aggressive warfare'.[130] In the event, Shishakli was unwilling to move out ahead of other Arab states who opposed the plan and he 'reiterated [the] Syrian inability [to] participate in [the] plan until existing UN resolutions re Palestine [are] made effective'.[131]

Domestic politics

Shishakli was close to the SSNP and he had staged his coup in cooperation with the party. He had promised SSNP members posts in his government and his first communiqué was written by the SSNP's Commissioner for Propaganda.[132] In a meeting with the SSNP leadership after the coup Shishakli proposed a three-stage plan in which the army would first destroy the communists, elections would then be held from which the communists and the People's Party would be excluded and then the SSNP would take over the government, in alliance with Hawrani's ASP, the Ba'th and a token representation from the National Party.[133]

The flaw in this plan was the intense hostility between the SSNP and the ASP/Ba'th alliance.[134] Hawrani and the Ba'thists refused to cooperate with Shishakli's plan, so in April the government issued a decree banning all political parties. While the ASP's newspaper was suppressed and the Muslim Brotherhood harassed, the SSNP's newspaper continued to appear, carrying government announcements.[135] Shishakli, however, kept his relationship with the SSNP informal and ambiguous and in his public pronouncements alternated the term 'Arab nation' with Sa'adah's 'Syrian nation'.[136]

Shishakli's decision to rule without the help of the established parties became clear in the autumn when he launched a new party, the Arab Liberation Movement (ALM).[137] He hoped that politicians from across the spectrum would join the movement which could then 'win' elections and provide a legitimate basis for his rule. However, even SSNP leaders refused to cooperate, regarding the move as a betrayal of his earlier promises.[138] Despite an expansion of radio broadcasts promoting the ALM's pan-Arab message, the movement remained a hollow organisation.

Since the breakdown of their discussions, the gulf between Shishakli and the Ba'th/ASP had become irreconcilable. Hawrani and his colleagues, however, only became a threat to Shishakli when they found a sympathetic audience in the army. Some officers had become disillusioned with their Chief of Staff both as a result of his personal conduct and the high-handed behaviour of his security officers.[139] An example of this tension was a confrontation which erupted at Qatana, home of the army's main armoured unit. In response to the death of an NCO while under interrogation by the Deuxième Bureau, the unit's officers sealed off their barracks and forbade entry to members of the security branch. Shishakli retaliated by posting the officers involved to distant parts of the country.[140] As frustrations mounted there was talk among junior officers of removing Shishakli. Hawrani and the Ba'th leaders fanned this discontent.[141]

During November and December bombs attributed to agents of Hawrani's ASP damaged ALM offices in Aleppo, Latakia and Hama.[142] Nonetheless, Shishakli felt secure enough to go ahead with an official visit to Cairo in mid-December. This was cut short when Ibrahim Husayni informed him that he had discovered plans for a coup. Shishakli swiftly ordered the arrest of around 40 officers, with 'Adnan Malki being identified as the ring-leader. His anger was, however, mainly directed at Hawrani and the Ba'thists. The army communiqué issued on 29 December blamed 'extremist political parties' which had persuaded officers to 'pursue political activities in the barracks'.[143]

Hawrani, Bitar, 'Aflaq and other politicians fled to Lebanon where they were granted political asylum and held press conferences publicising their criticisms of Shishakli. They claimed that they had been forced into exile by an increasingly repressive government which was spending its funds on maintaining a police state instead of promoting progressive legislation. Furthermore, they argued that Shishakli's government was seeking to join a Western defence pact and to abandon the Palestinian cause. Shishakli's press responded with vigorous counter-attacks and he closed the Lebanese border for four days to force Beirut to clamp down on the exiles' activities.[144]

Although *Le Monde* reported in January that 'The Shadow of Civil War is Discernable in Damascus', Shishakli emerged from the affair in an apparently strong position.[145] Although it was now clear that he was ruling despite the opposition of the majority of the political class, his security services had shown themselves capable of repressing any organised opposition.

By the summer of 1953 he felt confident enough to emerge from the shadows and institutionalise his leadership. In June a new constitution was promulgated which accorded greater powers to the president than under the 1950 constitution. On its approval in a July plebiscite he became President, with an absurd 99.6 per cent of the vote.[146] Parliamentary elections were held on 9 October in which the ALM won 60 of the 82 seats. Most of the others went to pliable independents and tribal leaders. Since it was clear to all observers that the elections were rigged, they served only to alienate his remaining allies in the SSNP who protested that several of their successful candidates had been denied seats by the government's ballot riggers.[147] Although the party did not join the opposition, thereafter it ceased to cooperate with the government.[148]

Meanwhile the opposition had been reorganising. In September, 143 political leaders signed a 'National Pact' denouncing Shishakli's 'individualistic' and 'unconstitutional' government and calling for its replacement by 'democratic' and 'representative institutions'. Prominent among the signatories were ex-President Hashim al-Atasi, Druze notable Sultan al-Atrash, the pro-Hashimite Hasan al-Hakim and Rushdi Kikhia from the People's Party.[149] Hawrani and the Ba'th leaders were allowed to return to Syria in mid-October.[150] While in exile they had merged their parties to form the Arab Ba'th Socialist Party (ABSP) and, although under close surveillance, began to forge contacts with other opposition elements.[151]

This tide of dissatisfaction provided Shishakli's foreign opponents with the opportunity for which they had been waiting ever since his coup. They were not slow to exploit it.

Shishakli and the inter-Arab struggle

Shishakli's good relations with Egypt and Sa'udi Arabia had been cemented by visits in early 1952. Improved relations with Lebanon had been marked by the conclusion of an economic agreement in February.[152] In March the post-'Abdallah Syrian–Jordanian *rapprochement* had been formalised by the signature of a treaty of friendship.[153] Even relations with Iraq had improved since early 1952 when the Iraqi Military Attaché had been doing his best to drive a wedge between Selu and Shishakli. Nuri al-Sa'id had met Shishakli in July and Iraq had finally recognised Selu's government on 2 December.[154] Nonetheless, Iraq had not given up its ambitions in Syria.

In January 1953 Nuri al-Sa'id became Defence Minister in a new Iraqi government headed by the 'reactionary' Jamil Madfai.[155] Encouraged by the instability inside Syria, this new government opened its arms to Shishakli's opponents. In April Shishakli complained to both the British and the Americans about the activities of Syrian officers who had received asylum in Iraq and were agitating among the tribes along the Iraqi border and in the north of Syria. This group was led by Colonel Muhammad Safa, who had been purged after the December 1952 coup attempt. Another of their leaders was 'Isam Mraywad, the officer who had commanded the executions of Za'im and Barazi. He had left Syria with Hinnawi in August 1950 but after Hinnawi's assassination had taken refuge in Iraq. The third prominent figure was Colonel Mustafa Dawilibi, brother of Shishakli's longtime opponent Ma'ruf Dawilibi. He had been jailed in December 1952 and fled to Iraq on his release. They were joined by Hinnawi's brother-in-law, As'ad Tallas and Mahmud Rifa'i, a former director of the Deuxième Bureau.[156]

This group styled itself the 'General Command of the Free Syria Forces'. In May they issued a declaration condemning Shishakli's 'despotic' methods, his creation of a 'gloomy atmosphere of terror', the shooting of 'girls, workers and women', his officers' 'immoral crimes against school mistresses', and the persecution, torture and internment of officers who opposed him.[157] Shishakli was clearly concerned by the movement. He reinforced his bodyguard and demanded that Britain force Iraq to cease its support for the group.[158] British officials denied any hand in the affair but were aware of the strength of Safa's movement and made no effort to rein in the Iraqis.[159]

In September Fadhil al-Jamali formed a new government in Baghdad comprising younger and more aggressive politicians. The government was 'obsessed' with Fertile Crescent unity and intensified efforts to oust the Syrian President. In October Safa announced the formation of a 'Free Syrian Government' in Baghdad, further unsettling Shishakli.[160]

The fall of Shishakli

From December 1953 to February 1954 Syria was convulsed by a series of clashes which eventually brought down the Shishakli regime. Three groups shared the aim of toppling the government but they proved unable to coordinate their moves and Shishakli defeated the first two threats, only to be ousted by the third. In the turmoil accusations of foreign interference were directed at Jordan, Israel, Britain and Iraq. While it is clear that Iraq played a major role, Israel may also have had a hand in events.

The signatories of the National Pact had agreed to coordinate moves against the government to take place in early 1954 but the various factions had their own agendas as well. In mid-December the ABSP and Communist Party organised demonstrations in Aleppo, Damascus and in several smaller towns. Shopkeepers and lawyers also went on strike. Shishakli overruled his security chief, Ibrahim Husayni, who wanted to respond vigorously and only two demonstrators were killed by the security forces. Subsequently, Shishakli attempted to combine concessions with firmness. Husayni was posted to Washington as the Military Attaché and a civilian appointed head of the police.[161] In late January some of Husayni's more notorious secret police colleagues were dismissed. At the same time, Shishakli ordered the arrest of the political leaders who had subscribed to the National Pact. In doing so he was probably acting on the basis of intelligence supplied by the French who were keen to undermine what they saw as a pro-Hashimite and pro-British opposition.[162] Rushdi Kikhia, Sabri 'Asali, 'Adnan Atasi, Akram Hawrani, Michel 'Aflaq and Salah al-Din Bitar were taken to jail during the night of 26/27 January while Hashim Atasi and the Druze Hasan al-Atrash were put under house arrest.[163] A strike of Syrian lawyers was called in protest, which resulted in the arrests of the lawyers' leaders.[164]

Deuxième Bureau officers also descended on the Jabal Druze to investigate rumours of a Druze plot.[165] They stumbled across Ba'thist leaflets being distributed by, among others, Mansur al-Atrash, Sultan Pasha Atrash's son. In the course of the arrests disturbances broke out which left four gendarmes dead.[166] The security men then called in army units and advanced on Atrash's home village of Quraya to arrest the Sultan. The Druze had, however, been stockpiling weapons, largely of Iraqi origin, ready for a move on Damascus. The plan had been to seize the weapons of army units in the Jabal and then use trucks sent from Damascus to collect agricultural produce to transport Druze fighters to Damascus.[167] Although Atrash was not ready to make his move, he quickly assembled his forces and resisted the army. A guerrilla war ensued which lasted for almost a fortnight.[168] Druze fighters took effective control of half of the Jabal Druze and at one point held 190 soldiers prisoner. The army responded with artillery and air bombardments and terrorised the villages under its control with 'looting and raping'.[169] Jordan's King Hussein refused the Druze's plea for arms and by 10 February Sultan Pasha persuaded the more aggressive young Druze leaders to call a halt. The Druze leadership then took refuge in Jordan, which refused Shishakli's requests to extradite them. While there the Druze fighters were re-supplied with arms by Iraqi convoys with which they rendezvoused in the Jordanian desert but they did not resume attacks on the army.[170]

During the fighting Shishakli alleged that 'unusual foreign activity had been observed ... in the Suweida Governorate' and that 'the arms seized were modern'.[171] At first he accused Jordan of arming the Druze but a visit by Jordanian Interior Minister Hazza al-Majali armed with promises of full cooperation indicated that this was not the case.[172] Israel was also accused of arming the Druze. Although there is no evidence of Israeli arms being supplied, the British Foreign Office concluded that 'a number of Druze have undoubtedly been in the pay of Israel'.[173]

Israel certainly did its best to inflame the situation. Earlier in the year Israel Radio had publicised the activities of Safa's 'government in exile' and now Israel took the opportunity to try to destabilise Shishakli's regime.[174] The press and parliament trumpeted the Israeli Druze community's anger at the attacks on Syrian Druze villages and their calls for diplomatic and armed intervention. Prime Minister Moshe Sharett received a delegation of Druze notables, while both the left- and the right-wing press demanded action. Mapam's newspaper *Al-Hamishmar* argued that 'everything should be done to come to the help of the Druze' and Israel Radio broadcast Herut's admonition that 'the events in Syria provide an excellent opportunity for Israel to take action'.[175]

Sharett, however, refused to accede to calls from his more aggressive advisors to take drastic action. In his diary entry for 1 February 1954, Sharett records that he resisted Chief of Staff Moshe Dayan's proposal to arm the Israeli Druze so that they could intervene in the fighting in the Jabal Druze.[176] A Foreign Ministry document dated 21 February summarising Israeli responses to the uprising noted that 'we are now seeking to determine the possibility of establishing a direct contact between us and the Druze in Syria and contact with rebel Syrian bodies under the leadership of Muhammad Safa'.[177] Whether any contacts were in fact forged remains a mystery. On the 25th Pinchas Lavon, the Minister of Defence, tried to persuade Sharett to act, saying: 'Syria is disintegrating' and urging that 'now is the time to move and seize the Syrian border positions which are beyond the demilitarized zone'.[178] Sharett continued to refuse to act, leading Lavon to castigate him on the 28th, claiming that Israel had 'missed a rare opportunity to become stronger'.[179]

The main concern of Shishakli and his supporters was, however, over British and Iraqi interference. A typical headline in the Syrian newspaper *al-Faiha'* proclaimed the existence of a British conspiracy to take control of Syria.[180] Egypt's General Neguib, for his part, put the 'Syrian people ... on their guard against this ... [imperialist] conspiracy' and Anwar Sadat, a member of the ruling Egyptian Revolutionary Command Council, pointed to the 'dirty fingers of Britain'.[181] As ever, these charges owed more to propaganda than fact as Britain sought to restrain Iraqi activism. In early February the British Ambassador in Baghdad 'begged Dr Jamali to leave the Syrians to settle their own affairs'.[182] In a meeting with the British Ambassador on 10 February Shishakli admitted that he did not feel that Britain was directly responsible for the uprisings but since Iraq was clearly involved, then Britain could not escape blame.[183]

There was certainly no doubt about the major role that Iraq was playing. For several months Iraqi weapons and aid had been reaching the Druze.[184] The Military Attaché in Damascus, Brigadier 'Abd al-Moutalib al-Amin, had been in close contact with opposition politicians and had distributed funds and subsidised anti-Shishakli newspapers in Beirut.[185] Safa's movement had acted openly with Iraqi backing and had attempted to coordinate its actions with Sultan Pasha Atrash.[186] Furthermore, it appears that the Iraqis were intimately involved in coordinating the planned uprising in January. Prime Minister Fadhil Jamali admitted afterwards to the Americans that his government had

had foreknowledge of the plans.[187] In the wake of the student demonstrations in December, Hashim al-Atasi had cabled to Jamali that the 'democratic forces' were about to act and requested Iraqi assistance.[188] Jamali complied by flying to Amman and Beirut in an attempt to muster support for the opposition.[189]

Shishakli was well aware of the Iraqi role. After the Druze had been crushed, Brigadier al-Amin was expelled along with an assistant, Lieutenant Colonel Salih Mahdi al-Samarra'i.[190] Perhaps surprisingly, however, the two governments did not indulge in an all-out propaganda war. On 10 February the Secretary General of the Syrian Foreign Ministry, Dr Ibrahim al-Ustuwani, lamented that 'a certain coolness' had overtaken relations with Iraq due to the 'permission granted by the Baghdad Government to certain common criminals to take refuge in its territory' and to 'conduct subversive activities' from Iraq.[191] The Iraqi government in its turn spoke the platitudes of brotherhood: 'Syria is dear to our hearts, and our Government desires ... that stability and security ... should prevail in Syria'.[192] On the whole Shishakli tried to play the events down, the Syrian press claiming that what had occurred were 'simple measures taken ... to safeguard security' that had been exaggerated by the Israeli and 'imperialist' media.[193] It was left to Cairo's 'Voice of the Arabs' to lambast the 'criminal objectives' of the imperialists and Zionists who were 'sowing seeds of discord' in the Arab world.[194]

In any case, towards the end of the month tensions seemed to be subsiding, with talk of a Lebanese or Egyptian mediation role.[195] The army rebellion which suddenly erupted in Aleppo thus took most observers by surprise.

It appears that a group of army officers had been plotting to move against Shishakli since the summer. Many of these officers had been involved in the December 1952 plot and had subsequently been either posted to remote parts of the country or retired from the army. While some of the conspirators had links with civilian politicians, there appears to have been no coordination between the uprisings in December/January and the Aleppo revolt in late February. By the time the army officers took action, Aleppo was reported to be quiet and 'most people appeared thankful that order had been maintained'. This, however, merely demonstrated the 'relatively unimportant role which popular attitudes play in the struggle for political power in Syria'.[196]

The plans for the revolt 'were originally concocted in Deir-ez-Zor' which 'had become something of a place of exile for Army officers' opposed to Shishakli.[197] A large proportion of the officers whom Shishakli distrusted came from the minorities, especially the 'Alawi and the Druze. The 'Alawis had been angered by the murder of Muhammad Nasir, regarded as their leader, in July 1950 and the Druze added Shishakli's repression in the Jabal to their list of grievances.[198] Two Druze officers, Colonel Amin Abu Assaf and Captain Muhammad al-Atrash planned the revolt with Captain Mustafa Hamdun, who was close to Hawrani.[199] In January 1954 Atrash and Hamdun found themselves commanding infantry companies in Aleppo and they won over Captain Kamal Malki, a fellow company commander. The deputy commander of the Aleppo garrison, Colonel Faysal Atasi, Hashim Atasi's nephew, was reportedly only brought into the conspiracy at the last minute. The conspirators had also agreed to cooperate with Colonel Jawwad Raslan, commander of the Latakia garrison and a relative of the Atasi family from Homs. The commander of the Homs garrison, Colonel Shawqat, had also indicated his sympathy.

On 24 February the plotters put their plan into action. The main opposition was likely to come from the Military Police and Deuxième Bureau officers who were hand-picked by Shishakli to ensure their loyalty. Colonel Atasi therefore telephoned the commander of the Military Police and 'sent him on a wild-goose chase into the country' and asked the Deuxième Bureau Commander to remain at home to await a visit from the garrison commander. The rebels then arrested the garrison commander, General Umar Tamir Khan, and occupied the radio station from where they broadcast news of their revolt. On the morning of the 25th Aleppo Radio broadcast 'the case against Shishakli':

> he launched a ruthless war against the people ... he stuffed mouths with iron and fire, ruled the people with whips and bullets, and used the most vile and beastly measures of oppression against anyone who dared to make any utterance. ... He also overburdened the small wage-earners with ... unmerciful taxes. ... He ... deposited, in his own name, huge sums in world banks. ... He opened for his brother the biggest debauchery- and gambling-place in Damascus; and gave him a free hand to direct a gang smuggling narcotics. ... He sewed up the country with a wide, terrifying spy-network [the Deuxième Bureau] ... He ... tore [the army] ... asunder. ... A senior officer began to fear his most junior men ... lest they be spying on him ... Finally, Shishakli wanted us, the soldiers ... to be slaves in satisfying his blood lusts, by working to kill our sons, fathers, mothers, brothers and sisters ... We announce ... that Shishakli is an aggressor and usurper, that his rule is not lawful, and ... we ... invite the people to ... set up their adored, popular, republican regime with their own hands and entirely by their own will.[200]

During the morning the garrisons in Homs and Hama announced

their support for the rebels who already controlled Aleppo, Dayr al-Zor and Latakia.[201] Shishakli responded by ordering the arrest of several politicians and ex-officers in Damascus, such as 'Adnan Malki, and alerted armoured units based at Qabun and Qatana near the capital. Chief of Staff Shawqat Shuqayr, however, urged caution, concerned to avoid civil war.[202] It was also becoming apparent that many of the army units stationed in the Jabal Druze had gone over to the rebels.[203] In a meeting with his cabinet and the General Staff during the evening of the 25th Shishakli decided to resign rather than fight it out. In his resignation statement he blamed officers 'subject to party influences' and expressed his desire to 'prevent bloodshed'.[204] Along with several close aides he drove to Beirut where he was given asylum in the Sa'udi embassy.

Chief of Staff Shuqayr then turned to the civilian politicians whom Shishakli had jailed in January and asked them to form a government. In discussions on the 26th these politicians agreed to support a return to the 1950 constitution and to re-appoint Hashim Atasi as President. In the meantime, however, a group of Shishakli loyalists had seized the initiative in Damascus. Led by Captain 'Abd al-Haq Shehadi, formerly Shishakli's assistant chief of Military Police, Captain Husayn Hiddi, who had been wounded in the attempt on Shishakli's life in October 1950, and Lieutenant Burhan Adham, commander of the Military Police in Damascus, these loyalists commanded armoured and military police units around the capital and so were able to apply pressure to Shuqayr.

During the morning of the 26th they arrested Shuqayr and forced him to appear before the pro-Shishakli parliament which then requested that the Speaker of the Chamber, Dr Ma'mun Kuzbari, take on the vacant Presidency. Orders were issued for the re-arrest of the politicians whom Shuqayr had released the day before, prompting them to take refuge in Homs. In Beirut Shishakli heard of his supporters' comeback and demanded to be flown back to Damascus to take command. The Lebanese and Sa'udis, however, refused to permit him and he 'eventually emplaned for Sa'udi Arabia against his will'.[205] In any case, Haq and his comrades rapidly lost control of the situation. With Aleppo Radio launching vitriolic attacks on the 'murderer' Haq, a group of anti-Shishakli officers coalesced in Damascus which prevented Haq from taking control of all the forces stationed in Damascus.[206] In the morning of the 27th Air Force units stationed in Mezze went over to the rebels and leftist demonstrators stormed the parliament, chasing out the pro-Shishakli deputies. In the afternoon the demonstrators also attacked the Damascus radio station which was controlled by Haq's troops. In the mêlée 40 civilians were killed or injured. By then, however, the loyalists had admitted defeat and asked Shuqayr to inform the rebels that they no longer supported the Kuzbari government.

In the morning of the 28th Damascus radio broadcast a series of communiqués announcing Kuzbari's resignation and the army's return 'to normal duties'.[207] That evening, however, pro-Shishakli forces and possibly communists seeking to destabilise the situation, carried out 'sporadic sniping' which caused 50 casualties, before being suppressed by 'stern counter-measures'. The loyalist officers left to take up posts as Assistant Military Attachés abroad and the Atasi government formally entered the capital on 1 March.[208]

The new government was warmly welcomed by Iraq which described Shishakli's regime as 'hateful' and 'tyrannical' and declared that 'the victory of Hashim al-Atassi is regarded as a victory for the forces of good in Syria'.[209] Ironically, however, it appears that Shishakli had been ousted in spite of Iraq's strenuous efforts. Colonel Safa and his colleagues played no role in the February coup. Indeed, Mraywad and Rifa'i were jailed by the rebels in Homs when they returned to Syria during the coup.[210] The officers who led the coup had been motivated by their personal opposition to Shishakli. They gained support from other officers as much for 'bureaucratical and organizational' reasons as for political.[211] While there were rumours of Iraqi assistance to the Aleppo rebels, no firm evidence has emerged. Although Iraqi sources later claimed responsibility for removing Shishakli, it is likely that they merely capitalised on a fortunate situation after their planned rebellion involving civilian politicians and the Druze collapsed.[212] As Glubb Pasha concluded, 'the Iraqis are so incredibly heavy-handed that their plots always fail'.[213]

Iraq was not the only government caught off guard by the army revolt. French officials had no doubt been pleased that Shishakli had acted on their warnings and pre-empted the National Pact plotters. The sudden appearance of the Aleppo rebels raised the spectre of a pro-Iraqi comeback and the French rushed to bolster Haq's officers with financial aid.[214] Sa'udi officials did likewise. During the summer of 1953 senior Sa'udi personages had been personally involved in distributing bribe money to counter Safa's movement. After Shishakli's precipitate flight to Beirut Sa'udi officials distributed up to LS300,000 to pro-Shishakli diehards in an attempt to prolong their resistance.[215]

All these efforts had, however, proved in vain. Once again, as after the fall of Za'im, the Syrian pendulum swung back towards Iraq.

4

Syria between Nasser and the West, 1954–56

The fall of Shishakli was followed by a return to constitutional government led by the civilian politicians whom Shishakli had ousted in 1951. A succession of weak and short-lived governments was not, however, conducive to stability. Shishakli's dictatorship had not united the country's political classes, it had only suppressed their differences. In the period following his departure it became evident that the loose alliances of traditional leaders, epitomised in the National and People's parties, were unable to resist the challenge of the more disciplined ABSP and SSNP. The communists and Muslim Brotherhood played supporting roles as the Ba'th and Syrian Nationalists fought it out, sidelining the old guard politicians in the process. These struggles were conducted not just in parliament and the streets but also within the army. The army emerged from the events of February 1954 deeply divided and riven with political factions. All of the political parties recognised the importance of controlling the military as this enabled them to use the full weight of the Deuxième Bureau and Military Tribunals against their opponents.

In this state of instability Syria was even more vulnerable to external influences than previously. Since all three of the international conflicts in which Syria was enmeshed were coming to the boil, the country was ever more a target for foreign interference and subversion.

The inter-Arab struggle for control of Syria intensified with the rise of Nasserism. Nasser's bid for leadership of the Arab world was staunchly opposed by the governments of Iraq and Lebanon, but in Syria the pro-Nasserite forces gradually gained the upper hand.

The Arab-Israeli conflict was fuelled by Israel's strategy of escalating military 'retaliations' against its neighbours in response to Palestinian infiltration from their territories, which culminated in the invasion of Sinai in October 1956. The frequent clashes inflamed passions on the Arab political scene, benefiting the more radical parties. The fear of Israeli aggression helped the cause of those in Syria who sought protection under the umbrella of Egypt and the Soviet Union.

By the mid-1950s the Great Powers were deeply embroiled in the Cold War. The British and Americans continued their efforts to contain the USSR and formed the Baghdad Pact. The Western powers, however, were divided by disparate commitments. The British retained their close ties to the Hashimites and were at odds with both Nasser's Egypt and King Sa'ud's Sa'udi Arabia. While the United States was more ambivalent towards Nasser and had good relations with the Sa'udis, it was hamstrung by its commitment to Israel. The French meanwhile incurred Anglo-American wrath by going their own way in the Levant. Although they cooperated with Britain against Nasser, they only came to share Anglo-American views on the danger of communism in Syria in 1956. The Soviet Union, meanwhile, rid itself of Stalin's dogmatic foreign policy and came to regard the Middle East as a vital arena of superpower confrontation. To neutralise the containment strategy Moscow sought to extend its influence in the region using the bait of arms sales to draw Egypt and Syria towards it.

These three arenas of international conflict combined with the instability of Syria's domestic scene to create a volatile brew. Various Middle Eastern and Great Power intelligence agencies were active in seeking to impose their favoured government on Syria. During 1954 and 1955 Egypt and Sa'udi Arabia used their influence to pull Syria away from Iraq and into a pact which rivalled the Baghdad Pact. Syria's leftward and pro-Nasserite course was confirmed when the Ba'th routed the SSNP in the wake of the Malki assassination, in April 1955. The assassination also marked the opening of armed hostilities between the SSNP and their opponents. During 1955 and 1956 the overt and covert efforts of the West were not enough to halt the rise of the left as Israeli raids escalated and pushed Syria into the arms of Egypt and the USSR. The Iraqis and British responded by backing the Syrian opposition in a major covert operation during 1956. The failure of this conspiracy merely strengthened their opponents.[1]

The struggle commences

When Hashim al-Atasi took office as President in March 1954 he asked Sabri al-'Asali, the National Party's Secretary-General, to form a cabinet which included the National and People's parties.[2] Shawkat Shuqayr stayed on as Chief of Staff of the army but many of the leftist officers who had been dismissed by Shishakli returned. Prominent among them was 'Adnan Malki who became Chief of Operations. Described by both contemporaries and historians as the leading officer of his era, Malki exerted an influence out of proportion to his rank but was modest enough to refuse the temptation to succeed Shuqayr. Sympathetic to the ABSP, Malki, however, assented to civilian control under Minister of Defence Ma'ruf Dawilibi.[3] Control of the gendarmerie, long a bone of contention between civilians and the military, was returned to the Interior Ministry. In protest at this self-effacement several of the pro-ABSP officers who had been involved in the anti-Shishakli rebellion plotted another coup. Captains Mustafa Hamdun, 'Abd al-Hamid Sarraj and Tu'mah Awadallah were the main conspirators. When discovered they were dealt with leniently, the latter two being posted as Military Attachés to Paris and Cairo respectively.[4]

In foreign policy, 'Asali's government entered into discussions with Iraq concerning union. Egypt and Sa'udi Arabia reacted strongly. Egypt's Military Attaché, Lieutenant-Colonel Jamal Hammad, did his best to persuade army officers to oppose union and his arguments that Syrian officers would lose seniority in a united army found a receptive audience. At the same time the Sa'udis channelled funds to Syrian politicians and the venal Syrian press in order to foster anti-Iraqi sentiment. 'Asali's government responded with a press campaign of its own which lambasted Egypt's 'repressive' military régime and accused Egypt of backing Shishakli's ALM. Nonetheless, the Egyptian and Sa'udi efforts served to reduce enthusiasm for a union.[5]

Frustrated by this stalemate, Iraq encouraged its former protégé, Colonel Safa, to plan a coup. He needed little encouragement as he had found himself in the cold since his return to Syria. Suspicious of his intimate ties with Iraq and 'a non-Arab, foreign state', the army High Command had not re-admitted him to the army.[6] He therefore plotted with several other officers to remove Shuqayr and make himself Chief of Staff. The plotters, however, got no further than printing some manifestoes and placing a few articles in the press before they were discovered. On 18 June six officers and about 60 other ranks were arrested and charged with preparing a coup. On the same day 'Asali's government fell, partly because the army High Command opposed its pro-Iraqi stance. The Safa arrests were probably timed to remind both army officers and politicians that the High Command remained opposed to any precipitate move towards Iraq.[7]

'Asali's cabinet was replaced by a non-partisan one under Sa'id al-Ghazzi which declared that its sole intention was to prepare for parliamentary elections the following August. In the event the elections were postponed until late September and the results 'reveal[ed] a trend away from Syria's traditional political parties towards the newer, more doctrinaire A[B]SP and towards Independents known for their nationalistic and, in some cases, their anti-Western views'.[8] During the elections the Iraqis had attempted to restore their position by financing candidates in the traditionally sympathetic north and had relied on Husni Barazi, to whom they had probably paid LS30,000, to lead their cause.[9] However, the French, who financed the pro-French Khalid al-'Azm, appear to have had more success. The Chamber which emerged reflected the army's preferences which coincided with France's, namely 'weak independents or left-wing partisans ... [who] assure[d] [that the] new chamber [was] too divided [to] challenge the army's ... autonomy or take steps (e.g. Syro-Iraqi union) detrimental [to] army interests'.[10] The 'most cohesive, though not the largest, bloc of seats' was controlled by Akram Hawrani.[11]

The strong showing of the leftists caused alarm in Washington and London, but their main concern was at French policy which appeared to be helping the Ba'th and the communists. The army was regarded as 'a French stronghold' due to France's monopoly on arms supply and training courses, while the French also exercised influence in the academic world and among newspapers which they bribed not to discuss French policies in North Africa. As ever, the French were concerned to preserve their 'special position' in the country and to thwart any move towards Iraq. To this end they backed both the army and 'Azm. This annoyed the State Department and the Foreign Office because 'Azm had cooperated closely with Hawrani's ABSP and Baqdash's communists during the election campaign.[12]

Although anti-Iraqi interests had scored during the elections, the power struggle subsequently shifted back to the army. In early October a pro-Iraqi and pro-SSNP officer, Colonel Mahmud Shawkat, informed the US Embassy of plans by officers who opposed Malki and the ABSP to install a new military leadership. The Embassy refused to get involved and Malki subsequently had several of the officers involved disciplined. Shawkat's compatriots, who included the SSNP officer Colonel Ghassan Jadid, struck back by persuading Shuqyar to transfer Ba'thist officers, such as Mustafa Hamdun, abroad.[13]

The Turkish-Iraqi pact

On 13 January 1955 a joint Turkish-Iraqi communiqué was issued which proposed the conclusion of a defence agreement. The agreement was concluded on 24 February and, with the accession of Britain in April, was to become the Baghdad Pact. The Pact put Syrian domestic politics at the centre of the regional agenda. The parochial intrigues of Syrian officers and politicians became of paramount importance to Arab and Western states as the Baghdad Pact struggled to be born.

Since the collapse of their plans for the creation of a Middle East Defence Organisation in 1953 the British and Americans had worked to establish a grouping of 'northern-tier' states bordering on the Soviet Union to contain the perceived Soviet threat to the Middle East and South West Asia. The alliance between Turkey and Iraq was to provide the basis for this grouping and it was hoped that other Arab countries would join.[14] Since it bolstered the Iraqis and was directed against the distant Soviet Union rather than the immediate threat of Israel, the Egyptians and Sa'udis were bound to oppose the Pact. Nasser, who had ousted General Neguib in April 1954, used this opportunity to take up the mantle of pan-Arabism. He opposed what he labelled a 'neo-imperialist' plot and made a bid for regional leadership by calling for a policy of neutralism in which the Arab states would join an Egyptian-led collective security grouping under the aegis of the Arab League.[15]

Once again, Syria was at the centre of the tug-of-war between rival camps, only this time the traditional battle between the Hashimites and their rivals was overlain by the urgency of the West's anti-communist crusade and Nasser's charismatic calls for Arab unity.

The first push came from Turkey and Iraq who tried to exploit the divisions in the Syrian officer corps to install a government sympathetic to their cause. By late January 1955 it was clear to the US Embassy that 'a group of civilians and Army officers generally favorable to close Syro-Iraqi relations ... has commenced active operations'. Apart from Colonel Shawkat, the leading conspirators were Nadhir Fansah, the late Husni Za'im's brother-in-law and now owner of the pro-Western newspaper *al-Nas*, as well as Husni Barazi, Hasan Hakim and the former Ambassador to London, Edmond Homsi. They sought the return of Ibrahim Husayni, still serving as Military Attaché in Rome.[16] The conspirators claimed to have recruited senior army officers in Aleppo, Homs and Qunaytra to their cause and to have ties with 'Adnan Atasi, the President's son. The group received financial support from the Iraqi Minister in Damascus, 'Abd al-Jalil al-Rawi. On 26 January, the formation of a new party, dedicated to the cause of unity with Iraq was announced. Although the leaders of the party were second rank politicians and former officials, it was clear that the Fansah group was behind it.[17]

Turkey was also concerned at the 'general neutralist drift in Syria' and determined to 'procure Syrian adherence to the Baghdad communiqué ... by extraordinary measures' if necessary. Its Military

Attaché in Damascus began to forge contacts with sympathetic officers and canvassed replacements for Chief of Staff Shuqayr, suggesting in particular General Anwar Bannud or Brigadier Said Hubbi.[18] The Turkish Chargé meanwhile, who 'express[ed] disgust' at 'French machinations in the Levant detrimental to Western interests', promised the Fansah group his support.[19]

The United States welcomed these efforts. During 1954 its Embassy had become increasingly concerned at the 'pro-Soviet and anti-Western orientation in the Syrian press' and the 'unprecedentedly bitter [press] campaign against the United States'. While recognising that this was largely due to US support for Israel and Soviet support for the Arabs at the United Nations, the Embassy concluded that it was also the result of 'subsidization of the press and other Soviet activities in the field of propaganda'. Judging that 13 of the 38 Syrian political publications were 'wholly or in part supported by Soviet or local Communist Party funds' US diplomats and CIA officers discussed proposals to engage in counter-subsidisation. Although the USIS gave some aid to 'objective' papers, a large-scale operation was advised against on the grounds that such an operation was likely to be ineffective so long as US policy over Palestine did not change.[20] In regard to Syrian politics more generally, the State Department had lamented in December 1954 that 'Syria is ... wholeheartedly devoted to a neutralist policy with strong anti-Western overtones'.[21] The US Ambassador to the UN reported to Secretary of State Dulles that, 'the way Syria acts at the UN, she is a Soviet satellite'.[22]

Thus, when Fansah and his compatriots approached the US Embassy for help, they were warmly received and Ambassador Moose recommended they should be given 'discreet encouragement' at the 'proper time'.[23]

The pro-Baghdad Pact forces were, however, amply countered by Egyptian, Sa'udi and French counter-pressures. Faris al-Khuri's government, in office in Damascus since the elections, had reacted mildly to the Turkish-Iraqi communiqué and at an Arab League Premiers' Conference summoned by Egypt at the end of January, Khuri had refused to condemn Nuri al-Sa'id's policy outright.[24] This had infuriated the agreement's internal and external opponents and they combined to bring the cabinet down on 7 February. Although the main reason for the government's collapse was 'personal rivalries which embittered relations between the two coalition parties', President Atasi insisted that Sa'udi, Egyptian and French pressure had played an important role. He argued that 'Saudi agents [were the] most troublesome' as they encouraged ex-President Quwatli, now back in Syria, and some of the tribal deputies to coordinate their campaign to 'wreck' the Khuri cabinet.[25] Other reports stated that the Saʻudis had spent LS600,000 to remove Khuri's cabinet.[26] The State Department sympathised with Atasi and sought to bring the French into line but without success.[27]

Sabri ʻAsali took up the Prime Ministership once again but this time with a cabinet dominated by leftists. Khalid al-ʻAzm became Foreign Minister and worked closely with the left in the hope of gaining their support for the Presidency. Hawrani and the ABSP were happy to cooperate with him as long as he followed their policy preferences. Negotiations with Egypt got under way immediately and on 2 March Syrian and Egyptian officials signed a communiqué rejecting the Baghdad Pact in favour of an Arab defence pact. Four days later Syria joined with Egypt and Saʻudi Arabia to announce a 'federal union' including a unified military command.[28] Although this union, known as the Egypt-Syrian-Saʻudi (ESS) Pact, had little practical content, it heightened Western fears and led the US Embassy to argue that the 'continuation of [the] Asali Cabinet endangers US interests by giving [the] opportunity to Communist-infiltrated A[B]SP [to] gain control of essentials of power within [a] few months'.[29]

The agreement had been championed by ʻAzm, Chief of Staff Shuqayr and their military supporters such as Sarraj, who had threatened to mount a coup if the agreement was not approved by the government. To oppose them President Atasi had turned to the Iraqis and Turks for support. The Iraqis were alarmed enough to promise that they would invade the country and establish a 'legal government' if the leftists carried out their threat. The United States and Britain swiftly warned Baghdad of their opposition to such a destabilising move and Atasi was forced to go along with the ESS proposals.[30] Although Iraqi fears were lessened as negotiations over implementation of the agreement made slow progress, Shuqayr and Malki moved to tighten their grip on the army in any case. In mid-April Colonel Muhammad Maruf, a former colleague of Safa, and Muhammad Sulayman al-Ahmad, a former National Party Deputy, were arrested and several pro-Iraqi or SSNP officers, including the SSNP's Ghassan Jadid and Hinnawi's former intelligence chief, Mahmud Rifaʻi, were dismissed from the army.[31]

The Malki assassination

The intra-army power struggle exploded into violence on Friday 22 April. The army's top brass were gathered in the Damascus Municipal Stadium, giving up their day off to support the army's football team in a match against a visiting Egyptian coast-guard team. Shuqayr,

Malki, the Egyptian Ambassador as well as other ambassadors and senior military officers were seated together in the VIP area of the grandstand, guarded by a detachment of scarlet-bereted Military Police. Partway through the game, at 4.40pm, a Military Police sergeant descended the grandstand, drew his revolver and fired two rounds into Malki from behind. The Colonel was killed almost instantly. The assassin then put the gun to his head but it jammed. He pulled a second pistol and shot himself dead. In the confusion the other security men were slow to react, unlike Shuqayr who 'deserted unobtrusively in a private automobile' and the Russian Ambassador who hurdled a four and a half foot fence as he fled the scene.[32]

Within hours it was announced that the assassin, Yunis 'Abd al-Rahim, was a member of the SSNP. Two other SSNP members, Sergeants Badi' Makhluf and 'Abd al-Mun'im Dubussy, who had been at the scene to act as back-ups for Yunis, were quickly apprehended. Over the next few days Sarraj, who had been appointed to head the Deuxième Bureau by Shuqayr in February, launched a massive round-up of SSNP officers and civilians as the Ba'thists and Military Command pinned the blame on the SSNP.[33]

The Malki assassination has been a source of controversy in Syrian politics ever since. The Syrian military and the Ba'thists built him up as a martyred hero for their cause. During Malki's funeral service at the Ummayad Mosque in old Damascus on 23 April, Shuqayr eulogised that 'the entire Army has the spirit of 'Adnan'.[34] At the time of writing President Hafiz al-Asad's private residence in Damascus is overlooked by the heroic statue of Malki which dominates the Colonel's mausoleum. At the same time, however, the history of the affair has been rewritten to suit current political realities. The pro-Ba'thist prosecutors of the 1950s implicated the SSNP as a whole in the murder. Mustafa Tlass, Asad's Defence Minister, however, recently sought to clear the party's name by suggesting that the party leader acted without party authorisation in arranging the operation, and that Egypt and even Sarraj himself sponsored the murder.[35] Since the splintered remnants of the party are now allied with the Syrian regime, the motives for this rewriting of official history are clear.

It is therefore worth examining the case in some detail, both to set the historical record straight and because the murder and subsequent persecution of the SSNP had a lasting effect on the power struggle inside Syria.

Pro-Ba'thist and leftist officers seized on the murder as a chance to discredit the SSNP. The subsequent trials should be seen in this light, but nonetheless provide a starting point for the historian. The army prosecutors claimed that they had discovered evidence that the murder was the first step in a coup which the SSNP was planning to mount on behalf of Iraq and the United States. On 29 June the Military Prosecutor indicted 68 members of the party: 31 of them were charged in relation to the assassination, while the others were charged for activities relating to their membership of the party. As US diplomats judged, there was only really evidence against four of the 31 charged with involvement in the murder, the others being prosecuted for their involvement with the SSNP. Unsurprisingly, the trials bore more relation to Soviet-style show trials than to legal processes and were a 'travesty of justice'.[36] For instance, the SSNP was only declared an illegal organisation retroactively in order to deal with its adherents.[37] Furthermore, most of the defendants retracted their written confessions in court stating that they had been extracted under torture.[38]

The prosecution charged that Ghassan Jadid was the leader of the plot, pointing to the fact that he was, like Yunis, an 'Alawi from the village of Qurdahah. Georges 'Abd al-Masih (SSNP President), Iskandar Shawi (a Parliamentary Deputy and SSNP Defence Commissioner), Sami Khuri (SSNP Culture Commissioner) and Fu'ad Jadid (Ghassan's brother) were all charged with organising the plot and condemned to death. Makhluf and Dubussy, whose task had been to shoot Malki if Yunis failed, or to kill Yunis if he did not commit suicide, also received the death sentence.[39]

During the trial, the prosecution and leftist press made strenuous efforts to link the accused with foreign powers, notably the United States. A week after the murder Shuqayr told the press that 'the crime was not aimed only at eliminating a person ... rather it was aimed at eliminating all of Syria' and that 'we are in the presence of a great conspiracy against the security ... of Syria'. Prime Minister 'Asali likewise publicly accused the SSNP of being in league with a foreign power.[40] At the trial the prosecution relied largely on gossip. One story, current in Damascus to this day, was that the wife of the American Military Attaché had drunkenly told Malki to accept a posting abroad as his life was in danger. Another was that the American Director of Security for Tapline had asked his Syrian interlocutor 'who was next' if Malki were to be eliminated. In addition, the party was accused of passing intelligence information to the USIS in Damascus.[41]

Apart from these snippets of hearsay, the prosecution submitted three items of correspondence discovered in the house of Sa'adah's widow, Juliette al-Mir. The first was a letter to the party President from Hisham Sharabi, an SSNP member teaching at Georgetown University in Washington, DC. He recounted a meeting with a prominent personality, who later turned out to be the staunchly pro-American Lebanese Ambassador Charles Malik, in which cooperation between the United States and the SSNP was discussed.[42] Sharabi requested that 'Isam Mahaiyri be sent to the United States to discuss the offer. The second document was the memorandum of a discussion of the Sharabi letter by 'Abd al-Masih and other party leaders. In this memorandum the SSNP leaders interpreted Malik's approach to mean that the United States wanted SSNP cooperation in mounting a coup in Syria with the intention of bringing Syria into the Baghdad Pact. The party leaders discussed the pros and cons of the offer, but in the end decided not to send Mahaiyri. The third document indicated the party's desire for closer cooperation with the Lebanese government.[43]

Although the United States did regard the SSNP as a useful anti-communist force and was sorry to see it weakened during the trials, contacts with the party went no further than the occasional exchange of information. As SSNP members now recall, these documents were no more than topics for discussion which were never acted upon. Nonetheless, the prosecution made effective use of them to smear the SSNP.

It is clear that the prosecution's attempts to implicate the United States as well as its wholesale witchhunt for party members were motivated by a desire to crush the SSNP rather than to discover the truth about the assassination plot. Nonetheless, the evidence against the principal accused was strong and some of the party leadership were indubitably implicated in the murder. In recent interviews some of Malki's former colleagues have admitted the political nature of the trial, but remain convinced that Ghassan Jadid planned the killing.[44]

The truth behind the incident was only uncovered during the internal SSNP investigation into the affair which followed the dissolution of the party in Syria. In the course of researching this episode, the writer obtained interviews with party members involved in the investigation.[45] The party's committee of enquiry, chaired by 'Abdallah Kobecsy, gained access to Makhluf and Dubussy while they were in prison. On the basis of their evidence and that of other party members, the party charged Georges 'Abd al-Masih with carrying out the operation without the party's authorisation and, in October 1957, expelled him. To this day Masih leads a rival faction of the SSNP.

The investigation concluded that Ghassan Jadid was not involved in the plot. He had been dismissed from the army, both as a result of his SSNP activities and since he led the 'Alawite faction in the army. However, it appears that Shuqayr had as large a role in his dismissal as Malki. In any case, intermediaries had arranged a meeting between him and Malki to patch up their differences. This meeting was due to take place during the week after 22 April. While absolving Jadid, the investigation placed the full weight of blame on 'Abd al-Masih. Masih had become party President after Sa'adah's death but had always had a stormy relationship with his colleagues due to his autocratic behaviour. In 1951 he had been accused of authorising the assassination of Riyad al-Sulh without clearing it with the party's Supreme Council and in 1954 had temporarily resigned as president.[46] In the spring of 1955 Masih found his position threatened both from within the party and without. He was aware of moves afoot in the Supreme Council to depose him and wanted to send a message to his rivals that would warn them off crossing him. At the same time, Malki's annoyance at Masih's arrogant behaviour boiled over.

Malki was angered by the clout that Masih enjoyed within the army, complaining that when Masih visited the Homs Academy or Damascus Officers' Club he was treated with more respect by SSNP officers than Malki himself received. In mid-April, Malki told 'Isam Mahaiyri 'I have nothing against the party but I don't like Georges 'Abd al-Masih'. A few days before the assassination Malki ordered Masih to leave Syria. Since Masih was under sentence of death in Lebanon and would have to give up the presidency if he went into exile this was a deadly threat to his position. According to Adib Qaddurah, then President of the party's Council, if Masih had left Damascus then he would have been 'a finished man for ever'.

Masih vented his fury at a Council meeting where he described Malki as the biggest enemy of the SSNP in Syria. More concretely, he persuaded Iskandar Shawi, the party's Defence Commissioner, that the party's survival and honour depended on removing Malki. Shawi had been training several of the SSNP's members in the army for just such missions and put Masih in touch with Makhluf. Makhluf refused to carry out the actual shooting, but passed Masih along to Yunis 'Abd al-Rahim. Masih met with Yunis on 21 April to arrange the operation and must have realised that he had found the perfect instrument. Yunis was well educated and from a good family, but Malki had personally denied him admission to the Homs Officers Academy, thwarting the soldier's ambitions and provoking a deep hatred. Yunis further resented the Sunni Malki's feud against 'Alawite officers and men in the army. These personal grudges combined with Shawi's ideological indoctrination to make Yunis leap at the opportunity offered by Masih. Even other members of the highly-disciplined SSNP describe Yunis as exceptionally dedicated, a characteristic gruesomely demonstrated by his determined efforts to shoot himself even after his weapon jammed.

The evidence that Masih and Shawi plotted the killing for their own reasons seems compelling. Their colleagues on the Supreme Council were caught unawares by the news of the murder. Nonetheless, questions still remain as to whether Masih received any foreign encouragement. Mustafa Tlass's account of the affair accuses the CIA of having been behind Masih and points the finger at both the Egyptian Ambassador, Mahmud Riad, and Sarraj. His evidence against Riad centres on a telephone conversation which has become notorious among Syrian conspiracy theorists. Malki's sister recounted that she received a call from Riad on the Friday afternoon as Malki was preparing to leave to visit his fiancée. The football game had already started and Riad insisted that Malki should attend to encourage his team as the players had been disappointed to see the Colonel's chair vacant. When the sister replied that Malki had already left the Ambassador allegedly replied that he knew this was not the case, indicating that he had the house under surveillance.[47]

While Malki did arrive at the game late there is no other evidence to back up this conspiracy theory. There also seems little reason why the Egyptian Ambassador should have involved himself in a plot to remove the fairly pro-Egyptian Malki. For what it is worth, Bourhan Kassab-Hassan and 'Adnan Hamdun, both former army colleagues of Malki with ties to Tlass, dismiss the allegations. As noted above, these probably owe more to the demands of contemporary Syrian politics and propaganda than to historical fact.

Although the details of the assassination plot remain disputed in some quarters, the aftermath does not. The trials and purges which followed the murder were to have far-reaching effects on Syrian politics over the following years in two respects. First, and most obviously, were the gains made by the Ba'thists and their leftist allies. US diplomats observed that the trials 'demonstrate how [the ABSP] ... and its collaborators within and outside the Army are able by the calculated use of intimidation to exert a disproportionate influence over Syria's ... policy' and argued that the trial 'illustrates [the] extent ... of Leftist Influence in Syria'.[48] The Foreign Office in turn was 'gloomy' as it saw that a 'group of hotheaded young officers is now the dominant factor in Syrian politics'.[49] As the trials continued the military command tightened its grip and forbade officers to have contact with foreign diplomats, provoking Foreign Office ire at what it labelled this 'xenophobic military ascendancy'.[50] With the SSNP rooted out of the army the Ba'thists were in a stronger position to call the shots in both Syria's domestic and foreign policies.

The second legacy of the affair was the SSNP's turn to violence. Although the party had, and has, a reputation for violence, in fact it has generally only taken up arms when provoked. However, when it does so its discipline and paramilitary traditions make it a formidable opponent. As the party has put it: 'anyone who has opened an account with the SSNP can be sure that the SSNP will settle this account with him and in a final way'.[51] During the trials the party responded characteristically. Sa'id Taqi al-Din, the party's acting Commissioner for Propaganda, issued a leaflet condemning the 'horrid conspiracy' being perpetrated against it and warned that 'anyone who attempts to liquidate the Party shall be liquidated'.[52] In September SSNP agents shot at the prosecutor, Hamdi al-Salih, and blew up the house of one of the trial judges.[53] When the military court finally issued eight death sentences in December, the US Ambassador judged that the sentences may never be carried out due to the 'awareness of ... [the Syrian] authorities that [the] SSNP would probably attempt [to] avenge its members'.[54]

By driving the SSNP underground the Ba'thists weakened it but also encouraged the party's militarists and forced it to seek assistance from foreign powers. The wilder accusations of the prosecutors thus became self-fulfilling prophecies as over the next three years the party dedicated itself to waging a covert battle against Sarraj and his colleagues.[55] This enmity has lasted until the present time and party members still regard Sarraj as being high on their hit list.[56]

The presidential elections

Although the Malki assassination was ably exploited by the Ba'th and their allies to remove the SSNP from the political field and to drum up anti-Western feeling, the country's political future still hung in the balance. The power struggle see-sawed back and forth as the politicians fought for advantage in the run-up to the August presidential elections. Interested foreign powers redoubled their covert efforts to manipulate events. Egypt, Sa'udi Arabia and France continued to back the 'leftists' while Iraq, encouraged by Britain and the United States, tried to recover its position.

A word should be said about French policy since, in view both of that country's Cold War alliance with the United States and Britain and its subsequent cooperation with Britain against Nasser, its backing for pro-Soviet and pro-Egyptian elements may seem strange. Since French documents for this period are not available, her policy can only be reconstructed from US and British accounts, but these do concur with traditional French concerns. The Quai d'Orsay considered 'the maintenance of a type of Syrian independence acceptable to France more importan[t] than ... a common Western policy for the defense of the Middle East'.[57] In particular, the French continued to be alarmed at suspected Iraqi and British intrigues in favour of the Fertile Crescent scheme. They argued that the pursuit of such schemes was the main threat to Syrian stability since they would divide the country, as well as removing French influence. 'Azm, they suggested, was only supporting the left as a response to Iraqi intrigues. French officials dismissed Anglo-American fears of communist influence in the ABSP and army, arguing that Western security guarantees against Israel and Turkey would wean officers and Ba'thists away from Nasser and the USSR.[58]

This policy predisposition was reinforced by reporting from the French Embassy in Damascus. According to their American and British counterparts, French diplomats in Damascus relied on 'uncritically slanted reports from Foreign Minister ... 'Azm ... [as well as Shuqayr and other French-trained officers who are] old friends of the French from the days of the Mandate'.[59] Based on such sources, the French Embassy reported Syria 'as a veritable paradise of order, stability and prosperity, and alleged that rumours to the contrary were inventions of the Anglo-Saxons put out to further their designs'.[60] Reflecting 'Azm's perspective, French criticisms focused primarily on Iraqi subversive activities supposedly designed to lead to a Syro-Iraqi union and down-played Egyptian and Sa'udi activity.

The 'Anglo-Saxons', mesmerised by the 'Red Menace', regarded French complacency *vis-à-vis* the leftists as dangerously naive. In June the Special Assistant to the US Secretary of State minuted: 'the drift towards a leftist, anti-US and anti-UK position in Syria has not been arrested and governmental weakness and confusion may provide increasing opportunities for infiltration and behind-the-scenes direction for the numerically small and ably-led Communist movement'.[61] In July the Operations Coordinating Board (OCB) judged that the 'Communist Party of Syria ... is ... the largest, best organized and best led ... in the Arab world' and that it had 'made considerable progress in infiltrating the Army' as well as 'educational and religious institutions', the labour movement and 'front groups'. The OCB warned that 'if the present trend continues there is a strong possibility that a Communist-dominated Syria will result, threatening the peace and stability of the area and endangering the achievement of our objectives in the Near East'.[62]

The US Ambassador recognised that the ABSP was 'not Communist-controlled' but reported that it was 'certainly Communist-penetrated'. He could see 'no easy solution ... to the problem of stopping the accelerating Syrian drift to the left', but recommended that the United States 'lay a restraining hand' on Egypt, France and Sa'udi Arabia who, along with the Soviet Union, 'aid ... left wing and opportunist elements ... by means of bribes, threats or promises'. However, there was 'no way for the US to secure popular Syrian support for its N[ear] E[ast] objectives without some modification of US policy toward Israel'.[63]

Such a modification was not on the cards, so the United States could do no more than encourage the 'rightists' to continue their struggle. President Atasi continued to be one of the Ba'th's staunchest opponents. In the wake of the Malki assassination he tried to prevent them from exploiting the case politically and refused the army's requests that he declare martial law. In retribution the Deuxième Bureau-backed newspaper, *Rai al-Am*, called on him to resign.[64] Atasi received support in late June when a group of officers led by Brigadier Sa'id Hubbi, Brigadier Talib Daghistani, Brigadier Amin Abu Assaf and Colonel Mahmud Shawkat made plans to threaten Prime Minister 'Asali with a coup if he did not dismiss 'Azm and Shuqayr.[65] This group appears to have had Iraq's blessing as well as some financial support but Sarraj, now a Major, pre-empted the move in mid-July by arresting six junior officers and two civilians who had been involved in the plot. A warrant was also issued for the arrest of Husni Barazi, forcing him to flee to Lebanon and to abandon his pro-Western newspaper, *al-Nas*.[66]

This display of might by Sarraj and his colleagues, coming just a month before the presidential elections, may have been the cause of Shuqayr's sudden change of course a few days later.[67] As a Lebanese Druze, he had for a long time managed to remain above the factional fighting dividing his officers, but with the rise of the Ba'thist officer clique his authority had been undermined and many observers had come to regard him as a weak and pliable mouthpiece for the leftists.[68] Possibly fearing that he could be the next victim of the Deuxième Bureau, he went through Nadhir Fansah to arrange a secret meeting with Iraq's Dr Fadhil Jamali. The two met on 18 July and Shuqayr agreed to drop charges against As'ad Tallas, the editor of *al-Nas*, but refused to do the same for Husni Barazi. More importantly, Shuqayr informed his Iraqi interlocutor that he wanted to change course and would support a candidate acceptable to Iraq in the presidential elections. Previously, the army and Ba'thists' candidate had been 'Azm. Iraq and the United States, however, preferred Rushdi Kikhia, with Lutfi Haffar their second choice and Sabri 'Asali third choice. In the meeting Shuqayr expressed his preference for Nazim Qudsi.[69] Although Shuqayr and Jamali seem to have reached no agreement on whom to support, Shuqayr subsequently withdrew the army's backing for 'Azm declaring that the army did not favour any candidate.[70]

In the event, Iraq's preferred candidates declined to stand, but it became clear that 'Azm would not get enough votes to win.⁷¹ Instead, Shukri Quwatli presented himself as a compromise candidate. Quwatli had returned from his five-year exile in August 1954 to the delight of his National Party. In the run-up to the election he made overtures to the army and declared his neutrality between Egypt/Sa'udi Arabia and Iraq. With the help of Sa'udi agents, who were paying out LS10,000 a month to sympathetic Syrian newspapers, he garnered the support of the People's Party and a group of Independents.⁷² On 18 August he beat 'Azm on a second ballot by 91 votes to 41.⁷³

On the face of it 'Azm's defeat should have been a cause of relief in Baghdad, London and Washington. Quwatli declared his intention to remove the army from politics and steer a neutral course between Egypt and Iraq. Days after the election Shuqayr sent a message to the Ba'thists by arresting five leftist officers.⁷⁴ However, though he was disliked by many army officers, Quwatli retained intimate relations with Egypt and Sa'udi Arabia. He had spent his exile as their guest and was still in their pay.⁷⁵ Although his election was a blow to the Ba'th and communists it could only mean greater impetus for the ESS pact, the implementation of which had made little progress since the spring.

Egypt and Sa'udi Arabia moved swiftly to capitalise on this election result. On 20 October the ESS was given substance by the signing of military agreements between Syria and Egypt and between Sa'udi Arabia and Egypt. The Foreign Office judged that the agreements put Syria firmly into the Sa'udi/Egyptian camp and gave the Egyptian army significant influence over the Syrian army, and hence, politics. Israel reacted, as it had done previously when progress had been made in such matters, by ambushing a Syrian patrol and machine-gunning a village on the Syrian border. Sa'udi Arabia meanwhile rewarded the Syrian government with a $10 million loan.⁷⁶

The United States, Britain and Iraq responded to the situation with heightened alarm and became more frantic in their search for a remedy. The US Ambassador believed that the 'Communist threat in Syria [is] now substantially greater than that estimated in May. Without any definite move, Communists may soon have enough control of [the] government to defeat any US attempt to pursue its objectives in Syria. ... The fall of Syria would spread communist "poison" to neighbouring states, ... [and] expose Turkey's southern flank, thereby undermining [the] NATO structure.'⁷⁷ He argued that 'there is no ... time to waste if [the] US and other western nations intend to take remedial action' but warned that any pro-Western group that came to power would, 'unless supported by outside military force', have to rely on the support of leftists and have to take a hostile line on Palestine.⁷⁸

The Foreign Office shared American concerns, arguing that Britain could not 'idly watch Syria go over to the other side'. However, while the United States toyed with the idea of Nasser taking a greater role in Syria in order to neutralise the communist threat, Britain put its faith in Iraq.[79] Complaining that the Iraqi case had gone 'by default' in Syria as Iraq had given up countering Sa'udi subsidisation of newspapers, the Foreign Office pressed Prime Minister Nuri al-Sa'id to 'adopt a more forward policy ... to make Iraqi influence felt in Syria'.[80] The Foreign Office regarded closer Syrian-Iraqi ties as 'very favourable' for the United Kingdom and sought for 'some way of ensuring a pro-Iraqi regime in Damascus'. To achieve this, London proposed that the Iraqi and British Chiefs of Staff plan for a possible military intervention, and that secret discussions be opened

> with Nuri [on] ways and means of extending Iraqi influence over Syria. These would include everything from straight economic assistance to the subversion of the Syrian Army. ... In the last resort we should be prepared to coerce or disrupt Syria. ... [In the meantime, the ground should be prepared by] bribery in [which] ... the Syrian Army should be the main target; ... the rapid build up of Iraqi forces; ... propaganda in Syria; ... efforts to subordinate Syria's economy to Iraq's (eg a loan); ... measures, overt and covert, to counter Saudi influence in Syria.[81]

The British Ambassador in Baghdad relayed this advice to Nuri, urging him to spend 'money on the Syrian Press and on influencing individual politicians either by direct bribery or indirectly in some way' and suggested he 'enlist ... [Turkish] cooperation'.[82]

Nuri Sa'id certainly did not need the British to tell him of the necessity of taking action in Syria. On 5 October he described the Syrian situation as 'going from bad to worse' and argued that the country was in the 'grip of an evilly disposed minority' which was making trouble for the IPC, an Iraqi 'vital interest', and was allowing Syria to fall under communist control.[83] He had heard rumours that Syria had threatened to cut the oil pipeline and that the 'Egyptians and Saudi Arabians were ... getting set to strangle Iraq through the Communist element in Syria'.[84] After the signing of the ESS military agreement, Foreign Minister Bashayan concluded that 'Quwwatli and [Syrian Prime Minister] Ghazzi have yielded to [the] extremist element in [the] Syrian Army'.[85] The Iraqi government was particularly concerned at 'the flow of Saudi money to the hands of Communist and terrorist elements in Iraq and in other parts of the Middle East' and the infiltration of communist cadres across the Syrian-Iraqi border.[86]

Iraqi intelligence had not been as inactive as the Foreign Office seemed to think. As well as encouraging the rightist officers in their plot in July, the Military Attaché had given money to the SSNP's 'Isam Mahaiyri and during May attempts had been made to infiltrate Iraqi army officers and arms into Syria.[87] At the time of the Syrian presidential elections Iraq had not only backed its preferred candidates but also worked with its former *bête noir*, Adib Shishakli. In coordination with the Lebanese government and the SSNP, Shishakli had returned to Beirut and had talks with Jamali. He had travelled *incognito* to Damascus to drum up support among officers for a coup if 'Azm won the election. After Quwatli's election he left the region, reportedly saying that he would wait and see how the new President behaved before he took any action.[88]

However, by the autumn Nuri was sceptical about the possibility of changing the Syrian government from within. He complained that 'all Syrians [are] ... the same and all equally useless' and argued that it was a waste of money bribing Syrian politicians and newspapers because they could only be trusted so long as Sa'udi Arabia did not offer them more.[89] He pleaded in vain that the United States and Britain freeze ARAMCO's payments to the Sa'udi government, arguing that if 'credit [was] frozen for ... six to twelve months ... he could stabilize the situation'.[90] His preferred option was to intervene overtly and decisively. To the British Ambassador he revealed his plan to invade Syria, hold a plebiscite and establish some form of union. He requested that Britain and the United States ensure French and Israeli acquiesence in the plan. Both London and Washington, however, warned him against 'premature action by Iraqi forces' since they believed that an invasion would not succeed and would in any case arouse too much international opposition.[91] With his strategy thwarted by the Great Powers he reluctantly followed British proddings on the propaganda front, but with little enthusiasm. Information offices were opened in Damascus, Beirut and Amman and a newspaper started in Beirut. In April Iraqi money sponsored an article by Hasan al-Hakim in a Damascus newspaper calling for the Arabs to unite behind Nuri. The Iraqi government, however, refused to increase its payments to individual Syrian politicians.[92]

Exiles and arms deals

Unhindered by an angry but inactive Iraq, the Syrian leftists meanwhile tightened their grip on power. One manifestation of their confidence was the Deuxième Bureau's more aggressive pursuit of its opponents abroad. An instance of this was a campaign to deter Syrian Druze from cooperating with Israel. In September two Palestinians from the Bureau's Palestinian unit, which had been set up to conduct espionage missions in Northern Israel and was made up of Palestinians who originally came from the region, tracked down a Druze defector to his Upper Galilee village.[93] Yussuf al-Safadi had been sentenced to death *in absentia* for espionage and the two Syrian operatives carried out the sentence. In December five other Druzes were condemned to death for espionage and collaboration with Israel.[94]

The Bureau's covert battle against the SSNP was of more importance. When they had fled from Syria in the wake of the Malki assassination the SSNP's leaders had been given refuge in Lebanon. Although the Lebanese authorities had not forgiven the party for killing Riyad al-Sulh, Foreign Minister Malik regarded it as a dedicated anti-communist force of which it was important to make use.[95] Sarraj sought to hunt down the fugitives, but his first effort ended in farce. An agent was sent to the Lebanese tribal leader Dandash and offered him LL50,000 if he could deliver Ghassan Jadid. Dandash informed the party of the offer and they decided to play along. First Dandash insisted on a down payment, which the party pocketed. Then he arranged a meeting in a restaurant on the Beirut seafront with the Deputy Director and the Chief Financial Officer of the Bureau, who was carrying the LL50,000 cheque. SSNP 'waiters' staking out the meeting point kidnapped the two officers and took them to the party's headquarters in Dayr al-Shuwayr, Sa'adah's home village. SSNP officers, including Jadid, used the opportunity to interrogate the two men, in particular getting details of the LL300,000 per month that the Bureau was paying to Lebanese newspapers to publish anti-SSNP propaganda.

After the two officers had been missing for 24 hours the Syrian Defence Minister, Rashad Barmada, came to Beirut and demanded that Lebanese Chief of Staff Fu'ad Chehab find and return the Syrians. Chehab contacted the SSNP who, having cashed the cheque, extracted maximum humiliation from the affair by insisting on a formal military handover of their prisoners to the Lebanese Minister of Defence.[96] After this embarrassment the Syrian authorities stiffly demanded that the Lebanese Prime Minister, Rashid Karamah, order the arrest of Jadid and six other SSNP leaders. That this order was not satisfactorily fulfilled is evident from the US Military Attaché's report of a conversation with the Lebanese gendarmerie commander, Colonel Zouain:

> action to implement this government decision seems hardly such as to produce a successful manhunt. Gendarmerie posts have been given ... instructions to arrest the men *if* they see them. As he told this Colonel

Zouain's attitude was definitely 'tongue in cheek,' and he smiled broadly as he emphasized the word 'if'.[97]

Sarraj took the lessons of this humiliating episode to heart. Never again would he rely on the Lebanese to help him deal with the SSNP and never again would he send desk officers and accountants into the Lebanese underworld.

Sarraj, however, did not have much time to nurse his wounded pride. The power struggle in the High Command and government continued to rage. As 1955 drew to a close the all-consuming question concerned arms supplies. The Israeli Defence Forces (IDF) were mounting ever more destructive raids into Jordan and Egypt and firefights on the disputed Syrian-Israeli border were frequent.[98] Tensions had been heightened by Israel's plans to carry out irrigation work in the Upper Galilee which would divert water from the Jordan river. The Syrian press and parliament fumed and threatened war if Israel began work.[99] In September Nasser revealed his historic arms deal with the Soviet Bloc.[100] Leftist Syrian officers were keen to follow his lead. In February 1955 Syria had purchased some World War II-vintage German tanks from the Soviet Union, but Shuqayr and Quwatli were reluctant to take the plunge of committing themselves to the USSR so irrevocably.[101]

Although the military entered into negotiations with the Eastern Bloc over arms purchases, Shuqayr expressed his preference for Western equipment. He was 'determined [to] conclude no ... agreement [with the USSR] unless [the] US rejects [the] Syrian request'.[102] He asked the United States to supply trucks and anti-aircraft guns and Britain to sell more Meteor jets. Both the US and British Embassies urged their governments to be forthcoming as a last chance to block Soviet influence. Britain had supplied the Syrian Air Force previously and now approved the sale of seven Meteor jets.[103] The United States, however, procrastinated, insisting on guarantees that the weapons would only be used for defence and that classified material would be protected.[104] As these negotiations were in progress Sarraj struck another blow at his rivals by dismissing from the army the pro-Iraqi officers detained in July.[105]

On 11 December the IDF launched an unprecedently large attack against Syrian military positions around Lake Tiberias: 48 Syrian soldiers and policemen were killed along with eight civilians.[106] A wave of shock and humiliation swept the country, with popular anger being directed against the West for supporting Israel.[107] Egypt was quick to exploit the situation, publicly donating money to purchase arms.[108] The Deuxième Bureau also went to work spreading rumours that blamed Shuqayr for the disaster.[109] The US Embassy realised that a critical psychological juncture had been reached: 'should [the] US not approve [the] pending arms req[uest], resentment here would be so profound that for all practical purposes Syria could thereafter be considered [an] unfriendly country, whether Communists took over or not'.[110] This plea fell on deaf ears in Washington.

Despairing of the Great Powers, Shuqayr and Quwatli made one last effort to fend off the Soviet embrace. In mid-February the Turks helped the Chief of Staff and President to open channels to the Iraqis, as a result of which Nadhir Fansah was despatched to meet Nuri. He carried with him proposals for economic and military agreements and there were even suggestions that Iraqi commandoes be sent into Syria to arrest 'undesireables [sic]'.[111] Despite British encouragement for the mission, however, Nuri refused to see the emissary as he did not believe Fansah represented a significant pro-Iraqi lobby.[112] Instead, the Iraqi strongman reiterated his plea for the Great Powers to restrain Turkey and Israel so that he could send in the Iraqi army 'in response to an appeal from elements in Syria as a result of some local Syrian situation "arising"'.[113]

The failure of this mission was the last straw for Shuqayr and Quwatli. They acceded to demands that Syria's new-found wealth, from an agreement on transit fees with IPC, be spent on East Bloc arms.[114] In February the army contracted for 15,000 Czech sub-machine guns. The next month a $23 million deal was concluded with Czechoslovakia for tanks, aircraft, artillery, small arms, trucks and medical equipment. Twenty MiG jets and 60 T-34 tanks were to be supplied from Egypt's stocks of Soviet equipment.[115]

The Iraqi plot

In the autumn of 1956 Syrian counter-intelligence announced the discovery of a planned uprising subsequently labelled the 'Iraqi plot'. This conspiracy, which united Shishakli, the SSNP, conservative politicians and officers, Iraq, the SIS and the CIA was the most powerful counter-thrust organised by opponents of Syria's move towards Egypt and the USSR. Its failure enabled the leftists to consolidate their grip on power to such an extent that subsequent attempts to remove them were virtually doomed to fail.

Previous researchers have provided useful accounts of aspects of the plot. Seale used Iraqi sources to examine Baghdad's role.[116] Gorst and Lucas used US and British archives to highlight the Anglo-American contribution, known as Operation Straggle.[117] The account provided here draws an overall picture of the affair using a range of sources. Details of the conspiracy and Iraq's role are taken from the trials of the plotters held in Damascus in early 1957 and the trials of former Iraqi officials held after the Iraqi coup in 1958. The British and US roles are examined using official archives.

For details of the CIA's role researchers have tended to rely heavily on the memoirs of former CIA agent Wilbur Crane Eveland.[118] Unfortunately, Eveland's credibility is as low as Copeland's was in relation to the Za'im coup. An internal CIA review of the book noted that 'its author does not know or understand much about the Arab east' and his obvious errors of fact make 'one skeptical of other, uncheckable, statements'.[119] A former Director of the CIA wrote to this writer that 'I regard ... Eveland as [an] unsatisfactory source'.[120] Reviewing the book in the *Middle East Journal*, a former US Ambassador in the Middle East argued that, although the book was 'extraordinarily interesting', it was 'a ... self-serving apologia, conspiratorially sensational, ... and not always accurate in its facts'. He warned the reader to take care to 'separate the wheat from the chaff'.[121] Eveland's claims must therefore be treated with the utmost caution.

London and Washington develop 'Straggle'

The Anglo-American conviction of the necessity for stronger action in Syria evolved during the spring and summer of 1956. Britain led the way in pushing for drastic action and, with Iraq, formulated plans for a major paramilitary operation to oust the Syrian government and the leftist officers. Washington was equally concerned at the situation but was at first unwilling to act so precipitately. The United States persisted in its efforts to bolster right-wing politicians and officers, believing that there was still a chance of change from within. In the autumn, however, the US administration came round to Britain's pessimistic view and threw its weight behind the Anglo-Iraqi scheme. Although the transatlantic partners grew more estranged as the Suez Crisis heated up, they continued to coordinate their Syrian plans until the last moment.[122]

The British government's conversion to an all-out covert offensive came in March. As demonstrated above, there had been mounting concern at the situation in Syria for a while. Nonetheless, the Foreign Office had until then recommended only the expansion of covert propaganda and political action measures. Nuri's more aggressive proposals had been rejected. The main reason for this was that Anglo-American Middle Eastern policy in late 1955 and early 1956 had been centred round secret attempts, codenamed Alpha, to persuade Nasser to cooperate with the West and to obtain 'a Palestine settlement by negotiation between Nasser and Ben-Gurion'.[123] Foreign Secretary Selwyn Lloyd visited Nasser in March, but concluded after their talks that Nasser preferred to accept Russian help to become leader of the Arab world rather than cooperate with the West in making peace in the Middle East.[124] On 10 March the Assistant Undersecretary of State responsible for the Levant minuted the Permanent Undersecretary of State:

> The collapse of Alpha last week removed the linch-pin [of British policy]. ... we are left without a Middle East policy of any kind. ... I think this is a situation of grave national emergency. ... Unless the Israelis commit an aggression, we are becoming daily more deeply committed to go to war against a Soviet-armed Arab world as soon as they feel strong enough or fanatical enough to attack Israel.[125]

King Husayn's dismissal of the British commander of the Arab Legion, General John Bagot Glubb, on 1 March had deepened the sense of crisis. On 21 March the cabinet met and concluded that Britain 'could not establish a basis for friendly relations with Egypt' so British policy must be to counter Egyptian policies 'to the utmost' and 'uphold our true friends'. Britain would seek to persuade the United States to join the Baghdad Pact, wean Sa'udi Arabia from Egypt and bring Jordan and Iraq closer together. Warned by Lloyd that 'unless some decisive action is taken in the near future, there is [a] danger of ... [Syria] drifting in effect into the position of a Communist satellite', the cabinet also ordered the Foreign Office and SIS to 'seek to establish in Syria a Government more friendly to the West'.[126] It appears that SIS, which was taken over in April by Sir Dick White, was encouraged by Eden to work aggressively to remove both Nasser and the Syrian government.[127] Although this led to differences with the Foreign Office in regard to Nasser (as the diplomats balked at plans to assassinate him), there appears to have been little disagreement on SIS's aggressive approach to Syria.[128]

In this atmosphere, Nuri's pleas for help fell on more receptive ears. Encouraged by the British Ambassador's assessment that he could 'bring about the merger of Syria with Iraq any time if given enough money', Lloyd recommended that Eden give approval to Nuri's efforts to 'create a situation' in which Syria would appeal for Iraqi intervention.[129] Discussions had been held with the Turkish Prime Minister, Menderes, who gave his pledge to give Nuri a free hand. The main task now was to ensure 'full American co-operation in any such effort' and Prime Minister Eden approved proposals to open discussions with Secretary of State J.F. Dulles and CIA Director Allen Dulles.[130]

Concern at Soviet encroachment in the Middle East had reached the highest levels of the Eisenhower administration by early 1956.[131] The Operations Coordinating Board assessed that the communists aimed to 'move step by step, to take over one country at a time until they have isolated India and Egypt' and that 'Soviet strategic planning for the Middle East calls for eventual incorporation of the nations of that area in a World Union of Soviet Socialist Republics'.[132] With the Soviet and Czech Legations in Damascus already acting as the 'center of all Soviet direction of Communist activites in the Middle East', it was believed that the Soviet Union's 'vigorous diplomatic offensive' would accelerate 'a Soviet-supported Syrian drift into a firmly anti-Western position'.[133] This high-level alarm pushed the national security bureaucracy into action. In January 1956 the OCB coordinated an inter-agency review which gave 'priority consideration' to 'developing courses of action in the Near East designed to affect the situation in Syria' and recommended 'specific steps to combat communist subversion in Syria'. Most of the conclusions of this review remain classified but the first two recommendations were to sell defensive equipment to Syria and to extend economic and technical assistance.[134]

The administration, however, remained unreceptive to proposals for more aggressive covert action. US officials were aware of Turkish and Iraqi plans to take action but counselled restraint.[135] They also rejected SSNP requests for assistance in mounting a coup since these plans 'are unlikely to be brought to a successful conclusion'.[136] Allen Dulles laid out his concerns in a memorandum to his brother: 'action today by Iraq in staging a coup in Syria would probably mean the end to any chance of early negotiation with Egypt, and would involve the danger of inter-Arab strife'.[137] John Foster concurred, telling Prime Minister Eden in January that none of the plans put forward concerning action in Syria 'seemed sufficiently sound to warrant our support'.[138]

Like the British, Eisenhower was placing his faith in the secret talks with Nasser. Eisenhower was confident that Nasser would cooperate with the West against the Soviet Union if Egypt was allowed to maintain 'its hegemony of the Arab countries'.[139] Just in case he did not cooperate, J.F. Dulles suggested preparing economic sanctions. The United States could take action on 'the waters of the Upper Nile – [where] we can strangle him if we want to' or ruin Egypt's cotton market.[140]

However, by mid-March Eisenhower and Dulles had, like Eden and Lloyd, to recognise the failure of Alpha. On 12 March Robert B. Anderson, who had been touring the Middle East as the President's personal representative, returned to Washington with a gloomy report. He told the President that:

he had made no progress whatsoever in ... arranging some kind of meeting between Egyptian officials and the Israelites [sic]. Nasser proved to be a complete stumbling block. ... Because he wants to be the most popular man in all the Arab world ... he ... concludes he should take no action whatsoever – rather he should just make speeches, all of which must breathe defiance of Israel. On the other side, the Israel[i] officials are anxious to talk with Egypt, but they are completely adamant in their attitude of making no concessions whatsoever in order to obtain peace.[141]

With no immediate prospect of winning over Nasser or solving the Arab-Israeli conflict, US leaders cast about for a new approach which would limit damage to the American position. Although Eisenhower indulged in some tough talking, telling the Chiefs of Staff that 'the time may well be coming when we will have to serve some notice on certain of the Middle Eastern countries', the adminstration did not adopt London's hard line.[142] Instead, the President approved a series of measures suggested by John Foster Dulles on 28 March. As Dulles put it,

the primary purpose [of these measures] would be to let Colonel Nasser realize that he cannot cooperate ... with the Soviet Union and at the same time enjoy most-favored-nation treatment from the United States. We would want for the time being to avoid any open break which would throw Nasser irrevocably into a Soviet satellite status and we would want to leave Nasser a bridge back to good relations with the West.[143]

There were five key elements in Dulles's proposals. First, Nasser would be put under pressure by continuing to deny Egypt arms supplies, stalling negotiations over financing of the Aswan Dam and delaying action on requests for foodstuffs and other aid. Second, the United States would 'give increased support to the Baghdad Pact without actually adhering to [it]'. The idea of joining the Pact was dismissed as this would necessitate giving a security guarantee to Israel, which would make Iraq leave the Pact. Instead Dulles suggested participating more actively in the Pact's military discussions and its counter-subversive committee.[144] Third, King Sa'ud would be built up as a rival Arab leader 'in the thought that mutually antagonistic personal ambitions might disrupt the aggressive plans that Nasser is evidently developing'. Eisenhower, himself was particularly keen on the idea that Sa'ud could become first spiritual and then political leader of the Muslim Arab states. Dulles suggested increasing arms supplies to Sa'udi Arabia, encouraging Britain to settle its territorial dispute over the Buraimi oasis, and convincing King Sa'ud of the danger which Nasser posed to him. Fourth, Israel would be dissuaded from 'taking ... precipitate steps which might bring about hostilities'. Fifth, pro-Western elements in the region would be supported. Thus the United Kingdom would be encouraged to 'prevent a ... pro-Egyptian coup d'état' in Jordan and friendly elements in Lebanon would be helped by economic aid 'for projects designed to create the most favorable impact on public opinion'.

The US administration recognised the desireability of coordinating its new approach with Britain. In talks with the British Defence Staff in April, Eisenhower emphasised 'the importance of our information, propaganda, and political warfare activities in the region' and 'thought that the United States and the UK should do a great deal toward concerting activities in this field'.[145] Steps were taken to counter the effective propaganda of Radio Cairo and Radio Moscow, for instance by assisting Iraq in building up its broadcasting facilities.[146]

However, so far as Syria was concerned, the United States did not, at first, feel it necessary to buy into the Anglo-Iraqi operation. Indeed, CIA officials expressed alarm at SIS's aggressive proposals and the reliance of George Young, SIS's Middle East operations officer, on Iraq.[147] To the Americans, there still seemed plenty that could be done to encourage anti-communist elements to change the situation from within. Two projects which came up for discussion during the summer seemed to offer good opportunities for implementing Dulles's fifth suggestion. The first was a proposal to offer Syria cooperation in using radioisotopes for medical research. The OCB argued that this offer, under the 'Atoms for Peace' Programme, would be 'very significant' in influencing Syrian public opinion.[148] The second and more significant opportunity was Syria's plan to construct a new oil refinery at Homs. A Czech company put in the lowest bid which provoked US fears that 'the Soviet[s] ... [intend to] use this refinery project as a means of infiltrating and influencing developments in the ... Middle Eastern oil industry' and led the State Department to argue that 'it is important that every effort be made to secure the awarding of the Syrian refinery contract to a reliable Western firm'.[149] Although lengthy discussions ensued on the feasibility of subsidising the rival Italian-American bidder, Procon, no action was taken in time and the Czech company won the contract.[150]

On the covert side, State and the CIA retained the hope that by encouraging, and financing, rightist officers and politicians, the march of 'communism' could be halted.[151] Damascene political manoeuvrings in June and July proved cause for both pessimism and optimism. In June Ghazzi's cabinet, which had been in power since Quwatli's election, resigned. Attempts to form a conservative cabinet under the pro-Iraqi Lutfi Haffar failed. On 14 June Sabri 'Asali again became

Prime Minister in an all-party cabinet which nonetheless represented a victory for the Ba'thists, who got the Ministries of Foreign Affairs and National Economy. US and British diplomats concluded that the cabinet had been formed largely at the instigation of the Egyptian Ambassador, Mahmud Riad, who had developed close ties with the ABSP, and also of the Sa'udis, who had paid 'Asali a large bribe.[152]

The Ba'thists capitalised on their success by pushing proposals for closer Syrian-Egyptian union. Hawrani and his colleagues demanded that the government issue a declaration proclaiming the union of Egypt and Syria which would be open to all Arab states who were not members of other defence pacts. Sarraj and Mustafa Hamdun backed up the demands by threatening to mount a coup if they were not accepted.[153] The Ba'thist move galvanised their opponents into action. Colonel Nafuri, who led an anti-Sarraj/Hamdun faction of officers, approached the Iraqi Minister, 'Abd al-Jalil al-Rawi, for help. The Minister introduced Nafuri to Mikhail Ilyan, a staunch pro-Western politician in Iraq's pay and 'Asali's main rival in the National Party.[154] In their talks Nafuri put forward proposals to forge an alliance between his officers, the Arab Liberation Movement (ALM) and rightist politicians.[155] Iraq's facilitating role in these talks was strongly encouraged by London which had blamed the fall of the Ghazzi government on the Iraqis' 'failure ... to make their influence felt' and had urged the British Ambassador in Baghdad to 'do your best to instil some urgency into Nuri and get him ... to do something'.[156]

The Ba'thists, however, got their way on 27 June when 'Asali issued a declaration calling for an eventual Syrian-Egyptian union. The right struck back and forced Shuqayr to resign as Chief of Staff on 7 July. Shuqayr had backtracked on his approaches to Iraq since the spring, instead aligning himself with leftist army officers. Along with Sarraj, he had done his best to isolate the new and more right-wing Minister of Defence, Raslan. With support among rightist politicians and Nafuri's officers, Raslan forced Shuqayr out and replaced him with Tawfiq Nizam al-Din, who the British regarded as 'pro-West but ... weak'. Raslan and his allies tried to go further, having Sarraj and Hamdun transferred out of their influential positions, but this failed as the Ba'thists were able to mobilise enough opposition.[157]

The replacement of Shuqayr by al-Din was to be only a temporary setback to Sarraj and the Ba'thists, but the United States was optimistic. At the end of July, US intelligence agencies concurred in the judgement that 'conservative elements appear in recent weeks to have regained some strength, especially within the Army'.[158] At the same time, the prospects for divorcing the Sa'udis from Egypt appeared to be improving. The Sa'udis had recently been hedging their bets, having hosted Shishakli since March.[159] In July and August both the Foreign Office and State Department detected signs of a growing rift between Egypt and Sa'udi Arabia since the latter was concerned at the growth of leftist influence in Syria. The prospect of an Egyptian-Syrian republic, as envisioned in the Ba'thists' proposals, was certainly not welcomed by the Sa'udi monarchy.[160]

Hoping that its cautious approach would continue to bear fruit, the US administration continued to warn against the destructive consequences of a 'British-inspired Iraqi move against Syria'.[161] Nonetheless, during August and September the CIA got involved. By 18 October Allen Dulles could tell his brother that he was in the know concerning British plans for Syria, even though the British were keeping Washington in the dark concerning their planning with France and Israel to attack Egypt.[162] What appeared to have changed Washington's view was the news that Quwatli was planning to forge closer economic and military ties with Moscow. Soviet Foreign Minister Shepilov had visited Damascus in June and Quwatli was scheduled to lead a delegation to Russia at the end of October.[163] US archives remain silent on the discussions which must have accompanied this change of heart, but presumably the Dulles brothers concluded that Quwatli's proposed trip indicated the defeat of the government and army right-wingers.

The plan

With CIA approval, the British and Iraqis could go ahead with their plan. Despite claims that the British Military Attaché in Beirut attended some of the conspirators' meetings, there is no hard evidence of the role played by British agents in organising the operation. Nonetheless, the British government's decision in March 1956 to remove the Syrian government enables one to interpret the scattered archival references. On 2 May Foreign Secretary Lloyd was assured by an assistant that 'covert action to diminish Nasser's influence in other Arab countries is being actively prepared'.[164] In a 30 May briefing for Lloyd on the Middle East, Syria was dealt with under the heading 'Straggle'.[165] Combined with the evidence of constant pressure for action which the British exerted on Nuri, one can reasonably conclude that the Foreign Office, or at least the SIS, were not only well acquainted with the plans but took a hand in drawing them up.

Iraq's role, and that of the Syrian conspirators, is more fully documented thanks to the evidence of Syrian investigators and the subsequent Iraqi revolutionaries. Both sets of trials need to be treated with caution. Many contemporary Syrian lawyers regarded much of the evidence presented in the trials of the conspirators as 'utterly fantastic and liable to expose the courts to ridicule'.[166] The trials of *ancien régime* figures held after the July 1958 Iraqi revolution were clearly show trials designed to make a political point rather than to discover the truth.[167] Nonetheless, by judicious use of the trial transcripts, diplomatic and press reports of the trials and a few other sources, it is possible to piece together a fairly accurate picture of events.

Already in 1954 the Iraqi General Staff had drawn up plans for a military invasion of Syria, at Nuri Sa'id's request. However, when Ghazi Daghistani became Deputy Chief of Staff he advised the Iraqi leadership that the plan, 'Operation X', would be logistically unfeasible and would leave the door open for Israeli military intervention. Acting on this advice Nuri dropped the military plans and ordered his officers to put together a covert operation which Iraq could orchestrate from behind the scenes.

The conspirators were a disparate and fractious group which included the SSNP, followers of Adib Shishakli and of Muhammad Safa. Various conservative and pro-Iraqi politicians were among the plot's leaders. Iraqi agents were intimately involved at all levels of the affair from initially bringing together those involved to coordinating their political and military preparations. Initial discussions were held during the spring of 1956 and the plot took on a solid outline over the summer. The conspiracy was organised on two levels, political and military, each coordinated by a committee which kept the details of its planning secret from the other.

The political leadership of the plot included Mikhail Ilyan as well as two Iraqi protégés, Jalal Sa'id and Muhammad al-Fadil. Sami Kabbara, Justice Minister after Hinnawi's coup in 1949, was brought into the plot by Muhammad Maruf, who had been Hinnawi's Chief of Police. Ex-officer Husayn al-Hakim played a key role in bringing the leaders together. Sa'id Taqi al-Din represented the SSNP in the plotters' discussions. Subhi al-Amari, who had fled Syria after his involvement in the summer 1955 coup attempt was brought into the discussions early on and offered the post of Defence Minister in the post-coup government. Munir 'Ajlani was brought into the plot in June to head the Committee and to conduct the overt political struggle in Damascus. Adil 'Ajlani was also a key player.

Adib Shishakli was Nuri's preferred choice to lead the coup and take over Syria. His brother, Salah, brought him to Beirut in July where he held talks with several of the plotters. Claiming that he disapproved of the plans, he refused to cooperate and returned to Paris, taking with him 10,000–15,000 dinars of Iraqi money.[168] Salah and Muhammad Maruf, however, persuaded him to listen to further Iraqi representations and he subsequently met Iraqi Deputy Chief of Staff Ghazi Daghistani and Foreign Minister Bashayan in Geneva.[169] Nonetheless, the talks do not seem to have made any progress and Adib played no significant part in the plot. Without Shishakli's consent to act as a figurehead, the plotters hoped instead to make Hashim al-Atasi President. His son, 'Adnan Atasi, was approached in August to inform him of the conspirators' plans, but it is unclear to what extent Hashim al-Atasi became aware of the plottings.

The military side of the plot was largely controlled by the SSNP. Iraqi government officials believed that only a 'group of adventurers such as ... [the SSNP]' had the 'courage' to actively 'correct [the] Syrian situation'.[170] The party's setback in the wake of Malki's assassination had given Iraq the chance to offer assistance, which had previously been refused by the party, suspicious of Iraq's ties with 'imperialist' Britain. An SSNP delegation had visited Baghdad in late 1955. They had been formally received by the Palace and entered into talks with Iraqi officials. The meetings, however, broke up when the delegation's leader, Adib Qaddurah, objected to the Iraqis' heavy-handed attempts to bribe the delegation. None the less, in Beirut in January 1956 Ghassan Jadid, who had become the party's Defence Commissioner, and Taqi al-Din, met the Iraqi Military Attaché, Salih Mahdi al-Samarra'i, and the head of Iraqi Military Intelligence for discussions on military cooperation. Although the SSNP was to provide the plot's paramilitary backbone, Iraq's old Syrian military protégés, Muhammad Safa and Muhammad Maruf, complained at Samarra'i's and Daghistani's over-reliance on the party and were also appointed to the Military Committee.

By late summer, despite endless bickering and power struggles among the plotters, military and political planning had coalesced and preparations were well in hand to mount the operation in late October. Daghistani and Samarra'i in Beirut arranged the supply of Iraqi money and arms to the Syrian conspirators. According to the evidence of Burhan Adham, an ex-Syrian officer who acted as Sarraj's informer among the conspirators, Daghistani requested that Baghdad supply LS1.5 million and 1,500 weapons to the plotters. The CIA put up one-third of this money, which was handed over by Wilbur Eveland. The Agency also arranged to supply 2,000 small arms via the British airbase at Habbaniyya.[171] The cash was distributed by the Political Committee inside Syria to buy support. The Druze leader Hasan Atrash, for instance, asked for 100,000 dinars in return for his help, but negotiations reduced this to what the plot's paymasters considered a reasonable sum. He and various tribal leaders in the Suwayda' and eastern desert districts were budgeted LS250 for each fighter they supplied. In addition, some of the money was earmarked for propaganda, such as starting up new newspapers.

The SSNP's military plans were also ready. Lebanon's pro-Western President Chamoun regarded Syria as 'the most serious threat to the stability of the Middle East' and his Chief of Staff, General Chehab, kept a discreet but benevolent eye on the evolution of the plot.[172] Ghassan Jadid organised training camps in the Biqa' valley and the Matn where about 3,000 SSNP militiamen were trained. Iraqi Military Intelligence supplied arms to the training camps. One source stated that a total of 60 light-machine guns, 2,500 rifles and 60,000 rounds of ammunition were supplied. Some were dropped by parachute from Iraqi aircraft over the Biqa'. One planeload of 30 tons of small arms was brought in through Beirut airport, at a time when Jadid had arranged to have SSNP loyalists in the control tower. Arms were also smuggled into Syria across the desert by tribesmen and cached in safe houses in Damascus and other Syrian towns. Jadid also made efforts to get in contact with other ex-Syrian officers and offered them up to LS300 per month to join him in Beirut. Some of these officers were delegated to mobilise SSNP loyalists in the military who had escaped the post-Malki purges.

The plan called for rebel units to move into Syria from Lebanon and link up with sympathetic officers and tribes who would coordinate their risings. SSNP units of about 300 men in Syrian military uniforms under Jadid and other officers were detailed to move on Homs, Hama and Aleppo where SSNP officers would take control of their garrisons and join up with the rebels. Muhammad Maruf was detailed to lead a revolt in the 'Alawite mountains. An SSNP unit in police uniforms was to enter Damascus and use the arms stored in safe houses to take over key installations. The air force was largely loyal to the SSNP and it was hoped to use the anti-aircraft cannon at the Damascus airfield to counter any movement of government tanks from their base at Qatana. Atrash's Druze fighters, stiffened by an SSNP contingent, would meanwhile take over government installations in the Jabal Druze. Bedouin tribesmen, trained in Iraqi camps near the Syrian border, were to back up the rebels by tying down Syrian troops in the east of the country. Government and army leaders would be arrested or killed.

On the international front, the Iraqis had gained the support of Turkey in addition to Britain and the United States. Turkish-Syrian relations, already tense due to Turkish fears of a pro-communist Syria, deteriorated during the summer of 1956. Turkish determination to stop the endemic smuggling on their common border led to frequent armed clashes. Numerous Syrian civilians and soldiers fell victim to Turkish mines laid on the border and Turkish troops frequently pursued suspects into Syrian territory. After one incident in which the Turks arrested 38 Syrians, Damascus had threatened to take the issue to the UN Security Council. Turkey had its own Syrian exiles whose plotting it encouraged. Husni Barazi was the most notable of these, but he was not involved in the Iraqi plot. Turkey was quite happy for Baghdad to make the running, merely promising not to intervene.[173]

With most of the pieces in place, the plotters disagreed at the last minute on the date for the operation. First, a date was set for just before Quwatli's trip to Moscow on 31 October. The leaders then decided to wait until he was in Russia. Finally, the conspirators decided to postpone the operation until he returned so that they could arrest him. They feared that he may otherwise take refuge in Egypt and lead an exile government. However, on 29 October Israeli forces invaded the Sinai. Jadid immediately ordered his men to postpone the operation and other leaders told Iraq that they could not now go ahead since any move against the Syrian government would be regarded as being in league with Israel and the West.[174]

Eisenhower was furious at British duplicity over the Suez intervention, fuming 'that nothing justifies double-crossing us'.[175] On the 30th Allen and John Foster Dulles discussed 'Straggling' and agreed that it 'would be a mistake to try to pull it off'. The CIA Director commented that 'if the assets can be held together for a few days more without taking action we would much prefer it'. His brother made the case for caution, 'what will happen if you get hooked in this and get friends in and fighting starts – it will put us in a difficult position – they will turn against us'. The British were pressing to go ahead with the operation but Allen Dulles was 'suspicious of our cousins and if they want a thing he thinks we should look at it hard. Not before Nov. 1.'[176]

Under British pressure to go ahead and so coincide with the Anglo-French invasion of Egypt, the conspirators sent Kabbara to Rome to try to persuade Ibrahim Husayni to help them carry out the plan despite the new circumstances. Husayni, however, refused to work with the SSNP and Kabbara returned empty-handed.

The plotters had no second chance as on 3 November the Deuxième Bureau announced its discovery of the plot and began to round up those of the 47 suspects who were in Syria. The incident which led to the unravelling of the affair had been the chance arrest by policemen of a driver smuggling arms who was involved in a road accident. His load was part of a consignment smuggled in from Iraq on 25 October by Druze chieftain Shakib Wahhab. Wahhab had hired cars and trucks to collect the weapons from an Iraqi army truck in the desert and delegated the running of the operation to Hayil Srur, a Parliamentary Deputy and leader of the Suwayda'–based Mseid tribe. Srur brought in 500 rifles and four machine-guns which Wahhab distributed among Atrash's forces and SSNP militiamen in the Jabal Druze and kept 300 rifles and two machine-guns for his own followers to use in the uprising.

Sarraj later claimed in a newspaper interview that he had known of the plot since its inception. This may well have been partially true. According to the Iraqi Minister in Damascus at the time, in mid-1955 Colonel Samarra'i had indiscreetly sounded out Sarraj in an attempt to recruit him. Sarraj subsequently used what he had learned from Samarra'i to uncover further details of the plot and managed to infiltrate Burhan Adham, who had been a security officer under Shishakli, into the plotters' counsels. Although Adham was not privy to all the details of the preparations his information was clearly highly valued by Sarraj who subsequently appointed him head of the Deuxième Bureau's Internal Affairs Section.[177]

The aftermath

The trials and purges which followed the discovery of the Iraqi plot shattered the right in Syria. The verdicts were handed down on 26 February 1957 with 12 of the accused being sentenced to death and 29 to varying terms of imprisonment.[178] Those politicians and officers not in jail were in exile. Although they continued to conspire, they had few influential friends left inside Syria. As subsequent plots were to demonstrate, it was henceforth very difficult for foreign agents to find any significant support for a move against the leftist leadership in Damascus.

At the same time as the trials were destroying Syria's right-wing, Nasser's political victory in Suez excited public opinion and further boosted the pro-Nasserites in Damascus. On Nasser's orders Syrian troops did not intervene against Israel but did move into Jordan. The Syrian population was put on a war footing by the mobilisation of the state militia, the Popular Resistance Organisation. On 2 November Syria broke diplomatic relations with France and Britain. On 3 November the IPC pipeline transiting Syria was closed down by explosions at three pumping stations. This came after previous Syrian warnings of just such a move if the British attacked Egypt and was carried out by Sarraj's men according to a plan previously agreed with Nasser. Despite American pressure, the Syrian government refused to allow repairs to begin on the line until British, French and Israeli forces withdrew from Suez.[179]

Syria's leading politicians, 'Azm, Hawrani and 'Asali, rode the wave of pro-Nasserism and anti-Westernism generated by the conjunction of Suez and the Iraqi plot trials. External attempts to reverse the rise of the Syrian left had only accelerated the rise.

5

Battling the Eisenhower Doctrine, 1957–58

As 1956 drew to a close, power in Damascus was clearly in the hands of the 'leftists'. On 31 December Sabri al-'Asali formed a new government which excluded the People's Party and right-wing National Party politicians. Real power, however, was in the hands of the triumvirate of Hawrani, speaker of Parliament, 'Azm, leader of a 'progressive' bloc in Parliament and Sarraj at the Deuxième Bureau.[1] Domestic opponents were scattered and discredited. The main threat to the Damascus power brokers now came from outside. On 5 January President Eisenhower made a speech before Congress which formed the basis of the doctrine which was to bear his name. The Eisenhower Doctrine aimed to fill the 'vacuum' left by the collapse of British influence after Suez by pledging US support for local anti-communist forces. In the course of the year the pressure intensified as the governments of Lebanon, Jordan, Sa'udi Arabia and Iraq all accepted Eisenhower's umbrella. A French observer described the Syrian political scene:

> During the summer of 1957, the anxieties aroused by Baghad's ambitions and by Beirut's complaisance to the United States ... and above all the fear of renewed Turkish pressure, developed in Syria a feeling of isolation which provoked a truly ... [obsessive] fever.[2]

During 1957 the SSNP battled Syrian intelligence while the United States launched its own covert operations and marshalled Syria's neighbours for action. This pressure only served to further entrench the leftists in power. This entrenchment, epitomised by Colonel 'Abd al-Hamid Sarraj at the Deuxième Bureau, was reflected in a more aggressive Syrian foreign policy. In cooperation with Egyptian intelligence, Syrian covert operators began to hit back at their opponents abroad and took the battle to Jordan and Lebanon. In Jordan King Hussein reversed his country's previously pro-Nasserist course and, despite the efforts of Syrian intelligence, took Jordan into the opposing camp. In Lebanon, Sarraj coordinated a campaign against the Chamoun regime which became increasingly violent as the year went on. These activities foreshadowed the subversive turmoil of the United Arab Republic period.

Terrorism and the SSNP

The only organised opposition group among the numerous Syrians forced into exile during the tumult of the previous two years was the SSNP. The arrests and purges which had followed the Iraqi plot had finally rooted out the party's clandestine members in the army and frustrated plans for a coup from within Syria. Badly weakened, the party made a tentative attempt at reconciliation with Nasser and the Syrian government. Sarraj sabotaged this approach by having two of the party's emissaries killed at a secret meeting on the Syrian-Lebanese border. The party therefore returned to the fight, using terrorism as the only weapon available to it.

The party's view of the situation was expressed in a 1958 pamphlet:

> Nearly four years ago, Egyptian apparatuses, backed by International Communism, began to prepare and direct a number of police actions in the Republic of Syria, aiming at the liquidation of the mature, anti-communist, nationalist elements, which form an invincible wall in the face of all foreign expansion in Syria. ... The Party ... engaged in widespread battles against communist infiltration allied with Nasser's expansion in Syria, Lebanon and Jordan.[3]

Party leaders now admit that their aim was only to keep the Syrian regime off balance; they realised they could not hope to overthrow it by such means. There were still plenty of arms, cached inside Syria during 1956, and plenty of party members willing to make use of them. The covert war between the SSNP and Sarraj's men developed into a vicious struggle in which the Deuxième Bureau used assassination to counter the party's terrorism.[4]

The SSNP did not take the arrest and trial of their members involved in the Iraqi plot lying down. On 2 February 1957 several of their agents threw bombs at buildings in Aleppo. The town's officers' club, the offices of the ABSP and of the Communist Party, as well as the homes of the branch secretaries of both parties were all hit but without loss of life. The authorities subsequently arrested 26 SSNP members and the party responded to their trials in its usual fashion, bombing other political offices in late March.[5]

Sarraj, meanwhile, had struck back at the SSNP's military brain,

Ghassan Jadid. Jadid had been one of those on trial *in absentia* during the Iraqi plot trials and his role as the SSNP's military mastermind made Sarraj more determined than ever to get him. At 2.45 pm on 19 February Jadid had just turned his car into the Ras Beirut street where the SSNP press office was located. A Deuxième Bureau sergeant named Izzat Sh'ath had been observing Jadid's movements for the past three days under the cover of his broom-selling business. Suddenly he stepped out into the road and opened fire on the car with a sub-machine gun. Jadid was hit by 12 bullets and died instantly. The assassin fled the scene but was pursued by a passer-by and took refuge in a nearby building. A gendarmerie unit surrounded the building and engaged in a ten-minute fire fight which ended in Sh'ath's wounding and capture. As he was brought out of the building an SSNP member by the name of Aziz Ziub broke through the police cordon and fired two bullets into Sh'ath, killing him.[6] The Lebanese authorities responded to the killings by requesting that the Syrian Deuxième Bureau reduce its 200–strong contingent in its Beirut office, which was thinly disguised as a military logistics office in the port. Ghaleb Kayyali, Acting Director of Political Affairs at the Syrian Foreign Ministry, expressed satisfaction at the killing and told the Italian Ambassador that it 'would help Lebanon understand Syria'.[7]

Fadlallah Abu Mansur, who had been one of Za'im's executioners and had been intimately involved in preparing the Iraqi plot, replaced Jadid as the SSNP's Defence Commissioner. In April he held discussions with Iraqi Military Attaché Colonel Samarra'i and the National Party's Mikhail Ilyan concerning plans for another coup attempt in Syria scheduled to coincide with Syria's National Day, 17 April. Archibald Roosevelt, the CIA's officer responsible for Syria, met the plotters and agreed to finance their operation via Iraq.[8] On the afternoon of the 17th Allen Dulles spoke to his brother saying that the NSC staff 'are keeping their fingers crossed re Syria for today'.[9] In the event, nothing came of the plan. Fadlallah nonetheless continued the covert war. In September SSNP men were arrested after bombing the Egyptian Embassy and Khalid al-'Azm's home in Damascus. The Soviet Embassy was also bombed. In October a Syrian army communiqué announced the discovery of an SSNP arms cache in the 'Alawite mountains and accused Muhammad Maruf of training the party's paramilitaries in Lebanon. However, it is probable that this arms dump was left over from the Iraqi plot as the party no longer had the resources to smuggle in large quantities of arms during 1957. On 4 January 1958 Deuxième Bureau agents bombed the Beirut apartment of the brother of SSNP member Lieutenant Mahmud Nahmah. Nahmah had just escaped from Mezze prison where he was on trial for his part in a subversive plot. He was not in the apartment at the time but the three occupants were killed. A week later SSNP members were probably responsible for dynamiting the Club d'Orient in Homs.[10]

By early 1958, however, the dirty war between the SSNP and the Deuxième Bureau had become subsumed in the wider covert struggle between Syria and Lebanon.

Subverting Lebanon

Lebanon's hospitality to the SSNP was a reflection of its generally hostile attitude to the Syrian ruling clique and to Nasser's ambitions. In November 1956 President Chamoun had dismissed the pro-Egyptian cabinet led by Sa'ib Salam and 'Abdallah Yafi.[11] Their replacements, Prime Minister Sami al-Sulh and Foreign Minister Charles Malik, took a robust pro-Western line. At the Beirut Arab Summit which followed the tripartite invasion of Egypt, they refused Egypt's demands that Lebanon not only break off relations with Britain and France but also allow Syrian troops to be stationed in Lebanon. On 16 March 1957 the government announced its acceptance of the Eisenhower Doctrine. An exchange of state visits between Chamoun and Turkish President Celal Bayar further enraged the power brokers in Damascus.[12]

Damascus was particularly concerned at Lebanon's harbouring of Syrian exiles. In November 1956 Deuxième Bureau agents had tried to kidnap Mikhail Ilyan from the St Georges Hotel in Beirut so that he could stand trial in Damascus, but the agents were apprehended, beaten up and imprisoned by Lebanese security forces. The Bureau responded by stepping up its efforts against the Lebanese government. In late November the Lebanese police seized an oil tanker filled with arms coming from Damascus. Syrian agents also increasingly co-operated with Egyptian military intelligence. When the Egyptian Military Attaché in Beirut, Hasan Khalil, was declared *persona non grata* for organising a series of bombings of official buildings, there was evidence that Syrian agents had worked with him.[13]

By early 1957 the Lebanese government was so concerned at the Syrian threat that it had re-orientated its military posture away from defence against Israel and towards resisting a possible Syrian attack. Chief of Staff Chehab told the British Military Attaché that he was preparing for Syria to move small military units into Lebanon to act as focal points for launching a guerrilla offensive. The Lebanese army was making preparations to sabotage likely approach roads and was arming villagers in areas it considered threatened.[14]

In this state of barely concealed hostility, the June parliamentary elections provided the opportunity for a dress rehearsal of the all-out covert war that was to erupt the following year. The elections were hotly contested by Chamoun's supporters and opponents in Lebanon and a variety of interested foreign powers threw their weight behind their preferred candidates.[15] The Foreign Office, which strongly backed the Chamounists, correctly observed that 'elections in Lebanon have never been wholly free'. Nonetheless, governmental intimidation and ballot-rigging 'were used as seldom before', leading General Chehab to complain that 'corruption, bribery and skullduggery ... had reached proportions never before seen in Lebanon'.[16]

Foreign interference on all sides was blatant. Egypt helped the anti-Chamounists with stepped-up propaganda attacks on the government and paid up to £200,000 to opposition groups which staged demonstrations on 30 May in which seven people were killed.[17] In April several Syrian intelligence agents had been arrested and charged with attempting to influence the elections.[18] In June the US Military Attaché in Beirut received documents from 'a usually reliable source' which indicated the extent of Deuxième Bureau activity in Lebanon. These documents listed 29 alleged Deuxième Bureau officers who had visited agents, as well as the name of a Beirut café which was supposedly used as a rendezvous point.[19] In addition to financial aid, Syrian intelligence also provided arms to opposition groups, as well as orchestrating some terrorist acts.[20] For instance, the Lebanese gendarmerie alleged that the Deuxième Bureau was responsible for an incident in June when dynamite was thrown from a Syrian-licenced car in Beirut.[21] Syrian officers even proffered their services to one sympathetic candidate, offering to kidnap any of his rivals he chose. The Foreign Office concluded that 'there is ample evidence of Egyptian, Syrian and possibly Russian interference, including bribery and distribution of arms'.[22]

The Western powers meanwhile supported the Chamounists. The US Ambassador argued that 'our interest is to prevent the election of a majority or even a large minority of the candidates who are grouping around ex-President Bechara Khouri ... unquestionably [backed] by Egyptian and Syrian money and ... by hidden Soviet funds'. He noted that the 'Bechara Khouri-ESS crowd are prepared to spend a minimum of around *two* million dollars to get their deputies elected' and urged that Washington provide enough funds to support the Chamounists.[23] The CIA responded by pouring money into Chamoun and Sami al-Sulh's campaign chests. The Foreign Office did its best to publicise Syrian and Egyptian subversive activity in the British press. Probably of more significance was King Sa'ud's change of policy. Responding to American promptings and his own fears of the spreading wave of

Nasserism, he had backed away from the Egypt-Syrian axis and halted Sa'udi payments to Lebanese opposition politicians. This was an important factor in the eventual rightist victory, when pro-Chamounist candidates won two-thirds of the parliamentary seats.[24] US officials described the results as 'a great victory for ... the West'.[25]

Having failed to remove the government through the electoral process, Sarraj and his Egyptian colleagues stepped up their efforts to destabilise the country. Sa'ib Salam and 'Abdallah Yafi visited Damascus for talks with Syrian leaders. Syrian agents concentrated on distributing money to opposition politicians in the Tyre-Sidon, Mount Harmal and Tripoli areas. Kamal Junblatt's Druze militia was supplied with arms and assisted in carrying out operations such as the 17 August bombing of the Damascus-Beirut railway-line.[26] Sarraj also began to make use of the Deuxième Bureau's Palestinian unit. Under the Syrian officer Akram Safadi, the unit was withdrawn from its espionage duties inside Israel and put to work in Lebanon. Although the unit was officered by Syrians, its men were Palestinian refugees. This gave Syrian operations a degree of deniability as the operatives often could not be identified with the Bureau. Furthermore, the men were able to exploit their family contacts among Palestinian refugees in Lebanon to recruit more agents.[27]

It appears that this unit was responsible for the majority of the terrorist operations which took place after the elections.[28] On 30 July the Jordanian Embassy and the USIS offices in Beirut were bombed and twelve Palestinians subsequently arrested. In August a Palestinian who admitted to working for 'Syrian officers' was arrested while preparing to dynamite the US Embassy. In the middle of August the President's summer residence was bombed as was a pipeline bringing water into Beirut. In the night of 25/26 August six members of a paramilitary team were arrested by the gendarmerie after they had attempted to blow up a bridge. The police also began to seize modern Czech weaponry being smuggled into the country from Syria. On 12 September a gun battle between gendarmes and arms smugglers near the Syrian border left three policemen and eight smugglers dead. In September a Syrian-backed gang sent threatening letters to embassies and newspapers in the name of the 'Society for the Liberation of the Usurped Land'. This was followed by the bombing of five newspaper offices in Beirut and also a Jewish school. On 5 November the owner of the newspaper *al-Rasid* was murdered. The Lebanese authorities arrested 30 suspects in the wake of this bombing spree, some of whom confessed to working for the Syrians.[29] In December paramilitary units operating from across the Syrian border attacked two gendarmerie posts in isolated areas.[30]

The Lebanese government and their Western allies reacted to the Syrian offensive with alarm. In September Malik told Foreign Secretary Lloyd that 'it was a matter of life and death for Lebanon and the other neighbours of Syria that the present regime in Syria should be changed'.[31] Britain and the United States were worried enough to offer Chamoun military intervention if he asked for it.[32] Their anxiety was heightened by the fact that Syrian and Egyptian subversion was not confined to Lebanon. Jordan's King Hussein was also coming under intense pressure.

Subverting Jordan

Since 1955 pro-Nasserist forces had been gaining the upper hand in Jordan. Britain's attempts to get Jordan to join the Baghdad Pact had led to widespread riots in December 1955 and January 1956 in which Egyptian- and Sa'udi-backed mobs attacked Western installations. The tide of nationalist sentiment led to the dismissal of British officers from the Arab Legion and the opening of negotiations over the replacement of the British subsidy under the Anglo-Jordanian treaty by an Arab one.[33] In the view of the Foreign Office, the signing of a Syrian-Egyptian-Jordanian military agreement in October 1956 had finally turned Jordan into a 'satellite of Egypt ... committed to ... [Nasser's] "positive neutralism"'.[34] The Israeli reprisal raids which Nasser's *fedayeen* provoked had excited popular opinion and the Suez Crisis brought a wave of support for pro-Nasserists. More concretely, the entry of Syrian forces into Jordan on 30 October under the terms of the military treaty had given Syrian intelligence a secure base from which to operate. Just before the Suez war, Sulayman Nabulsi had formed a strongly pro-Nasserist government with a Ba'thist, 'Abdallah al-Rimawi, as Foreign Minister. Nabulsi and Rimawi ardently proclaimed their support of 'positive neutralism' and declared: 'we will not cooperate with the West because it wants to exploit us ... and make us underlings'.[35]

King Hussein at first went along with this trend, but in early 1957 he was convinced by his more conservative advisors of the dangers that the tide of Nasserism and 'communism' posed and he began to take a strong anti-communist line.[36] This reversal was watched with concern in Cairo and Damascus whose intelligence services had done much to foster the anti-Western trend. Egypt's radio stations had poured out propaganda and Sarraj had spent up to £110,000 in 1956 to secure the election of the Nabulsi government.[37] As the crisis between Hussein and his government loomed, Syrian and Egyptian covert operators did what they could to help their allies.

The crisis came to a head in April.[38] On 13 March the Anglo-Jordanian treaty had been terminated and on 2 April Nabulsi informed the king of his government's intention to establish diplomatic relations with the Soviet Union. On the 8th the First Armoured Car Regiment under Captain Nazir Rashid threw up a cordon around Amman, leading the British and King Hussein to fear that a coup was under way. The unit, however, returned to barracks on Hussein's orders.[39] It appears that Nabulsi was unaware of Rashid's motives. Indeed, he feared the operation had been ordered by the king to force out the government. The aim of the cordon, however, appears to have been to pressure the king into dismissing Bahjat Talhuni, his security chief.[40] Some observers point to Rashid's subsequent close ties to Sarraj and suggest that the Syrian spymaster may have orchestrated the move.[41]

On the 10th Nabulsi resigned as Prime Minister and an open struggle ensued over who would succeed him. The pro-Nasserite Chief of Staff, 'Ali Abu Nuwar, had been close to Nabulsi's government and had made a point of promoting 'progressive' officers at the expense of the Bedouin who traditionally formed the backbone of the army and the core of the monarchy's support. He was the nominal leader of a 'Free Officers' group in the army, modelled on Nasser's movement.[42] On 13 April Abu Nuwar and Assistant Chief of Staff 'Ali Hiyari informed Hussein that the army demanded that 'Abd al-Halim al-Nimr be allowed to form a new government. They also ordered the Bedouin Third Infantry Regiment away from camp on a desert night exercise. Suspecting that a coup was planned, the unit mutinied and in the fighting at the garrison town of Zerqa there were twenty casualties. King Hussein dashed to the scene where he was acclaimed by his supporters, who threatened to kill Abu Nuwar for his supposed treachery.[43]

In the turmoil Hussein asked the Western powers and Iraq for their help. Observing that 'the pot appears to be boiling over in Jordan', the Foreign Office made clear its determination 'to sustain King Hussein against this Syro-Egyptian plot'. Plans were made to reinforce the Royal Air Force detachment at Mafraq with Venom jets from Cyprus but it was thought that the Iraqis were in a better position to help militarily. Nuri al-Sa'id promised to do so and immediately despatched a brigade to the pipeline station, H3, in the desert. He also pledged to counter any move by Syrian forces in the north of Jordan, only requesting that the RAF support his forces if Syrian and Egyptian jets became involved. The United States moved the Sixth Fleet into the Eastern Mediterranean, urged restraint on Israel and encouraged Sa'udi Arabia to prepare for military intervention. The White House followed up these measures with a $10 million loan.[44]

In the event these precautions proved unnecessary. Syrian troops based at Mafraq did coordinate their movements with the plotters and took over the joint Syrian-Jordanian army intelligence centre, sealed off several villages and cut communications lines between Jordan and Iraq. These manoeuvres had been ordered by Sarraj in conjunction with the Egyptians but without authorisation from the Syrian government. When Bahjat Talhuni telephoned President Quwatli to complain, Quwatli was taken by surprise and ordered the troops back to barracks.[45] There was also evidence that the Egyptian Military Attaché and the Egyptian Operations Officer at the Joint Command HQ in Amman had helped Abu Nuwar to plan his moves.[46]

After the failure of the plot, King Hussein appointed a hard-line conservative government, under Ibrahim Hashim with Samir Rifa'i as Foreign Minister, which imposed martial law and moved against the Nasserists. Trials of the plotters were held, the king being convinced that he had narrowly averted a large-scale conspiracy orchestrated by Sarraj aimed at absorbing Jordan into a Greater Syrian Republic.[47] The British Ambassador, Charles Johnston, however, concluded that the 'conspiracy was an amateurish performance of disparate and ill-coordinated elements'. In any case, Abu Nuwar took asylum in Syria. 'Ali Hiyari followed him there and Syrian troops facilitated the flight of numerous lesser personages who were sought by the new government.[48] Abu Nuwar, Hiyari and members of Nabulsi's government denied that there had been a plot, arguing that Hussein had engineered a crisis in order to remove them.[49] In his autobiography Abu Nuwar wrote that when he met Sarraj in Damascus the Syrian asked him 'how goes the coup?' Abu Nuwar replied, 'What coup?'[50] Indeed, the evidence presented at the subsequent trials was not sufficient to convince US diplomats that there had been a conspiracy to remove the king.[51] Nonetheless, the important thing was that Hussein believed in the existence of the plot.

Relations between Syria and the Rifa'i government rapidly deteriorated as Hussein decisively threw in his lot with the British anti-Nasserist campaign. The British Embassy supplied Hussein with intelligence 'about ... Egyptian and Syrian subversive activities in Jordan' and Jordanian security forces apprehended and turned a team of Egyptian and Syrian assassins. On 14 May Johnston reported that the government's 'attack on Egyptian subversive activities could not be more vigorous'. Syrian troops had been confined to their barracks and surrounded by Jordanian soldiers; 'from being a centre of subversion they are being converted into something like a hostage of fortune'.[52] The British and Americans were, however, concerned for the king's personal safety. During the Zerqa incident there had been an attempt to kill him with a car bomb and a subsequent plot to kill Queen Zein, the Queen mother, was foiled. The United States also had 'knowledge [of an] Egyptian sponsored plot to assassinate Hussein'.[53] After hearing that the Egyptian Military Attaché to Sa'udi Arabia had planted a bomb in one of King Sa'ud's palaces, Johnston opined 'I wish I could share [the king's confidence] in his personal security arrangements'.[54]

At the end of May Damascus and Amman radios traded invective, with Amman castigating the Syrian army which has 'assumed the character of a political police force directing its aggression against the citizens', and lambasting the 'hypocritical' and 'lying' rulers in Damascus.[55] The Foreign Office chortled that: 'this splendid piece of dirty-linen washing in public should put another nail in the coffin of Syro/Jordanian relations' and expressed relief at the withdrawal of the Syrian troops, completed on 27 May.[56] King Hussein also sought to build bridges to the Syrian opposition. Salah Shishakli was invited to Amman for an audience with the king, as was the SSNP's President. The SSNP arranged to supply men to work with Jordanian security officers to foil Syrian assassination teams during a visit by King Sa'ud.[57]

The battle soon became violent with both Jordanian and Syrian intelligence seeking to carry out terrorist operations against each other. In July Jordanian intelligence sent a Muslim Brotherhood agent named Adib al-Dessuki into Syria to assassinate Syrian leftist leaders and kidnap Jordanian exiles.[58] The wide scale of Jordanian operations was demonstrated by Charles Malik's remarks to Selwyn Lloyd in September that 'Jordan was already providing arms for the Druzes and the Alawites' in Syria.[59]

The Syrian-Egyptian campaign of terrorism and black propaganda was on a larger scale. The aim was to destabilise the Jordanian government by giving the impression that there was wide-spread popular opposition to it and that a revolutionary situation was brewing.[60] Syrian officers visited Jordan and recruited agents to bomb government and Western targets. At the same time a 'whispering campaign' in the press was orchestrated by the Syrian Legation to the effect that the king would soon bend to 'popular pressure' and ask Nabulsi back to form a government. The Egyptians used their diplomatic bag to smuggle in anti-royalist propaganda leaflets.[61]

The terrorist campaign began in mid-August when a Deuxième Bureau officer toured Jordan recruiting agents who let off bombs in Amman and Hebron and attempted to plant bombs in Ramallah and Irbid. A would-be bomber was arrested while carrying explosives intended for the British or US Consulates in Jerusalem. In September bombs went off outside the USIS office, the Turkish Embassy and the house of the Military Governor in Amman. On 27 September the car of the Military Governor of Nablus was blown up by a mine and its driver wounded. At the same time Jordanian security forces began discovering caches of weapons smuggled in from Syria. The police also discovered that many Syrian intelligence personnel had recently married Jordanian women from the West Bank so that they could more easily travel to Jordan and deliver money and instructions.[62]

On 7 October the house of the US Assistant Military Attaché was badly damaged by a bomb, prompting more vigorous official action. On the 10th the army carried out house-to-house searches in three Palestinian refugee camps near Amman, uncovering caches of fuses. Similar searches in a Jerusalem school run by a Ba'th sympathiser, where Egyptian teachers had been working, uncovered a cache of explosives and Communist Party pamphlets. The next day a bomb went off in the Ministry of the Interior and a timebomb was subsequently discovered in the house of a government minister. Explosions in Zerqa on the 23rd were followed by more searches which located gelignite and fuses in a nearby refugee camp.[63]

By November the 'Jordanian security system ... [was] about as efficient as is possible in an Arab country'. A Royal Guard regiment under Sharif Nasir, the king's uncle, had been formed and the 'extraordinary [security] precautions ... [around] the King's person' had shown their worth. The terrorist campaign waned as Syrian diplomats were expelled and Syrian agents were brought before Jordanian military courts.[64] Syria and Egypt switched their tactics and intensified their overt propaganda campaign against the monarchy. A Jordanian government in exile was established in Damascus. In the hope of 'incit[ing] nationwide disturbances' Cairo and Damascus Radios denounced Hussein as a traitor willing to settle with Israel.[65] The broadcasts found a sympathetic ear since the Jordanian government had 'no perceptible following in any sector of Jordanian political life'.[66] They were especially well received among the Palestinian refugees who chafed under the government's heavy hand. Nonetheless, the campaign did not achieve any significant success. In the State Department's judgement this was because the king had decapitated the opposition movement by jailing or driving into exile his opponents and because the agitators who had previously organised demonstrations, such as Egyptian teachers, had either been thrown into jail or deported.[67]

As the year drew to a close the Western powers could conclude with satisfaction that 1957 had seen Jordan turn from an Egyptian 'satellite' into a 'determined opponent' of Nasser and the communists and were pleased with their prompt action which had exploited this 'unique opportunity ... to encourage [a] realignment of forces in Near East'.[68] Nonetheless, the main struggle was still being fought to the north. By the autumn of 1957 US attempts to topple the Syrian government had blown up into a major international crisis.

The American plot

During 1957 the Western powers watched apprehensively as Syria's relations with Nasser and the Soviet Union grew closer and her intelligence services sowed mayhem in Lebanon and Jordan. However, with the destruction of the Syrian right there was little that the West could achieve with propaganda or political action. America attempted to use covert action but eventually resorted to isolating Syria and seeking to prevent the further spread of Soviet influence.

When the Eisenhower Doctrine was announced in January the Syrian government had rejected the notion of a communist threat to Syria and the United States' attempts to control the region. In March the attempts of President Quwatli and the relatively pro-Western Chief of Staff Nizam al-Din to transfer Sarraj and other leftist officers were thwarted by 'Azm, now Defence Minister, and Hawrani.[69] In the May by-elections leftist candidates swept the board and the US Ambassador reported that the victory of the 'A[BS]P-Communist-fellow traveler-opportunist vanguard of proletariat' made 'it plain that conservatives ... cannot win at the polls under existing circumstances'.[70] The by-elections were followed by transfers of army officers which further strengthened Sarraj and the leftists. Burhan Adham was appointed head of the Deuxième Bureau's Counter-Intelligence Branch while an 'extreme leftist' was made chief of Military Police. In July Quwatli made a speech in which, for the first time, he labelled the United States an 'overt foe'. Robert Strong, the US Chargé d'Affaires, reported that the speech was 'indistinguishable from Communist propaganda'.[71]

Military and economic ties with the Soviet Union were also strengthened. In December 1956 Selwyn Lloyd had told a NATO meeting that Soviet intentions appeared to be to re-equip and expand the Syrian army, provide a pool of equipment for use by Egypt and other friendly states and preposition equipment for use by Soviet 'volunteers' in any future crisis. Contrary to press reports, no Soviet aircraft had arrived in Syria and 'before Syria can be used as an operational base for Soviet type aircraft, a considerable amount of airfield and logistical development is necessary'.[72] Nonetheless, £20 million worth of tanks, armoured personnel carriers and artillery had been delivered and 20 MiG 15s were being assembled in Egypt for despatch to Syria. Soviet military advisors had arrived with the equipment and were also reported to be working with the Deuxième Bureau's interrogation branch at Mezze prison giving instruction in the use of 'truth drugs'.[73] In January 1957 the US Military Attaché reported that 'the Syrian port of Latakia is jammed with military supplies'.[74]

Syria's trade remained predominantly with Western countries. Even in late 1957 her trade with NATO countries totalled $54.3 million as against $19.5 with the East Bloc.[75] However, in late September 1957 'Azm led a delegation to Moscow which resulted in the announcement of an LS400 million loan and Soviet help in oil prospecting. The Foreign Office concluded that 'Syria can now be regarded as a Soviet satellite'.[76]

The bright spot for London and Washington amidst all this gloom was that France and Sa'udi Arabia had switched sides. France had belatedly become alarmed at the effect its support for 'Azm was having and during 1956 had reversed course. Shishakli had been approached about the prospects for mounting a coup and Paris was now coordinating its policy with London and Washington to counter Egyptian and Soviet penetration. In November 1956 the French Ambassador warned the State Department that 'Syria is becoming increasingly a tool of the Soviet Union, and that something must be done'.[77] In similar fashion, King Sa'ud had become alarmed at the success of 'Azm and the Ba'thists. Encouraged by the United States, he cut his links with Nasser and the Syrian regime. Sa'udi money began to flow into the pockets of the opposition.[78]

The addition of France and Sa'udi Arabia to the Anglo-American camp, combined with the reversal of Jordan's position and the Lebanese election results, were causes for celebration in London and Washington. Nonetheless, the two governments still had to tackle Syria. Britain and Iraq, smarting from the collapse of their elaborate covert operation in November 1956, remained inactive. The initiative now shifted to Ankara and Washington.

Turkey shared Washington's view of the communist and Egyptian 'threat' in Syria and its Foreign Secretary had suggested to the US Ambassador in October 1956 that 'internal medicine will not do, surgery is required for cancerous growth'. The Turks thought the SSNP was the 'best possibility for [the] time being'.[79] In November Prime Minister Menderes informed the US government of Turkey's assessment of the situation. Praising the tripartite attack on Egypt for destroying and dispersing the Soviet weaponry accumulated by Egypt, Menderes noted that the USSR was 'concentrating all its military attention and activity on Syria'. He warned that: 'we are now witnessing Syria become a Russian military base' as part of the Soviet Union's strategy 'to surround and isolate Turkey.'[80]

Turkey responded to the threat with military and subversive sabre-rattling. In December 1956 Damascus lodged a formal complaint with Ankara and the United States about Turkish troop movements on its borders and airspace violations by Turkish jets.[81] In February and March 1957 there was an exodus of up to 200 Syrian exiles from Beirut to Turkey, spurred by Jadid's assassination and 'the habit of agents of the present Syrian régime of descending on ... [the exiles] and whisking them back to Syria'.[82] Turkey welcomed the exiles and backed their plottings. During the summer Mikhail Ilyan was encouraged to approach the British and Americans with demands for Iraqi action in Syria[83]

It was, however, up to the United States to take the lead. In the wake of the Suez Crisis the State Department had drawn up revised policy plans for the Middle East which recognised that 'the French are no longer able to play a constructive role in the area' and that Britain's position 'has been seriously prejudiced'. Therefore 'the US must assume leadership in maintaining and restoring the Western position in the area'.[84] The US administration had been especially disturbed by the interruption of oil supplies during the Suez Crisis due to the blocking of the Suez Canal and the sabotage of the IPC pipeline. Europe had faced oil shortages and it was feared that Soviet influence over both the Suez Canal and the trans-Syrian pipelines would enable them to strangle the West.[85] John Foster Dulles argued that 'a vacuum has been created in the area with the virtual elimination of British influence' and 'the Soviets are likely to take over the area, and they could thereby control Europe through the oil on which Europe is dependent and even Africa as well'.[86]

With regard to Syria, the US administration adopted a policy of maintaining 'minimum official contacts with [the government] while endeavoring [to] discreetly encourage elements opposed [to] present [Syrian] policies'.[87] Foreign Minister Bitar's castigation of US support for 'reactionary, dictatorial, police regimes' and requests for aid 'without political conditions' were listened to politely and ignored.[88] Foreign Service and CIA officers were constantly on the look-out for potential opponents to the regime. Contacts with the SSNP were good and both the Embassy in Damascus and the Consulate in Aleppo received regular reports on SSNP activities.[89] However, after the 17 April plot misfired the CIA turned its attention elsewhere. Allen Dulles told his brother 'we have to start new planning. It is not hopeless.'[90]

About this time, sources differ on whether it was in April or June,

Kermit Roosevelt, the CIA officer responsible for the Middle East, transferred a new station chief to Damascus.[91] The previous station chief, Vernon Cassin, had forged contacts with a dissident Syrian general earlier in the year but nothing had come of it.[92] The new appointee was Howard Stone, a legendary covert operator who had been involved in the 1953 coup in Iraq. Roosevelt hoped that his appointment would 'light a fire' under covert action efforts. Under intense pressure from his superiors to achieve fast results and not speaking Arabic or French, Stone organised an insecure and 'sloppy' operation that ultimately backfired.[93] State Department professionals describe the affair as amateurish and intensely embarrassing and the Chargé in Damascus was unsympathetic to Stone's efforts. However, with covert action being coordinated between the Dulles brothers, there was little that Foreign Service officers lower down the ladder could do.[94]

Stone and his CIA colleagues, Arthur Close and Frank Jeton, were unable to interest any senior Syrian officers in their plans. They got in touch with four officers, one of whom was a Druze and two Armenian, none of them above the rank of Lieutenant-Colonel. Several meetings were held with the officers, first in a safe-house and then in Close's apartment. Two female secretaries from the Embassy were included in the meetings to provide cover and up to $3 million in bribes were handed out. The plan agreed upon by the conspirators was probably due to take place on 13 or 14 August. The intention was for the director of the Armoured School to use his tanks to cordon off Qatana and seize key installations in Damascus. Other units from Latakia, Aleppo, Homs and Suwayda' would then join the putschists.[95]

The CIA also contacted Ibrahim Husayni in Rome and he was smuggled into Damascus to meet the conspirators. Unimpressed, he returned to Rome. There is disagreement between sources as to whether Adib Shishakli was directly involved. Arthur Close claims that although Husayni may have contacted Adib Shishakli, the CIA men did not meet him. The Syrian government, however, claimed that Shishakli had also visited Damascus and met the conspirators. This was confirmed to the writer by a former Foreign Service officer with intimate knowledge of the affair.[96]

Whether or not Shishakli was involved in the end made no difference. The Deuxième Bureau had had the CIA men under surveillance as a result of earlier meetings they had had with SSNP loyalists. The Bureau found out about the meetings, turned one of the Syrian officers and kept the plotters under surveillance. It was probably Husayni's visit on 11 August that persuaded Sarraj he had better halt the conspiracy before it went any further. On 12 August the Syrian government announced the discovery of an 'American plot'.[97] According to the Syrian communiqué, 'American imperialism was not happy to see Syria free' and sent its 'most skilful expert on conspiracy, one Warren Stone' to 'replace [the] system of government in Syria'.[98]

Stone and Jeton were declared *persona non grata*. Close was not expelled but was put under close surveillance. The Military Attaché, Colonel Robert Molloy, was also expelled. It is unclear whether he had been involved in the plot. One American Foreign Service source claimed that he constructed bombs which Stone planned to use during the coup, possibly to assassinate senior Syrian officers. Close, however, denies that Mallory was involved. In any case, he had 'made a point of getting into the hair of the Syrian military leadership' and aggressively exercising his rights to observe Syrian military exercises. Once he had even been involved in an altercation with Sarraj in which punches were thrown. Sarraj therefore probably used the opportunity to get rid of the Colonel.[99]

The aftermath and the Turkish crisis

Sarraj and his allies used the furore over the American plot to consolidate their hold on power. Husayni was dismissed from his post as Military Attaché in Rome. More importantly, Nizam al-Din lost his job and 'Afif al-Bizri became Chief of Staff. Bizri had presided over the Iraqi plot trials and was vehemently anti-Western. Western governments regarded him as a communist.[100] His appointment was accompanied by a purge of senior officers. At the same time, Sarraj took the opportunity to extend the reach of the Deuxième Bureau. Earlier in the year he had succeeded in transforming the civilian Department of General Security into a subordinate arm of the Bureau and now Military Intelligence officers were assigned to all government ministries. A senior Soviet intelligence officer, General Serov, was brought in to assist in a re-organisation of the security services.[101]

The Foreign Office concluded that these events 'mark the consolidation of real power in the hands of left wing elements in the Army ... [and] the final obliteration of elements in the Army prepared to oppose complete control by the left wing officers around Sarraj'.[102] John Foster Dulles assessed that 'there is evidence in Syria of the development of a dangerous and classic pattern' of Soviet infiltration which, as in Czechoslovakia, will result in the country falling under 'the control of International Communism and becom[ing] a Soviet satellite'.[103] The situation was 'wholly unacceptable' to the United States and he concluded that 'it seems to us that there is now little hope of correction from within and that we must think in terms of the external assets reflected by the deep concern of the Moslem states having common borders with Syria.' British Prime Minister Harold Macmillan concurred, arguing that the United States and Britain should encourage the Arab states to expose the Syrian regime as 'Communist stooges'.[104]

Acting on this approach Dulles sent a flurry of telegrams to America's allies on 21 August.[105] To King Sa'ud he cabled 'I trust that you will exert your great influence to the end that the atheistic creed of Communism will not become entrenched at a key position in the Moslem world.'[106] To the Israelis: 'I hope I can proceed on the assumption that no action will be taken which would involve the Syrian matter in aspects of the Arab-Israeli dispute.'[107] To Selwyn Lloyd he urged: 'we must perhaps be prepared to take some serious risks to avoid even greater risks and dangers later on.'[108] These urgings were accompanied by accelerated arms shipments to Iraq, Jordan and Sa'udi Arabia.[109]

An envoy, Loy Henderson, was despatched to the Middle East in an attempt to drum up an anti-Syrian campaign. He found that, at least in private, Syria's neighbours were ever more alarmed by the latest turn of events. In Jordan Samir Rifa'i warned of the imminent 'subversion or overthrow' of the Jordanian and Iraqi monarchies.[110] In Baghdad Nuri Sa'id, although out of office, talked of instigating a tribal uprising in Syria which would give a pretext for Iraqi military intervention. He was, however, deterred by the relatively strong Syrian Air Force.[111] Lebanon's Charles Malik told Dulles that if the current government became entrenched in Syria then he believed Jordan would fall in a month, Lebanon in three months, Iraq in six and Sa'udi Arabia in 'perhaps a year'.[112] The Turks were the most concerned and the most willing to take action. Menderes believed that Syria was now 'a Soviet satellite' and 'on her way to becoming a springboard for covert aggression'. He warned: 'little time remains to us in which to do something about this dangerous, unfortunate situation.'[113]

On Henderson's return, Dulles gave the United States' regional allies the green light to act, declaring that 'Syria has become, or is about to become, a base for military and subversive activities in the Near East designed to destroy the independence of those countries and to subject them to Soviet Communist domination'. He pledged US support to any of Syria's neighbours who took military action under Article 51 of the UN Charter, i.e. in self defence.[114] A NATO meeting gave its members a free hand by concluding that 'indirect aggression' was already underway in the form of Syrian infiltration into Lebanon and Jordan. Senior US officers were despatched to

Turkey to discuss military plans, Turkish troops were massed on the Syrian border and US strategic nuclear forces were put on alert to deter the Soviet Union from intervening.[115] Ibrahim Husayni was received as an honoured guest in Ankara.[116] Meanwhile the State Department and USIS launched a 'stepped up psychological campaign'.[117]

Dulles reacted strongly to the leftist moves in Syria because he saw this as the 'period of greatest peril ... since the Korean War ended'. This was due to his belief that the developments represented a Soviet takeover and Khrushchev's 'intention to step up the Cold War'.[118] Robert Strong, the US Chargé in Damascus, however, cautioned that Washington 'goes much too far now in foreseeing "complete" dependency on the Soviets'.[119] He argued that there were significant splits developing in the regime between the Ba'thists on the one hand and 'Azm and the leftist officers on the other as Hawrani was concerned at the growing influence of the communists and the Soviet Union. Unsurprisingly, Strong's nuanced analysis was lost in the atmosphere of crisis.[120]

Dulles's attempts to mobilise a campaign of external pressure against Syria were nonetheless thwarted by the unwillingness of Arab leaders to attack publicly a brother Arab state and by the Soviet Union's counter-pressures. King Sa'ud and Iraqi Prime Minister 'Ali Jawdat al-Ayubi both visited Damascus in late September in a show of Arab solidarity, prompting Assistant Secretary of State William Rountree to complain that 'what the Arabs [a]re saying publicly b[ears] little or no relation to what they are saying privately'.[121]

On 16 October the Syrian government took their complaints about the provocative Turkish military moves to the UN General Assembly.[122] The Syrian note protested that 'there exists an actual military threat to Syria [from Turkey] ... which presages imminent attack'.[123] The Soviet Union supported the Syrian protest with a propaganda campaign and Foreign Minister Gromyko warned of plans 'for an attack by Turkey on Syria'.[124] In the subsequent debates the Arab governments denied their concern at events inside Syria, feeling unable to side with Turkey against a member of the Arab League.[125] The Soviets encouraged the Turks to think again about their military bullying of Syria by carrying out joint manoeuvres with the Bulgarian armed forces near the Turkish border.[126] Egypt meanwhile scored a propaganda coup by landing a token military force in Latakia in a show of support for Syria.[127] The United States, worried lest unilateral Turkish military action create 'an extremely serious situation', urged the Turks to back down and encouraged the Sa'udis to arbitrate between Ankara and Damascus.[128] At the United Nations the Syrian complaint was 'pigeon-holed' after the parties had had their chances to speak and the crisis was gradually defused.[129]

In mid-October Strong summarised the failure of Dulles's hard-line approach:

> efforts to persuade moderate Arab leaders to take an overt hard line toward Syria having failed, what alternatives do we have? Force is ruled out. Clandestine activities would not succeed. A hard line from the West alone would only drive Syria closer to the Soviet Bloc. Unhappily there is no satisfactory alternative ... to leaving the handling of the problem to King Sa'ud and other moderate Arabs [with] behind the scenes [help from the United States]. Limited economic warfare measures which annoy but do not have any serious effect only justify the extremists in their course ... continuation of the Turkish military threats simply gives the Soviets and Syrian extremists another golden propaganda opportunity. The best we can hope for from Syria for a long time would be genuine neutrality.[130]

Formation of the United Arab Republic

The Western Powers had little choice but to adopt Strong's recommendations. Over the following weeks Britain, the United States and Jordan continued to work on joint propaganda programmes emphasising the communistic nature of the Syrian regime but the Syrian-Turkish frontier returned to its normal semi-tense state.[131] On 7 November Rountree and Bitar held talks in New York.[132] Although King Sa'ud and Nuri continued to hatch anti-Syrian plots, they did so quietly and without attracting any attention.[133]

In the event it was not American bluster, Turkish threats or Iraqi subversion which checked the communist rise in Syria but rather the Ba'th and Nasser. During December US diplomats reported an escalating struggle between Ba'thists and communists in Syria. 'Azm was reported to be working '100%' with the communists in the hope of winning their support for the Presidency but Hawrani and 'Asali had agreed to cooperate against him in order to forestall a communist victory in the following year's parliamentary elections. Bitar meanwhile complained of the undue influence of the Soviet Embassy and Military Attaché. In the army, Sarraj was seeking to oust Bizri and lead a Nasserist military government.[134]

Nasser meanwhile contacted the Americans to tell them he was also disturbed at the growing influence of the Soviets and the Communist Party in Syria. He promised to work against them and requested a halt to US propaganda attacks for three months to ease his task. The United States agreed and the American Ambassador to

Cairo, Raymond Hare, shared intelligence with Nasser on the situation in Syria. The struggle intensified over the following month as the Soviet Embassy in Damascus complained of Egyptian efforts to undermine its influence in Syria. Baqdash's communists coordinated a wave of strikes and 'Azm intrigued to remove 'Asali. Deputy Chief of Staff Nafuri defected to the communist side. Nonetheless, the Egyptian Chargé in Damascus expressed his optimism to Robert Strong that the combination of Quwatli, Sarraj, the Ba'thists and the National Party would prevail in the struggle. The rivalry between Sarraj and Bizri came out into the open and both men reinforced their bodyguards. Sarraj was even reported to have made overtures to the SSNP, offering to release their prisoners in return for the party's support.[135]

The Ba'thists eventually concluded that their best chance of blocking the communists was through union with Egypt.[136] On 12 January a delegation of officers flew to Cairo to plead for union. Nasser was reluctant to take on full responsibility for the country's turbulent domestic scene but eventually agreed to do so provided it was on his terms. Quwatli's attempts to negotiate a federal arrangement, which had been approved in principle by a joint session of the Syrian and Egyptian parliaments the previous November, were rejected and the formation of the United Arab Republic was proclaimed on 1 February 1958.[137]

6

The United Arab Republic, 1958–61

The three-year life of the United Arab Republic (UAR) comprised 'one of the richest spells of inter-Arab subversive activity'. As Yakov Caroz, former Deputy Director of the Mossad, put it:

> Jointly the two secret services [Egyptian and Syrian] outdid themselves in their unbridled subversive warfare against Lebanon, Iraq and Jordan. ... Clandestine action ... was at the time the principal form of communication between the UAR and the other three countries.[1]

In early 1958 Syria and Egypt appeared to stand together as the leaders of a wave of 'anti-imperialist' pan-Arabism. The ongoing pro-Nasserist agitation in Jordan and the overthrow of the Iraqi monarchy in July all suggested that the UAR would soon be joined by other 'progressive' republics. Syrian and Egyptian intelligence used covert operations and terrorism on an unprecedented scale to fan the flames of popular discontent and the West became so alarmed that Britain and the United States intervened militarily to prop up the Lebanese and Jordanian governments. By late 1958, however, the balance of forces had changed. The turmoil in Lebanon and Jordan had subsided. In Iraq the accession to power of Qasim ushered in an anti-Nasser reaction and a swing towards the Soviet Union. The covert war shifted, with Iraq becoming the target of the UAR's intelligence services. The battle with Jordan flared up again in 1960 but was subsequently patched up in the face of the common Iraqi threat.

Under the UAR Syrian intelligence services were, like the rest of the government, taken over by the Egyptians. As one observer put it: 'Egypt's organizational and governmental systems were transplanted to Syria as if she were one of its provinces'.[2] The Egyptian intelligence bureaucracy had been re-organised by Nasser during 1954 and 1955. The Directorate of Military Intelligence (DMI) had been established as a tri-service agency responsible for ensuring the loyalty of the military and for collecting military intelligence. The Directorate of General Investigations was a civilian body with responsibility for domestic counter-espionage. In late 1955 the Directorate of General Intelligence (DGI) had been set up to act as the paramount intelligence agency for both domestic and foreign activities. Egyptian Military Attachés abroad, the point men for the majority of Egyptian covert operations, held a dual brief for both the DMI and the DGI.[3]

On the formation of the UAR, the formerly dominant Syrian Deuxième Bureau was placed under the control of the DMI. With a new director, Colonel Muhammad Istambuli, its activities were restricted to counter-intelligence within the Syrian army (now the First Army of the UAR) and the collection of military intelligence.[4] The civilian Department of General Security, which Sarraj had subordinated to the Deuxième Bureau, became a branch of the Directorate of General Investigations and was subordinated to the Northern Province's Interior Ministry.[5] A new department, the Special Bureau, was established as a branch of the DGI. This Bureau was also subordinated to the Ministry of the Interior and became the lead security and intelligence agency. Its Internal Department concentrated on domestic counter-intelligence while its External Department was responsible for foreign intelligence gathering and covert operations.[6]

Due to the Egyptian takeover it became hard to speak of Syrian activity as such. In many cases Egyptian officers directed and participated in operations. Nonetheless, Syrian officers and agents continued to play a leading role in the Levant for two reasons. First, the authority of Sarraj himself. Regarded as Nasser's man in Damascus, his fortunes waxed during the UAR period. Upon declaration of the Union he was made Interior Minister of the Northern Province and in September 1958 became Chairman of the Syrian Provincial Council. Due to his intimate knowledge of politics and covert activity in the Levant, he appears to have had a great deal of leeway in planning and executing intelligence and covert operations.[7] On his move to the Interior Ministry he took with him many of his officers from the Deuxième Bureau, so ensuring that their talents and experience were not wasted.[8] The second reason was the experience and local knowledge of Syria's intelligence operatives. Syrian intelligence officers had been operating in Lebanon and Jordan for several years and had knowledge and contacts that Egyptian officers could not match. In both Lebanon and Jordan the case officers, agents and paramilitaries tended to be Syrians, or Palestinians recruited by Syrian officers.

Reactions to the Union

The formation of the Union posed a dilemma for the United States. Washington had long had mixed views regarding Nasser. In the immediate aftermath of the Free Officers' coup in 1952 Neguib and Nasser had been welcomed as nationalists. The CIA had even helped to train Egyptian intelligence officers.[9] 'Regionalists' in the State Department and CIA continued to support the view that he was a nationalist leader whose cooperation against the USSR could be secured by a conciliatory US approach. 'Globalists' in the US administration, led by John Foster Dulles but centred in the White House, however, took the view that Nasser could not be trusted and that his 'neutralism' was merely a euphemism for subservience to Moscow. The case of the 'globalists' had been strengthened by the failure of the Alpha plan and the increase of Soviet influence in Syria and Egypt. The 'regionalists', of whom Allen Dulles was a lukewarm supporter, saw some vindication of their approach during 1957. Ambassador Hare had been sent to Cairo in September 1956 with instructions to make a fresh start with Nasser and the upshot was Nasser's promise to counter communist influence in Syria.[10]

In its assessment of the impact of the union, the US administration sought to balance probable short-term benefits against possible long-term dangers. It was seen that, in the short term, the Union may be in US interests if Nasser cracked down on communist activity in Syria. This he did, with Sarraj's agents setting off bombs in Damascus as an excuse to round up communist sympathisers in mid-February.[11] At the same time the US administration saw long-term threats because the Union would facilitate Nasser's 'domination' of the Arab world, spread 'positive neutralism' and freeze Syria in an 'unnatural orientation'. These concerns led the United States to promise Syria's neighbours support in any action they took to disrupt the Union.[12] None the less, according to Ambassador Hare, the American attitude to the UAR was that 'it wasn't a matter of major concern or major rejoicing'.[13] While the United States did its best to counter the UAR's subversive activities, it also sought to keep the door open for a reconciliation.

The other states involved did not take such an ambivalent view. For Britain, Lebanon, Iraq, Turkey, Jordan and Saʻudi Arabia, the Union was a threat as it meant an expansion of Nasser's influence and resources. They were concerned less at his ties with the Soviet Union than with his aggressive attempts to lead the Arab world and bring other Arab states under his control.

The immediate response of some of these states was to launch some rather inept plots. The most notorious of these was the 'Sa'udi plot'. On 5 March Nasser announced the discovery of a conspiracy to kill him organised by King Sa'ud. The UAR charged that, in early February, King Sa'ud had despatched his father-in-law, Shaykh Asad Ibrahim, to meet Sarraj in Damascus. The emissary proposed to Sarraj that he lead a coup against the Union. In return, Sa'ud would pay him £22 million and ensure international recognition of the new regime. Sarraj obtained an advance of £1.9 million from the emissary and informed Nasser of the plot. When Nasser subsequently visited Damascus, the emissary allegedly offered Sarraj an extra £2 million if he would arrange Nasser's assassination by planting a bomb on the Egyptian President's aircraft.

The evidence supplied by Sarraj in the subsequent press conferences, which included copies of the Arab Bank cheques, appeared to be convincing. It is possible that Sa'ud, who attacked the Union as 'Egyptian colonialism', did authorise the operation.[14] Nonetheless, the ineptness and naivety shown by the emissary, who discussed the proposal with Sarraj in the latter's office thus enabling Sarraj to tape-record the meeting, made some observers suspicious. The Foreign Office, for instance, speculated that it may all have been an attempt by Sa'udi Crown Prince Faysal to undermine Sa'ud and so pave the way for a reconciliation between Riyadh and Cairo by discrediting Sa'ud's hostile attitude to the UAR.[15]

Another alleged plot came to light on 13 February when an army communiqué announced the arrest of several dozen communists and infiltrators. The authorities claimed that the agents had been sent by the Baghdad Pact countries and had been financed by the United States. Their aim had been to disrupt the referendum planned for 21 February, which had been called to approve the Union and Nasser's Presidency. Whether or not a foreign plot actually existed is hard to tell. It is equally likely that Nasser's security men were manufacturing an excuse to crack down on any potential opposition to the referendum.[16]

While these incidents were occurring, Turkey and Iraq discussed covert action but with no result. In June 'Abd ul-Ilah approached the United States requesting support for a scheme of Mikhail Ilyan's to stir up the Syrian tribes. The State Department dismissed the idea and the Iraqi revolution forestalled any further action.[17] Turkey backed Ilyan's schemes and kept up a limited degree of military pressure on the Syrian border but most of the skirmishes which occurred over the following years were related to smuggling and other criminal activities.[18]

Sarraj's response to foreign plots was as robust as ever. The plotters in the Sa'udi case fled to safety abroad but harsher methods were used against exiles based in Lebanon. In February the home of an SSNP leader in Lebanon was destroyed by a bomb days after he had been accused by the Syrian press of infiltrating armed units into Syria.[19] In August, a car containing two exiled Syrian politicians and the former Iraqi Military Attaché in Beirut, Colonel Salih Sammara'i, was machine-gunned in Beirut.[20]

On the whole, however, the UAR was relatively secure against foreign plots and the intelligence services did not have to devote a great deal of effort to defensive activities. Instead, they were free to take the offensive in Jordan and Lebanon.

Isolating Jordan

During the winter and spring Syrian and Egyptian intelligence had continued to operate in Jordan, helping local opposition groups to carry out a handful of bombings. In November a bomb had damaged the apartment of the Minister of the Economy. On New Year's Eve the offices of an American oil company were bombed. On 16 January bombs exploded at the Amman electricity station and at Zerqa post office. In March the printing press of a pro-government newspaper, *al-Jihad*, was destroyed, and in May the car of the Assistant American Military Attaché was blown up.[21]

In general, however, a combination of Jordan's tight security measures and reduced Syrian and Egyptian activity ensured a relatively stable climate. On 12 January Jordanian police arrested seven alleged Syrian agents who had entered the country on false papers and on 4 February a military court in Nablus handed down sentences for 45 subversives, several of whom had been trained in Syria. On 31 March the Egyptian Consul in Jerusalem was expelled, followed, on 6 June, by his secretary. They had been subsidising opposition groups. Predicting a period of stability, the government lifted the curfew and eased other martial law measures.[22]

The formation of the UAR pushed King Hussein to look to Iraq for security and on 14 February an Arab Union was established joining the two monarchies. Hussein and his cousin, King Faysal, portrayed this Union as reflecting the 'true' aspirations of the Arab peoples, unlike Nasser's UAR which had been imposed.[23] The Arab Union lasted for only five months as on 14 July the Iraqi monarchy was overthrown by army officers. The monarchy's leaders, including Nuri Sa'id, 'Abd ul-Ilah and Faysal were killed. Hussein reacted with an abortive military intervention but was soon fighting for his own survival.[24]

Nasser greeted the revolutionary regime in Iraq with open arms, hoping it would join the UAR.[25] In the meantime, he launched 'an all-out offensive against Jordan ... to take advantage of the psychological shock caused by the ... revolution'.[26] A mobile radio station, broadcasting as 'Jordanian People's Radio', was set up and operated just inside Syrian territory near Dera'. The station called for Hussein's overthrow: 'O Hussein, the throngs of our people will set out for your palace – the cell of dirty plotting – to demolish it. The people will crush your decaying head, your traitorous gang and your master, imperialism.'[27] In the aftermath of the Iraqi revolt the border with Jordan had been closed and on 3 August Syria closed its border with Jordan, leaving the port of Aqaba as Jordan's only access to the outside world apart from infrequent flights to Beirut and the Gulf. Since Jordan imported much of its needs, especially fuels, via Beirut and Latakia and exported most of its agricultural products to Syria and Iraq, these measures imposed a tremendous strain on the economy.

As well as psychological and economic measures, Sarraj's agents went to work organising subversive activities. On 20 July pamphlets were distributed in Amman denouncing the 'traitor king, fake parliament and British imperialism' and calling for a general strike the next day. The message was reinforced by the explosion of four 'noisemaker' bombs overnight. The next morning, however, Jordanian police had little trouble breaking the strike, forcing open shops which had remained closed.[28] In addition, Jordanian exiles in Damascus were helped by UAR intelligence to get in touch with a gang of smugglers who brought in rifles and machine guns with which it was hoped to arm opposition elements. Twenty-seven alleged smugglers were arrested and 25 subsequently convicted, with 13 receiving death sentences. The Jordanian security forces increased their surveillance of the Syrian border, as a result of which the UAR used Bedouin to smuggle weapons in from Gaza across the relatively porous Negev border.[29]

Syrian agents additionally sponsored a terrorist group which bombed the British Council and the Jordan Development Board offices in Amman and also planned to attack the USIS offices. Seventeen suspects were arrested after these attacks. It turned out that Syrian intelligence had made good use of its connections with Palestinian refugees and the Lebanese opposition. The bombs had been smuggled into Jordan by a Lebanese employee of UNRWA and hidden in Madaha refugee camp by one of the camp's UNRWA officers. The government discredited its case against the five defendants, all Palestinians, by bringing them to court still showing visible marks of the torture that was regularly used by Jordanian interrogators at the time. This provoked international criticism of police brutality but made little difference to the case. Two of the defendants were sentenced to death and three to terms of imprisonment.[30]

Hussein and his government responded to the UAR threat vigorously. The king used Jordanian radio to launch counter-attacks against Nasser. On 28 July Amman Radio called on the Arabs 'to "wake up" to the fact that 'Abd an-Nasir's associates understood liberty in terms of massacre'.[31] A week later Hussein proclaimed 'we will not permit Communism and atheism to penetrate our ranks ... we are going to defend Arab nationalism and the great Arab homeland'.[32] Diplomatic relations with the UAR were broken off and its Consulate and Embassy closed, measures which significantly reduced the capability of UAR intelligence. Wide-ranging and harsh security measures were instituted by the security forces. Even night-club artistes from Beirut were expelled because of the Lebanese connections of the Amman bombing gang.[33] As the appearance of the defendants at the Amman bombing trial had demonstrated, torture was frequently used by the security forces. Suspects were often beaten, burnt and had their fingernails extracted in the effort to force confessions from them. During this period the authorities displayed a 'callous indifference ... to due processes of law ... [which] resulted in [the] protracted detention of individuals without a single reason being given for their arrest'.[34]

The government's brutal reaction to the UAR threat was one factor which led to the United States' lukewarm response to Hussein's pleas for help. Immediately after the Iraqi revolution the king had approached Britain and the United States requesting assurances that military assistance would be provided if needed.[35] The US Embassy was reluctant to make a commitment to Jordan because it considered that 'aside from the internal opposition created by the pro-Western, anti-Nasser posture of the Rifa'i government, the regime has lost the support of practically the entire population of Jordan because of its arrogant injustice, rampant corruption and pervading inefficiency'. Dulles himself considered Jordan 'an artificial state' which had only been kept alive by foreign subsidies. 'The reason for its existence was that its disappearance might reopen the Arab-Israeli war'.[36] Although reluctant to support a monarchy propped up by 'bedouin bayonets', the United States nonetheless did come to Hussein's aid as it concluded that 'any effort to replace [Rifa'i's oppressive rule] with a more "popular" regime will start Jordan on a downhill slide into the Nasser camp'.[37]

Having considered these factors, America and Britain decided to respond to Hussein's requests. The United States organised an airlift of fuels from the Gulf and the Mediterranean to replace the supplies which had been cut off when the UAR closed the border. Britain landed a brigade of paratroops in Amman. Britain also supplied internal security equipment, including tear gas, riot shields and radios, to the Jordanian police force.[38]

By October the Jordanian government was back in firm control of the situation. The monarchy's intelligence services had been revamped and had managed to break up several coup attempts.[39] The release of detainees began, martial law restrictions were eased and on 20 October British troops started to withdraw.[40] However, in November an incident occurred which provided a controversial postscript to the summer's turmoil. On 11 November King Hussein took off from Amman airport, intending to take a holiday in Switzerland. He returned to Amman the same day, reporting that Syrian MiGs had intercepted his aircraft and tried to force it down. Hussein and his biographers have claimed that the Syrians wanted either to force the king to land so that he could be handed over for trial to a Jordanian exile group, or to make the aircraft crash so that the king's death would look like an accident.[41] The Syrian pilots involved later defected and admitted the attempt, though to what extent they had been coerced by Jordanian interrogators into making their confessions is a matter of speculation. However, it is significant that the MiGs did not attempt to shoot down Hussein's aircraft. That such an action would have been well within the bounds of possibility had been demonstrated in August. A Middle East Airlines Dakota *en route* to Beirut had inexplicably been ordered by Damascus tower to return to Damascus airfield. When it did so, Syrian anti-aircraft artillery opened fire on the aircraft, forcing the pilot to take evasive action. It became clear that this incident had been an attempt to shoot down a Jordanian aircraft which, at about the same time, had been *en route* to New York. The aircraft was carrying an official delegation heading for the United Nations to lodge a protest about UAR subversion. The Syrians had attacked the wrong plane.[42]

If UAR officials had been willing to take the blatant risk of shooting down a civilian Jordanian aircraft over Damascus, then it is surprising that they would have refrained from shooting down Hussein's aircraft over open desert. The UAR subsequently claimed that the Syrian fighters had merely been intercepting an unauthorised and unidentified aircraft.[43] This version of events is plausible as, since the formation of the UAR, aircraft overflying Syrian airspace had been required to pay a toll and fly along a restricted flight path. On several occasions when foreign aircraft had failed to do so they had been shot at or forced to land.[44] It is therefore possible that this attack was not directed at Hussein personally.[45]

Whatever the truth, Hussein's version of events was believed in

Jordan and he exploited the incident to boost his own popularity at Nasser's expense. Furthermore, the downturn in UAR-Iraqi relations distracted the attention of UAR intelligence agencies and on 29 November the Jordanian government felt confident enough to lift martial law.[46] With a combination of official ruthlessness and Western help the monarchy had survived the UAR's efforts at subversion. Such efforts, though, had been limited as UAR covert operators had carried out relatively few operations and their subversive activities had not been too difficult to counter.

Nasser vs Qasim

The Iraqi revolution had been led by two officers, Colonel 'Abd al-Salam 'Arif and Major-General 'Abd al-Karim Qasim.[47] 'Arif had become head of the new republic, with Qasim his Prime Minister. In September 1958 Qasim ousted 'Arif. Apart from personal rivalry, the main argument between the two men had been over 'Arif's enthusiasm for the UAR.[48] Qasim was determined not to fall under Nasser's influence and instead pursued a policy of Iraqi nationalism bolstered by close ties to the USSR.[49] A January 1959 State Department Intelligence Report outlined the situation:

> A man of limited intelligence and neurotic tendencies ... Qasim ... has manifested little positive leadership and has lost the respect of most of his governmental colleagues. ... The poor performance of the entire revolutionary regime – indecisiveness, economic stagnation and bureaucratic chaos, all reaching the point of anarchy – has by now caused dissatisfaction and loss of confidence at all levels of the population. ... The immediate issue, on which the revolutionary government has already openly split, is how far to go in assimilating to Nasir's United Arab Republic. ... The Communist Party of Iraq is winning, largely by default, a major victory. Its apparently well-calculated plan would make Iraq, although not an actual satellite, a major base for anti-Western propaganda and for penetration and agitation. ... The speed and vigor of the Communist thrust has been a revelation – especially to Nasir – of Soviet intentions and methods.[50]

Nasser felt threatened by Qasim's regime, both because it stole some of his 'anti-imperialist' limelight and because he feared that Qasim was an instrument of the communists who hoped to detach Iraq from the Arab world and use it as a base for further encroachment in the region. The Egyptian leader therefore took a 'public stand divorcing Communism from Arab nationalism ... [so giving] anti-Communists ... room for maneuver without inviting the stigma of "imperialist collaborator"'.[51] The chaotic situation in Iraq persuaded Nasser to 'leave the matter of union in abeyance' since 'a too precipitate drive toward union with the UAR, would risk long-drawn-out civil conflict'.[52] Instead, he led an aggressive campaign which sought to emphasise the communist nature of Qasim's regime. This campaign was to continue until Qasim's overthrow in 1963.[53]

Like Nasser's other campaigns of destabilisation in the Fertile Crescent, the anti-Qasim campaign comprised vitriolic radio propaganda and covert operations led by the UAR's intelligence agencies operating out of the Northern Province, usually under Sarraj's guidance. Iraqi officials claimed that Sarraj had a hand in two alleged plots during 1959, one to assassinate Qasim and the other to support a coup by Rashid Ali but few details of these alleged conspiracies remain.[54] The most significant event in which UAR intelligence was implicated was the March 1959 Mosul revolt.

In the months preceding the revolt there had been 'sporadic but insistent' reports from Mosul of opposition to the regime, sermons in the mosques againt communism and Ba'thist/Nasserist demonstrations.[55] On 6 March the Partisans of Peace, a Communist Party-led organisation, brought nearly 100,000 demonstrators into the city to 'throw down the gauntlet' to Mosul's Arab nationalists. The next day Arab nationalists held counter demonstrations which led to clashes with communists. This appears to have been part of a plan by the garrison commander, Colonel 'Abd al-Wahab Shawwaf, for the pro-Nasser demonstrators 'to cause an altercation in the streets which would give Shawwaf an opportunity to arrest the leaders of elements likely to oppose them'. He would then lead an army uprising to remove Qasim. Shawwaf ordered the arrest of about 350 communists as well as army officers not loyal to him, but his plan appears to have misfired from the start. First, he could count on the support of only part of the Mosul garrison. Second, fighters from the Shammar tribe, who were supposed to assist him in gaining control of Mosul, only appeared on the scene on 9 March.

As fighting escalated in Mosul between Shawwaf's troops and civilians and troops loyal to the government, Qasim announced a $28,000 reward for the rebel Colonel's head. On the 8th the rebel 'Mosul Radio' began to broadcast. Shawwaf lambasted Qasim as the 'mad tyrant' who was backed by a 'chaotic group leading the country and the regime into corruption', announced his desire for good relations with the West and called on other army units and towns to join his revolt and march on Baghdad.[56] The following day saw an intensification of the fighting. Two rebel air force planes made an unsuccessful bombing raid against Baghdad Radio's transmitting station. Shammar tribesmen rampaged through Mosul's Christian areas killing and looting, supposedly as they had been told that these were areas where communism was strongest. Government soldiers and militiamen, the Popular Resistance Forces, swept through the city massacring suspected rebels and looting their homes. The back of the revolt was broken when four air force planes rocketed Shawwaf's headquarters. It is unclear whether he was killed by the rockets or by soldiers who attacked the headquarters, but in any case with his death the revolt fizzled out. No other army units responded to his calls for assistance and the city was turned over to pro-government and pro-communist soldiers and militias. These extracted a bloody revenge, with impromptu 'People's Courts' executing suspects and hanging their bodies from lamp-posts. US diplomats concluded that, although the death total could not be given with any precision, it was probably around 2,000 to 3,000.

Qasim's government subsequently blamed the UAR for organising the revolt and expelled ten UAR diplomats, but historians have been divided on the role played by the UAR.[57] In their history of Iraq, the Slugletts argue that the UAR's intelligence services made no real effort to intervene.[58] Tabitha Petran, in contrast, argues that the revolt 'was largely a Syrian operation organized by Sarraj and the Ba'th'.[59] While he does not go as far as Petran, Nutting nonetheless claims that Shawwaf received substantial help in the form of Syrian army officers and military radios.[60] Batatu also takes this view, writing that the UAR 'had in the past backed ... [the anti-Qasim coalition] in a circumspect and half hearted manner', but 'despairing wholly of Qassim, ... undertook to give them unstinting support'.[61]

The limited evidence available appears to confirm Batatu's contention that the UAR promised Shawwaf support but then let him down. According to one of the officers who took part in the revolt, the plotters had talks with Syrian officials who promised to send a squadron of MiGs to provide air cover for the rebels. They also promised to send a battalion of commandos to assist if necessary.[62] The commandos never appeared but on 11 March witnesses observed 15 or 16 UAR MiGs flying over Mosul airport. By then there was little they could do to assist the rebels. UAR intelligence also assisted by providing weapons to tribesmen north of Mosul, this supply being coordinated by the ubiquitous Burhan Adham. Its main assistance, however, was in providing the transmitter for Radio Mosul. The Iraqi army had no transmitter in Mosul powerful enough for Shawwaf's purposes and a suitable unit was supplied by the UAR. This arrived late and out of order and so broadcasting only started on 8 March.[63]

The surprisingly inept performance of UAR intelligence in backing Shawwaf stands in marked contrast to its record in Lebanon and

Jordan. Probably this was because the UAR was caught off-guard by events in Mosul. Shawwaf's men had planned to coordinate their uprising with the UAR but something made the rebels act earlier than intended. This would also explain the puzzling fact that Shawwaf received no army support outside Mosul, even though several senior officers were known to be sympathetic. Why Shawwaf acted too early remains a matter of speculation. One possibility is that Qasim had sent the Partisans of Peace to provoke the Colonel, with whom he had recently had serious disagreements.[64] If this was the case, then Qasim's move proved more successful than he could have hoped.

The failed intervention of the UAR in Mosul enabled the Iraqi communists and Qasim to whip up an unprecedented storm of anti-Nasser agitation. In Baghdad effigies of Nasser were hung by demonstrators and the UAR rushed to evacuate its citizens.[65] In Basra mobs 'erupted into an orgy of killing and beatings of Nasir supporters' that left five dead.[66] Government officials and the press viciously attacked Nasser and sought to detach Syria from the Union. Mahdawi, the President of the Court trying the Mosul rebels, used especially blood-curdling rhetoric:

> We feel confident that the Syrian people will struggle against the despotic clique which is now swindling them in the name of Arab nationalism ... we must now say frankly that Syria and Egypt must be liberated from the despotic Fascist-Nasserist rule which has betrayed Egypt's cause ... (Oh Nasser and your stooges) have you forgotten Israel that you are now threatening to bomb Baghdad ... ? You cowardly scoundrels, you little monkeys, do you propose to assail the den of the lions ... ? The great people of Iraq have given thought to liberating the valiant Syrian people ... [h]owever, I feel that the brotherly Syrian people will liberate themselves.[67]

The UAR countered in kind and the enmity between the two regimes was sealed. On 11 March Nasser had responded to the revolt by attacking Qasim as the 'Divider of Iraq' who was backed by 'Communists ... separatists and ... opportunists'.[68] Thereafter an intense propaganda campaign was organised in Syria. The press and radio kept up a stream of anti-Qasim rhetoric and mass 'Victory in Iraq' rallies were held to whip up 'popular passions'. Sarraj claimed that he had received thousands of telegrams demanding he proclaim a *jihad* to liberate Iraq from communism.[69] These attacks on 'red communism', 'the communist spirit of hate and grudges', and the communists' role as 'agents of foreign masters' represented Nasser's first open attacks on communism. Particular criticism was directed at the Syrian and Lebanese communist parties and there were accusations that

Syrian communists were cooperating with Iraq to organise an armed revolt in Syria. Damascene newspapers also began to carry attacks on Khrushchev, portraying him as the mastermind behind the Iraqi communists.[70]

Iraqi exiles, meanwhile, were welcomed and incorporated into the UAR's propaganda machine as they trickled across the border into Syria.[71] On 30 August the Free Iraqis' Organisation, a group of exiles sponsored by the UAR, issued a statement in Damascus labelling Qasim 'the latter-day Nero' and proclaiming that the 'blood of Iraq's sons is being shed, its civilization is being destroyed, and its whole area subject to a Red reign of terror whose barbarism exceeds anything ever before witnessed by mankind'.[72]

In response to the escalating persecution of their party inside Iraq, the Iraqi Ba'th Party Regional Command took the decision to assassinate Qasim. The attack took place in Baghdad on 7 October but was a failure and only wounded its target.[73] At the subsequent trials of 78 persons accused of involvement in the attack the Iraqi prosecutor 'charged Nasser with having approved [the] plan whereby Baathists would carry out [the] assassination' and claimed the UAR was 'training volunteers, intriguers and traitors'.[74] The prosecutor also denounced Nasser as 'an instrument in [the] hands [of] capitalist monopolists like American, British and French imperialists' and sought to establish that the assassins had, rather improbably, received arms from the British, Bulgarian and Sa'udi Embassies.[75]

In court many of the defendants retracted confessions which had been extracted under duress. Most notably, Ayad Sa'id Thabit, organiser of the hit team, steadfastly refused to implicate the UAR in his testimony, despite the best efforts of the prosecutor.[76] Fu'ad al-Rikabi, Chief of the Iraqi Ba'th Party, was subsequently given asylum in the UAR but he was also censured by the Ba'th's National Command for ordering the assassination attempt without authorisation.[77] Evidence of UAR involvement in the plot is therefore rather sparse. Iraqi historian Majid Khadduri has argued that 'moral ... [and] ... material support appears to have been promised by the UAR', but in the event was not forthcoming.[78] The most that can reasonably be concluded is that Sarraj may have used his own contacts in the Ba'th party to encourage Rikabi to carry out the operation. This theory was propounded by historian John Devlin, who argued that Sarraj would have been acting against Nasser's wishes because, although he wanted Qasim removed, he did not sanction his assassination.[79] On the limited evidence available, it appears safe to conclude that the plot was largely of indigenous origin, although it is plausible that Sarraj gave the conspirators some encouragement.

Whatever the truth, Qasim's belief that the UAR backed the assassination attempt deepened his hostility to Nasser. The struggle for supremacy intensified but, although the UAR's propaganda barrage continued apace, covert action was on an insignificant scale. The main reason for this appears to have been that Sarraj was distracted by domestic discontent

Discontent in the Northern Province

The appeal of 'Arab unity' under Nasser was generally greater outside Egypt than at home, where the deadweight of the Nasserist police state and the 'socialist' economy were more evident. Similarly, in Syria the reality of unity proved less attractive than the dream. The UAR was not a partnership between equals, it had involved the wholesale takeover of Syria by Egypt. Syrian political parties were banned and Syrian army officers were given inferior positions. The heavy-handed Egyptian domination had aroused resentment even in the early days of the Union. In June 1958, following the purging and arrest of politically active army officers, there were signs of discontent which erupted into a shoot-out at an officers' club. There were also reports of strikes and demonstrations.[80]

By late 1959 disenchantment with the Union was widespread in Syria. In addition to the resentment felt by politicians and army officers, the Damascus government's rigid application of socialist economic policies had caused the alienation of the merchants of Syria's cities, while three successive years of drought had led to popular unrest. In August the Foreign Office received news of a coup being plotted among Syrian brigadiers. Nasser responded to the unrest by tightening his grip on the country. In October the joint committee of Syrian and Egyptian politicians set up to coordinate policy was dissolved and Marshal 'Abd al-Hakim 'Amir appointed to act as Nasser's proconsul.[81] In the view of a contemporary diplomatic observer: "Amer's assignment to Syria probably indicates the collapse of most of what may have remained of independent Syrian authority'.[82] Nasser also sacrificed his Ba'thist allies, blaming their economic radicalism for Syria's economic problems. The Ba'thist ministers in the Union government, Hawrani, Bitar and Hamdun, all resigned at the end of the year.[83]

These changes had both negative and positive effects on the position of Interior Minister Sarraj and his intelligence services. The State Department judged that Sarraj had annoyed Nasser by exceeding 'his directives, particularly in the operation of his secret intelligence apparatus in neighbouring countries, to the embarrassment of the regime; he has also systematically obstructed Egyptian intelligence activities in Syria and refrained from cooperating with them'. 'Amir's appointment thus circumscribed 'the somewhat free-wheeling role of ... Sarraj'.[84] None the less, he was still highly regarded by Nasser and the Syrian propaganda and information services were formally transferred to the Ministry of the Interior. Sarraj's response to the discontent was to intensify repression. The Deuxième Bureau, for instance, was re-organised to exert an even tighter grip over all domestic activities. The titles of seven of its fourteen functional branches give an idea of the importance of its re-invigorated domestic role: Surveillance Branch, Supervision of Foreign Embassies, Supervision of Intellectual Clubs, Supervision of Sporting Clubs, Bureau of Missing Persons, Supervision of Deputies, Supervision of Government Personnel and Prominent Civilians.[85]

The end of the United Arab Republic

The relative moderation in Nasser's foreign policy, exemplified by his cooperation with Jordan to protect Kuwait from Qasim's irredentist claims,[86] served to alienate many of the remaining pro-Nasserists in Syria who had been willing to accept Egyptian domination in return for the opportunity of sharing in the glories of a radical foreign policy.[87] With disillusionment and resentment against Egyptian rule on the rise, Marshal 'Amir sought to appease Syrian opinion in August by granting Syrian politicians more seats in the joint cabinet and by transferring Sarraj to Cairo to fill the symbolic post of Vice-President in charge of UAR security.[88] Sarraj rapidly resigned his post, protesting that 'Amir's actions would only make it easier for Syrian secessionists to make their move. He was proved right when on 28 September 1961 a group of officers led by Lieutenant-Colonel 'Abd al-Karim Nahlawi, backed by Jordan and Sa'udi Arabia, mounted a coup. They expelled 'Amir and announced Syria's secession from the union. Sarraj, who had returned to Damascus on the 26th to fight the secessionists on his own initiative, was arrested and imprisoned.[89]

Nasser reacted to this 'treacherous' uprising by putting his paratroops and troop transports on standby to intervene and reassert control.[90] In the event he refrained from making any significant military moves.[91] Instead, he 'resigned [himself] to doing no more than trying to isolate Syria, subvert its government, and appeal to the Syrian people'.[92] So began a new period in Syria's history.

Conclusion

The world portrayed in these pages, a world of amateur spies, casual plotters, hot-headed officers and part-time terrorists, is long gone. Since at least the 1970s the Middle East's underworld has become a more serious, professional and deadly milieu.

Arab politicians and officers continue to hatch plots against their governments but the regimes in power have shown remarkable durability. In the 1950s an officer with a handful of men and tanks was often the primary means of political change. No longer. The incumbent Arab regimes have been in place for over two decades. The free-wheeling international politics of the region, both overt and covert, has been replaced by a more static and security-conscious world.

The Arab intelligence and security services, like their states, have become institutionalised, bureaucratised and increasingly ruthless. As states have tightened their grip on society these agencies have grown and their roles have expanded. They have also increased their operational capabilities abroad. Whereas in the 1950s exiles often concentrated in easily accessible neighbouring countries, they have since moved further afield. The intelligence services have followed them.

The other services involved in this story have also seen major changes. The Americans have graduated from the early days of Miles Copeland and Wilbur Eveland and now deploy a huge intelligence bureaucracy. The British, French and, lately, the Russians are now mainly of importance insofar as they relate to the US intelligence establishment.

Despite this altered environment, the sorts of activities exposed in this book still go on in the region. Only hints and suspicions will come to public knowledge until well into the next century when researchers gain access to the official archives. Only then can future scholars embark on an authoritative study of today's secret wars.

The aim of such a study would be to fill in some of the gaps in our understanding of events, an understanding which is necessarily shaped by our perceptions of overt and publicly visible events. Such a study

CONCLUSION 161

would look at what sort of covert action was used, what the aims and methods were and how the actions affected the course of regional and national politics. These are the questions that this book has sought to answer with regard to the 1950s. Although recognising that it can only provide a partial picture, this book has brought out a variety of points regarding the uses and forms of covert action.

In the introduction covert action was classified into three types: *propaganda*, *political action* and *paramilitary*. The preceding chapters have provided examples in each category. Overt propaganda was widely used but only grey and black propaganda come within the category of covert action. Grey propaganda was disseminated primarily through newspapers in the target country. Most of the Syrian newspapers in the mid-1950s received funds from a variety of foreign states and in return supported their sponsors' policy lines or their sponsors' loyalists in Syria. The degree of foreign control over the newspapers varied. At one extreme, an organisation like USIS placed a few articles favourable to the US position while at the other, Iraqi agents in Beirut started up their own newspaper. Black propaganda generally took the form of clandestine radio stations and leafleting campaigns. Clandestine stations which broadcast against Nasser or the Jordanian monarchy generally purported to represent domestic opposition groups when in fact they were run by foreign intelligence services. Leaflets, such as those distributed by Egypt in Jordan in 1957/58, also falsely claimed to be the product of domestic groups.

Political action measures used during the period were more varied. Tactics included intriguing with politicians and army officers to seek a change in the balance of power in the target country. This type of activity was exemplified by the rival activities of Iraq, Egypt and Sa'udi Arabia in Syria in late 1949 and 1950, Iraqi intrigues with anti-Shishakli leaders in 1953 and early 1954 and the pro-Iraqi efforts of individuals such as Nadhir Fansah in the mid-1950s. Another method used was bribery of politicians. It was common for politicians to receive funds from foreign sources in return for adopting a favourable attitude. At times they would be paid for their votes in parliament on specific issues, as happened in Syria in early 1949 with respect to Tapline and in 1955 at the time of the presidential election. In other instances candidates would be assisted with their electoral expenses, as happened during the 1954 Syrian elections and the 1957 Lebanese elections. Army officers were also paid bribe money. Sometimes they received the money to support a general policy line, as with Sa'udi Arabia's payments to Syrian officers to persuade them to oppose union with Iraq during the early 1950s. On other occasions they were paid for taking specific actions, as was the case with Sa'udi payments to pro-Shishakli officers who held out against the insurgents in Damascus in February 1954.

A more drastic form of political action was to encourage officers to mount coups. Sometimes the plotters would be given financial aid, often they would be promised safe haven if they failed or recognition if they succeeded. Interestingly, most of the coup attempts which clearly had foreign backing were abortive. The Kallas-'Ajlani plot in 1950, Safa's coup attempt in 1954, Abu Nuwar's plot in Jordan in 1957 and the American plot in the same year were just the most notable examples where there was clear evidence of covert foreign support for plots which ended in failure. Most of those that succeeded do not appear to have been orchestrated by foreign intelligence services. Hinnawi's coup in 1949 probably had Iraqi backing but neither Za'im nor Shishakli nor the anti-Shishakli putschists in February 1954 appear to have had significant foreign help.

Paramilitary activities included the supply of weapons and other military equipment to plotters or rebels. The most noteworthy instances of this were Za'im's supply of weapons to the SSNP in 1949, Iraq's supplies of arms to the Druze in late 1953 and early 1954 and again to the SSNP and their allies in 1956, Syrian and UAR supplies of weapons to Jordanian and Lebanese opposition groups in 1957 and 1958, and the UAR's supply of equipment to Shawwaf in Mosul in 1959. On occasion, personnel would also be provided to bolster rebel forces. The most notable example was the infiltration of Syrian and Palestinian personnel into Lebanon in 1957 and 1958, but it should be recalled that Za'im also offered Sa'adah troops for use against Lebanon in 1949.

Another type of paramilitary activity was the sponsorship or support of terrorism. This tactic only became prevalent in the late 1950s. In the early 1950s there were a few isolated instances of this activity, most notably in 1950 in Syria. Between 1957 and 1961, however, various parties began to employ terrorism. The SSNP used indiscriminate bombings to counter the Syrian state's repression of the party and Syrian intelligence responded with assassinations of party leaders. Syrian intelligence mounted indiscriminate bombing campaigns in Jordan and Lebanon during 1957 and 1958 in order to destabilise the governments and to encourage popular opposition to the regimes. In 1960 Syrian intelligence initiated a campaign of assassinations in Jordan designed to demoralise and provoke the regime. Jordan responded by organising indiscriminate bombings in Syria designed to avenge the Syrian attacks and to discredit the UAR authorities. In most cases, terrorism was used by intelligence agencies and sub-state groups as a last resort. The SSNP only took up terrorism in

1957 after its attempts to mount a coup had failed. Syria only began to use terrorism in Jordan after the failure of Abu Nuwar's coup attempt and in Lebanon after the Chamounists' victory in the June 1957 elections. Syrian attempts to assassinate Jordanian leaders in 1960 came at a time when there remained no Jordanian opposition movement to support.

Rewriting Syrian history

In addition to providing an account of the nature of covert operations in the Middle East, this study has sought to add to our understanding of recent Syrian history. It has done so both by using new source material and by using the novel perspective of covert activities to delve beneath the surface of events. This approach adds significantly to the few published accounts which deal with this period.

The research presented here has shown how the Syrian state changed from being primarily a victim of covert action and terrorism to being primarily a perpetrator. This change provides the basis for viewing the period in two phases, defensive and offensive, as suggested in the introduction.

From 1949 to 1957 Syria's sovereignty was frequently undermined by the covert activities of both Arab and Western states. During this period it was virtually a routine part of diplomacy for interested foreign parties to buy support among politicians, officers and the press. It was only slightly less common for foreign governments to encourage officers and politicians to stage coups. On occasion, intelligence services also sought to foment armed insurrections or to sponsor terrorist campaigns. The Syrian state was not entirely on the defensive during this period. Under Za'im, efforts were made to overthrow the Lebanese government and in the mid-1950s Syrian exiles were pursued abroad. However, there was no significant Syrian subversive activity in Lebanon, Jordan or Iraq. Quite simply, the Syrian state and intelligence agencies were too weak and too much on the defensive to act aggressively.

It was only between 1957 and 1961 that Syria adopted a more aggressive posture. This change was due to the consolidation in power of Syrian leftists and Sarraj's control of the Syrian intelligence apparatus. The defeat of the Syrian 'right' reduced opportunities for foreign intrigue in Syria and enabled Syria's rulers to take the fight abroad. During this period Syrian intelligence was extremely active in engaging in political action and propaganda activities, backing coup attempts abroad, arming and funding rebel groups and sponsoring and supporting terrorist operations.

Turning to the detailed findings of this work, the use of new source material has enabled this book to illuminate modern Syrian history in three ways. First, by fleshing out the historical record. Second, by covering incidents which have not previously been adequately studied. Third, by challenging the findings of recent research.

The areas in which earlier research has been supplemented with previously unknown details are in relation to the intrigues of Iraq, Egypt and Sa'udi Arabia in Syria during 1949 and 1950 and in the struggle between Nasser and his opponents from the end of Shishakli's regime to the collapse of the Iraqi plot. This research has detailed the twists and turns of Cairo, Baghdad and Riyadh's policies and their covert relationships with Syrian politicians and officers.

The accounts of the 1954 uprisings against Shishakli, the Iraqi plot and the American plot also add to the existing historical record. In all of these instances more detail is provided about the roles of foreign powers in the events than has previously been published. Although Seale did discuss Iraq's role in backing the 1954 revolt, he did not have access to the documents which have been used here to give a fuller picture of events. Seale likewise covered the 'Iraqi plot', but dealt only with the Iraqi and Syrian aspects. Gorst and Lucas, meanwhile, focused primarily on the Anglo-American perspective. The account presented here puts the plot into the context of escalating Iraqi and Anglo-American concerns at the situation in Syria, pulls together for the first time the international, regional and local aspects of the affair and gives a full account of the SSNP's leading role in the conspiracy. As for the 'American plot', Seale, Lesch and Little all provide only cursory descriptions of the affair. The account provided here is the first comprehensive discussion of the operation.

In some cases the accounts of the episodes discussed here differ from previously published research. For instance, the description of Hinnawi's coup and the executions of Za'im and Barazi is notably different from that of Seale who accepts Abu Mansur's version. In other cases this study has uncovered political manoeuvrings which were previously unknown. An example are the discussions of the 1955 Syrian presidential elections and the 1956 Soviet arms deal. The revelations of Shuqayr's approaches to the Iraqis deepen our understanding of the course of events. Furthermore, the descriptions of certain events, notably those of the Sa'adah affair and the Malki assassination, use such a wealth of untapped sources that the accounts presented here are significantly more accurate and comprehensive than previous ones.

This study has also discussed several episodes which have remained almost wholly unstudied up until now. The Hashimite-backed conspiracy and the Saʻudi/Egyptian terrorist campaign in Syria in 1950 come under this heading. More significantly, the covert battles waged during 1957 between Syrian intelligence on the one hand and the SSNP and the Jordanian and Lebanese governments on the other have been neglected. The chapter on the UAR likewise covers a period which remains largely unresearched. Works on Jordan, Lebanon and Iraq have touched on their relations with the UAR but there has been no comprehensive study of these relations.

The only event on which my conclusions differ radically from those of a recent researcher is the Zaʻim coup. Working solely from US archives, Douglas Little supported Copeland's claims that the CIA backed Zaʻim's coup. Combining a reappraisal of the US documentation with new material from British archives, as well as several interviews, I have argued here that the CIA role was probably insignificant.

The evidence presented here also enables some contribution to be made to the historical debate now underway regarding the supposed communist threat in the Middle East in the 1950s and the effect of the Eisenhower administration's policies on this 'threat'. Until Russian archives are opened it is not possible to ascertain conclusively whether Eisenhower and Dulles did seriously overestimate and misunderstand the communist challenge in the region. Nonetheless, this study has shown that US policies did help to push Syria towards Nasser and the Soviet Union. The CIA's covert meddling merely hastened this development. The United States was hamstrung by a simple and inescapable dilemma – its commitment to Israel. As long as Washington was not willing to sell arms to Syria then, despite their preference for ties with the West, Syrian officers were pushed to turn to the Russians. Britain was similarly hamstrung by its commitment to the Hashimites. Hashimite influence not only split the old-guard nationalists but also aroused the opposition of all the radical parties. Whatever government was in office, the United States and the United Kingdom could do little to reconcile these intrinsically incompatible interests.

There remains, however, the question of the real degree of communist influence. The Nasserist and Baʻthist officers in Damascus in late 1957 and early 1958 were frightened into rushing precipitately towards union by the growth of communist and Soviet influence. As those most intimately involved, these officers are probably our best guides to the real level of communist influence and, by late 1957, this influence was clearly substantial. However, it is also evident that in the years preceding this, such as in 1949 when the United States pushed Zaʻim to take action against the Communist Party, communism loomed much larger in Western than in Syrian minds. To a large extent it was the unpopularity of Western policies that fuelled the growth in communist influence.

Past, present and future

These concluding remarks would be incomplete without some more general observations. These will hopefully be taken as they are meant, merely as points for consideration regarding current issues.

Comparison of the events recounted in this book with similar ones occurring more recently suggests that the changing nature of states and societies in the Middle East has altered the nature of covert action. In the 1950s most of the states in the region had fairly open political structures. Although military rulers such as Shishakli could for a time clamp down on political activity, there were plenty of opportunities for intelligence agencies to intrigue and bribe politicians and officers and so influence a country's policies. Over the last two decades, however, all the states in question have centralised power and, to a greater or lesser degree, have become police states. This has reduced the scope for the type of freewheeling political action so prevalent in the 1950s. At the same time the modernisation of societies and the creation of modern administrative structures has reduced the autonomy of traditionally rebellious groups, such as the Syrian Druze or tribes in the Syrian/Iraqi deserts. Foreign states now have less opportunity to foment uprisings among such groups.

This is not to say that opportunities for subverting a state by aiding a rebellious group no longer exist. At times of severe internal dislocation intelligence services still find it possible to do so. An example was the Muslim Brotherhood uprising in Syria in the late 1970s and early 1980s, which Jordan and other states probably exploited.[1] On the whole, however, Syria, Jordan, Egypt, Iraq and Sa'udi Arabia are much less susceptible to the tactics used in the 1950s. The exception has been Lebanon. With a weak central government and a society in which ethnic groups retain considerable autonomy, Lebanon has been highly susceptible to all forms of covert action over the past two decades. Unable to subvert their opponents at home, Arab governments have often fought out their differences through Lebanese proxies in an environment which remained until recently as open to foreign influences as were most of the Middle Eastern states during the 1950s.

The reduction in the opportunities for most forms of covert action is probably one reason for the increasing use of terrorism between states.[2] Since the late 1960s Middle Eastern states have increasingly relied on terrorist tactics as an adjunct to diplomacy and the nature of terrorism has changed. The notion of Syrian intelligence officers touring Jordan employing civilians to throw bombs for them, as recounted in this study, now seems rather quaint. Three factors have contributed to the increased prevalence and changed nature of state-sponsored terrorism. First, the strengthening of central authority discussed above has meant that more subtle options are unavailable. Second, changes in weapons and communications technology have made terrorists more deadly and more mobile. Most terrorism in the 1950s involved casually employed agents setting off crude bombs outside buildings in an opponent's capital. Now agents can use more sophisticated weapons against targets anywhere in the world. Third, there is the proliferation of sub-state groups as a result of the factionalisation of the Palestinian movement in the late 1960s. Whereas in the 1950s it was common for Military Attachés to recruit terrorists and coordinate their operations, over the last two decades it has been more common for states to 'contract out' operations to sub-state groups, a practice which reduces the risk of the sponsoring state being identified.

A more general observation concerns the conspiracy theory mentality. A finding of this study has been that covert machinations have played a significant role in the region's recent history. A comprehensive picture has been provided of the almost constant intrigues to which Syria and its neighbours were subjected and to which they subjected each other. Given this legacy, researchers should not dismiss out of hand conspiratorial explanations. This applies whether the researcher is seeking explanations for historical or contemporary events. At the same time however, this research has demonstrated that conspiratorial explanations for events in the region were often exaggerated in two respects.

First, many of the successful conspiracies did not owe much to external covert help but were indigenously inspired. The coups which succeeded, such as Za'im's in 1949 and Shishakli's in 1949 and 1951 had little need of foreign support. In these cases the officers and politicians involved were determined and organised enough to do without foreign help. Once conspirators sought foreign help, as was the case with the SSNP in 1949 in Lebanon or in 1956 in Syria, this was a fair sign that the movement was too weak to be effective. The often complex and sprawling nature of foreign-led operations also made them more vulnerable to discovery.

Second, one can conclude that the common belief in the Middle East, and among some Western researchers, that one or other of the Great Powers is behind events should be treated with great scepticism. Although Middle Eastern conspiracy theories concerning the 1950s often give pride of place to the CIA or SIS, these agencies were in fact less active than their regional counterparts. In both the Za'im and the Malki affairs accusations of a CIA role cannot be substantiated. In the struggle against the Syrian leftists and Nasserites, it was Iraqi covert operators who led the way and the Lebanese and later Sa'udi governments also became involved. The only cases where the CIA was directly involved were the Iraqi plot, the April 1957 SSNP plot and the American plot. The SIS was only directly involved in the Iraqi plot. In other cases, the Americans and British backed and encouraged their regional allies but they did not take the lead operationally.

A concluding observation concerns the place of 'dirty tricks' in Middle Eastern politics in general. As argued in the introduction, Michel Seurat was wrong to argue that Syria's use of terrorism abroad during the 1980s represented an effort to 'establish it as a new code of international relations'. All the states discussed in this thesis used covert action to further their foreign policy goals in the Middle East during the 1950s and most employed terrorism in some form. There is no reason to suppose that they have changed their ways. Tactics and targets may have changed and terrorism may have become more significant than other forms of covert action, but no state can claim to have clean hands. We must wait for the archives to open before writing a comprehensive history of covert action in the contemporary Middle East but there is little reason to doubt that intelligence agencies have continued to play a leading role in the region's politics.

Notes

Introduction

1. P. Seale, *Asad: The Struggle for the Middle East* (London: IB Tauris & Co, 1988), p. 461.
2. M. Seurat, *L'État de Barbarie* (Paris: Editions du Seuil, 1989), p. 43.
3. For a discussion of this phenomenon, see D. Pipes, 'Dealing with Middle Eastern conspiracy theories', *Orbis*, Vol. 36, No. 1 (Winter 1992), pp. 41–56.
4. R. Deacon, *The Israeli Secret Service* (London: Hamish Hamilton, 1977); R. Payne, *Mossad: Israel's Most Secret Service* (London: Bantam Press, 1990); D. Eisenberg, U. Dann and E. Landau, *The Mossad* (New York: Paddington Press, 1978). An exception is I. Black and B. Morris, *Israel's Secret Wars* (London: Hamish Hamilton, 1991).
5. On SIS and SDECE, see: J.T. Richelson, *Foreign Intelligence Organizations* (Cambridge, MA: Ballinger Publishing Co, 1988), pp. 26, 163; C. Andrew, *Secret Service: The Making of the British Intelligence Community* (London: Heinemann, 1985), pp. 488–94; R.J. Aldrich, 'Secret intelligence for a post-war world: reshaping the British intelligence community, 1944–51', in R.J. Aldrich, ed., *British Intelligence, Strategy and the Cold War, 1945–51* (London: Routledge, 1992), pp. 15–49. On US activities, see: J.T. Richelson, *The U.S. Intelligence Community* (Cambridge, MA: Ballinger Publishing Co, 1989), p. 344; J. Prados, *Presidents' Secret Wars* (New York: William Morrow and Co, 1986), pp. 28–60; S. Ambrose, *Ike's Spies: Eisenhower and the Espionage Establishment* (Garden City, NY: Doubleday and Co, 1981).
6. The two most widely cited are M. Copeland, *The Game of Nations* (London: Weidenfeld and Nicolson, 1969) and W.C. Eveland, *Ropes of Sand: America's Failure in the Middle East* (New York: W.W. Norton and Co, 1980).
7. There is only one survey of Arab secret services in English. Y. Caroz, *The Arab Secret Services* (London: Corgi, 1978).
8. In American intelligence circles the label 'special activities' is also used. The British terminology is 'special political action'. Richelson, *Foreign Intelligence Organizations*, p. 26. The Soviet term 'active measures' seems to include a rather broader range of activities. A.N. Shulsky, *Silent Warfare: Understanding the World of Intelligence* (Washington, DC: Brasseys, 1991), p. 76.
9. Richelson, *The U.S. Intelligence Community*, p. 3. Italics in the original.
10. Ibid., p. 3.
11. G.F. Treverton, *Covert Action: The Limits of Intervention in the Postwar World* (New York: Basic Books Inc, 1987), p. 13.
12. This typology is taken from Treverton and Richelson. Shulsky provides a slightly different one. Shulsky, *Silent Warfare: Understanding the World of Intelligence*, pp. 76–90.
13. P. Wilkinson, *Terrorist Targets and Tactics: New Risks to World Order*, Conflict

Studies No. 236 (London: Research Institute for the Study of Conflict and Terrorism, 1990), p. 1.

14. T.P. Thornton, 'Terror as a weapon of political agitation', in H. Eckstein, ed., *Internal War* (London: Collier-Macmillan, 1964), p. 73.

15. These phenomena were identified by Brian Jenkins in 1974 when he wrote that states may 'employ [terrorist groups] ... or their tactics as a means of surrogate warfare against another nation'. B.M. Jenkins, *International Terrorism: A New Kind of Warfare* (Rand P-5261, 1974), p. 13. Wilkinson formally incorporated them into an academic typology in 1977, when he introduced the concept of 'proxy' or 'camouflaged' war between sovereign states. P. Wilkinson, *Terrorism and the Liberal State* (London: Macmillan, 1977), pp. 177–80.

16. J. F. Murphy, *State Support of International Terrorism: Legal, Political, and Economic Dimensions* (London: Mansell Publishing & Westview Press, 1989), p. 34. Murphy includes the following as types of support which may be given: intelligence support, training (both basic military and specialised terrorist), use of diplomatic assets, provision of high technology, provision of weapons and explosives, provision of logistics, transportation, permitting use of territory, financial support, rhetorical support, and tacit support (having foreknowledge and failing to act), pp. 32–3.

17. P. Seale, *The Struggle for Syria* (New Haven, CT: Yale University Press, 1986), pp. 1–3.

18. Examples include: D.T. Pritchett, 'The Syrian strategy on terrorism, 1971–1977', *Conflict Quarterly* (Summer 1988), pp. 27–48; 'The unmasking of Assad', *US News & World Report*, Vol. 101, No. 19 (10 November 1986), pp. 26–30; D. Pipes, 'Terrorism: the Syrian connection', *The National Interest* (Spring 1989), pp. 15–28; US Department of State, *Syrian Support for International Terrorism: 1983–1986*, Special Report No. 157 (Washington DC; Department of State, December 1986).

19. President Asad has claimed that 'our country is one of the countries most subjected to terrorism'. 'Interview: Hafiz al-Asad: Terrorism and the anti-Syria campaign', *Journal of Palestine Studies*, Vol. XV, No. 4 (Summer 1986), p. 3. See also: 'Khaddam, Al-Shar', Talas, Rajjuh condemn terrorism', *Foreign Broadcast Information Service*, 6 May 1986, p. H 1.

20. For a discussion of Syrian historical writings, see U. Freitag, *Geschichtsschriebung in Syrien 1920–1990* (Hamburg: Deutsches Orient-Institut, 1991).

21. G.H. Torrey, *Syrian Politics and the Military 1945–1958* (Ohio: Ohio State University Press, 1964); N. Van Dam, *The Struggle for Power in Syria* (London: Croom Helm Ltd, 1979).

22. They all rely heavily on Seale's account of the 1950s. T. Petran, *Syria* (London: Ernest Benn Ltd, 1972); D. Hopwood, *Syria 1945–1986: Politics and Society* (London: Unwin Hyman, 1988); V. Perthes, *Staat und Gesellschaft in Syrien: 1970–1989* (Hamburg: Deutsches Orient-Institut, 1990).

23. I. Rabinovich, *The Road Not Taken: Early Arab-Israeli Negotiations* (Oxford: Oxford University Press, 1991); A. Gorst and W.S. Lucas, 'The other collusion: Operation Straggle and Anglo-American intervention in Syria, 1955–56', *Intelligence and National Security*, Vol. 4, No. 3 (1989), pp. 576–95; D. Little, 'Cold War and covert action: the United States and Syria 1945–1958', *The Middle East Journal*, Vol. 44, No. 1 (1990), pp. 51–75; D.W. Lesch, *The United States and Syria, 1953–1957: The Cold War in the Middle East* (PhD Thesis, Harvard University, 1990).

24. Seurat, *L'État de Barbarie*, p. 91.

1 Syria in its environment

1. Geographical Syria, as described by the ancients, includes the present-day territories of Syria, Lebanon, Jordan, Israel and parts of Iraq and Turkey. A.H. Hourani, *Syria and Lebanon: A Political Essay*, (London: Royal Institute of International Affairs/Oxford University Press, 1946), p. 4. On Ottoman rule, see: J.P. Pascal, 'La Syrie à l'époque ottomane', in A. Raymond, ed., *La Syrie d'aujourd'hui* (Paris: Centre d'études et de recherches sur l'Orient arabe contemporain, 1980), pp. 31–53; G. Haddad, *Fifty Years of Modern Syria and Lebanon* (Beirut: Dar al-Hayat, 1950), pp. 28–33; J.B. Glubb, *Syria, Lebanon, Jordan* (London: Thames and Hudson, 1967), pp. 105–18. On earlier Syrian history, see: P.K. Hitti, *History of Syria* (London: Macmillan, 1951).

2. D. Fromkin, *A Peace to End All Peace* (London: Andre Deutsch, 1989); P. Mansfield, *The Ottoman Empire and its Successors* (London: Macmillan, 1973), pp. 34–63.

3. E. Kedourie, *In the Anglo-Arab Labyrinth: The McMahon-Husayn Correspondence and its Interpretations 1914–1921* (Cambridge: Cambridge University Press, 1976).

4. See: Z.N. Zeine, *The Struggle for Arab Independence* (Beirut: Khayats, 1960), Chapter I. The documentation is in G. Antonious, *The Arab Awakening* (London: Hamish Hamilton, 1938), pp. 413–30.

5. See H.N. Howard, *The King-Crane Commission* (Beirut: Khayats, 1963).

6. Haddad, *Fifty Years of Modern Syria and Lebanon*, pp. 57–68; Zeine, *The Struggle for Arab Independence*, pp. 25–188. The text of the Mandate is in Hourani, *Syria and Lebanon: A Political Essay*, pp. 308–14.

7. On Mandate Syria, See: S.H. Longrigg, *Syria and Lebanon under the French Mandate* (London: Royal Institute of International Affairs/Oxford University Press, 1958); Hourani, *Syria and Lebanon: A Political Essay*, pp. 163–307; A.H. Hourani, *Minorities in the Arab World* (Oxford: Oxford University Press, 1947), pp. 75–90; A. Raymond, 'La Syrie, du Royaume Arabe à l'independence (1914–1946)', in Raymond, ed., *La Syrie d'aujourd'hui*, pp. 55–85.

8. On the French suppression of this uprising, see: D. Omissi, *Air Power and Colonial Control* (Manchester: Manchester University Press, 1990), pp. 189–96.

9. The text of the treaty is in Hourani, *Syria and Lebanon: A Political Essay*, pp. 314–20.

10. For a succinct account of the emergence of these political leaders, see: D. Hopwood, *Syria 1945–1986: Politics and Society* (London: Unwin Hyman, 1988), pp. 22–7.

11. Haddad, *Fifty Years of Modern Syria and Lebanon*, pp. 98–100; A.B. Gaunson, *The Anglo-French Clash in Lebanon and Syria, 1940–45* (New York: St Martin's Press, 1987); S. Mardam Bey, *Syria's Quest for Independence 1939–1945* (Reading, MA: Ithaca Press, 1994).

12. Brief descriptions of the main parties can be found in: M. Amine, *Le Développement des partis politiques en Syrie entre 1936 et 1947* (PhD Thesis, University of Paris, 1950), pp. 78–191; G.H. Torrey, *Syrian Politics and the Military 1945–1958* (Ohio: Ohio State University Press, 1964), pp. 49–62; M. Harb Farzat, *Al Hayah al-hizbiyah fi Suria (Party Life in Syria)* (Damascus: Dar al-Ruad, 1955), pp. 222–48.

13. 'Un grand parti politique à Damas patronné par Djémil Mardam Bey', *La Bourse Egyptienne*, 1 January 1947.

14. P. Rondot, 'Tendances particularistes et tendances unitaires en Syrie', *Orient*,

2e année, 1er trimestre, numéro 5 (1958), p. 136; 'La physionomie de la nouvelle Chambre syrienne', *La Bourse Egyptienne*, 15 October 1947.

15. My thanks to Faisal Qudsi, Nazim's son, for emphasising these distinctions. Interview with Faisal Qudsi, 24 June 1992, London.

16. The party was originally called the Syrian National Party, but French officials mistranslated the Arabic word for 'national' as 'popular', hence the tendency in Western sources to call the party Parti Populaire Syrien – PPS. In 1948 Sa'adah reformulated the party's ideology, placing greater stress on its 'social nationalist' aspect, hence the subsequent use of the name Syrian Social Nationalist Party (SSNP). A hagiographic account of Sa'adah's life is given in Syrian Social Nationalist Party Information Bureau, *Antoun Sa'adeh: Leadership and Testimony*, (n.p.: n.d.), pp. 7–19.

17. *The Principles and Aims of the Syrian Social Nationalist Party* (Beirut: SSNP, 1949); L. Zuwiyya Yamak, *The Syrian Social Nationalist Party: An Ideological Analysis*, Harvard Middle Eastern Monographs XIV (Cambridge, MA: Center for Middle Eastern Affairs, Harvard University, 1966), pp. 76–110; H.A. Kader, *The Syrian Social Nationalist Party* (Beirut: n.pb., 1990), pp. 21–82; M. Maatouk, *A Critical Study of Antun Sa'ada and his Impact on Politics, The History of Ideas and Literature in the Middle East* (PhD Thesis, School of Oriental and African Studies, 1992), Part III.

18. See for example, D. Pipes, *Greater Syria: The History of an Ambition* (Oxford: Oxford University Press, 1990), p. 101. Appearing to add weight to this charge is the fact that the party symbol resembles a swastika. Founding members of the party, however, argue that their symbol is a combination of the Christian cross and the Islamic crescent and that its four arms represent the party's four key values.

19. *The Principles and Aims of the Syrian Social Nationalist Party*, p. 30.

20. For an account of the party's early history and ideology, see: J.F. Devlin, *The Ba'th Party: A History from its Origins to 1966* (Stanford University, Stanford, CA: Hoover Institution Press, 1976), pp. 7–45, and A.Y. El-Khalil, *The Socialist Parties in Syria and Lebanon* (PhD Thesis, American University, Washington, DC, 1962), Chapters III and IV. A good contemporary description is provided by W. Kirkpatrick, Information Officer at the British Legation in Damascus, writing in 1949. See: Public Records Office (hereafter PRO), Foreign Office (hereafter FO) 371/1018/63, Damascus to FO, 18 August 1949.

21. 'Fermeture des locaux communistes en Syrie', *La Bourse Egyptienne*, 18 December 1947.

22. W.Z. Laqueur, *Communism and Nationalism in the Middle East* (London: Routledge & Kegan Paul, 1956), p. 154.

23. On the Communist Party, see: Laqueur, *Communism and Nationalism in the Middle East*, pp. 141–70. On Baqdash, see: M. Khadduri, *Arab Contemporaries* (Baltimore, MD: Johns Hopkins University Press, 1973), Chapter IX. For a discussion of socialism in Syria, see: J. Rastier 'A la recherche de socialism Syrien', *Orient*, 1re année, 4e trimestre, numéro 4 (1957), pp. 169–76.

24. The emergence of the Muslim Brotherhood is recounted in O. Carré and G. Michaud, *Les Frères Musulmans (1928–1982)* (Paris: Éditions Gallimard/Julliard, 1983), and J. Heyworth-Dunne, *Religious and Political Trends in Modern Egypt* (Washington, DC: The author, 1950). On the Syrian branch, see: U.F. Abd-Allah, *The Islamic Struggle in Syria* (Berkeley, CA: Mizan Press, 1983), pp. 91–101.

25. After the 1947 parliamentary elections, *La Bourse Egyptienne* ran the headline 'Le Triomphe du Front Religieux aux Élections Syriennes' even though the Brotherhood won only three seats. *La Bourse Egyptienne*, 18 July 1947.

26. PRO, FO 371/75541/E14487, Broadmead to FO, 28 November 1949.
27. Laqueur, *Communism and Nationalism in the Middle East*, pp. 255–7.
28. P. Seale, *The Struggle for Syria* (New Haven, CT: Yale University Press, 1986), p. 8.
29. The Hashimite monarchy had been temporarily ousted in 1941 after a coup led by Rashid 'Ali al-Gaylani but had been restored by British troops.
30. The text is in J.C. Hurewitz, *Diplomacy in the Near and Middle East: A Documentary Record: 1914–1956* (Princeton, NJ: D. Van Nostrand, 1956), p. 236.
31. Although as pan-Arabism gained in popularity, 'Abdallah tended to portray the plan as the first step on the road to Arab unity. On the Greater Syria projects, see: M. Khadduri, 'The scheme of Fertile Crescent unity: a study in inter-Arab relations', in R.N. Frye, ed., *The Near East and the Great Powers* (Cambridge, MA: Harvard University, 1951), pp. 137–77; Pipes, *Greater Syria: The History of an Ambition*, pp. 71–88; I. Gershani, 'King 'Abdallah's Concept of a "Greater Syria"', in A. Sinai and Allen Pollack, eds, *The Hashemite Kingdom of Jordan and the West Bank* (New York: American Academic Association for Peace in the Middle East, 1977), pp. 139–47.
32. For an account of the rivalry between Nahhas and King Faruq which accompanied the adoption of Egypt's Arab policy, see: J.W.D. Gray, 'Abdin against the Wafd', *Middle East Forum*, Vol. XXXVIII, No. 2 (February 1962), pp. 17–20, 48.
33. On the formation of the League, see: C.A. Hourani, 'The Arab League in Perspective', *Middle East Journal*, Vol. 1, No. 2 (April 1947), pp. 125–36. The conversations leading up to the Alexandria Protocols appear in: 'Document sur les origines de la Ligue des États Arabes', *Orient*, 4e année, 2e trimestre, numéro 14 (1960), pp. 177–216.
34. The text of the pact is in Hurewitz, *Diplomacy in the Near and Middle East: A Documentary Record: 1914–1956*, pp. 246–9.
35. P.J. Vatikiotis, *Conflict in the Middle East* (London: George Allen & Unwin Ltd, 1971), p. 93.
36. On the Sa'udi-Hashimite conflict between the wars, see: R. Lacey, *The Kingdom* (London: Hutchinson, 1981), pp. 181–200; H. St John Philby, *Sa'udi Arabia* (London: Ernest Benn Ltd, 1955), Chapter 10.
37. In May 1953 US Secretary of State John Foster Dulles had a conversation with General Adib al-Shishakli, then Chief of Staff. It was noted that Shishakli 'sees the facts as they are. ... [H]e recognizes that the state of Israel is a real and living thing. He does not want arms to push Israel into the sea.' Memorandum of Conversation (hereafter MemCon), 16 May 1953, *Foreign Relations of the United States, 1952–1954, Vol. IX* (Washington, DC: US Government Printing Office, 1986) (hereafter *FRUS* with year and volume), p. 58. Although Shishakli was at the time asking the United States for arms supplies, he argued that these were necessary to defend Syria against Israeli aggression.
38. The borders between the Mandates of Syria and Palestine had been established by the Paulet-Newcomb Accord in 1922 after negotiations between Britain and France. On UNTSO, see: S. Bhutani, *The United Nations and the Arab-Israeli Conflict* (New Delhi: The Academic Press, 1977), pp. 38–47.
39. F.J. Khouri, 'Friction and Conflict on the Israeli-Syrian Front', *Middle East Journal*, Vol, 17, Nos 1 & 2 (Winter and Spring 1963), pp. 14–34; Lieutenant General E.L.M. Burns OBE, DSO, MC, *Between Arab and Israeli* (London: George G. Harrap and Co Ltd, 1962), pp. 113–18; N. Bar-Yaacov, *The Israeli-Syrian Armistice* (Jerusalem: Magnes Press, 1967).
40. Z. Schiff, 'The dispute on the Syrian-Israeli border', *New Outlook*, (February 1967), p. 8.

41. An early clash occurred on the Sea on 12 July 1950 when Syrian troops fired at Israeli police launches in the north-east corner of the Sea. For a detailed overview, see: E. Berger, *The Covenant and the Sword* (London: Routledge & Kegan Paul Ltd, 1965), pp. 105–23.
42. Clark to Department of State (hereafter DoS), 18 October 1951, *FRUS, 1951*, Vol. V, p. 1082.
43. On the background to the British position in the Middle East, see: E. Kedourie, *England and the Middle East* (London: Bowes & Bowes, 1956). On British strategic thinking, see: D.R. Devereux, *The Formulation of British Defence Policy Towards the Middle East, 1948–56* (London: Macmillan, 1990), pp. 1–42 and S. Ball, 'Bomber bases and British strategy in the Middle East, 1945–1949', *Journal of Strategic Studies*, Vol. 14, No. 4 (December 1991), pp. 515–33.
44. For the text of the Anglo-Iraqi treaty, see: Hurewitz, *Diplomacy in the Near and Middle East: A Documentary Record: 1914–1956*, pp. 178–81. The Anglo-Egyptian treaty is in ibid., pp. 203–11.
45. The text of the draft treaty is in Hurewitz, *Diplomacy in the Near and Middle East: A Documentary Record: 1914–1956*, pp. 271–3.
46. 'Iraq cabinet shift aids Britain in Middle East', *Christian Science Monitor*, 28 January 1949.
47. The text of the treaty is in Hurewitz, *Diplomacy in the Near and Middle East: A Documentary Record: 1914–1956*, pp. 296–9.
48. 'Message of the President to Congress', *Department of State Bulletin*, Vol. XVI, No. 403, 23 March 1947, p. 536.
49. 'American position', *FRUS, 1947*, Vol. V, p. 513.
50. 'The American Paper', *FRUS, 1947*, Vol. V, p. 575.
51. Discussions within the State Department on these issues can be found in the section entitled, 'Chronological summary of correspondence and exchanges of views leading up to the discussions with the British on the Middle East', *FRUS, 1947*, Vol. V, pp. 488–96.
52. One has to be wary of ascribing this rivalry as a motive for British or American actions as the historical record is clouded by Soviet propaganda. Anglo-American rivalry was a constant theme of Soviet propaganda and influenced the analyses presented in various media outlets. See, for instance, a report of Anglo-American rivalry in Iran put out by the Soviet-backed Azerbaijani Democratic Party Radio on 12 June 1949, BBC Summary of World Broadcasts (hereafter SWB), Part IV, No. 9, 21 June 1949. Also 'Arab rumors hold U.S. rivals Britain', *New York Times*, 2 May 1949; 'Talk of rivalry between Britain and U.S. rises in M.E. as aides tour area', *New York Times*, 9 June 1949.
53. W.R. Louis, *Imperialism at Bay, 1941–1945* (Oxford: Clarendon Press, 1977), pp. 123–4. Louis provides a detailed account of Anglo-American differences on this subject.
54. An example of the tension between the United States' desire for cooperation with Britain and its desire to mollify indigenous nationalisms was the debate over Anglo-Egyptian relations. See: P.L. Hahn, *The United States, Great Britain, and Egypt, 1945–1956* (Chapel Hill, NC: University of North Carolina Press, 1991).
55. In 1948, 38.6 per cent of Western Europe's oil came from the Middle East. Under the European Reconstruction Programme, this was planned to rise to 82.1 per cent by 1951. PRO, FO 371/75115/E6196, M.E. (O) W.P. 5, 14 May 1949.
56. By 1948, UK interests produced 31.2 million tons of oil per annum, while US interests produced 24.55 million tons. PRO, FO 371/75115/E6196, M.E. (O) W.P. 5, 14 May 1949.
57. The IPC was jointly owned by Anglo-Persian, Near East Development,

Anglo-Saxon Petroleum (a British-Dutch company) and the Compagnie Française des Pétroles.
  58. On the development of the oil industry, see: B. Shwadran, *The Middle East, Oil and the Great Powers* (New York: Council for Middle Eastern Affairs, 1959), pp. 223–64, 306–42; S.H. Longrigg, *Oil in the Middle East* (London: Oxford University Press, 1954), Chapters III, V–XII; I.H. Anderson, *Aramco, the United States and Saudi Arabia* (Princeton, NJ: Princeton University Press, 1981); D.S. Painter, *Oil and the American Century* (Baltimore, MD: Johns Hopkins Press, 1986).
  59. PRO, FO 93/33/391.
  60. PRO, FO 371/75051/E 937, 'Anglo-French cooperation in the Levant states'.
  61. Keeley to Secretary of State (hereafter SS), 10 January 1950, *FRUS, 1950*, Vol. V, p. 1203.
  62. On the background to Anglo-French relations in the Levant, see: J. Marlowe, *Perfidious Albion: The Origins of Anglo-French Rivalry in the Levant* (London: Elek Books, 1971). For a graphic depiction of Anglo-French rivalry at the local level, see: Sir Alec S. Kirkbride, *A Crackle of Thorns* (London: John Murray, 1956), Chapter 19.
  63. See B. Rubin, *The Great Powers in the Middle East, 1941–1947* (London: Frank Cass, 1980), pp. 162–222.
  64. On Soviet perceptions, see: W.Z. Laqueur, *The Soviet Union and the Middle East* (London: Routledge & Kegan Paul, 1959), pp. 136–58; E. Karsh, *The Soviet Union and Syria* (London: Royal Institute of International Affairs/Routledge, 1988), pp. 1–4; D. Dallin, *Soviet Foreign Policy After Stalin* (New York: J.B. Lippincott Co, 1961), pp. 385–400.

2 Coups and covert action

  1. For a summary of events, see: G. Kirk, 'Cross currents within the Arab League: the Greater Syria plan', *The World Today*, Vol. IV, No. 1 (January 1948), pp. 15–25.
  2. 'Der Besuch König Abdullah's in Ankara', *Neue Züricher Zeitung*, 12 January 1947; 'La Grande Syrie', *La Bourse Egyptienne*, 16 January 1947; 'Transjordan and Turkey', *The Times*, 20 January 1947; 'La Transjordanie et la Grande-Syrie', *La Bourse Egyptienne*, 3 February 1947; 'Plans for a Greater Syria', *Manchester Guardian*, 14 February 1947.
  3. Government of Jordan, *Al-Kitab al-Urdunni al-abyad* (*The Jordanian White Book*) (Amman: n.pb., n.d.).
  4. 'La Grande Syrie, clé de la situation', *La Bourse Egyptienne*, 4 August 1947.
  5. 'Effervesence dans Le Djebel Druze', *La Bourse Egyptienne*, 2 July 1947; 'Big Arab states merger urged', *Scotsman*, 12 August 1947; 'Préparait-on une révolte dans le Hauran?', *La Bourse Egyptienne*, 25 September 1947.
  6. 'Expulsion d'un agent britannique de Damas', *La Bourse Egyptienne*, 24 March 1947; 'Greater Syria', *The Times*, 15 July 1947; 'Syrian crisis', *Scotsman*, 6 September 1947.
  7. 'Arab kings in dispute', *The Daily Telegraph*, 1 September 1947; 'Egypt will abide by League pact', *Egyptian Mail*, 5 September 1947. During the 1924–25 war in which Ibn Sa'ud captured the Hijaz, British pressure had prevented him capturing Aqaba and Ma'an, instead incorporating them into Transjordan. G. Troeller, *The Birth of Saudi Arabia* (London: Frank Cass, 1976), pp. 222–30.
  8. 'Que sortira-t-il de la nouvelle Chambre syrienne?', *La Bourse Egyptienne*,

26 July 1947; 'Pour la révision de la constitution Syrienne', *La Bourse Egyptienne*, 8 November 1947; 'Syrian President renamed', *New York Times*, 19 April 1948; M. Amine, *Le développement des partis politiques en Syrie entre 1936 et 1947* (PhD Thesis, University of Paris, 1950), pp. 192–8.

9. 'Police fire in Damascus', *News Chronicle*, 2 December 1948; 'Ausbreitung der Unruhen', *Neue Züricher Zeitung*, 3 December 1948; Public Records Office (hereafter PRO), Foreign Office (hereafter FO) 371/68808/E15804.

10. 'Le Cabinet syrien a été constitué', *La Bourse Egyptienne*, 17 December 1948; PRO, FO 371/75528/E765.

11. Although earlier willing to compromise with the French, Mardam had felt betrayed by the French rejection of the 1936 treaty. Thereafter he adamantly opposed French influence. He also believed in the possibility of an Arab economic union and hence opposed economic ties with France. Anonymous interview 1.

12. 'M. Khaled el Azem entreprend la liquidation de la désastreuse expérience Mardam', *Le Monde*, 29 January 1949.

13. PRO, FO 371/75528/3445; 68808/E2581.

14. PRO, FO 371/75528/5441. On Israeli-Syrian relations in 1949, see: I. Rabinovich, *The Road Not Taken: Early Arab-Israeli Negotiations* (Oxford: Oxford University Press, 1991), Chapter 3.

15. For the military details of the coup, see B. al 'Ayf, *Al-Inqilab al-Suri: 30 adhar 1949 (The Syrian Coup: 30 March 1949)* (Damascus: Maktabat Muhammad Husayn al-Nuri, 1949), pp. 21–36. For general accounts of events, see: P. Seale, *The Struggle for Syria* (New Haven, CT: Yale University Press, 1986), pp. 41–5; E. Be'eri, *Army Officers in Arab Politics and Society* (London: Praeger, 1970), pp. 55–60; G.H. Torrey, *Syrian Politics and the Military 1945–1958* (Ohio: Ohio State University Press, 1964), pp. 121–40.

16. PRO, FO 371/75530/E4208, Broadmead to FO, 31 March 1949. In a subsequent report, First Secretary Man put forward the theory that the Homs-based Atasi family and the Hama-based families of 'Azm, Hawrani and Barudi had conspired to remove Quwatli. He argued that, after the fall of Mardam's government, Hashim al-Atasi had not formed a government as Quwatli would not agree to his terms which sought to restrict the role of the President. The Atasis and their allies had then turned to the army by way of Bahij Kallas. They agreed that a People's Party cabinet, with Za'im as Defence Minister, would follow a coup. After the coup Faydi Atasi tried to form a cabinet, but Za'im reneged on the deal and appointed himself Prime Minister. PRO, FO 371/75540/E10944, Man to Attlee, MP, 3 September 1949.

17. PRO, FO 371/75533/E4901, Broadmead to FO, 11 April 1949; E4860, enclosing MA/SEC/42, D'Oyly Harmar, to de Lisle, 6 April 1949; 'Military coup in Syria', *The Times*, 31 March 1949. For the decrees and communiqués of the coup, see: Le Bureau des Documentations Syriennes et Arabes, *Bulletin de la Presse Syrienne*, No. 108, Supplement No. 12 and No. 109, Supplement No. 13.

18. Tabitha Petran, for instance, uncritically endorses claims that the United States backed Za'im's coup. T. Petran, *Syria*, (London: Ernest Benn Ltd, 1972), p. 96.

19. 'Communiqué', enclosed in PRO, FO 371/75533/E3675, Broadmead to FO, No. 10/65/49, 9 April 1949. One outside observer echoed these views. According to the then-President of Aleppo College, the reasons for the removal of the Quwatli administration were its 'incapacity in the affairs of state, and [its] turning of public power to personal ends' A. Carleton, 'The Syrian coups d'état of 1949', *Middle East Journal*, Vol. 4, No. 1 (January 1950), p. 11. Some observers have portrayed Za'im's coup in sociological terms as the victory of the petit bourgeoisie over the aristocracy.

For a Marxist analysis of events, see: B. Ghalioun, *Etat et luttes des classes en Syrie, 1945-1970* (PhD Thesis, University of Paris VIII, 1974), pp. 124-65.

20. Qasim Alwan, whose unit captured the Damascus radio station during the coup, recalls that his units suffered from chronic shortages of ammunition during the fighting around Nazareth. Qasim Alwan interview, 10 August 1993, Cairo. 'Abd al-Ghani Qannut, who Za'im appointed as chief of Military Police for Damascus, recalls a similar sense of dissatisfaction. 'Abd al-Ghani Qannut interview, 16 May 1993, Damascus.

21. Carleton, 'The Syrian coups d'état of 1949', p. 3.

22. K. al-'Azm, *Mudhakkirat Khalid al-'Azm (Memoirs of Khalid al-'Azm)* (Beirut: Dar al-muttahida lil-nashr, 1973), Vol. 2, p. 181. One Syrian politician recalls an incident when 'Azm summoned Za'im to his office and then kept him waiting in his anteroom for two hours. Anonymous interview 1.

23. Al-'Azm, *Mudhakkirat Khalid al-'Azm*, pp. 181-3. The ghee and weapons story is confirmed by Nassuh Babil, then a prominent journalist. N. Babil, *Sahafa wa-seyasa (Journalism and Politics)* (London: Riyad al-Rayyes Books, 1987), p. 363.

24. Some of Za'im's former colleagues recall that the coup was planned by Adib Shishakli and that Za'im stayed out of the way, with an escape route to Lebanon planned, until he was sure the coup had succeeded. Qasim Alwan interview, 10 August 1993.

25. PRO, FO 371/75530/E 4271, FO to Damascus, 4 April 1949.

26. On these events see Seale, *The Struggle for Syria*, pp. 47-57.

27. PRO, FO 371/68810/E15809, Broadmead to McNeil, 8 December 1948.

28. PRO, FO 371/75530/E4338, Houstoun-Boswell to FO, 2 April 1949.

29. PRO, FO 371/75530/E4413, Gordon to FO, 4 April 1949.

30. 'Les espoirs que le coup d'état en Syrie avaient fait naître à Amman se dissipent', *La Bourse Egyptienne*, 16 April 1949.

31. In June rumours surfaced that Nuri had assisted Za'im in his coup with Iraqi soldiers. After conducting investigations, the Foreign Office concluded that the allegations were 'nonsense'. PRO, FO 371/75537/E7403, Broadmead to FO, No. 329, 15 June 1949; E7566, Mack to FO, 18 June 1949.

32. PRO, FO 371/75550/E4605, Mack to FO, 9 April 1949.

33. PRO, FO 371/75550/E4606, Mack to FO, 9 April 1949.

34. PRO, FO 371/75550/E4889, Mack to FO, 18 April 1949; E4890, Mack to FO, 19 April 1949. The text of the proposed military agreement and the correspondence concerning it were published by *Al-Misri* on 6 June 1949. A translation of the texts can be found in PRO, FO 371/75551/E8974, 15 July 1949.

35. PRO, FO 371/75532/E4685, Kirkbride to FO, 9 April 1949.

36. 'Azzam Pasha est parti, hier, pour Damas', *La Bourse Egyptienne*, 18 April 1949.

37. Al-'Ayf, *Al-Inqilab al-Suri: 30 adhar 1949*, p. 191.

38. 'Après la visite du Colonel Zaim à S.M. le Roi Farouk', *La Bourse Egyptienne*, 22 April 1949.

39. 'Zayim recognized by 3 Arab states', *New York Times*, 24 April 1949.

40. Damascus Radio, 26 April, BBC Summary of World Broadcasts (hereafter SWB) Part IV, No. 2, 3 May 1949.

41. Damascus Radio, 28 April, SWB Part IV, No. 2, 3 May 1949.

42. 'Syria is annoyed by talk of merger', *New York Times*, 27 April 1949; 'Syrians dig in on frontier', *Egyptian Gazette*, 29 April 1949; PRO, FO 371/75535/E5252, Minute, 28 April 1949; *Bulletin de la Presse Syrienne*, Nos 116, 117, 118.

43. PRO, FO 371/75536/E5378, Broadmead to FO, 28 April 1949.

44. PRO, FO 371/75535/E5342, Houstoun-Boswell to FO, 27 April 1949.

45. PRO, FO 371/75535/E5369.
46. 'Assassins sentenced', *New York Times*, 27 April 1949; 'M. Choucri El-Kouatly sera autorisé à quitter la Syrie', *La Bourse Egyptienne*, 16 June 1949.
47. PRO, FO 371/75532/E5367, Kirkbride to FO, 29 April 1949.
48. PRO, FO 371/75550/E6127, Mack to FO, 14 May 1949.
49. PRO, FO 371/75550/E5876, Broadmead to FO, 10 May 1949; E6120, Mack to FO, 12 May 1949.
50. PRO, FO 371/75550/E6617, Mack to FO, 26 May 1949; E6649, Mack to FO, 28 May 1949; E7166, Broadmead to FO, 11 June 1949. Lebanese-Syrian relations are discussed below.
51. 'Syria dissolves political parties', *The Daily Telegraph*, 30 May 1949.
52. PRO, FO 371/75551/E7212: FO to Mack, 16 June 1949; Mack to FO, 12 June 1949.
53. A report to the UN by the Syrian Women's League described the widespread use of torture, midnight raids by the political police and the holding of 500 political prisoners. 'Husni Zaim fait régner en Syrie un régime de terreur', *L'Humanité*, 28 July 1949. The State Department believed that the Women's League was a communist front organisation. National Archives Record Group 263, The Murphy Collection, Records of the CIA: International Communism 1917–1958 (hereafter RG 263), Box 113, Keeley to DoS, 10 July 1950.
54. 'Le Colonel El Zaim repond à la concentration de troupes Irakiennes par une concentration de troupes syriennes', *La Bourse Egyptienne*, 16 June 1949; 'Iraq denies moving troops to frontier', *New York Times*, 17 June 1949. The Syrian army at the time, however, was so weak that Za'im's moves were a bluff, he dug in and camouflaged trucks near the border in the hope that the Iraqis would think they were tanks. Anonymous interview 2.
55. 'Colonel Zaim's Plebiscite', *Manchester Guardian*, 18 June 1949; PRO, FO 371/75551/E7418, Scott-Fox to FO, 17 June 1949; E7392, Broadmead to FO, 15 June 1949.
56. Arab News Agency (hereafter ANA), 22 June, SWB Part IV, No. 10, 28 June 1949.
57. ANA, 22 June, SWB Part IV, 28 June 1949. At the same time, Ibn Sa'ud was asking Britain and the United States to provide him military aid in case of a Hashimite attack. These appeals left 'no doubt that the King ... [was] going through one of his acute phases of apprehension about the Hashimites'. PRO, FO 371/75077/E7496, Scott-Fox to FO, 19 June 1949.
58. 'Syrian President chosen unopposed', *New York Times*, 26 June 1949. Za'im himself 'admitted [to a CIA informant] ... that the ... elections ... [were] "cooked"'. 'Syrian coup d'état', CIA Information Report, No. SO23547, 28 April 1949. Obtained from the CIA under the Freedom of Information Act (FOIA).
59. Voice of Israel, 26 June, SWB Part IV, No. 11, 5 July 1949; 'Syrian munitions blow up; blasts shake Damascus, *New York Times*, 27 June 1949.
60. PRO, FO 371/75537/E8037, Broadmead to FO, 26 June 1949.
61. PRO, FO 371/75542/E8932, Man to FO, 20 July 1949.
62. 'La politique exterieure de la Syrie a l'egard des Pays Arabes et des grandes puissances', *La Bourse Egyptienne*, 6 July 1949.
63. 'Zaim's plan to aid poor', *Egyptian Gazette*, 10 July 1949.
64. Quoted in 'Moscow', *New York Herald Tribune*, 19 April 1949.
65. 'Le coup d'état syrien est un nouvel épisode de la rivalité anglo-américaine en Moyen-Orient', *Combat*, 1 April 1949.
66. 'Le pacte du Proche-Orient à la recherche d'un Prophète au Manteau Vert', *La Tribune des Nations*, 22 April 1949.

67. PRO, FO 371/68810/E11422, Minute, 'Syrian government as constituted on 23rd August 1948', 27 August 1948; 68809/E9654, Broadmead to FO, 8 July 1948.
68. PRO, FO 371/68809/E12909, Minute, 'Approach by the Syrian government for an Anglo-Syrian defence agreement', 20 September 1948.
69. Quoted in 'Syria and Britain', *Egyptian Gazette*, 20 February 1949.
70. PRO, FO 371/75556/E1691, Minute, 'British policy towards the Levant states with particular reference to the possible conclusion of defence agreements', 19 January 1949.
71. PRO, FO 371/68809/E16430, Broadmead to Burrows, 21 December 1948. Houstoun-Boswell in Beirut concurred with this criticism, writing: 'British policy in the Levant seems to be purely negative. On the other hand, the Americans are being very active while the French are definitely positive in their policy.' E214, Houstoun-Boswell to FO, 28 December 1948.
72. PRO, FO 371/75529/E3531, Intelligence Summary 61, Syria 24121/GI enclosed in Broadmead to FO, 16 March 1949.
73. PRO, FO 371/75529/E4071, Broadmead to FO, 28 March 1949.
74. PRO, FO 371/75529/E4072, FO to Broadmead, 30 March 1949.
75. PRO, FO 371/75533/E5062, Minute, 'Recognition of the Syrian government', 15 April 1949.
76. PRO, FO 371/75530/E4248, FO to Bagdad [sic], 3 April 1949.
77. PRO, FO 371/75531/E4631, FO to Bagdad [sic], 10 April 1949.
78. PRO, FO 371/75542/E7357, Houston-Boswell to FO, 15 June 1949.
79. PRO, FO 371/75538/E9335, 'The Syrian situation', 19 July 1949.
80. PRO, FO 371/75556/E9520, Man to FO, 2 August 1949.
81. National Archives and Record Administration, Annex, Suitland, MD, Damascus Legation/Embassy Post Files, Record Group 84 (hereafter NARG 84), Confidential File 350 (hereafter CF 350), Joint Weeka, 5 August 1949; Confidential File 350C (hereafter CF 350C), Harrison to Acheson, 11 August 1949.
82. PRO, FO 371/75561/E4309, Broadmead to FO, 3 April 1949; E6118, Broadmead to FO, 14 May 1949.
83. PRO, FO 371/75560/E7327, Harmar to War Office, MA/SEC/58, 21 May 1949; Harmar to de Lisle, MA/SEC/60.
84. The War Office argued that the only arms available in Britain's straitened circumstances were small arms and artillery. PRO, FO 371/75560/E510, 'War Office memorandum on supply of military equipment to foreign countries', 29 December 1948.
85. PRO, FO 371/75561/E7018, Broadmead to FO, 8 June 1949; E7072, Broadmead to FO, 8 June 1949.
86. PRO, FO 371/75560/E7500, Minute, 'Arms for Syria', 11 June 1949; E7313, Chadwick to Loughnane, 22 June 1949; 75556/E6916, Houstoun-Boswell to FO, 6 June 1949; 75561/E7564, Broadmead to FO, 21 June 1949.
87. PRO, FO 371/75560/E9580, Man to FO, 4 August 1949.
88. PRO, FO 371/75547/E7841, Houstoun-Boswell to FO, 25 June 1949.
89. PRO, FO 371/75531/E 4455, Harvey to FO, 5 April 1949; FO to Paris, 7 April 1949.
90. 'French influence in Syria', *Scotsman*, 15 July 1949.
91. J.C. Chadwick, Assistant Head of Department, did express concern over large French arms shipments to Za'im, asking 'are the French building up a stronger army in Syria than the Iraqis have?' but did not disagree with his colleagues comments. PRO, FO 371/75560/E9074, Trevelyan to Bevin, 15 July 1949. See minutes attached to PRO, FO 371/75547/E8164, Helm to FO, 4 July 1949.

92. National Archives and Records Administration Group 59 (hereafter NARG 59, Keeley to Acheson, 890D.00/1-1749.
93. PRO, FO 371/75051/E6268, Houstoun-Boswell to FO, 16 May 1949.
94. PRO, FO 371/75547/E8164, Helm to FO, 4 July 1949.
95. NARG 59, Keeley to Acheson, 890D.00/6-1049.
96. PRO, FO 371/75549/E8731, Houstoun-Boswell to FO, 16 July 1949.
97. Paris Radio, 22 April, SWB Part IV, No. 1, 26 April 1949. PRO, FO 371/75560/E7327, Harmar to de Lisle, MA/SEC/60.
98. PRO, FO 371/75560/E6545, Harvey to FO, 26 May 1949.
99. 'Inquiétudes au Quai d'Orsay', *La Bourse Egyptienne*, 22 March 1949.
100. 'A. Arslan, *Dhikrayat al-Amir 'Adil Arslan an Husni al-Za'im (Memoirs of Amir 'Adil Arslan about Husni al-Za'im)* (Beirut: Dar al-kitab al-jadid, 1962), pp. 29-35.
101. 'La politique exterieure de la Syrie a l'egard des Pays Arabes et des grandes puissances', *La Bourse Egyptienne*, 6 July 1949.
102. Seale, *The Struggle for Syria*, p. 36, n. 18. Italics in original.
103. This proposal was dismissed with the scathing comment: 'In view of the comparative shortage of arms and the relative unimportance of the Syrian army I do not think it matters whether we or the French or both arm them.' Thirkell note in PRO, FO 371/75547/E7841, Houstoun-Boswell to FO, 25 June 1949.
104. PRO, FO 371/75556/E 1691, Minute, 'British policy towards the Levant states with particular reference to the possible conclusion of defence agreements', 19 January 1949.
105. Quoted in Seale, *The Struggle for Syria*, p. 36.
106. Moscow Radio, 1 July, SWB Part IV, No. 12, 12 July 1949.
107. M. Copeland, *The Game of Nations* (London: Weidenfeld and Nicolson, 1969), pp. 40-5.
108. M. Copeland, *The Game of Nations*, pp. 41-2.
109. D. Little, 'Cold War and covert action: the United States and Syria 1945–1958', *The Middle East Journal*, Vol. 44, No. 1, (1990), pp. 55-7. Little's comments regarding McGhee are purely speculative and, on current evidence, cannot be supported. McGhee's own account of his visit does not mention the subsequent coup. He does, however, give the impression that coordinating political action was the last thing on his mind. Until late February he had been employed as the State Department's Coordinator for the Greek-Turkish Aid Program, but in early March was suddenly appointed Special Assistant with responsibility for the Arab refugee problem. His account of his visit to Damascus, which followed his attendance at a meeting of the Palestine Conciliation Commission in Beirut, gives the impression of someone overwhelmed by and immersed in his new task. G. McGhee, *Envoy to the Middle World* (New York: Harper and Row, 1983), pp. 28-33. See also Rabinovich's treatment of the State Department record: Rabinovich, *The Road Not Taken: Early Arab-Israeli Negotiations*, pp. 82-91.
110. H.N. Howard, *The King-Crane Commission* (Beirut: Khayats, 1963).
111. NARG 59, Meminger to Acheson, 890D.00/12-447.
112. PRO, FO 371/75527.
113. NARG 84, CF 350, Joint Weeka, 24 December 1948.
114. On the Turco-Syrian dispute, see: A.K. Sanjian, 'The Sanjak of Alexandretta (Hatay): its impact on Turkish-Syrian relations (1939–1956)', *Middle East Journal* Vol. 10, No. 4 (Autumn 1956), pp. 379-94. For an outline of Turkey's importance in the US's Cold War strategy, see O. Soysal, *An Analysis of the Influence of Turkey's Alignment with the West and of the Arab-Israeli Conflict upon Turkish-Israeli Relations and Turkish-Arab Relations* (PhD Thesis, Princeton University, 1983), Part I.

115. Central Intelligence Group (CIG) Report ORE-15 'The Hatay question', 28 February 1947, President's Secretary's Files, Intelligence File, Box 254, Harry S. Truman Presidential Library, Independence, MO (hereafter Truman Library).
116. On these claims, see: Appendix F to CIG Situation Report-1, 'Soviet territorial demands on Turkey', President's Secretary's Files, Intelligence File, Box 258, Truman Library.
117. 'La question d'Alexandretta évoquée à la Chambre syrienne', *La Bourse Egyptienne*, 15 October 1947. See also 'Activités turques dans le nord-syrien', *La Bourse Egyptienne*, 15 April 1947; 'Wedge in Arab-Turkish bloc', *Egyptian Gazette*, 6 June 1947.
118. Mardam, as well as other politicians such as Qudsi and Kikhia, were adamantly opposed to the existence of Israel and hoped that the refugees would form a 'ring of fire' around the Zionist state. Faisal Qudsi interview, 24 June 1992, London.
119. Copeland, *The Game of Nations*, p. 42.
120. 'Zayim dissolves Syrian parliament', *New York Times*, 3 April 1949.
121. NARG 59, Memcon 'Syrian ratification of the Tapline convention', 890 D.6363/5-2549.
122. 'Communism curb pledged by Zayim', *New York Times*, 4 April 1949.
123. 'Et en Syrie', *La Bourse Egyptienne*, 18 April 1949.
124. PRO, FO371/75531/E4578, Broadmead to FO, 6 April 1949; NARG 84, CF 350, Joint Weekas, 8 and 15 April 1949.
125. 'Autour du rapprochement turco-syrien', *La Bourse Egyptienne*, 12 July 1949; PRO, FO 371/75548/E5760, Eyres to FO, 6 May 1949.
126. PRO, FO 371/75548/E5039, Campbell to Wright, 18 April 1949.
127. 'Une axe Ankara-Damas protégé par L'Amerique?', *La Bourse Egyptienne*, 19 July 1949.
128. 'Zaim wants Atlantic Pact for M.E.', *Egyptian Gazette*, 10 August 1949.
129. Arslan, *Dhikrayat al-Amir 'Adil Arslan an Husni al-Za'im*, pp. 15-28. Before his coup Za'im is reported to have had contacts with Israeli intelligence officers. A. Shlaim, 'Husni Za'im and the plan to resettle Palestinian refugees in Syria', *Journal of Palestine Studies*, Vol. XV, No. 4 (Summer 1986), pp. 68-80.
130. Acheson to Keeley, 13 May 1949, *Foreign Relations of the United States, 1949, Vol. VI*, (Washington, DC: US Government Printing Office) (hereafter *FRUS* with year and volume), pp 1007-8.
131. NARG 84, CF 350, Joint Weeka, 25 February 1949.
132. NARG 84, CF 350, Joint Weeka, 4 March 1949. In the process of the reforms, Fakri Barudi, the head of the army's counter-espionage service, lost his job. Copeland, giving the story a different twist, recalls that Barudi was undermined as a result of a plot hatched by Copeland, Meade and Za'im which resulted in a shoot-out in Copeland's home. M. Copeland, *The Game Player* (London: Aurum Press, 1989), p. 94.
133. NARG 59, Keeley to Acheson, 890D.oo/3-149.
134. Mardam may have been coordinating this opposition to undermine the government. NARG 84, CF 350, Joint Weeka 18 February 1949.
135. NARG 59, Keeley to Acheson, 890D.oo/3-149 and 3-1649.
136. PRO, FO 371/75562/E3148, Broadmead to Bevin, 1 March 1949; E2404, Houstoun-Boswell to Bevin, 10 February 1949.
137. NARG 59, Keeley to Office of Near Eastern Affairs, 890D.oo/1-2749.
138. NARG 84, CF 350, Joint Weeka, 18 February 1949.
139. NARG 59, Keeley to Acheson, 890D.oo/2-1449.

140. PRO, FO 371/75530/E4408, FO to Washington, 6 April 1949; 75531/E4507, Harvey to FO, 6 April 1949.
141. PRO, FO 371/75533/E5031, FO to Washington, 21 April 1949.
142. DoS to Paris, 15 April 1949, *FRUS, 1949, Vol. VI*, p. 1630, note 2.
143. Acheson to Truman, 25 April 1949, *FRUS, 1949, Vol. VI*, p. 1630.
144. NARG 84, CF 350, Joint Weeka, 1 April 1949.
145. PRO, FO 371/75561/E6119, Broadmead to FO, 14 May 1949.
146. PRO, FO 371/75561/E6118, Broadmead to FO, 14 May 1949; E6543, Broadmead to FO, 26 May 1949. However, this statement may have been merely a ploy by Jabbara. Minutes of the meetings between Za'im and Tapline representatives leading up to ratification show that Tapline refused Syrian requests for a loan, but suggested that the matter could be discussed after ratification. NARG 59, Damascus to DoS, 890D.6363/7–649.
147. NARG 84, CF 350, Joint Weeka, 1 April 1949.
148. NARG 84, CF 350, Joint Weeka, 22 April 1949.
149. NARG 84, CF 350, Joint Weeka, 13 May 1949.
150. NARG 84, CF 350, Joint Weeka, 12 August 1949.
151. NARG 59, Keeley to Acheson, 890D.6363/4–1449.
152. Copeland, *The Game Player*, p. 94.
153. Deane Hinton, Political Officer in the US Legation at the time, recalls of Copeland that 'hyperbole was his middle name' and that he 'let everyone in sight … know that he was … a bigger bigshot than the Minister'. Letter from Deane R. Hinton, 27 September 1992. Richard Bissell, a former colleague of Copeland in the CIA, believes that Copeland 'did exaggerate [his] … role in the major events of the period …'. Letter from Richard M. Bissell, Jr, 22 October 1992.
154. 'The game of nations: the amorality of power politics', *Studies in Intelligence*, Vol. 14, No. 1 (Spring 1970), pp. 107–12. Obtained from the CIA under the FOIA.
155. Anonymous communication 1.
156. PRO, FO 371/75528/E5673; 'Zayim decorates Americans', *New York Times*, 24 July 1949.
157. Copeland claims that the Joint Weeka reports to the Pentagon were fabricated by Legation staff as a prank. If this was the case, then this raises the question of how reliable the reports of Meade's conversations are. More likely, this claim casts further doubt on Copeland's reliability. Copeland, *The Game Player*, pp. 103–6.
158. NARG 84, CF 350, Joint Weeka, 3 December 1948.
159. NARG 84, CF 350, Joint Weeka, 11 February 1949.
160. NARG 84, CF 350, Joint Weeka, 4 March 1949.
161. On Za'im's promises see also: NARG 84, CF 350C, Memo by Meade, 'Syrian army commander's plans to seize power', 10 March 1949.
162. NARG 84, CF 350, Joint Weeka, 18 March 1949.
163. NARG 84, CF 350, Joint Weeka, 18 March 1949.
164. NARG 84, CF 350, Joint Weeka, 25 March 1949.
165. This appears to have been gained through their mutual friend Farid Chehab, commander of the Lebanese Sûreté.
166. According to Deane Hinton, Political Officer in the Legation, Keeley 'was out of step with the President'. Letter from Deane R. Hinton, 27 September 1992.
167. NARG 84, CF 350C, Keeley to Berry, 16 December 1949.
168. Letter from Richard M. Bissell, Jr, former CIA officer, 22 October 1992.
169. Sulh was shot by a three-man SSNP team on his way to Amman airport. In line with its tradition of dedication to the cause, two of the assassins killed themselves rather than be captured. Interview with an SSNP member who was a friend

of Mishal al-Dik, one of the assassins. Bachir Mousli interview, 11 July 1993, Damascus. See also: 'Arab statesman assassinated', *The Times*, 17 July 1951. The President of the Military Court, Ghassan Sharbil, was subsequently shot, and crippled, by SSNP member Husayn al-Shaykh. Bechara al-Khuri, the Lebanese President, was not pursued by the SSNP since he let them know that it was Sulh and not he who was responsible for Sa'adah's execution. Interviews with party members, June 1993, Beirut; letter from SSNP officer Hisham Abu Jaoude, 27 November 1993.

170. For a summary of events, see: E. Rabbath, *La Formation Historique du Liban Politique et Constitutionnel* (Beirut: Librarie Orientale, 1986), pp. 558–9.

171. A. Sa'adah, *Mukhtarat fi al-mas'alah al-lubnaniyah – 2 – al-ini'zaliyah 'aflasat (Selected Writings in the Lebanese Question – 2 – Isolationism Failed)* (Beirut: SSNP, 1976), p. 28. On the 1932 to 1947 period, see: H.A. Kader, *The Syrian Social Nationalist Party* (Beirut: n.pb., 1990), pp. 85–99.

172. M.M. Bodron, *Violence in the Syrian Social Nationalist Party* (MA Thesis, American University of Beirut, 1970), pp. 14–47; 'Vers le classement de l'affaire Saadé', *La Bourse Egyptienne*, 11 April 1947; 'Le "Fuhrer" libanais Antoun Saadé a établi son Q.G. dans la Montagne', *La Bourse Egyptienne*, 9 September 1947.

173. Rabbath, *La Formation Historique du Liban Politique et Constitutionnel*, p. 441.

174. On the National Pact see: Farid el-Khazen, *The Communal Pact of National Identities*, Papers on Lebanon, No. 12 (Oxford: Centre for Lebanese Studies, 1991).

175. H. Sharabi, *Al-Jism wa-al-ramad (The Body and the Ashes)* (Beirut: Dar al-tali'ah lil-tiba'ah wa-al-nashr, 1978), pp. 226–7.

176. NARG 84, CF 350, Joint Weeka, 1 April 1949.

177. PRO, FO 371/75549/E4844, Houstoun-Boswell to FO, 14 April 1949.

178. PRO, FO 371/75536/E6614, Harmar to de Lisle, MA/SEC/59, 23 May 1949. On the incident in general, see: 'La Syrie ferme ses frontières avec le Liban', *La Bourse Egyptienne*, 19 May 1949; 'Syria and Lebanon reopen frontier', *New York Times*, 25 May 1949; 'Syria scores victory', *New York Times*, 3 June 1949. PRO, FO 371/75536/E6848, Broadmead to FO, 2 June 1949; E9903, Houstoun-Boswell to FO, 9 August 1949.

179. PRO, FO 371/75528/E9475.

180. Interview with 'Abdallah Kobecsy, then Sa'adah's private secretary, 27 February 1992, Beirut; *Bulletin de la Presse Syrienne*, No. 115, Rubrique III.

181. Interview with Bachir Mousli, then active in the SSNP's Damascus branch, 11 July 1993, Damascus.

182. As recounted by Adib Qaddurah, who accompanied Sa'adah in the meeting. Interview with Adib Qaddurah, 8 July 1993, Beirut. Qaddurah also discusses the Sa'adah affair in his autobiography: A. Qaddurah, *Haqa'iq wa-mawaqif (Facts and Opinions)* (Beirut: Dar mu'assasat al-fikr, 1989), pp. 107–17. Elias Georgi Kunayzah, Sa'adah's private secretary, recalls that after the meeting Sa'adah commented that Za'im had exaggerated a lot and doubted that he would deliver on his promises. Interview with Elias Georgi Kunayzah, 8 July 1993, Dayr al-Shuwayr.

183. 'Les "Kataebs" font echouer un complot contre les ministres libanais', *La Bourse Egyptienne*, 11 June 1949; 'Au Liban', *La Bourse Egyptienne*, 18 June 1949. On 20 July the President issued a decree dissolving all militias and forcing them to become purely political parties or cease operations, so the move against the SSNP could be seen as the first step towards a general strengthening of the state. Beirut Radio, 20 July, SWB Part IV, No. 14, 26 July 1949; 'Swift moves in Lebanon', *Egyptian Gazette*, 30 July 1949.

184. Sharq al-Adna, 11 June, SWB Part IV, No. 9, 21 June 1949. Sharq al-Adna

was financed by SIS. A. Weir, J. Bloch, P. Fitzgerald, 'Sun sets over the other empire', *The Middle East* (October 1981), No. 84, p. 39.

185. NARG 59, Pinkerton to Acheson, 890E.00/6-1349.

186. Kobecsy also states that a proposed retaliatory attack on a *Kata'ib* base was called off when it was discovered that the base was being protected by ISF units. Kobecsy interview, 27 February 1992; interview with Joubran Hayek, former editor of the SSNP's newspaper, 13 February 1992, Beirut.

187. Beirut Radio, 11 June, SWB Part IV, No. 9, 21 June 1949; PRO, FO 371/75318/E12106. There are no reliable figures for the strength of the SSNP in Lebanon, but a report received by the British Legation in Beirut in April 1949 put membership at around 4,000, of whom 500 were armed. PRO, FO 1018/62, 'PPS in Lebanon', 2 April 1949.

188. Mousli interview, 11 July 1993.

189. Kobecsy interview, 27 February 1992; Georgi interview, 8 July 1993; 'Zayim called plotter', *New York Times*, 25 September 1949.

190. This is why he called the action 'the first revolution', not because he expected it to fail as some observers thought. See: 'The communiqué of the National Socialist leadership of the first revolution, about the revolution, its methods and its goals', in A. Sa'adah, *Mukhtarat fi al-mas'alah al-lubnaniyah – 2 – al-ini'zaliyah 'aflasat*, pp. 202–207. Sharabi argues the latter case. Sharabi, *Al-Jism wa-al-ramad*, pp. 226–7.

191. In the weeks following the *Jamayzah* incident SSNP agents had made two vain attempts to blow up al-Sulh's car. J. Jabrij, *Ma' Antun Sa'adah (With Antun Sa'adah)* Vol. 4 (Beirut: n.pb., 1984), p. 176.

192. Bachir Mousli was responsible for distributing the arms. Mousli interview, 11 July 1993. Sharabi claims that King 'Abdallah supplied weapons, but this is denied by the party members most involved who recall that Sa'adah had poor relations with 'Abdallah. Sharabi, *Al-Jism wa-al-ramad*, pp. 226–7.

193. Mousli interview, 11 July 1993. The *New York Times* reported that some of the arms captured from SSNP men were part of a recent French delivery to the Syrian gendarmerie. 'Zayim held hurt in "Betraying" ally', *New York Times*, 10 August 1949.

194. Approximately 50 men came from Syria. The number from Lebanon was greater, but is not known. Mousli interview, 11 July 1993.

195. In published accounts it has been claimed that some of the attacks took place on the 2nd. The timings here are taken from the diary which Bachir Mousli kept at the time and to which he kindly allowed the author access. For other accounts, see: A.A. Freiha, *L'Armée et l'État au Liban (1945–1980)* (Paris: Librairie Générale de Droit et de Jurisprudence, 1980), p. 61; Sharabi, *Al-Jism wa-al-ramad*, p. 228.

196. Interviews with Georgi, 8 July 1993; Mousli, 11 July 1993; 'Abdallah Mohsin, 9 July 1993, Beirut. All three were in Damascus with Sa'adah. Sharabi claims that when he heard of the failure of the revolt, Sa'adah fled for Jordan, but turned back to Damascus when he reached Dera'. This was denied by all the above interviewees. Sharabi, *Al-Jism wa-al-ramad*, pp. 228–9.

197. The Lebanese journalist Ghassan Tueni was jailed for three months by the Lebanese government for publishing the story. 'Lebanon man held for court critique', *New York Times*, 12 July 1949; Damascus Radio, 11 July, SWB Part IV, No. 13, 19 July 1949; *Bulletin de la Presse Syrienne*, No. 137, Rubrique IV.

198. Chehab later claimed that Rifa'i, acting on Sulh's orders, asked Sa'adah to get out of the car at one point on their journey. Fearing that Rifa'i would seek to kill Sa'adah 'while he was attempting to escape', Chehab refused to let Sa'adah out of the car. Kobecsy interview, 27 February 1992.

199. His lawyer was not permitted time to study the brief and withdrew to be replaced by a military officer. Sharabi, *Al-Jism wa-al-ramad*, pp. 235–7; 'Lebanon executes would-be Hitler after party's rebellion collapses', *New York Times*, 9 July 1949; 'Antoun Saadé, l'auteur du dernier mouvement insurrectionnel, a été jugé, condamné et exécuté en moins du vingt-quatre heures', *La Bourse Egyptienne*, 9 July 1949. Twelve other party members were subsequently condemned to death, six were executed on 16 July. 'Six more shot in Lebanon', *Egyptian Gazette*, 21 July 1949.
200. PRO FO 371/75528/E9475.
201. PRO, FO 371/75320/E8912, Extract from Damascus MA/SEC/69, 9 July 1949.
202. The trucks which delivered the arms were driven by military police NCOs. Since Za'im's 'dirty tricks' assistant, Ibrahim Husayni, was Chief of the Military Police it is clear that this delivery was directly under Za'im's orders. Bachir Mousli provided names of the truck drivers, interview 11 July 1993.
203. NARG 59, Pinkerton to Acheson, 890E.00/7-749. In official British correspondence Sa'adah was invariably labelled a fascist. Sulh, on the other hand, was regarded as friendly. PRO, FO 371/75549/E7826, Houstoun-Boswell to FO, 25 June 1949.
204. Syrian Social Nationalist Party Information Bureau, *Antoun Sa'adah: Leadership and Testimony* (n.p: n.d.), p. 25.
205. Georges 'Abd al-Masih, who became party president after Sa'adah's death, goes further and argues that 'the ... Syrian and Lebanese governments laid a plan for the liquidation of the party, after the leader (Antun Sa'adah) demonstrated ... the danger of the plot against our country by the Jews'. Quoted in Freiha, *L'Armée et l'État au Liban (1945–1980)*, p. 62, n. 214.
206. 'Le secret de l'homme qui a été vengé deux fois', *La Bourse Egyptienne*, 14 August 1951.
207. He was Sulh's brother-in-law. PRO, FO 371/75540/E10944, Man to Attlee, 3 September 1949.
208. Rumour had it that Sulh paid Barazi LL20,000 for Sa'adah. Kobecsy interview, 27 February 1992; Qaddurah interview, 8 July 1993; Jabrij, *Ma' Antun Sa'adah*, pp. 181–2.
209. See Fansah's account of the affair: N. Fansah, *Ayyam Husni al-Za'im – 137 yawman hazzat Suria* (*Days of Husni al-Za'im – 137 Days that Shook Syria*) (Beirut: Dar al-afaq al-jadidah, 1973), pp. 77–82.
210. 'Zayim held hurt in "Betraying" ally', *New York Times*, 10 August 1949.
211. For details, see: PRO, FO 957/79, British Middle East Office: Economic Levant States – Syro-Lebanese Economic Agreement; *Bulletin de la Presse Syrienne*, No. 137, Rubrique II.
212. Radio Damascus, 14 August, SWB Part IV, No. 18, 23 August 1949.
213. F. Abu Mansur, *A'asir Dimashq* (*Damascus Storms*) (Beirut: n.pb., 1959), pp. 75–6. Seale concurs with this account. Seale, *The Struggle for Syria*, p. 75. See also Be'eri, *Army Officers in Arab Politics and Society*, pp. 60–3 and Torrey, *Syrian Politics and the Military*, pp. 143–58.
214. PRO, FO 371/755440/E10779, Harmar to de Lisle, MA/SEC/98, 11 August (dated wrongly) 1949.
215. NARG 84, CF 350, Joint Weeka, 19 August 1949.
216. Abu Mansur, *A'asir Dimashq*, pp. 70–1.
217. Kobecsy interview, 27 February 1992. After the killings, SSNP officers brought Za'im's bloodstained coat to Sa'adah's widow as proof that her husband had been avenged. Mousli interview, 11 July 1993.

218. The plotters feared that they would lose control of this unit if it reached the Jabal. Several of the Druze officers also feared it would be used against their villages. PRO, FO 371/75538/E9864, Man to FO, 16 August 1949; Seale, *The Struggle for Syria*, pp. 74-5.
219. PRO, FO 371/75528/E10946.
220. PRO, FO 371/75538/E9966, Man to FO, 15 August 1949.
221. Alwan interview, 10 August 1993. Alwan himself was posted as an instructor to the Homs Military Academy.
222. For Abu Mansur's account of the plot, see: Abu Mansur, *A'asir Dimashq*, pp. 60-70.
223. PRO, FO 371/75540/MA/SEC/108, Harmar to de Lisle, 30 September 1949.
224. Fath as Mukayil Saqaal, *Min dhikrayat hukumat al-za'im Husni al-Za'im* (*From the Memoirs of the government of General Husni al-Za'im*) (n.p.: n.pb., 1952), p. 142. Saqaal was Za'im's Minister for Public Works.
225. Radio Damascus, 14 August, SWB Part IV, No. 18, 23 August 1949.
226. Acheson to Truman, 19 September 1949, *FRUS, 1949, Vol. VI*, p. 1635; Seale, *The Struggle for Syria*, pp. 73-5; 'Military coup in Syria', *The Times*, 15 August 1949.
227. This 'cloud of oppression' had darkened in the weeks preceding the coup when Za'im had proposed large tax increases to finance a higher military budget. PRO, FO 371/75528/E10946. On press attitudes compare *Bulletin de la Presse Syrienne*, No. 137, Rubrique II with No. 146, Rubrique III.
228. 'Les evenements de Damas', *La Bourse Egyptienne*, 15 August 1949.
229. 'Syrian coup may stall reforms', *Christian Science Monitor*, 15 August 1949.
230. 'Le nouveau putsch Syrien', *Le Monde*, 16 August 1949.
231. See Radio Prague, 16 August; Warsaw Radio, 17 August, Radio Ravag, 17 August, SWB Part IV, No. 18, 23 August 1949.
232. 'La Grande-Bretagne reconquiert ses positions dans le Moyen-Orient', *Combat*, 16 August 1949.
233. 'L'Opinion de la presse parisienne', *Le Monde*, 16 August 1949.
234. 'France and Syria', *Yorkshire Post*, 17 August 1949.
235. 'Der Staatsreich in Syrien', *Neue Züricher Zeitung*, 16 August 1949.
236. PRO, FO 371/75547/E14119, Mack to Burrows, 11 November 1949.
237. PRO, FO 371/75529/E1650, 29 January 1949.
238. 'Les Anglais souhaitent le maintien d'une politique franco-brittanique commune en Moyen-Orient', *Le Monde*, 17 August 1949.
239. PRO, FO 371/75552/E11978, Man to Burrows, 26 September 1949.
240. IPC had two pipelines running from Kirkuk to Tripoli, carrying 6.5 million tons of crude oil per annum between them. It hoped to begin construction of a larger pipe, terminating in Banias, with a capacity of 13 million tons in 1950. MEPL's proposed pipeline, which would go from Abadan and Kuwait to Tartus would have a capacity of 25 million tons. Tapline, which was due to be completed in early 1951, would have a capacity of 16 million tons. PRO, FO 371/82844/EY1532/2, Minute 'Oil pipelines in Syria', 15 March 1950.
241. 'Britain faces challenge in Middle East oil fields', *Christian Science Monitor*, 30 August 1949.
242. PRO, FO 371/75543/E11141, Ashley-Clarke to Wright, 6 September 1949.
243. Seale, *The Struggle for Syria*, p. 73. Some of Za'im's former colleagues argue that Hinnawi was just a figurehead for others, such as Mraywad, who they saw as Iraqi agents. Alwan interview, 10 August 1993; Qannut interview, 16 May 1993.
244. 'Tout est possible', *La Bourse Egyptienne*, 22 August 1949.

245. PRO, FO 371/75538/E10009, FO to Bagdad [sic], 15 August 1949 and 16 August 1949.
246. PRO, FO 371/75539/E10048, Trevelyan to FO, 17 August 1949.
247. Acheson to Truman, 19 September 1949, *FRUS, 1949, Vol. VI*, p. 1635.
248. Radio Beirut, 24 August, SWB Part IV, No. 19, 30 August 1949.
249. 'Army gives reins to Syrian Cabinet', *New York Times*, 16 August 1949; 'New Syrian cabinet faces old job of reform', *Christian Science Monitor*, 19 August 1949.
250. PRO, FO 371/75551/E10496, Man to FO, 28 August 1949; 75552/E12008, Broadmead to FO, 3 October 1949.
251. PRO, FO 371/75551/E10696, FO to Man, 2 September 1949.
252. PRO, FO 371/75552/E11326, Man to FO, 17 September 1949.
253. PRO, FO 371/75552/E11529, Ministry of Defence to Burrows, 20 September 1949; 75546/E14903, Furlonge Minute, 10 December 1949.
254. Serious differences remained concerning the form of union. The Iraqis proposed a confederation, while the Syrian side argued in favour of a more centralised administration with a single parliament. PRO, FO 371/75552/E11670, Man to FO, 25 September 1949; 'Three Arab states negotiating for a union', *Daily Telegraph*, 17 September 1949.
255. Some observers, however, believed that Mikhail Ilyan was the real power in the party. PRO, FO 371/75540/E13662, Broadmead to FO, 10 November 1949.
256. 'Syrian Bloc favors union now with Iraq', *New York Times*, 30 September 1949; PRO, FO 371/75540/E10825, Man to FO, No. 498, 4 September 1949.
257. 'Sous un jour nouveau', *La Bourse Egyptienne*, 8 November 1949. In fact, Israel regarded the plans as a security threat. 'Israelis fear crisis if Syria and Iraq unite', *New York Herald Tribune*, 16 October 1949.
258. PRO, FO 371/75555/E12954, Campbell to FO, 25 October 1949. On the contacts between Quwatli's supporters and army officers such as Major Ahmad al-'Azm, Director of Police and Security, see PRO, FO 371/75541/E14465, Harmar to Hewitt, MA/Top/58, 22 November 1949. US sources broadly concurred with these findings. NARG 84, CF 350C, Caffrey to Acheson, 3 November 1949.
259. PRO, FO 371/75544/E15275, FO to Jedda, 31 December 1949.
260. PRO, FO 371/75552/E11330, Trevelyan to FO, 17 September 1949.
261. PRO, FO 371/75552/E11930, Broadmead to FO, 30 September 1949; E11978, Man to Burrows, 26 September 1949; 75555/E13287, Mack to Burrows, 25 October 1949.
262. Acting Secretary of State to Truman, 6 October 1949, *FRUS, 1949, Vol. V*, p. 181; Acheson to Truman, 14 October 1949, *FRUS, 1949, Vol. V*, pp. 182–3; PRO, FO 371/75555/E12940, Campbell to FO, 26 October 1949.
263. PRO, FO 371/75553/E12053, Broadmead to FO, 5 October 1949; 'Abdallah serait opposé à une union de la Syrie et de l'Irak', *L'Aube*, 13 October 1949.
264. W.F. Stirling, *Safety Last* (London: Hollis and Carter, 1953).
265. NARG 84, CF 350C, Knight to DoS, 16 December 1949.
266. 'Le Colonel Stirling blessé a Damas', *Le Monde*, 8 November 1949; 'Colonel Stirling recovering', *The Times*, 15 November 1949.
267 PRO, FO 371/75540/E13396, Broadmead to FO, 7 November 1949; E13577, Broadmead to FO, 8 November 1949; 75541/E13663, Broadmead to FO, 10 November 1949; E14034, Harvey to FO, 21 November 1949.
268. NARG 84, Confidential File 370, Keeley to Acheson, 7 November 1949.
269. 'Le Gouvernement provisoire syrien démissione', *Le Monde*, 15 December 1949. PRO, FO 371/75541/E14487, Broadmead to FO, 28 November 1949.
270. PRO, FO 371/82785/EY1015/4, Broadmead to McNeil, 31 December 1949.

271. PRO, FO 371/75541/E14264, Minute, 'Syrian elections', 22 November 1949; E14465, Harmar to Hewitt, MA/Top/58, 22 November 1949.
272. NARG 84, CF 350C, Keeley to Acheson, 20 December 1949.
273. Damascus Radio, 19 December, SWB Part IV, No. 36, 30 December 1949.
274. For instance, the army had had to discharge 2,000 new recruits as it did not have sufficient uniforms. NARG 84, CF 350C, Memo by Lt Col Mitchell, 6 October 1949.
275. PRO, FO 371/75541/E15047, Broadmead to FO, No. 659, 19 December 1949; E15053, Broadmead to FO, 19 December 1949; E15264, Harmar to Halliday, MA/SEC/121, 20 December 1949.
276. PRO, FO 371/82785/EY1015/4, Broadmead to McNeil, 31 December 1949.
277. PRO, FO 371/75541/E15196, Broadmead to FO, 21 December 1949.
278. PRO, FO 371/75544/E15197, Mack to FO, 22 December 1949.
279. Tass, 20 December, SWB Part IV, No. 36, 30 December 1949.
280. 'Nouveau coup d'état en Syrie', *L'Humanité*, 20 December 1949.
281. 'Aflaq was Minister of Education and Hawrani Minister of Agriculture. NARG 59, Memcon 'Tapline difficulties in Syria: decision to commence construction work', 890D.6363/10–2449; On Western concerns at the activities of Hawrani and 'Aflaq, see: PRO, FO 371/75562/E11575, Man to FO, 23 September 1949.
282. NARG 84, CF 350, Joint Weeka, 2 September 1949.
283. NARG 84, CF 350, Joint Weeka, 23 September 1949.
284. NARG 84, CF 350, Joint Weeka, 28 October 1949.
285. NARG 84, CF 350C, Harrison to Acheson, 12 October 1949.
286. Copeland, *The Game Player*, p. 108.
287. Fawzi Selu had commanded the Syrian contingent in the French attack on Damascus in 1945 and Anwar Bannud had been the only Syrian to reach the rank of Colonel under the French. NARG 59, Keeley to Acheson, 890D.00/12–2149.
288. PRO, FO 371/82790/EY1022/2, Harvey to FO, 4 January 1950.
289. NARG 59, Keeley to Acheson, 890D.00/12–2149.
290. 'Réactions égyptiennes', *La Bourse Egyptienne*, 26 December 1949; 'Egypt in warning to Iraq and Jordan on moves in Syria', *New York Times*, 27 December 1949.
291. Kirkbride had countermanded this order. He complained: 'I wish that Syria would settle down because the longer the present uncertainty continues the greater the danger that, some day, someone will get out of control and intervene'. PRO, FO 371/82790/EY1022/4, Kirkbride to Furlonge, 28 December 1949.

3 The Shishakli era

1. For overviews of events, see: J.S. Roucek, 'Syria: a lesson in geopolitics', *Current History* (April 1952), pp. 221–6 and G.H. Torrey, *Syrian Politics and the Military 1945–1958* (Ohio: Ohio State University Press, 1964) pp. 164–202.
2. National Archives and Record Administration Annex, Suitland, MD, Damascus Legation/Embassy Post Files, Record Group 59 (hereafter NARG 59), Keeley to Acheson, 890D.00/12–2149; Crocker to Acheson, 12–3149.
3. NARG 84, Confidential File 350C (hereafter CF 350C), Keeley to Acheson, 21 December 1949. Husayni had been imprisoned during Hinnawi's coup but then released and appointed to a regional police post. NARG 59, Keeley to Department of State (hereafter DoS), 783.521/5–350.
4. NARG 84, CF 350C, Keeley to Acheson, 28 December 1949.

5. 'La Crise Syrienne', *La Bourse Egyptienne*, 27 December 1949; 'Khaled El Azem', *L'Aube*, 29 December 1949.

6. In January the Secretary-General of the Ministry of Foreign Affairs, 'had the Iraqi Military Attaché on the mat ... and told him not to interfere in politics'. Public Records Office (hereafter PRO), Foreign Office (hereafter FO) 371/82791/ EY1024/1, Broadmead to FO, 30 January 1950; NARG 59, Harrison to Acheson, 783.00/1-1850.

7. PRO, FO 371/82784/EY1013/2.

8. PRO, FO 371/82787/EY1016/1, Minute, 6 February 1950; 82790/EY1022/ 11, Campbell to FO, 18 January 1950; 82791/EY1024/2, Broadmead to FO, 3 March 1950.

9. Keeley to Acheson, 24 February 1950, *Foreign Relations of the United States 1950, Vol. V* (Washington, DC: US Government Printing Office) (hereafter *FRUS* with year and volume), p. 1205; Keeley to Acheson, 10 January 1950, *FRUS, 1950, Vol. V*, p. 1203.

10. The Legation in Beirut had been bombed the day before. *Bulletin de la Presse Syrienne*, No. 210, Rubrique III.

11. NARG 59, Keeley to DoS, 611.83/4-1950.

12. 'Bombs hit U.S. Legations at Damascus and Beirut', *New York Times*, 20 April 1950; NARG 59, Mitchell report, 611.83/4-1450. Subsequently, the US Minister complained bitterly to his British counterpart of the State Department's policy which he believed had harmed US-Syrian relations. PRO, FO 371/82796/ EY10345/2, Broadmead to Furlonge, 22 April 1950.

13. PRO, FO 371/82796/EY10345/1, Broadmead to FO, 19 April 1950; NARG 59, Joint Weeka, 21 April 1950, 783.00(W)/4-2150.

14. 'Tripartite declaration regarding security in the Near East, 25 May 1950', *Department of State Bulletin*, Vol. XXII, No. 570, June 5, 1950, p. 886.

15. In January 1951, Qudsi told the British: 'you cannot expect Syria to support any resolution which may lead to war, so long as you refuse to provide her with arms and so long as the United States provides Israel with funds to enable her to prepare for another attack on the Arab world'. PRO 371/91846/EY1022/3, Montagu-Pollock to FO, 19 January 1951. On press reaction, see: *Bulletin de la Presse Syrienne*, No. 227, Rubrique III.

16. On these rumours, see: Memorandum from Hillenkoetter, Director of Central Intelligence, 27 April 1950, Declassified Documents Reference System (hereafter DDRS), 1978, 20B.

17. Acheson to the Legation in Syria, 28 April 1950, *FRUS, 1950, Vol. V*, pp. 1210-12; PRO, FO 371/82784, EY1013/4; EY1013/5.

18. PRO, FO 371/82792/EY1025/2, Minute 'Syria and communism', 14 June 1950.

19. The Union had been dissolved after Lebanon had refused to respond to 'Azm's protests that the existing system was to Syria's disadvantage. 'Franchise Douanière Totale Pour: Blé, Beurre, Viande, Légumes, Coton', *L'Orient*, 15 March 1950; 'Syrian cabinet quits amid disintegration', *New York Times*, 30 May 1950.

20. 'Syrian caretaker regime sits on economic volcano', *Christian Science Monitor*, 15 June 1950.

21. In September he permitted British military transport aircraft to fly through Syrian airspace *en route* to the Far East. PRO, FO 371/82784/EY1013/10.

22. PRO, FO 371/82788/EY1017/1, Harmar to Halliday, MA/SECRET/3, 10 January 1950.

23. NARG 59, Owen Jones to Acheson, 783.551/8-750.

24. PRO, FO 371/82785/EY1015/24, Montagu-Pollock to FO, 7 August 1950.

25. PRO, FO 371/82786/EY1015/60, Montagu-Pollock to FO, 18 December 1950. To this day, Qannut claims it was Husayni who pulled the trigger, not himself. Qannut interview, 16 May 1993, Damascus.
26. 'Comment fut assassiné le commandant de l'aviation syrienne', *La Bourse Egyptienne*, 4 August 1950; 'Situation in Syria', *Scotsman*, 20 January 1951; Damascus Radio, 2 October, BBC Summary of World Broadcasts (hereafter SWB) Part IV, No. 103, 7 November 1950; *Bulletin de la Presse Syrienne*, No. 282, Rubrique III.
27. PRO, FO 371/82784/EY1013/9.
28. Faysal al-'Asali had been suspected of being involved in the attack on Stirling, but was cleared. PRO, FO 371/75528/(December 48); 82784/EY1013/8. The two parties amalgamated in October 1951. 91842/EY1015/25.
29. PRO, FO 371/82784/EY1013/7.
30. PRO, FO 371/82784/EY1013/9.
31. PRO, FO 371/82786/EY1015/34, Montagu-Pollock to Younger, 9 September 1950. A translation of the constitution is enclosed in EY1015/39, Montagu-Pollock to FO, 25 September 1950.
32. This according to the British Legation. The Arab News Agency (hereafter ANA) reported that three army officers were sentenced. PRO, FO 371/91841/EY1013/2; ANA, 29 January, SWB Part IV, No. 128, 6 February 1951. See also: ANA, 18 December, SWB Part IV, No. 117, 29 December 1950; 'Syrian army arrest', *Daily Telegraph*, 12 September 1950; 'Nouvelles arrestations prévus en Syrie', *La Bourse Egyptienne*, 30 September 1950; *Bulletin de la Presse Syrienne*, No. 266, Rubrique III and No. 278, Rubrique III.
33. Israel Radio, 19 October, SWB Part IV, No. 100, 27 October 1950.
34. PRO, FO 371/82785/EY1015/10, Kirkbride to Furlonge, 15 February 1950.
35. PRO, FO 371/82788/EY1017/3, Minute 'Reports of a possible coup d'etat in Syria', 17 July 1950.
36. PRO, FO 371/82786/EY1015/45, Kirkbride to Bevin, 10 October 1950.
37. PRO, FO 371/82797/EY10380/1, Montagu-Pollock to Attlee, 2 October 1950.
38. PRO, FO 371/91851A/EY10380/1, Montagu-Pollock to Bevin, 5 February 1951.
39. Ibid.
40. Ibid.
41. *Bulletin de la Presse Syrienne*, No. 285, Rubrique III and No. 287, Rubrique III.
42. PRO, FO 371/91851A/EY10380/1, Montagu-Pollock to Bevin, 5 February 1951.
43. On the 28th Qudsi and Fawzi Selu met 'Abdallah in Amman. 'Abdallah continued to urge Syria to unite with Jordan and bitterly attacked Sa'udi Arabia, where 'anarchy and oppression prevail' and Egypt, which, he said, was characterised by 'disgraceful scandals'. King 'Abdallah of Jordan, *My Memoirs Completed: 'Al Takmilah'* trans. H.W. Glidden (London: Longman, 1978), pp. 28–37.
44. *Bulletin de la Presse Syrienne*, No. 266, Rubrique III and No. 267, Rubrique III.
45. This name is taken from British and American diplomatic reports. Arabic sources have called it *Kata'ib al-Fida' al-Arabi*, the 'Battalions (or Phalange) of Arab Sacrifice'. Y. Sayigh, 'Reconstructing the paradox: the Arab Nationalist Movement, armed struggle and Palestine, 1951–1966', *Middle East Journal*, Vol. 45, No. 4 (Autumn 1991), pp. 608–29.
46. Damascus Radio, 12 October, SWB Part IV, No. 98, 20 October 1950; ANA, 24 October 1950, SWB Part IV, No. 101, 31 October 1950; 'Hussein Tewfick

impliqué dans le complot contre Chichakly', *La Bourse Egyptienne*, 18 October 1950; 'Alleged terrorist gang in Syria', *The Times*, 31 October 1950; NARG 84, CF 350C, Box 21, Davies to Acheson, 6 August 1949.

47. PRO, FO 371/91842/EY1015/50, Montagu-Pollock to Morrison, 19 March 1951.

48. 'Un reportage sur Hussein Tewfik', *La Bourse Egyptienne*, 22 December 1950.

49. PRO, FO 371/91842/EY1015/50, Montagu-Pollock to Morrison, 19 March 1951.

50. Ibid.

51. ANA, 24 December 1950, SWB Part IV, No. 118, 2 January 1951. PRO, FO 371/82786/EY1015/50, Montagu-Pollock to Bevin, 21 October 1950.

52. The Sha'lan were a prominent Bedouin tribe traditionally powerful in the Syrian desert.

53. PRO, FO 371/82786/EY1015/46, Paterson to FO, 17 October 1950; EY 1015/44, Minute, 19 October 1950.

54. ANA, 18 November, SWB Part IV, No. 108, 24 November 1950.

55. ANA, 15 November, SWB Part IV, No. 107, 21 November 1950; 'Syria to review charges', *New York Times*, 19 November 1950; 'La Cour de Cassation de Damas maintient la condamnation à mort de Hussein Tewfik', *La Bourse Egyptienne*, 3 May 1951; PRO, FO 371/82786/EY1015/52, Montagu-Pollock to FO, 14 November 1950.

56. PRO, FO 371/82784/EY1013/11.

57. NARG 59, Jones to Acheson, 783.00/10-2750; Acheson to the Legation in Syria, 25 October 1950, *FRUS, 1950, Vol. V*, p. 1214; Cannon to Acheson, 1 November 1950, *FRUS, 1950, Vol. V*, pp. 1215-17. Cavendish W. Cannon had replaced Keeley as Minister on 20 September 1950.

58. 'Hussein Tewfik et Amer condamnés à mort', *La Bourse Egyptienne*, 13 March 1951; 'Syria frees 15 in plot', *New York Times*, 15 May 1951; 'La condemnation de Hussein Tewfik et de ses deux compagnons', *La Bourse Egyptienne*, 31 December 1951; *Bulletin de la Presse Syrienne*, No. 309, Rubrique III.

59. PRO, FO 371/91842/EY1015/7, Damascus to FO, 23 May 1951; EY1015/14, Damascus to FO, 11 June 1951.

60. PRO, FO 371/82786/EY1015/57, Montagu-Pollock to Bevin, 4 December 1950.

61. Extract from the Confidential Report of the Syrian Military Prosecutor, enclosed in PRO, FO 371/82786/EY1015/57, Montagu-Pollock to Bevin, 4 December 1950.

62. NARG 59, Jones to Acheson, 783.00/10-1850.

63. American sources subsequently identified a Deuxième Bureau agent named Sami Juma' who had 'prepared much of the bogus documentation of the Ajlani-Kallas Conspiracy and whose name has been linked with past bombings of American buildings in Damascus'. Juma' 'will do anything for money' and it is quite possible he assisted the Phalange on behalf of the Bureau. NARG 59, Moose to DoS, 783.00/6-2855.

64. I make the assumption with regard to the United States as he was described by US diplomats as 'well disposed' towards America. NARG 59, Clark Memo, 783.521/1-2854.

65. PRO, FO 371/82852/EY1651/4, Montagu-Pollock to Bevin, 4 September 1950; 'Syrian leader shot dead', *Manchester Guardian*, 31 October 1950; 'Slaying jolts pro-Hashemites', *Christian Science Monitor*, 15 November 1950; *Bulletin de la Presse Syrienne*, No. 271, Rubrique III.

66. PRO, FO 371/81913/E1024/16, Cairo to FO, 21 December 1950.
67. Acheson to Certain Diplomatic and Consular Offices, 6 December 1950, *FRUS, 1950, Vol. V*, p. 1223.
68. Agreed Conclusions of the Conference of Middle Eastern Chiefs of Mission, Istanbul, 14–21 February 1951, *FRUS, 1951, Vol. V*, p. 63.
69. 'Manifestations à Damas', *La Bourse Egyptienne*, 26 January 1951.
70. Memcon prepared by the Deputy Director of the Office of Near Eastern Affairs (Kopper), 17 May 1951, *FRUS, 1951, Vol. V*, p. 135. See also the formal paper, National Security Council (hereafter NSC) 47/5, 14 March 1951, *FRUS, 1951, Vol. V*, p. 95.
71. PRO, FO 371/91200/E1057/8, Memo 'Middle East Policy'.
72. On Britain's perceptions of its strategic needs in the Middle East, see: E. Monroe, *Britain's Moment in the Middle East 1914–1956* (London: Chatto & Windus, 1963), Chapter 7.
73. Turkey backed the proposal as she sought United States' guarantees vis-à-vis the USSR but realised that the US preferred multilateral rather than bilateral agreements. J. Stewart, *Aspects of Lebanon's Reaction to the Middle East Policy of the United States (May 1950–August 1958)* (MA Thesis, American University of Beirut, 1959), p. 18.
74. W.S. Poole, *The History of the Joint Chiefs of Staff, Vol. IV, 1950–1952*, (Washington, DC: Historical Research Division, Joint Secretariat, Joint Chiefs of Staff, 1979), pp. 336–53.
75. The rejection was accompanied by an escalation in clashes between British troops and Egyptian demonstrators and saboteurs.
76. For a summary of the issue, see: National Intelligence Special Estimate, SE–23 (Prospects for an inclusive MEDO), 17 March 1952, *FRUS, 1952–1954, Vol. IX*, pp. 195–9.
77. *Inaugural Address of Harry S. Truman*, 20 January 1949 (Washington, DC: Government Printing Office, 1949).
78. PRO, FO 371/81963/E1193/27, Minute, 'Syria and Lebanon in relation to Middle East defence', 9 October 1950.
79. Cannon to DoS, 9 February 1951, *FRUS, 1951, Vol. V*, pp. 1074–5.
80. PRO, FO 371/91867/EY1195/1, Montagu-Pollock to Bevin, 12 February 1951.
81. McGhee raised a storm of protest after a speech in which he implied that neutralism was losing ground and that Syria was pro-Western. 'Consulate in Aleppo bombed', *New York Times*, 21 January 1951; G. McGhee, *Envoy to the Middle World* (New York: Harper and Row, 1983), pp. 349–50. The bomb at the US Residence caused $15,000 worth of damage. National Archives RG 319, Hill to DoS, 19 April 1951, Army Intelligence Project Decimal File. There was speculation that the Aleppo bomb had been thrown by partisans of the Muslim Brotherhood, but no one was arrested for either bombing. PRO, FO 371/91841/EY1013/2.
82. 'Struggle for power in Syria', *The Times*, 15 March 1951; 'Ein Neues Kabinett in Syrien', *Neue Züricher Zeitung*, 30 March 1951.
83. Clark to DoS, 28 May 1951, *FRUS, 1951, Vol. V*, p. 1076. Another reason may have been that French bankers were in competition with the State Department in Syria and had encouraged the pro-French 'Azm to reject Point IV. 'French financiers rival U.S. in Syria', *New York Times*, 14 June 1951.
84. Exchanges of fire across the border in late March culminated in the killing of seven Israeli policemen on 4 April. The Israeli Air Force (IAF) bombed Syrian army positions in retaliation on 5 April and on 11 April an Israeli aircraft was shot down in a dogfight. On 16 May the UN Security Council condemned the IAF for

bombing a Syrian border village; on the 20th twenty Syrian soldiers and four Israelis were killed in firefights. On 29 May the UN Chief of Staff in Palestine, General Riley, called on Israel to end its irrigation work pending settlement of the border dispute. 'Developments of the quarter', *Middle East Journal*, Vol. 5, No. 3 (Summer 1951), pp. 349–50; *Facts on File, 1951*, pp. 98, 107, 143, 172.

85. 'Syrian cabinet resigns as civil workers strike', *New York Herald Tribune*, 2 August 1951; 'M. Hassan Hakim a constitué un gouvernement de coalition', *Le Monde*, 11 August 1951.

86. 'Syrian moderates dominate cabinet', *New York Times*, 11 August 1951.

87. Cannon to DoS, 12 August 1951, *FRUS, 1951, Vol. V*, p. 1081.

88. On numerous instances Acheson came under pressure both from US politicians and Israeli leaders not to arm the Arab states. See for instance, Acheson Memcon with Senator Herbert Lehman, 10 March 1950 and Acheson Memcon with Prime Minister David Ben-Gurion, 8 May 1951, Papers of Dean Acheson, Memoranda of Conversations, Truman Library.

89. Clark to DoS, 18 October 1951, *FRUS, 1951, Vol. V*, p. 1082. Clark's plea probably fell on deaf ears as Acheson is recorded as complaining in late 1951 that 'I just don't understand what's going on in Syria at all. I just can't understand it.' Quoted in Edwin A. Locke, Oral History Interview No. 33, Truman Library.

90. PRO, FO 371/91841/EY1013/11.

91. 'Syrian government resigns', *Observer*, 11 November 1951.

92. 'President resigns in Syria's crisis', *New York Times*, 3 December 1951; 'New regime in Syria', *The Times*, 4 December 1951.

93. 'Control of the police', *Manchester Guardian*, 30 November 1951; PRO, FO 371/91842/EY1015/28, Montagu-Pollock to FO, 29 November 1951; EY1015/29, Montagu-Pollock to FO, 29 November 1951.

94. Damascus Radio, 3 December, SWB Part IV, No. 215, 11 December 1951. The Foreign Office regarded Shishakli's move in a more cynical light: he 'acted solely in order to save himself from being cast aside by the Dawilibi government'. PRO, FO 371/98916/EY1016/1, Montagu-Pollock to Eden, 9 January 1952.

95. Damascus Radio, 2 December, SWB Part IV, No. 214, 7 December 1951.

96. PRO, FO 371/91842/EY1015/4, Montagu-Pollock to FO, 16 March 1951; EY1015/8, Montagu-Pollock to FO, 20 March 1951.

97. PRO, FO 371/91843/EY1015/50, Troutbeck to FO, 8 December 1951.

98. *Christian Science Monitor*, 30 November 1951. The Soviet media labelled Shishakli the 'American Colonel'. Moscow Radio, 4 December, SWB Part IV, No. 214, 7 December 1951.

99. 'Foe of U.S. heads new Syria cabinet', *New York Times*, 29 November 1951.

100. NARG 59, Cannon to Acheson, 611.83/7–951. When Jadid became Military Attaché in Washington the personal link was maintained through Major 'Adnan Malki. Shishakli's interest in the United States as an arms source may have been spurred in July by the French decision to supply aircraft to Israel. Leonard to Acheson, 611.83/7–3051.

101. Acheson to Damascus, 14 December 1951, *FRUS, 1951, Vol. V*, p. 1090.

102. Acheson to Damascus, 20 December 1951, *FRUS, 1951, Vol. V*, pp. 1095–6.

103. PRO, FO 371/91843/EY1015/53, Minute 'Syria', 6 December 1951.

104. PRO, FO 371/91845/EY1016/30, Minute 'The Syrian crisis', 29 November 1951.

105. 'King Abdullah assassinated', *Daily Telegraph*, 21 July 1951; 'Exiled Jordanians' revived hope', *The Times*, 24 July 1951.

106. PRO, FO 371/91841/EY1013/9.

107. PRO, FO 371/91843/EY1015/58, Kirkbride to FO, 11 December 1951.

Relations between 'Abd ul-Ilah and Talal were poor as 'Abdallah had made moves in late 1950 to disinherit Talal and name the Iraqi Regent or Faysal his heir in order to ensure the creation of Greater Syria after his death. *Background Memoranda on visit to the United States of His Majesty King Faisal II, King of Iraq and His Royal Highness Abd al-Ilah al-Hashimi Regent of Iraq August–September, 1952*, pp. 9–10, Box 43, State Department, Correspondence, 1952, Truman Library.

108. PRO, FO 371/91844/EY1015/81, Troutbeck to FO, 29 December 1951.

109. PRO, FO 371/91843/EY1015/34, Troutbeck to FO, 3 December 1951; EY1015/35, FO to Bagdad, [sic] 5 December 1951; EY1015/52, Minute 'Syria', 4 December 1951.

110. P. Rondot, 'Tendances particularistes et tendances unitaires en Syrie', *Orient*, 2e année, 1er trimestre, numéro 5 (1958), p. 143; 'New Syria laws put foreigners in uneasy spot', *New York Herald Tribune*, 23 March 1952; 'The new regime in Syria', *The Times*, 30 May 1952; PRO, FO 371/104965/EY1011/1. In March 1952 the government put restrictions on foreign cultural centres after accusing them of 'going beyond their duties'. Subsequently, a bomb damaged the US Information Centre, killing an employee. The police made little effort to investigate, prompting speculation that the attack was designed to reinforce the government's warning. FO 371/98914/EY1013/4; 'Syria bombing of US office baffles police', *New York Herald Tribune*, 30 March 1952.

111. Information on the history of Syrian security services was obtained during an interview with General Michel Sema'n, Chef D'État Majeur, Lebanese Internal Security Forces, February 1992, Beirut.

112. P. Khoury, *Syria and the French Mandate* (London: IB Tauris & Co, 1987), p. 78. During the British occupation of Syria, from 1941 to 1945, internal security was handled by detachments of the Intelligence Corps. As the British began their withdrawal in 1945, responsibility for security was turned back over to the Sûreté. H.O. Dovey, 'Security in Syria, 1941–45', *Intelligence and National Security*, Vol. 6, No. 2 (April 1991), pp. 418–46.

113. In March 1953 gendarmerie NCOs came under the authority of the Defence Ministry. NARG 59, 783.00/4–753.

114. For a US assessment of Communist Party activities in Syria, see: NARG 59, 'Analysis of communist propaganda', Office of Intelligence Research, Department of State, Intelligence Report No. 5714.5, 30 May 1952.

115. NSC 129/1, April 24, 1952, *FRUS, 1952–1954*, Vol. IX, p. 223. The incoming Eisenhower administration was advised by the CIA that the worldwide threat from the USSR was more of 'Communist exploitation' of 'political and economic difficulties' than of general war. 'Current policies of the government of the United States of America relating to national security', Vol. 1, 1 November 1952, p. I-1, President's Secretary's Files, NSC, Box 194, Truman Library.

116. As Raymond Hare, who became US Ambassador to Cairo in 1956, put it, MEDO was 'the same thing essentially [as MEC] except command was a bad name for it', Raymond Hare, Oral History 189, Eisenhower Library, p. 19.

117. Dulles to Certain Diplomatic Missions, CA-442, July 30, 1953, *FRUS, 1952–1954*, Vol. IX, p. 406. On his return Dulles instituted a review of defence policy which concluded in NSC 162/2, issued in October 1953, that a MEDO based on Egypt was not feasible. Instead attention should be focused on building a northern tier alliance of countries bordering on the USSR. R.J. Watson, *The History of the Joint Chiefs of Staff: Vol. V, 1953–1954* (Washington, DC: Historical Division, Joint Secretariat, Joint Chiefs of Staff, 1986), p. 331.

118. Zafir al-Rifa'i's declaration to *Al-Ahram* broadcast on Damascus Radio, 30 July, SWB Part IV, No. 282, 6 August 1952.

119. Moose to DoS, January 6, 1953, *FRUS, 1952–1954, Vol. IX*, pp. 1093–4. The US, UK, and French Legations in Damascus had been upgraded to Embassies in August 1952.
120. Moose to DoS, November 6, 1952, *FRUS, 1952–1954, Vol. IX*, pp. 1042–4.
121. Acting Secretary of State Bruce to Damascus, November 15, 1952, *FRUS, 1952–1954, Vol. IX*, p. 1064.
122. Memcon between His Excellency Dr Zafir Rifa'i, Syrian Foreign Minister, and Assistant Secretary of State for Near Eastern Affairs, Henry A. Byroade, November 15, 1952, pp. 1056–3; Moose to DoS, November 25, 1952, *FRUS, 1952–1954, Vol. IX*, p. 1071.
123. Moose to DoS, December 8, 1952, *FRUS, 1952–1954, Vol. IX*, p. 1078. The State Department recognised clearly that Shishakli's 'willingness [to] meet United States proposals on Palestine and MEDO is directly proportional to [the] amount [of] military aid [the] United States [is] willing [to] give [to] Syria'. Syria, Summary Paper STA D–5, May 5, 1953, *FRUS, 1952–1954, Vol. IX*, p. 1205.
124. Memcon between Acheson and Israeli Ambassador Abba Eban, January 5, 1953, *FRUS, 1952–1954, Vol. IX*, pp. 1088–93.
125. Memo of Discussion at the 147th Meeting of the NSC, June 1, 1953, *FRUS, 1952–1954, Vol. IX*, p. 381.
126. Memcon between Syrian Ambassador Zeineddine and Mr Jernegan, NEA, September 29, 1953, *FRUS, 1952–1954, Vol. IX*, pp. 1332–6.
127. On Israel's retaliation policy, see: B. Blechmann, 'The impact of Israel's reprisals on behaviour of the bordering Arab nations', *Journal of Conflict Resolution*, Vol. XVI, No. 2 (June 1972), pp. 155–81 and B. Morris, *Israel's Border Wars, 1949–1956* (Oxford: Clarendon Press, 1993).
128. 'Trends in Israeli policy toward the Arabs', November 1953, *FRUS, 1952–1954, Vol. IX*, pp. 1406–9.
129. On the river project, see: Jordan-Yarmuk River Projects, STA D–1/6, May 4, 1953, *FRUS, 1952–1954, Vol. IX*, pp. 1185–8. For Israel's position, see: Memcon Ambassador Eban and Mr Byroade, NEA, November 20, 1953, *FRUS, 1952–1954, Vol. IX*, pp. 1426–30.
130. Dulles to Johnston, October 13, 1953, *FRUS, 1952–1954, Vol. IX*, p. 1351.
131. Moose to DoS, January 4, 1954, *FRUS, 1952–1954, Vol. IX*, pp. 1477–8. The Johnston plan was eventually vetoed by the USSR in the UN Security council on 22 January 1954. *Facts on File, 1954*, p. 27.
132. NARG 59, Clark to DoS, 783.00/1–2753; Kobecsy interview, 27 February 1992, Beirut. Kobecsy himself had been promised the governorship of Latakia, but these promises were never fulfilled.
133. PRO, FO 371/91844/EY1015/77, Montagu-Pollock to Furlonge, 11 December 1951. Mousli interview, 11 July 1993, Damascus. Shishakli had close ties to Hawrani, whom he relied upon to mobilise support among the upcountry peasantry. See: N.M. Kaylani, 'The rise of the Syrian Ba'th, 1940–1958: political success, party failure', *International Journal of Middle East Studies*, Vol. 3, No. 1 (1972), pp. 3–23.
134. The British Minister regarded the Ba'th as an 'insignificant satellite' of the ASP at the time. PRO, FO 371/98916/EY1016/1, Montagu-Pollock to Eden, 9 January 1952.
135. PRO, FO 371/98916/EY1016/8, Montagu-Pollock to Eden, 8 April 1952; 'New Syrian party seen regime's aim', *New York Times*, 8 April 1952. The Brotherhood had been banned in January and there had been numerous clashes between its supporters and the security forces. 'Dissolution de l'association des Frères musulmans', *Le Monde*, 21 January 1952; 'Beirut', *New York Times*, 26 January

1952; PRO, FO 371/98916/EY1016/2, Montagu-Pollock to Eden, 22 January 1952.
136. E. Picard, *Espaces de Reference et Espace d'Intervention du Mouvement Rectificatif au Pouvoir en Syrie 1970–1982* (Paris: n.pb., n.d.), p. 105. According to Joubran Hayek, then editor of the party's paper, relations were worsened by the personal rivalry between Shishakli and Georges 'Abd al-Masih, SSNP president since Sa'adah's death. Masih tried to assert his authority over Shishakli, who refused to accept it. Hayek interview, 13 February 1992, Beirut.
137. 'Army chief pushes sole Syrian party', *New York Times*, 25 October 1952.
138. Mousli interview, 11 July 1993; PRO, FO 371/104965/EY1011/1; FO 371/98915/EY1015/12, Samuel to Ross, 5 September 1952.
139. Ibrahim Husayni had become Chief of Military Police after the coup and replaced Fu'ad Aswad as Director General of Police and Sûreté in June. 'A la tête de la police syrienne', *La Bourse Egyptienne*, 4 August 1952; NARG 59, Moose to DoS, 783.00/1–253.
140. Interviews with Bourhan Kassab-Hassan, 10 May and 8 June 1993, Damascus. Kassab-Hassan was one of the officers involved in the incident.
141. 'Nombreuses arrestations en Syrie', *Le Monde*, 30 December 1952.
142. 'Arrest of Syrian army officers', *The Times*, 29 December 1952; NARG 59, Moose to DoS, 783.00/1–1353.
143. PRO, FO 371/104967/EY1015/4, Montagu-Pollock to Eden, 13 January 1952. See also: FO 371/104967/EY1015/3, Montagu-Pollock to Ross, 2 January 1953; FO 371/98916/EY1016/21, Montagu-Pollock to FO, 27 December 1952; '18 Syrian officers ousted', *New York Herald Tribune*, 30 December 1952.
144. '3 leaders politiques syriens se réfugient au Liban', *L'Orient*, 4 January 1953; 'Syrian fugitives in Lebanon', *The Times*, 5 January 1952; 'Le Gouvernement syrien ordonne a tous ses ressortissents qui se trouvent au Liban de rentrer dans les 48 heures', *La Bourse Egyptienne*, 8 January 1952; NARG 59, Moose to DoS, 783.00/1–1953; PRO, FO 371/104967/EY1015/5, Samuel to Ross, 30 January 1953. In June the Lebanese authorities deported Hawrani, 'Aflaq and Bitar to Switzerland. 'Liban', *Le Monde*, 24 June 1953.
145. 'L'Ombre de la guerre civile se profile a Damas', *Le Monde*, 20 January 1953.
146. 'Constitution for Syria', *The Times*, 22 June 1953; 'Le général Chichackly a été plébiscité', *Le Monde*, 14 July 1953; M.L. Manley, 'The Syrian constitution of 1953', *Middle East Journal*, Vol. 7, No. 4 (Autumn 1953), pp. 520–38.
147. The Interior Minister resigned in the run-up to the elections protesting at government interference in the electoral process. PRO, FO 371/111137/VY1011/1.
148. Although the SSNP had helped Shishakli draft his constitution, they had been denied any senior government or military posts. After the election, the party had one member in parliament, but its leaders believed that they owed this fortune to a 'mistake' on Shishakli's part. Mousli interview, 11 July 1993; Kobecsy interview, 27 February 1992; PRO, FO 371/104966/EY1013/10; FO 371/104966/EY1013/11; 'Syrian parliament set', *New York Times*, 11 October 1953.
149. NARG 59, Caffery to DoS, 783.00/2–2654; Geren to DoS, 783.00/9–2853.
150. Bombs which exploded in March in the grounds of Shishakli's residence and in April at an office of the ALM may have been planted by members of the ASP. NARG 59, 783.00/3–2053; PRO, FO 371/104966/EY1013/5.
151. PRO, FO 371/104966/EY1013/11. The Ba'th-ASP alliance unravelled when Hawrani became estranged from 'Aflaq and Bitar during Dawilibi's secessionist government in 1962. Nonetheless, the Ba'th have retained the title ABSP since. J.F. Devlin, *The Ba'th Party: A History from its Origins to 1966* (Stanford University, Stanford, CA: Hoover Institution Press, 1976), p. 64; O. Roberts, *The Ba'th and*

the Creation of Modern Syria (London: Croom Helm, 1987), pp. 52–3.
152. 'Quatre mois de dictature militaire bicéphale', *Le Monde*, 8 April 1952.
153. Arab News Agency, 20 March, SWB Part IV, No. 245, 28 March 1952.
154. PRO, FO 371/98920/EY10393/2, Montagu-Pollock to Wardrop, 14 January 1952; EY10393/12, Samuel to Ross, 18 July 1952; EY10393/13, Samuel to FO, 4 December 1952.
155. PRO, FO 371/110986.
156. NARG 59, Moose to DoS, 783.00/4–1053; Moose to DoS, 783.00/4–2253; PRO, FO 371/104986/EY1591/1, Montagu-Pollock to FO, 13 April 1953; EY1591/2, Washington to FO, 11 April 1953.
157. PRO, FO 371/104967/EY1015/18.
158. PRO, FO 371/98246/EY1013/6.
159. PRO, FO 371/104967/EY1015/20, Montagu-Pollock to Ross, 26 May 1953.
160. 'Un gouvernement de la "Syrie libre" est constitué a Bagdad', *Le Monde*, 17 October 1953; PRO, FO 371/104986/EY1591/6, Gardener to Falla, 4 November 1953.
161. This was Hamdi Salih. NARG 59, Moose to DoS, 783.00/2–1254; PRO, FO 371/111139/VY1016/1. It was also suggested that Husayni was dismissed because he was plotting with opposition leaders against Shishakli. NARG 59, Moose to DoS, 783.00/1–454; Moose to DoS, 783.00/12–1553; PRO, FO 371/111138/VY1013/1.
162. The French had been especially annoyed by British attempts to break into the Syrian arms market by supplying jets and radar equipment to the Air Force. NARG 59, Moose to DoS, 783.00/3–454.
163. 'Political arrests in Syria', *The Times*, 28 January 1954; 'Disorders in Syria', *The Times*, 29 January 1954; PRO, FO 371/111139/VY1016/2.
164. PRO, FO 371/111139/VY1016/6.
165. This according to 'Adnan Hamdun, who commanded an army unit in the region. The Foreign Office believed that they had been sent to arrest Sultan Pasha al-Atrash. PRO, FO 371/111138/VY1013/2; interview with 'Adnan Hamdun, 5 June 1993, Damascus.
166. PRO, FO 371/111139/VY1016/2.
167. Hamdun interview, 5 June 1993.
168. Several bombs were detonated in Damascus during the fighting, possibly by Druze fighters. NARG 59, Moose to DoS, 783.00/2–54.
169. PRO, FO 371/111139/VY1016/12.
170. 'Sanglants combats au Djebel Druze', *Le Populaire*, 30 January 1954; PRO, FO 371/111139/VY1016/18; VY1016/29, Furlonge to FO, 15 February 1954.
171. Arab News Agency, 2 February, SWB Part IV, No. 438, 9 February 1954; 'Al-Aslihah al-hadithah fi Muhafazat al-Suwayda', *al-Faiha'*, 2 February 1954.
172. 'La Jordanie assure à la Syrie son entière collaboration', *La Bourse Egyptienne*, 5 February 1954; PRO, FO 371/111140/VY1016/78.
173. PRO, FO 371/111139/VY1016/37.
174. On Safa, see: Israel Radio, 30 June, SWB Part IV, No. 377, 7 July 1953; Israel Radio, 6 August, SWB Part IV, No. 388, 14 August 1953.
175. Israel Radio, 1 February, SWB Part IV, No. 438, 9 February 1954; 'Druze M.K.'s score Syrian aggression', and 'Shishakly has foes all over', *Jerusalem Post*, 2 February 1954; 'Knesset committee debates Druze plea', *Jerusalem Post*, 3 February 1954.
176. M. Sharett, *Personal Diary* (Tel Aviv: n.pb., 1978), Vol. II, p. 333. (in Hebrew). My thanks to Ronnie Bregman for locating and translating the *Diary* extracts used here.

177. 'The events in Syria', 21 February 1954, 2408/20/c, Foreign Ministry Files, Israel State Archives. My thanks to Itai Yemeni for searching the archives on my behalf and to Ronnie Bregman for translating the document.
178. Sharett, *Personal Diary*, Vol. II, p. 374.
179. Sharett, *Personal Diary*, Vol. II, p. 379.
180. 'Tafsilat mu'amarat al-inkliz al-kubra 'ala istiqlal Suriah', *Al-Faiha'*, 2 February 1954.
181. NARG 59, Caffery to DoS, 783.00/2-154; Cairo Radio, 1 February, SWB Part IV, No. 438, 9 February 1954.
182. PRO, FO 371/111140/EY1016/41, Minute, Iraq and the Syrian Disturbances, 16 February 1954.
183. PRO, FO 371/111139/VY1016/29, Gardener to FO, 10 February 1954.
184. PRO, FO 371/111139/VY1016/17, Furlonge to FO, 5 February 1954; Hamdun interview, 5 June 1993. Glubb Pasha reported that the revolt in the Jabal Druze was 'organised and paid for by the Iraqi Government'. PRO, FO 371/111139/VY1016/8.
185. PRO, FO 371/111140/VY1016/42, 'Political background on recent events in Syria'.
186. Shishakli's agents discovered a letter from Safa to Atrash in the latter's home. PRO, FO 371/111139/VY1016/25, Gardener to FO, No. 78, 8 February 1954.
187. NARG 59, Berry to DoS, 783.00/3-554.
188. NARG 59, Moose to DoS, 783.00/2-54.
189. PRO, FO 371/111140/EY1016/41, 'Iraq and the Syrian disturbances', 16 February 1954.
190. 'La Syrie demande le rappel de l'Attaché Militaire Irakien', *La Bourse Egyptienne*, 6 February 1954; *Bulletin de la Presse Syrienne*, No. 598, Rubrique III.
191. Radio Damascus, 10 February, SWB Part IV, No. 440, 16 February 1954.
192. Arab News Agency, 2 February, SWB Part IV, No. 438, 9 February 1954.
193. Damascus Radio, 2 February, SWB Part IV, No. 438, 9 February 1954.
194. 'Voice of the Arabs', 4 February, SWB Part IV, No. 439, 12 February 1954.
195. 'Les entretiens Chichakly-Yafi', *La Bourse Egyptienne*, 19 February 1954.
196. NARG 59, Moose to DoS, 783.00/3-1254.
197. Most of the details of the plot are taken from NARG 59, Moose to DoS, 783.00/3-1154. See also PRO, FO 371/111140/VY1016/57, Gardener to FO, 26 February 1954; VY1016/85, Gardener to Eden, 8 March 1954.
198. According to Bourhan Kassab-Hassan, who was dismissed from the army on his release from prison in mid-1953, 70–80 per cent of the army's NCOs were from the minorities. Kassab-Hassan interviews, 10 May and 8 June 1993.
199. Muhammad al-Atrash was, like his cousin Mansur, a Ba'thist.
200. Aleppo Radio, 25 February, SWB Part IV, No. 444, 2 March 1954; 'Syrian rebels seize radio station,' *Christian Science Monitor*, 25 February 1954.
201. However, this only gave them control of about 7,500 troops out of a 37,000-strong army. NARG 59, Moose to DoS, 783.00/3-454.
202. Shuqayr was a Lebanese Druze officer who had been made Chief of Staff by Shishakli.
203. 'Adnan Hamdun, Mustafa's brother, was stationed in the Jabal Druze and recalls arresting two pro-Shishakli officers in his unit, one an SSNP member and one a Palestinian, on hearing the first Aleppo radio broadcast. Hamdun interview, 5 June 1993.
204. NARG 59, Moose to DoS, 783.00/3-454.
205. NARG 59, Moose to DoS, 783.00/3-454; PRO, FO 371/111140/VY1016/

69, Chapman Andrews to FO, 27 February 1954. An arrangement between the Iraqi Embassy in Beirut and Lebanese Druze leaders to assassinate him was called off when he left for Sa'udi Arabia. He was assassinated in Brazil on 27 September 1964 by a Druze seeking revenge for the repression in the Jabal Druze. P. Seale, *The Struggle for Syria* (New Haven: Yale University Press, 1986), p. 146; *Cahiers de L'Orient Contemporarian* LVI (1964), p. 469.

206. This group was led by Colonel Tal'at 'Abd al-Qadir, formerly Ibrahim Husayni's assistant, and Captain 'Abd al-Hamid Sarraj, commander of a unit which had freed Shuqayr from his temporary arrest.

207. For a summary of the rival radio broadcasts during these events, see: SWB Part IV, No. 445, 5 March 1954, pp. 53–63; *Bulletin de la Presse Syrienne*, No. 604, Supplement No. 225.

208. NARG 59, Moose to DoS, 783.00/3-454; On the struggle for power between 25 February and 1 March, see: PRO, FO 371/111140/VY1016/64, Gardener to FO, 27 February; VY1016/65, Gardener to FO, 27 February 1954; VY1016/66, 27 February 1954; VY1016/71, 28 February 1954; 'Syria fears strife as Shishakly unit holds Damascus', *New York Times*, 27 February 1954; 'Loyal Syrian troops battle rebels in Damascus streets', *New York Herald Tribune*, 28 February 1954; 'Atassi is Syrian President', *New York Times*, 1 March 1954.

209. Baghdad Radio, 1 March, SWB Part IV, No. 445, 5 March 1954; 'Bagdad', *Le Monde*, 2 March 1954.

210. NARG 59, Moose to DoS, 783.00/3-454.

211. Many officers were concerned at Shishakli's increasingly arbitrary treatment of them in ordering summary transfers and retirements and cancelling pensions. NARG 59, Moose to DoS, 783.00/3-1154.

212. The Lebanese deputy, Emile Bustani, had earlier offered Shishakli a million dollars to take Syria into a union with Iraq. After Shishakli's downfall, Bustani boasted that since Shishakli had refused 'we' therefore spent the money on backing the coup. Recounted to Bachir Mousli by 'Isam Mahaiyri. Mousli interview, 11 July 1993. Iraqi military documents subsequently made public appeared to show that 21,000 dinars had been paid out during the revolt. *Bulletin de la Presse Syrienne*, No. 1049, Rubrique III.

213. PRO, FO 371/111140/VY1016/42, Melville to Thompson, 16 February 1954.

214. NARG 59, Moose to DoS, 783.00/3-454; 'Vers le Croissant Fertile', *Le Monde*, 27 February 1954.

215. PRO, FO 371/104967/EY1015/23, 'Iraqi-Syrian-Jordanian relations'; 111140/VY1016/75, Gardener to FO, 1 March 1954; NARG 59, Moose to DoS, 783.00/3-454.

4 Syria between Nasser and the West

1. For overviews of events, see: H. Laurens, *Le Grand Jeu: Orient Arabe et Rivalités Internationales* (Paris: Armand Colin, 1991), pp. 157–61 and G.H. Torrey, *Syrian Politics and the Military, 1945–1958* (Ohio State University Press, 1964), pp. 245–331.

2. On this period see: P. Seale, *The Struggle for Syria* (New Haven, CT: Yale University Press, 1986), pp. 164–85.

3. Bourhan Kassab Hassan, who was reinstated to the army as Director of Information and Education in 1954, recalls a meeting in which Malki castigated two politically active officers, Riyad Malki, his brother, and 'Abd al-Ghani Qannut

for carrying out political activity in the army. Kassab-Hassan interviews, 10 May and 8 June 1993, Damascus.
    4. National Archives and Records Administration, Record Group 59 (hereafter NARG 59), Moose to Department of State (hereafter DoS), 783.00/4–254.
    5. NARG 59, Clark to DoS, 783.00/5–1854; Clark to DoS, 783.00/5–1954; Public Records Office (hereafter PRO), Foreign Office (hereafter FO) 371/111138/VY1013/6; 111140/VY1016/92, Gardener to Eden, 14 May 1954; 111148/VY 10316/1, Gardener to Falla, 19 May 1954.
    6. *Bulletin de la Presse Syrienne*, No. 634, Supplement No. 240.
    7. NARG 59, Moose to DoS, 783.00/6–2154; PRO, FO 371/111141/VY1016/103, Gardener to Eden, 22 June 1954; *Bulletin de la Presse Syrienne*, No. 633, Rubrique III and No. 640, Rubrique III.
    8. NARG 59, Strong to DoS, 783.00/10–2054. The results were: Independents: 71; People's Party: 31; National Party: 19; ABSP: 16; SSNP: 2; Socialist Co-operative: 2; Communist: 1. PRO, FO 371/111138/VY1013/10; VY1013/11.
    9. However, Baghdad refused the Iraqi Minister's requests for up to 100,000 dinars to finance anti-ABSP candidates in the Hama area. PRO, FO 371/111141/VY1016/114, Damascus to FO, 14 September 1954; NARG 59, Yost to DoS, 783.00/2–2558.
    10. NARG 59, Strong to Secretary of State (hereafter SS), 783.00/9–2854.
    11. NARG 59, Strong to DoS, 783.00/9–3054.
    12. NARG 59, Strong to DoS, 783.00/10–654; PRO, FO 371/111149/VY 10317/3, Gardener to Falla, 10 November 1954; VY 10317/4, Gardener to Falla, 21 December 1954.
    13. NARG 59, Strong to DoS, 783.00/10–2754; Strong to DoS, 783.00/10–754; Strong to DoS, 783.00/10–2054.
    14. R.J. Watson, *The History of the Joint Chiefs of Staff: Volume V, 1953–1954* (Washington, DC: Historical Division, Joint Secretariat, Joint Chiefs of Staff, 1986), p. 345. On Iraq's foreign policy at the time, see: M. Khadduri, *Republican Iraq* (London: Oxford University Press/Royal Institute of International Affairs, 1969), p. 53. On the USSR's reactions to the Pact, see D.J. Dallin, *Soviet Foreign Policy After Stalin* (New York: J.B. Lippincott Co, 1961), pp. 201–3.
    15. On Nasser's turn to pan-Arabism and neutralism, see: P. Mansfield, *Nasser* (London: Methuen Educational Ltd, 1969), pp. 92–9.
    16. NARG 59, Moose to DoS, 783.00/1–2555.
    17. NARG 59, Moose to DoS, 783.00/2–455.
    18. NARG 59, Moose to DoS, 783.00/2–1555.
    19. NARG 59, Moose to DoS, 783.00/2–155.
    20. NARG 59, Moose to DoS, 783.00/5–2354; Strong to DoS, 783.00/10–454. The Operations Coordinating Board (OCB) did, however, discuss the possible 'targets of opportunity' suggested by the Damascus Embassy. Bishop to Mc-Causland, 9 June 1954, White House Office (hereafter WHO)/National Security Council Staff (hereafter NSC)/OCB Central Files (hereafter OCBCF), Eisenhower Library. The OCB had been established by President Eisenhower in September 1953 to achieve inter-agency coordination of the United States' 'overt and covert capabilities – political, psychological, military, economic, cultural, and informational' in the Cold War. 'Memorandum for the Executive Secretary, National Security Council', 2 September 1953 and Rockefeller to Eisenhower, 22 December 1955, OCB 5214 Gp/Confidential Files (hereafter CF)/Dwight D. Eisenhower White House Central Files (hereafter DDEWHCF), Eisenhower Library.
    21. Briefing paper, 'Syria and Lebanon', 17 December 1954, *Foreign Relations of the United States, 1955–1957, Vol XIII* (Washington, DC: US Government

Printing Office)(hereafter *FRUS* with year and volume), pp. 513–14.
  22. J.F. Dulles to A.W. Dulles, telephone call, 27 December 1954, Telephone Calls Series (hereafter TC)/J.F. Dulles Papers (hereafter JFD), Eisenhower Library.
  23. NARG 59, Moose to DoS, 783.00/2–155.
  24. *FRUS, 1955–1957, Vol. XIII*, pp. 514–15.
  25. PRO, FO 371/121856/VY1011/1; *FRUS, 1955–1957, Vol. XIII*, pp. 514–15; NARG 59, Moose to SS, 783.00/2–2155.
  26. NARG 59, Moose to DoS, 783.00/6–2855.
  27. NARG 59, Moose to SS, 783.00/2–2655; Dulles to Damascus, 16 February 1955, *FRUS, 1955–1957, Vol. XIII*, p. 516.
  28. NARG 59, Joint Weeka, 783.00(W)/3–1155.
  29. *FRUS, 1955–1957, Vol. XIII*, p. 518 and Moose to DoS, 8 March 1955, p. 519.
  30. NARG 59, Gallman to SS, 783.00/4–1355; Moose to SS, 783.00/4–1655; Gallman to SS, 783.00/4–1455; Dulles to Baghdad, 783.00/4–1355; Dulles to Damascus, 783.00/4–1355.
  31. NARG 59, Moose to SS, 783.00/4–1655.
  32. In the chaos it was unclear to some observers whether the assassin had committed suicide or was shot by someone else. The autopsy identified the bullets in Malki as coming from a different gun from those which killed the assassin. This led to false stories that the sergeant was shot either by the chief of the Military Police detail, Akram Dayri, or by one of his own accomplices. Mousli interview, 11 July 1993, Damascus; Qaddurah interview, 8 July 1993, Beirut; NARG 59, Moose to DoS, 783.00/4–2755; PRO, FO 371/115945/VY1015/31, Gardener to Macmillan, 27 April 1955; *Bulletin de la Presse Syrienne*, No. 716, Rubrique III and No. 733, Supplement No. 300.
  33. NARG 59, Joint Weeka, 783.00(W)/2–2555.
  34. NARG 59, Moose to DoS, 783.00/4–2755.
  35. M. Tlass, *Mir'at hayati (Mirror to my Life)* (Damascus: Dar al-Tlass, n.d.), pp. 465–84.
  36. NARG 59, Moose to SS, 783.00/12–1555.
  37. *Bulletin de la Presse Syrienne*, No. 726, Rubrique III.
  38. Transcripts of the trials are held in the Jafet library, American University of Beirut (AUB). For the indictments, see: Malki Trial, File 4, Middle East Files, Jafet Library, AUB. See also NARG 59, Moose to SS, 783.00/7–1955 and Moose to DoS, 783.00/9–2355.
  39. NARG 59, Moose to SS, 783.00/7–1955; *Bulletin de la Presse Syrienne*, No. 733, Supplement No. 300 and No. 779, Supplement No. 347.
  40. 'Shuqayr yu'akkid wujud addilah kashafat al-mu'amarah', *Lisan al-Sha'b*, 28 April 1955; *Bulletin de la Presse Syrienne*, No. 717, Rubrique III.
  41. *Bulletin de la Presse Syrienne*, No. 756, Supplement No. 324; NARG 59, Moose to DoS, 783.00/9–2355. Kassab-Hassan interviews 10 May and 8 June 1993; Alwan interview 10 August 1993, Cairo. For other accusations see, NARG 59, Moose to DoS, 783.00/11–155.
  42. Two weeks after the assassination Malik remarked to John Foster Dulles that the 'situation in Syria is bad and it is a matter of days before … it will be under Communist control'. J.F. Dulles to A.W. Dulles, telephone call, 5 May 1955, TC/JFD, Eisenhower Library.
  43. Sitting 8/30, Testimony of 'Isam Mahaiyri, Malki Trial, File 2, Middle East Files, Jafet Library, AUB, pp. 3–4; 'Al-watha'iq allati tudin al-hizb al-qawmi al-Suri', *Barada*, 8 May 1955; *Bulletin de la Presse Syrienne*, No. 749, Rubrique III and No. 754, Supplement No. 321.

44. Interviews with Bourhan Kassab-Hassan, 10 May and 8 June 1993; 'Adnan Hamdun, 5 June 1993, Damascus; Qasim Alwan, 10 August 1993.
45. Interviews with Bachir Mousli, 11 July 1993; 'Abdallah Kobecsy, 27 February 1992, Beirut; Adib Qaddurah, 8 July 1993. See also: A. Qaddurah, *Haqa'iq wa-mawaqif (Facts and Opinions)* (Beirut: Dar mu'assasat al-fikr, 1989), pp. 147–53.
46. Bodron, *Violence in the Syrian Social Nationalist Party*, pp. 59–64.
47. Tlass, *Mir'at hayati*, pp. 477–8.
48. NARG 59, Moose to DoS, 783.00/11-555.
49. PRO, FO 371/115945/VY1015/35, Gardener to Rose, 3 May 1955.
50. PRO, FO 371/115945/VY1015/39, Gardener to Rose, 1 June 1955.
51. NARG 59, Moose to DoS, 783.00/6-2955.
52. NARG 59, Moose to DoS, 783.00/6-2955.
53. PRO, FO 371/115946/VY10345/1, Damascus to FO, 28 September 1955; *Bulletin de la Presse Syrienne*, No. 754, Rubrique III; Torrey, *Syrian Politics and the Military*, p. 296.
54. NARG 59, Moose to SS, 783.00/12-1555. Makhluf and Dubussy were eventually executed on 3 September 1956. Quwatli, deterred by rumours of SSNP hit squads waiting to take revenge, had refused to authorise the executions but eventually succumbed to ABSP pressure. PRO, FO 371/121858/VY 1015/44, Gardener to FO, 30 June 1956; 121859/VY1015/62, Damascus to FO, 5 September 1956.
55. Soon after the assassination the Syrian press had reported that foreign states were helping the SSNP to stockpile arms in the 'Alawite mountains and that fugitives were being protected by the Lebanese security services. At the time these stories were probably untrue but during the next year both things took place. *Bulletin de la Presse Syrienne*, No. 718, Rubrique III and No. 719, Rubrique III.
56. Party members recall an abortive plot to kill Sarraj when he visited Beirut for medical treatment in the mid-1960s. At the time of writing, Sarraj lives in retirement in Egypt under the protection of Egyptian intelligence, and keeps well away from the SSNP's strongholds in Lebanon. Interviews with various party members, July 1993, Beirut; letter from SSNP officer Hisham Abu Jaoude, 27 November 1993.
57. NARG 59, Moose to DoS, 783.00/6-1555.
58. NARG 59, Hoover to Damascus, 783.00/5-1355; Memcon 'Exchange of views with French Foreign Ministry representatives', 783.00/6-655.
59. NARG 59, Moose to DoS, 783.00/6-1555.
60. PRO, FO 371/115946/VY1015/45, Beaumont to Gardener, 27 June 1955.
61. NARG 59, 'Intelligence note: crisis in Syria', 783.00/6-355.
62. 'Analysis of internal security situation in Syria', 7 July 1955, *FRUS, 1955–1957, Vol. XIII*, pp. 530–7.
63. NARG 59, Moose to SS, 783.00/5-755; Moose to SS, 783.00/6-455.
64. NARG 59, Moose to SS, 783.00/5-255.
65. NARG 59, Moose to SS, 783.00/6-2455.
66. PRO, FO 371/115946/VY1015/50, Gallagher to Macmillan, 20 July 1955; NARG 59, Moose to DoS, 783.00/11-2155.
67. Shuqayr told the US Military Attaché that Sarraj had had his full authority in carrying out the arrests. However, it seems likely that this was just to cover up the fact that 'the power ... [was] in Sarraj's hands with Shuqayr as [a] front'. NARG 59, Army Attaché to SS, 783.00/7-1455.
68. PRO, FO 371/115946/VY1015/50, Gallagher to Macmillan, 20 July 1955.
69. NARG 59, Moose to SS, 783.00/7-2055.
70. NARG 59, Moose to SS, 783.00/7-2955.

71. The election was among parliamentary deputies.
72. A colourful example of Sa'udi influence was provided by 'Isam Husayni, Ibrahim's brother and former head of archives at the Deuxième Bureau. He reported that a notorious Bureau agent, Sami Juma', who had lost his job just before the 1954 coup, had been reinstated into the service after the intervention of Amin Nakhli, a Lebanese poet and Sa'udi client who was friendly with Sabri 'Asali. Nakhli used Sa'udi money to pay off Juma''s debts and the latter now acted as a 'procurer' for the homosexual Nakhli and 'Asali. NARG 59, Moose to DoS, 783.00/6-2855.
73. PRO, FO 371/121856/VY1011/1; 115946/VY1015/58, Gallagher to FO, 18 August 1955; NARG 59, Moose to SS, 783.00/5-2555; Moose to SS, 783.00/8-1755; Moose to SS, 783.00/8-1855.
74. NARG 59, Moose to SS, 783.00/8-2355.
75. PRO, FO 371/115946/VY1015/68, 'The new president of Syria', 19 August 1955.
76. NARG 59, Joint Weeka, 783.00(W)/10-2855; Joint Weeka, 783.00(W)/11-1855; PRO, FO 371/121856/VY1011/1.
77. Moose to DoS, 14 October 1955, *FRUS, 1955–1957, Vol. XIII*, pp. 553–7.
78. NARG 59, Moose to SS, 783.00/10-2455; Moose to SS, 783.00/10-3055.
79. PRO, FO 371/115954/VY10393/10, Record of Conversation in the State Department, 27 October 1955. Harold Macmillan, Foreign Secretary until September, describes British fears of Soviet encroachment in his memoirs. H. Macmillan, *Tides of Fortune, 1945–1955* (London: Macmillan, 1969), pp. 635–60.
80. PRO, FO 371/115954/VY10393/1, FO to Baghdad, 8 October 1955.
81. PRO, FO 371/115954/VY10393/7, Arthur Minute: 'Iraq and Syria: the Fertile Crescent', 10 October 1955.
82. PRO, FO 371/115954/VY10393/1, FO to Baghdad, 8 October 1955; VY 10393/8, Hooper to Rose, 12 October 1955. See also A. Nutting, *No End of a Lesson: The Story of Suez* (London: Constable, 1967), p. 41.
83. PRO, FO 371/115954/VY10393/1, Hooper to FO, 5 October 1955.
84. Gallman to DoS, 4 October 1955, *FRUS, 1955–1957, Vol. XIII*, pp. 543–4.
85. NARG 59, Gallman to SS, 783.00/10-2455.
86. PRO, FO 371/121665, Wright to FO, 28 January 1956; 115954/VY10393/5, Shuckburgh to FO, 7 October 1955.
87. NARG 59, Gallman to SS, 783.00/5-955; PRO, FO 371/121870/10393/21, Gardener to Rose, 28 May 1956.
88. NARG 59, Moose to SS, 783.00/8-2655; Heath to SS, 783.00/8-3055; PRO, FO 371/115946/1015/66, Tesh to FO, 22 August 1955.
89. PRO, FO 371/115954/VY10393/8, Hooper to Rose, 12 October 1955; 115947/VY1015/94, Stewart to Rose, 6 December 1955.
90. NARG 59, Gallman to SS, 783.00/11-255.
91. PRO, FO 371/115954/VY10393/1, Hooper to FO, 5 October 1955; FO to Baghdad, 8 October 1955; VY10393/7, Arthur Minute: 'Iraq and Syria: the Fertile Crescent', 10 October 1955; Dulles to Baghdad, 6 October 1955, *FRUS, 1955–1957, Vol. XIII*, pp. 545–6.
92. PRO, FO 371/121870/VY10393/6, Wright to FO, 28 February 1956; VY 10393/20, Gardener to FO, 28 April 1956.
93. Since 1951 the Syrian army had used Palestinian refugees to gather intelligence in the Galilee and sabotage Israeli construction equipment in the DZs. B. Morris, *Israel's Border Wars, 1949–1956*, (Oxford: Clarendon Press, 1993) p. 66.
94. Y. Caroz, *The Arab Secret Services* (London: Corgi, 1978), pp. 264–5; 'Syrie', *Le Monde*, 23 December 1955.
95. NARG 59, Memcon 'Situation in Syria', 783.00/5-555.

96. RG319, ID File, R–414–55, 18 October 1955, Declassified Documents Project, Centre for Lebanese Studies, Oxford (hereafter CLS); Mousli interview, 11 July 1993.
97. CLS, RG319, ID File, R–454–55, 15 November 1955.
98. For details see: S/3319 and Annex IV to S/3373, *Security Council Official Records* (hereafter *SCOR*), *Supplement, 1954*; S/3660 and S/3685, *SCOR*, *Supplement, 1955–1956*.
99. PRO, FO 371/121858/VY1015/4, Gardener to Rose, 14 February 1956.
100. Nasser had concluded a preliminary agreement with Czechoslovakia in February, in response to the Turkish-Iraqi treaty. See: U. Ra'anan, *The USSR Arms the Third World* (Cambridge, MA: MIT Press, 1969), Part I.
101. Syria had bought 45 Mk IV tanks at the knock-down price of $2,408 each. Before these arrived, Syria had only one armoured brigade of 50 Sherman tanks. PRO, FO 371/115967/VY1192/1, 'Form at a glance: Syria', M14(b)2170, March 1955; Memorandum from Allen to Dulles, 25 June 1956, *FRUS, 1955–1957, Vol. XIII*, pp. 574–8.
102. NARG 59, Joint Weeka, 783.00(W)/11–2555.
103. PRO, FO 371/121856/VY1011/1
104. NARG 59, Joint Weeka, 783.00(W)/11–1855; Moose to DoS, 10 September 1955, *FRUS, 1955–1957, Vol. XIII*, pp. 540–2; Moose to DoS, 9 October 1955, p. 547; Memorandum from Allen to Hoover, 11 October 1955, pp. 550–1 and 8 December 1955, pp. 558–60.
105. NARG 59, Moose to DoS, 783.00/11–2155.
106. Nine soldiers were wounded. S/3516, *SCOR*, *Supplement, 1955–1956*. See also: Morris, *Israel's Border Wars, 1949–1956*, pp. 281–2.
107. The Lebanese newspaper *L'Orient* attributed 'Abd al-Hamid Sarraj's subsequent uncompromising hostility to the United States to the shock of this disaster. 'La Syrie sous le néo-socialisme', *L'Orient*, 30 August 1957.
108. PRO, FO 371/115947/1015/96, Gardener to FO, 15 December 1955.
109. NARG 59, Joint Weeka, 783.00(W)/12–3055.
110. NARG 59, Joint Weeka, 783.00(W)/12–1655.
111. Presumably 'undesireables' included the communist organisers of labour troubles which took place in Aleppo on 8 and 9 February. PRO, FO 371/121858/VY1015/1, Bowker to FO, 14 February 1956; VY1015/2, Rose Minute 'Iraq and Syria', 22 February 1956 and Gardener to FO, 16 February 1956.
112. Additionally, and rather tactlessly, Fansah's plan involved replacing Nuri with an Iraqi Prime Minister more acceptable to Syrian public opinion. PRO, FO 371/121858/VY1015/8, Bowker to Shuckburgh, 28 February 1956.
113. PRO, FO 371/121858/VY1015/13, Stevens to FO, No. 187, 10 March 1956.
114. The agreement, ratified in December, brought Syria $42 million. NARG 59, Joint Weeka, 783.00(W)/12–955.
115. Memorandum from Allen to Dulles, 25 June 1956, *FRUS, 1955–1957, Vol. XIII*, pp. 574–8. Defence Minister Muhammad Rashad Barmada records Czech deliveries of MiG 15s, 17s and BTR armoured personnel carriers as well as the T-34s. M.R. Barmada, *Dhikrayat wa-ara'* (*Memoirs and Opinions*) unpublished manuscript kindly loaned to this writer.
116. Seale, *The Struggle for Syria*, pp. 263–82.
117. A. Gorst and W.S. Lucas, 'The other collusion: Operation Straggle and Anglo-American intervention in Syria, 1955–56', *Intelligence and National Security*, Vol. 4, No. 3, (1989). One source claims that the US side of the operation was codenamed 'Wakeful'. J. Prados, *Presidents' Secret Wars* (New York: William Morrow and Co, 1986), p. 129.

118. W.C. Eveland, *Ropes of Sand: America's Failure in the Middle East* (New York: W.W. Norton and Co, 1980), Little, Gorst and Lucas all made extensive use of the book as do other accounts. See: J. Bloch and P. Fitzgerald, *British Intelligence and Covert Action* (Dingle: Brondon, 1983); Prados, *Presidents' Secret Wars*, pp. 128–30; W. Blum, *The CIA: A Forgotten History: US Global Interventions since WW2* (London: Zed Books, 1986), p. 91.

119. 'Ropes of sand: America's failure in the Middle East', *Studies in Intelligence*, Vol. 27, No. 3 (Fall 1983), pp. 105–6. Obtained from the CIA under the Freedom of Information Act (hereafter FOIA).

120. Anonymous communication 1.

121. H.F. Eilts, 'Ropes of sand: America's failure in the Middle East', *Middle East Journal*, Vol. 38, No. 2 (Spring 1984), pp. 324–7. These views were reiterated in an interview with Ambassador Eilts. Interview with Herman Eilts, August 1992, Washington, DC.

122. On the Suez Crisis in general, see: K. Love, *Suez: The Twice Fought War* (London: Longman, 1969); K. Kyle, *Suez* (London: Weidenfeld and Nicolson, 1991).

123. For the background to Alpha, see: S. Shamir, 'The collapse of Project Alpha', in W.R. Louis and R. Owen, eds, *Suez 1956: The Crisis and its Consequences* (Oxford: Clarendon Press, 1989), pp. 73–100.

124. S. Lloyd, *Suez 1956* (London: Jonathan Cape, 1978), pp. 45–8.

125. PRO, FO 371/121235/V1054/70, Shuckburgh to Kirkpatrick, 10 March 1956.

126. PRO, CAB 128/30, CM 24(56), Cabinet Meeting 21 March 1956; FO 371/121858/VY1015/15, Minute 'Syria' from Secretary of State to Prime Minister, 15 March 1956; Lloyd, *Suez 1956*, pp. 59–60; H. Macmillan, *Riding the Storm* (New York: Harper and Row, 1971), pp. 97–102.

127. Eden's paranoia regarding Nasser was notorious. In September he wrote, 'the seizure of the Suez Canal is ... the opening gambit in a planned campaign designed by Nasser to expel all Western influence and interests from Arab countries'. Sir Anthony Eden, *Full Circle: The Memoirs of the Rt Hon Sir Anthony Eden KG, PC, MC* (London: Cassell, 1960), p. 465.

128. W.S. Lucas, *Divided We Stand: Britain, The US and The Suez Crisis* (London: Hodder & Stoughton, 1991), pp. 101–3; C. Andrew, *Secret Service: The Making of the British Intelligence Community*, (London: Heinemann, 1985), p. 495.

129. E. Shuckburgh, *Descent to Suez* (New York: W.W. Norton and Co, 1986), pp. 289–90.

130. PRO, FO 371/121858/VY1015/15, Minute 'Syria', from Secretary of State to Prime Minister, 15 March 1956.

131. On the development of US policy in 1955 and 1956, see: D.W. Lesch, *The United States and Syria, 1953–1957: The Cold War in the Middle East*, (PhD Thesis, Harvard University, 1990), pp. 157–71.

132. OCB, 'Communism in the Middle East', 20 October 1955, WHO/NSC/OCBCF, Eisenhower Library.

133. OCB, 'Communism in Syria', 21 September 1955, WHO/NSC/OCBCF, Eisenhower Library; NARG 59, 'The new Soviet approach to Syria', 661.83/12-2155.

134. OCB, 'Preparation of courses of action against communism in Syria', 9 January 1956, WHO/NSC/OCBCF, Eisenhower Library.

135. NARG 59, Memcon 'Turkish interest in possible coup', 783.00/1-556; Dunn to DoS, 783.00/1-2856.

136. DoS to Damascus, 13 January 1956, *FRUS, 1955–1957*, Vol. XIII, p. 565.

137. Allen Dulles Memorandum, n.d., JFD/White House Memoranda Series (hereafter WHM), Eisenhower Library.
138. Memcon Dulles and Eden, 30 January 1956, *FRUS, 1955–1957, Vol. XIII*, p. 567.
139. Memcon Eisenhower, Anderson and Dulles, 11 January 1956, JFD/WHM, Eisenhower Library.
140. J.F. Dulles to Hoover, telephone call, 27 September 1955, TC/JFD, Eisenhower Library.
141. Memcon with Hoover and Anderson, 13 March 1956, Dwight D. Eisenhower Diaries Series (hereafter WDDE), Ann Whitman Files (hereafter Whitman Files), Eisenhower Library.
142. Memcon with Chiefs of Staff, 16 March 1956, WDDE, Whitman Files, Eisenhower Library.
143. Memorandum for the President, 'Near Eastern policies', 28 March 1956, Box 13, WDDE, Whitman Files, Eisenhower Library.
144. Memorandum for the President, 'Near Eastern policies', 28 March 1956, Box 13, WDDE, Whitman Files, Eisenhower Library; J.F. Dulles to A.W. Dulles, telephone calls, 17 April 1956, TC/JFD. Dulles had backed the original 'Northern Tier' proposals of a Turkish-Pakistani alliance, but had opposed Iraq's membership as this would split the Arab world. He complained in April 1956 that the Pact had been taken over by London and 'run ... as an instrument of British policy'. Eisenhower to JFD, telephone call, 7 April 1956, WDDE, Whitman Files, Eisenhower Library.
145. Goodpaster Memcon, 3 April 1956, WDDE, Whitman Files, Eisenhower Library. The joint UK-US campaign to isolate Nasser was codenamed Omega. Lucas, *Divided We Stand: Britain, The US and The Suez Crisis*, pp. 110–25.
146. Memorandum for the President, 'Near Eastern policies', 28 March 1956, Box 13, WDDE, Whitman Files, Eisenhower Library. On Iraqi broadcasting plans, see: NARG 59, Dunn to DoS, 783.00/1–2856.
147. Gorst and Lucas, 'The other collusion: Operation Straggle and Anglo-American intervention in Syria, 1955–56,' pp. 585–6.
148. Gustin to Staates Memo, 24 April 1956, WHO/NSC/OCBCF, Eisenhower Library.
149. Memorandum from Allen to Hoover, 16 July 1956, *FRUS, 1955–1957, Vol. XIII*, pp. 582–6; Gustin Memorandum, 'Status of Syrian oil refinery', 19 September 1956, WHO/NSC/OCBCF, Eisenhower Library.
150. Memorandum from Rountree to Murphy, 18 March 1957, *FRUS, 1955–1957, Vol. XIII*, pp. 614–17.
151. A. Roosevelt, *For Lust of Knowing: Memoirs of an Intelligence Officer* (London: Weidenfeld and Nicolson, 1988), pp. 443–4.
152. NARG 59, Moose to SS, 783.00/6–656; Moose to SS, 783.00/7–756; Strong to SS, 783.00/6–1756; Strong to SS, 783.00/6–1856.
153. Ghaleb Kayyali, then Acting Director of the Political Department in the Syrian Foreign Ministry, described in a recent interview how foreign policy at the time was controlled by the army officers. Civilian politicians had little influence over, or interest in, foreign affairs. Ghaleb Kayyali interview, 22 November 1992, Damascus.
154. A former US Foreign Service officer based in Damascus at the time wrote to this writer that 'I regard [Ilyan] as having been a CIA agent first and foremost'. Anonymous communication 2.
155. PRO, FO 371/121858/VY1015/39, Gardener to FO, No. 323, 23 June 1956; VY1015/37, Gardener to FO, 20 June 1956.

156. PRO, FO 371/121858/VY1015/28, Rose Minute 'Syria', 5 June 1956 and FO to Baghdad, 5 June 1956.
157. PRO, FO 371/121858/VY1015/42, Gardener to FO, 28 June 1956; VY 1015/44, Gardener to FO, 30 June 1956; VY1015/50, Gardener to FO, 8 July 1956; 121859/VY1015/55, Gardener to Rose, 18 July 1956; NARG 59, Moose to SS, 783.00/7–856; Joint Weeka, 783.00(W)/7–1356.
158. Special National Intelligence Estimate Number 30–3–56, 'Nasser and the Middle East situation', 31 July 1956, p. 24. Obtained from the CIA under the FOIA.
159. NARG 59, Carrigan to DoS, 783.00/3–3156.
160. PRO, FO 371/121864/VY10316/15, Trevelyan to Ross, 14 July 1956; NARG 59, Moose to SS, 783.00/8–156.
161. 'Nasser and the Middle East situation', 31 July 1956, p. 29.
162. J.F. Dulles to A.W. Dulles, telephone call, 18 October 1956, JFD/TC, Eisenhower Library.
163. PRO, FO 371/121867/VY10338/4, Gardener to Lloyd, 27 June 1956; VY10338/15, Hayter to FO, 5 November 1956; VY10338/20, Hayter to FO, 12 November 1956.
164. PRO, FO 800/723, Walson Minute 'Egypt', 2 May 1956. Lloyd did, however, express 'doubts ... [whether Nuri's] operation affecting Syria' would 'ever tak[e] place'. Lloyd, *Suez 1956*, p. 106.
165. PRO, FO 800/723, Shuckburgh to Lloyd, 29 May 1956.
166. PRO, FO 371/128221/VY1015/25, Johnston to Watson, 20 February 1957. The Foreign Office's accounts of the trials are in: PRO, FO 371/121617/VY1015/6, Beirut to FO, 18 January 1957; VY1015/9, Beirut to FO, 25 January 1957; 128221/VY1015/17, Beirut to FO, 7 February 1957; VY1015/23, Beirut to FO, 22 February 1957; VY1015/35, 15 March. The State Department's accounts of the trials are in: NARG 59, Moose to DoS, 783.00/1–1057; Moose to DoS, 783.00/1–2357; Moose to SS, 783.00/1–1757; Moose to DoS, 783.00/2–157; Moose to SS, 783.00/2–257; Moose to DoS, 783.00/3–157. Syrian press accounts are in *Bulletin de la Presse Syrienne*, Nos 871, 879, 883, all Rubrique III and Nos 895–6, Supplement No. 402. Details of the SSNP's role were obtained in interviews with Rajah Yazija, who assisted Ghassan Jadid during the preparations for the uprising, and Adib Qaddurah who was president of the party's High Council after the Malki assassination. Rajah Yazija interview, 30 June 1993, Beirut; Qaddurah interview, 8 July 1993. See also: Qaddurah, *Haqa'iq wa-mawaqif*, pp. 154–5. For Munir 'Ajlani's account of events, see: M. 'Ajlani, *Difa' al-duktur Munir al-'Ajlani amam al-mahkamah al-'askariyah bi-Dimashq* (*Defence of Dr Munir al-'Ajlani Before the Military Court in Damascus*) (n.p.: n.pb., 1957). Details of the CIA role were obtained in an interview with Arthur Close, deputy chief of the Damascus CIA station from 1953 to 1957. Arthur Close interview, 5 August 1992, Washington, DC.
167. For State Department accounts of the Baghdad trials, see: NARG 59, Gallman to SS, 787.00/8–1758; Gallman to SS, 787.00/8–1858; Gallman to SS, 787.00/8–2058; Gallman to SS, 787.00/8–2458; Gallman to SS, 787.00/8–2558; Gallman to SS, 787.00/8–2758; Gallman to SS, 787.00/8–3058; Gallman to SS, 787.00/8–3158; Gallman to SS, 787.00/9–258; Hart to SS, 787.00/9–1158; Gallman to SS, 787.00/9–1258; Gallman to SS, 787.00/9–1458; Gallman to SS, 787.00/9–1558; Gallman to SS, 787.00/9–1658; Gallman to SS, 787.00/9–2358; Gallman to SS, 787.00/9–2558; Gallman to SS, 787.00/9–258; Gallman to SS, 787.00/10–1858; Gallman to SS, 787.00/11–1158; Gallman to SS, 787.00/10–1858. Iraqi broadcasts are in the following BBC Summary of World Broadcasts Part IVs, all Baghdad Radio: 17 August, No. 631, 19 August 1958; 18 August, No. 633, 21 August 1958;

24 August, No. 638, 27 August 1958; 20 August, No. 636, 25 August 1958; 20 September, No. 660, 22 September 1958; 22 September, No. 663, 25 September 1958; 24 September, No. 666, 29 September 1958. Syrian press accounts are in: *Bulletin de la Presse Syrienne*, Nos 1038, 1040, 1041, 1043, 1044, 1045, 1048, 1049, 1052, 1054, 1056, 1059, all Rubrique III.

168. Eveland claims that his intervention led to Shishakli's departure as the CIA considered his presence not conducive to their attempts to build a rightist coalition in Syria. Eveland, *Ropes of Sand: America's Failure in the Middle East*, pp. 192–8.

169. There is a discrepancy in the evidence regarding Shishakli's trip to Beirut. Daghistani, for instance, claimed that he visited Shishakli in Switzerland *before* the latter went to Beirut. Baghdad Radio, 24 August 1958, SWB Part IV, No. 638, 27 August 1958.

170. NARG 59, Gallman to SS, 783.00/6–2556.

171. Daghistani claimed that the plotters asked for a million dinars and 20,000 weapons, but that in the end he handed over 120,000 dinars and 2,000 small arms, half supplied by the United States and half purchased in Italy. Baghdad Radio, 24 August 1958, SWB Part IV, No. 638, 27 August 1958.

172. PRO, FO 371/121862/VY1022/25, Middleton to Rose, 10 December 1956. On Syrian-Lebanese relations during 1956, see: FO 371/121617/VL10389/7, Duke to FO, 3 September 1956.

173. PRO, FO 371/121868/VY10344/1, Damascus to FO, 25 June 1956; VY 10344/7, Gardener to FO, 14 July 1956; VY10344/21, Ankara to FO, 6 November 1956; NARG 59, Kohler to DoS, 783.00/6–2656; Joint Weeka, 783.00(W)/7–2056.

174. Eveland claims that SIS changed the date so as to coincide with the Israeli invasion of Sinai, but there is no evidence to corroborate this.

175. Memorandum of conference with the President, 29 October 1956, 7.15pm, WDDE, Whitman Files, Eisenhower Library.

176. J.F. Dulles to A.W. Dulles, telephone call, 30 October 1956, TC/JFD, Eisenhower Library.

177. PRO, FO 371/121617/VY1015/12, Beirut to FO, 31 Januray 1957; Yost to DoS, 783.00/2–2558; 'Stampede to the left in Syria', *Manchester Guardian*, 23 February 1957.

178. PRO, FO 371/128221/VY1015/31, Scott to Watson, 7 March 1957.

179. Pumping only began on 11 March 1957. *FRUS, 1955–1957, Vol. XIII*, pp. 593–4 and p. 614; Moose to DoS, 3 November 1956, pp. 594–5; Hoover to Damascus, 13 December 1956, pp. 607–8; NARG 59, Moose to SS, 783.00/8–1356; Moose to SS, 783.00/11–556; M. Heikal, *Nasser: The Cairo Documents* (London: New English Library, 1972), pp. 111–12.

5 Battling the Eisenhower Doctrine

1. N.M. Kaylani, 'The rise of the Syrian Ba'th, 1940–1958: political success, party failure', *International Journal of Middle East Studies*, vol. 3, No. 1 (1972); Public Records Office (hereafter PRO), Foreign Office (hereafter FO) 371/128220/ VY1015/4, Rose Minute 'New Syrian government', 1 January 1957.

2. P. Rondot, 'Tendances particularistes et tendances unitaires en Syrie', *Orient*, 2e année, 1er trimestre, numéro 5 (1958), p. 146. For overviews of events, see: M. Ionides, *Divide and Lose: The Arab Revolt 1955–58* (London: Geoffrey Bles, 1960), Chapter XVI; H. Laurens, *Le Grand Jeu: Orient Arabe et Rivalités Internationales* (Paris: Armand Colin, 1991), pp. 161–5.

3. *The Lebanese Crisis as viewed by The Syrian Social Nationalist Party*, Pamph-

let in Middle East Files, Jafet Library, American University of Beirut.
  4. 'Abdallah Kobecsy interview, 27 February 1992, Beirut; Rajah Yazija interview, 30 June 1993, Beirut.
  5. PRO, FO 371/128221/VY1015/19, Scott to Watson, 7 February 1957; *Bulletin de la Presse Syrienne*, Nos 889, 890, 891, 895, 896, 904, 905, 909, 915, all Rubrique III; National Archives and Records Administration, Record Group 59 (hereafter NARG 59), Atherton to Department of State (hereafter DoS), 783.00/2–1457.
  6. 25,000 mourners turned out for Jadid's funeral. 'L'assassinat du leader PPS Ghassan Jédid', *L'Orient*, 20 February 1957; *Bulletin de la Presse Syrienne*, No. 894, Rubrique III; NARG 59, Heath to DoS, 783.00/2-2857; A. Qaddurah, *Haqa'iq wamawaqif (Facts and Opinions)* (Beirut: Dar mu'assasat al-fikr, 1989), pp. 155–166.
  7. NARG 59, Moose to Secretary of State (hereafter SS), 783.00/2-2257. Interestingly, J.F. Dulles interpreted the murder as an example of 'how far the Syrians were willing to go when pushed by the Russians'. This merely indicated his crude black and white picture of events in the region. 313rd National Security Council (hereafter NSC) meeting, 21 February 1957, NSC Series (hereafter WNSC), Eisenhower Library.
  8. This was recorded in Samarra'i's cables read out at the Baghdad trials. *Bulletin de la Presse Syrienne*, Nos 1052 and 1054, all Rubrique III.
  9. J.F. Dulles to A.W. Dulles, telephone call, 17 April 1957, Telephone Calls Series (hereafter TC) J.F. Dulles Papers (hereafter JFD), Eisenhower Library.
  10. NARG 59, Strong to SS, 783.00/10–1157; 'Un nouveau complot en Syrie', *L'Orient*, 11 October 1957; *Bulletin de la Presse Syrienne*, Nos 947, 956, 979, 982, all Rubrique III; 'Attentat à la bombe contre l'Ambassade d'URSS à Damas', *L'Orient*, 17 September 1957; 'Explosion à Achrafieh', *L'Orient*, 5 January 1958; '3 Syrians slain in Lebanon blast', *New York Times*, 5 January 1958; 'Die Wühlarbeit der panarabischen Nationalisten', *Neue Züricher Zeitung*, 11 January 1958.
  11. Chamoun had beaten Khuri in the September 1952 presidential elections. K.S. Salibi, *The Modern History of Lebanon* (London: Weidenfeld and Nicolson, 1965), p. 195.
  12. PRO, FO 371/128014/VL10389/1, Middleton to Lloyd, 31 January 1957; 128003/VL1022/13, Middleton to Lloyd, 11 April 1957; 'L'envoyé d'Eisenhower a "L'Orient"', *L'Orient*, 16 March 1957.
  13. PRO, FO 371/121617/VL10389/11, Middleton to FO, 24 November 1956; Centre for Lebanese Studies, Oxford (hereafter CLS), RG319, ID File, R–533–56, 4 December 1956.
  14. PRO, FO 371/128014/VL10389/2, Middleton to Ross, 28 January 1957.
  15. 'Elections in the Lebanese republic', *World Today*, Vol. 13, No. 6 (June 1957), pp. 260–5.
  16. PRO, FO 371/127999/VL1015/40, Middleton to Lloyd, 4 July 1957.
  17. Chehab blamed these disturbances on 'the machinations of the unholy alliance of Syria, Egypt and the Communists'. NARG 59, Heath to SS, 783A.00/6–157.
  18. CLS, RG319, ID File, R–92–57, 1 April 1957.
  19. CLS, RG319, ID File, R–208–57, 20 June 1957.
  20. 'Lebanon acts against terrorists', The Observer Foreign News Service, 12 November 1957. In a conversation with the US Ambassador in June, Chehab accused Syria of arming Bedouins in the Kermel district. CLS, RG319, ID File, Beirut to SS, No. 347, 1 June 1957.
  21. CLS, RG319, ID File, Beirut to SS, No. 619, 3 June 1957.
  22. PRO, FO 371/127999/VL1015/21, Middleton to FO, 30 May 1957; VL

1015/23, Middleton to FO, 31 May 1957; NARG 59, Heath to DoS, 783.00/6-1757.
23. NARG 59, Heath to SS, 683A.00/1-2757.
24. PRO, FO 371/127999/VL1015/28, Middleton to FO, 1 June 1957; VL1015/40, Middleton to Lloyd, 4 July 1957; W.C. Eveland, *Ropes of Sand: America's Failure in the Middle East* (New York: W.W. Norton and Co, 1980), pp. 249-51; interview with Stuart Rockwell, Deputy Director of the Bureau for Near-Eastern Affairs at the State Department during the elections, 3 August 1992, Washington, DC.
25. NARG 59, Heath to DoS, 783A.00/6-1257.
26. 'Des terroristes ont voulu faire sauter ce point', *L'Orient*, 18 August 1957.
27. In 1955 Sarraj had formed the unit out of volunteers who had family contacts in the Galilee. In the same year regular military conscription was extended to Palestinians in Syria, but the Bureau's unit remained volunteer only. Interviews with Khalid al-Fahum, ex-Speaker of the Palestine National Council, 8 June 1993, Damascus; Ahmad Sidqi al-Dajani, founder member of Palestine Liberation Organisation, 9 August 1993, Cairo; Qasim Alwan, 10 August 1993, Cairo; NARG 59, Heath to SS, 783A.00/11-2157.
28. The British Embassy concluded that this violence was 'almost certainly the work of Syrian agents'. PRO, FO 371/128000/VL1015/51, Beirut to FO, 12 September 1957.
29. PRO, FO 371/128000/VL1015/43, Beirut to FO, 2 August 1957; VL1015/48, Beirut to FO, 16 August 1957; VL1015/49, Scott to Lloyd, 22 August 1957; VL1015/56, Beirut to FO, 8 November 1957; CLS, RG319, ID File, R-275-57, 20 August 1957; 'Les saboteurs de Chouf étaient armés par le 2ième Bureau Syrien', *L'Orient*, 27 August 1957; 'Sanglant accrochage, à Deir el-Achayer, entre gendarmes et trafiquants d'armes', *L'Orient*, 13 September 1957; 'Red Hand terrorists send death threat to envoys', *News Chronicle*, 24 September 1957; 'Un ressortissant Jordanien arrêté par la police', *L'Orient*, 6 October 1957; 'Arrestation de 14 personnes', *L'Orient*, 7 November 1957; 'Beyrouth et le Liban', *L'Orient*, 25 December 1957.
30. 'Attaque-éclair, dans la nuit de jeudi à vendredi, contre la poste de gendarmerie de Machta-Hassan', *L'Orient*, 7 December 1957; 'Beyrouth et le Liban', *L'Orient*, 23 December 1957.
31. PRO, FO 371/128230/VY1015/271, Memcon Lloyd and Malik, 24 September 1957.
32. PRO, FO 371/128000/VL1015/55G, FO to Beirut, 14 November 1957.
33. 'Future United States policy towards Jordan', 19 April 1956, *Foreign Relations of the United States, 1955-1957, Vol. XIII*, (Washington, DC: US Government Printing Office) (hereafter *FRUS* with year and volume), pp. 37-9; Z. Raad, *King Hussein's Foreign Diplomacy: January 1956-December 1958* (PhD Thesis: Cambridge, 1993), pp. 30-96.
34. PRO, FO 371/127887/VJ10110/7, Johnston to Lloyd, 9 October 1957.
35. PRO, FO 371/127889/VJ1023/8, Johnston to FO, 16 March 1957; VJ1023/10, Johnston to FO, 6 April 1957.
36. For an overview of the spring crisis, see: Raad, *King Hussein's Foreign Diplomacy: January 1956-December 1958*, pp. 111-40.
37. PRO, FO 371/121859/VY1015/56, Gardener to Rose, 21 July 1956.
38. PRO, FO 371/127878/VJ1015/9, Johnston to FO, 1 March 1957; VJ1015/16, Johnston to FO, 4 April 1957; VJ1015/18, Mason to FO, 10 April 1957. See also: J. Lunt, *Hussein of Jordan: A Political Biography* (London: Macmillan, 1989), pp. 36-43. P. Snow, *Hussein: A Biography* (London: Barrie and Jenkins, 1972), pp.

NOTES TO CHAPTER 5

92–116. For King Hussein's account of these events, see: His Majesty King Hussein, *Uneasy Lies the Head* (London: Heinemann, 1962), pp. 126–51.

39. PRO, FO 371/127880/VJ1015/118, Johnston to Lloyd, 14 May 1957.

40. NARG 59, Merriam to DoS, 785.00/11–1857.

41. Rashid fled to Syria later in the month. After Sarraj's imprisonment by the secessionist government in 1961, Rashid helped him to escape from Damascus. Interview with Naim Abd al-Haadi, Minister of Public Works in the Nabulsi government, 28 July 1993, Amman.

42. Abu Nuwar had been made Chief of Staff in June 1956. Brigadier S. Ali al-Edroos, *The Hashemite Army 1908–1979* (Amman: The Publishing Committee, 1980), pp. 316–17. On Nuwar, Hussein and the army, see: P.J. Vatikiotis, *Politics and the Military in Jordan* (London: Frank Cass, 1967), pp. 126–35.

43. PRO, FO 371/127887/VJ10110/7, Johnston to Lloyd, 9 October 1957; 'Istid'a' al-Nabulsi lil-qasr al-maliki fajr ams', *Falastin*, 13 April 1957; 'Jalalat al-malik kallafa al-sayyid 'Abd al-Halim al-Nimr ba'd dhuhr ams bi-ta'lif al-wizarah', *Falastin*, 14 April 1957.

44. PRO, FO 371/127878/VJ1015/26, FO to Baghdad, 15 April 1957; VJ1015/27, Wright to FO, 15 April 1957; Dulles to Amman, 25 April 1957, *FRUS, 1955–1957, Vol. XIII*, pp. 112–13 and Joint Chiefs of Staff to Unified and Specified Commanders, 24 April 1957, pp. 107–8.

45. Ghaleb Kayyali confirmed in a recent interview the differences between Quwatli and Sarraj concerning Jordan. Kayyali interview, 22 November 1992, Damascus.

46. PRO, FO 371/127880/VJ1015/123, Johnston to Lloyd, 29 May 1957; VJ1015/129, Johnston to FO, 6 July 1957; B. Shwadran, *Jordan: A State of Tension* (New York: Council for Middle Eastern Affairs Press, 1959), p. 360; C. Johnston, *The Brink of Jordan* (London: Hamish Hamilton, 1972), p. 59.

47. PRO, FO 371/127879/VJ1015/55, Johnston to FO, 22 April 1957; 127880/VJ1015/135, BBC Monitoring, 18 July 1957.

48. PRO, FO 371/127879/VJ1015/54, Johnston to FO, 21 April 1957.

49. Mallory to DoS, 21 April 1957, *FRUS, 1955–1957, Vol. XIII*, pp. 100–2; Hamad Farhan, Undersecretary to Nabulsi's Minister of National Economy told this writer in a recent interview that 'I still feel [the incident at Zerqa] was staged'. Hamad Farhan interview, 2 August 1993, Amman.

50. Ali Abu Nuwar, *Hin talashat al-'arab* (*When the Arabs Wither*) (London: Dar al-Saqi, 1990), p. 325.

51. NARG 59, Merriam to DoS, 785.00/11–1857.

52. PRO, FO 371/127889/VJ1023/13, Johnston to FO, 14 May 1957.

53. Dulles to Damascus, 25 April 1957, *FRUS, 1955–1957, Vol. XIII*, pp. 111–12.

54. PRO, FO 371/127880/VJ1015/107, Johnston to FO, 6 May 1957; VJ1015/128, Johnston to FO, 19 June 1957.

55. PRO, FO 371/127897/VJ10389/1, Johnston to FO, 28 May 1957; VJ10389/3, Johnston to FO, 29 May 1957; 'Riposte d'Amman à Damas', *L'Orient*, 29 May 1957.

56. PRO, FO 371/127897/VJ10389/5, Minute 'Jordan-Syrian relations', 28 May 1957.

57. During the visit, Jordan accused the Egyptian Military Attaché of organising an attempt on Sa'ud's life and expelled him. PRO, FO 371/127897/VJ10389/6, Mason to Hadow, 5 June 1957; VJ10389/7, 'Jordan-Syria relations', 28 May 1957; 'Complot contre Seoud éventé à Amman', *L'Orient*, 11 June 1957.

58. 'Confession: he "went to Syria for murder"', *Egyptian Gazette*, 18 July 1957;

Bulletin de la Presse Syrienne, No. 932, Rubrique III; NARG 59, Strong to DoS, 783.00/7–1857.

59. PRO, FO 371/128230/VJ1015/271, Memcon Lloyd and Malik, 24 September 1957.

60. Some of the bombings were carried out by Jordanian opposition groups, like the Arab Nationalist Movement, though it is unclear whether they received any help from the Syrians. Y. Sayigh, 'Reconstructing the paradox: the Arab Nationalist Movement, armed struggle, and Palestine, 1951–1966', *Middle East Journal*, Vol. 45, No. 4 (1991), p. 612. As ever with intelligence operations, the situation could at times be murky. When a bomb of 'Czechoslovak make ... wrapped in an Egyptian flag' was found in an Amman electrical installation, the Foreign Office expressed surprise at the symbolism of the device and wondered 'whether this was an American plant'. PRO, FO 371/127881/VJ1015/161, Johnston to FO, 3 October 1957.

61. PRO, FO 371/127881/VJ1015/143, Johnston to FO, 13 August 1957; VJ1015/169, Dudgeon to Hadow, 9 October 1957; 'Anti-US pamphlets in Jordan', *Egyptian Gazette*, 19 August 1957.

62. PRO, FO 371/127881/VJ1015/140, Stewart to FO, 10 August 1957; VJ 1015/148, Johnston to FO, 3 September 1957; VJ1015/156, Stewart to FO, 26 September 1957; VJ1015/162, Johnston to FO, 25 September 1957; VJ1015/169, Dudgeon to Hadrow, 9 October 1957.

63. There were also several other minor bombings. PRO, FO 371/127881/VJ1015/166, Johnston to FO, 8 October 1957; VJ1015/168, Johnston to FO, 11 October 1957; VJ1015/170, Stewart to FO, 14 October 1957; VJ1015/173, Johnston to FO, 16 October 1957; 127882/VJ1015/180, Johnston to FO, 23 October 1957; NARG 59, Franklin to DoS, 785.00/10–1557; Mallory to SS, 785.00/10–1857; Amman to SS, 785.00/10–2457; 'Bombs go off by US homes in Amman', *Egyptian Gazette*, 9 October 1957; 'Dhabt asliha', *Al-Difa'*, 9 October 1957.

64. PRO, FO 371/127882/VJ1015/191, Johnston to FO, 12 November 1957 and Johnston to FO, 12 November 1957; VJ1015/199, Johnston to FO, 13 November 1957; VJ1015/211, Johnston to FO, 27 November 1957; 'Amman expulse les collaborateurs de l'attaché militaire Syrien', *L'Orient*, 29 September 1957.

65. The charges were given credence by widespread rumours that Hussein's grandfather had dealt with the Zionists. On the substance behind these rumours, see: A. Shlaim, *Collusion Across the Jordan* (Oxford: Clarendon Press, 1988).

66. NARG 59, Mallory to SS, 785.00/11–657.

67. PRO, FO 371/127897/VJ10389/29, Johnston to FO, 11 November 1957; 127980/VJ1681/2, Department of State Intelligence Brief, No. 2209, 21 November 1957, 'Jordan's King Husayn successfully withstanding Syro-Egyptian campaign'.

68. PRO, FO 371/127887/VJ10110/7, Johnston to Lloyd, 9 October 1957; Mallory to DoS, 3 May 1957, *FRUS, 1955–1957, Vol. XIII*, pp. 122–5.

69. Sa'udi Arabia backed Quwatli's move but Egyptian support for Sarraj and Hawrani counter-balanced this. A.W. Dulles to Goodpaster, 'Situation report on Syria', 22 March 1957, Declassified Documents Reference System (hereafter DDRS) 1981, 26 E; PRO, FO 371/128222/VY1015/40, Johnston to Watson, 27 March 1957; NARG 59, Moose to DoS, 783.00/4–1557. The United States may also have backed these attempts. D.W. Lesch, *The United States and Syria, 1953–1957: The Cold War in the Middle East* (PhD Thesis, Harvard University, 1990), pp. 215–19.

70. NARG 59, Moose to DoS, 783.00/5–2557; Moose to DoS, 17 May 1957, *FRUS, 1955–1957, Vol. XIII*, p. 618.

71. NARG 59, Strong to DoS, 783.00/7–1857; Moose to DoS, 783.00/5–2357

72. PRO, FO 371/121867/VY10338/35, 'Brief for the Secretary of State for NATO Meeting', 11-14 December 1956; VY10338/36, 'Syria and Soviet penetration in the Middle East', 11-14 December 1956; VY10338/37, Hayter to Brimelow, 7 December 1956.
73. NARG 59, Moose to SS, 783.00/5-1157.
74. Mrozinski to Staats, 25 January 1957, White House Office (hereafter WHO)/National Security Council (hereafter NSC)/Operations Coordinating Board Central Files (hereafter OCBCF), Eisenhower Library.
75. Mrozinski to Dearborn, 25 November 1957, Office of the Special Assistant for National Security Affairs (hereafter OSANSA)/Operations Coordinating Board Series (hereafter OCB)/ Subject Subseries (hereafter S), Eisenhower Library.
76. PRO, FO 371/128223/VY1015/88, Rose Minute 'Situation in Syria', 13 August 1957. On Syrian trade relations, see: NARG 59, Intelligence Report No. 7368, 'Syrian vulnerability to Sino-Soviet Bloc activities', 1 November 1956.
77. PRO, FO 371/121859/VY1015/80, FO to Paris, 3 December 1956; NARG 59, Yost to SS, 783.00/9-457; Memcon Alphand and Murphy, 17 November 1956, *FRUS, 1955-1957, Vol. XIII*, p. 605.
78. 'Briefing book for visit of King Saud to Washington DC, 30 January 1957', Confidential File (hereafter CF)/White House Central Files (hereafter WHCF), Eisenhower Library; PRO, FO 371/134381/VY1011/1, Middleton to Lloyd, 6 February 1958; NARG 59, Mallory to DoS, 785.00/11-2957; F.K. Barradah, 'Saudi Arabia's Foreign Policy 1945-1984' (Unpublished PhD Thesis, Aberdeen University, 1989), pp. 198-200.
79. NARG 59, Warren to SS, 783.00/10-1956.
80. Warren to SS, No. 1123, 14 November 1956, Dulles-Herter Series (hereafter WDH), Whitman Files, Eisenhower Library. That Turkey's fears were exaggerated is demonstrated by a February 1957 assessment by the US Joint Chiefs of Staff that even with its new equipment, the Syrian Air Force 'is not presently capable of defending Syria from any external attack'. JCS 2073/1365, 25 February 1957, DDRS, 1980, 57A.
81. NARG 59, Moose to DoS, 783.00/12-556.
82. PRO, FO 371/128269/VY1821/1, Bowker to Rose, 20 February 1957.
83. PRO, FO 371/128222/VY1015/37, Bowther to Watson, 15 March 1957; 128236/VY1022/9, Bowker to Ross, 23 May 1957; NARG 59, Strong to DoS, 783.00/7-857. At the time Turkey was cooperating closely with Israel and Iran on intelligence sharing related to the USSR and Syria. Y. Melman and D. Raviv, *The Imperfect Spies* (London: Sidgwick & Jackson, 1989), p. 89.
84. Hoover Memorandum, 'Near East Policy', November 1956, WDH, Whitman Files, Eisenhower Library.
85. Discussion at the 303rd Meeting of the NSC, 8 November 1956, WNSC, Whitman Files, Eisenhower Library.
86. Memcon with President, 20 December 1956, Goodpaster Memcon, Dwight D. Eisenhower Series (hereafter WDDE), Whitman Files, Eisenhower Library.
87. Dulles to Damascus, 28 May 1957, *FRUS, 1955-1957, Vol. XIII*, p. 619. See also: 'Outlook for the Syrian situation', Special National Intelligence Estimate 36.7-56, 16 November 1956, *FRUS, 1955-1957, Vol. XIII*, pp. 601-5.
88. Moose to DoS, 15 July 1957, *FRUS, 1955-1957, Vol. XIII*, pp. 620-5.
89. Interview with Alfred Atherton, Consul General in Aleppo in 1957 and 1958, August 1992, Washington, DC. Not all US officials were enamoured of this relationship. William Brewer, Chief of the Political Section in the Damascus Embassy from 1952 to 1955, commented that the SSNP 'was seized upon by some of our intelligence operatives because it was the only group willing to cooperate.

To me, that made it a pretty weak reed.' Letter from William Brewer, 25 August 1992.

90. J.F. Dulles to A.W. Dulles, telephone call, 7 May 1957, TC/JFD, Eisenhower Library. In the trials which followed the discovery of the August plot, SSNP leaders such as Abu Mansur were charged, along with Husayni and Shishakli, for participation in 'the American plot'. In reality, however, the SSNP and the Husayni plots were separate operations. *Bulletin de la Presse Syrienne*, No. 990, Rubrique III.

91. Details of the plot are from: Oral History Interview with Charles Yost (subsequently Ambassador to Syria), OH–416, Eisenhower Library, pp. 25–6; interview with Arthur Close, Deputy Chief of Damascus CIA station in 1957, Close interview, 5 August 1992, Washington, DC; interview with Stuart Rockwell, Deputy Director of the State Department's Bureau of Near-Eastern Affairs in 1957, 3 August 1992, Washington, DC; Anonymous communication 2; 'La Syrie saisit l'ONU du "complot" américain', *L'Orient*, 21 August 1957; *Bulletin de la Presse Syrienne*, No. 939, Supplement No. 415 and No. 945, Rubrique III; NARG 59, Strong to SS, 783.00/10–257.

92. Presumably these contacts were with either the Nafuri group of officers or the 'Damascene' group under Colonel Umar Qabbani, both of which groups Allen Dulles identified in March as working to oust Sarraj and the Ba'thists. Memorandum Allen Dulles to Goodpaster, 22 March 1957. Obtained from the CIA under the Freedom of Information Act (FOIA).

93. Some researchers have labelled this 'Operation Wappen', but the Foreign Service and CIA officers interviewed do not recall this term being used.

94. Rockwell interview, 3 August 1992; Anonymous communication 2.

95. NARG 59, Strong to SS, 783.00/10–257.

96. Anonymous communication 2.

97. A few days before they were exposed, Stone had reported to Allen Dulles that they were under surveillance and argued that the operation should be called off. Dulles nonetheless ordered Stone to carry on. This may indicate that the plot was not seriously intended to result in a coup, but merely to keep the Syrian government under pressure.

98. Damascus Radio, 12 August 1957, BBC Summary of World Broadcasts (hereafter SWB) Part IV, No. 322, 14 August 1957; NARG 59, Strong to SS, 783.00/8–1357.

99. Anonymous communication 2. The United States responded by expelling the Syrian Ambassador. Rountree to Herter, 13 August 1957, *FRUS, 1955–1957*, Vol. XIII, pp. 632–4.

100. For his description of the Arab 'people's' anger at the 'imperialist plots' of the 1950s, see: Afif al-Bizri, *Al-Nasiriyah fi jumlat al-isti'mar al-hadith* (*Nasirism in the Body of Modern Imperialism*) (Damascus: Dar al-Sharq lil-nashr wa al-tawzi', 1962), p. 239.

101. PRO, FO 371/128223/VY1015/89, Scott to FO, 16 August 1957; NARG 59, Strong to SS, 783.00/8–2157; 'Publicity-shy Syrian', *New York Herald Tribune*, 13 March 1958; Eveland, *Ropes of Sand: America's Failure in the Middle East*, pp. 256–7.

102. PRO, FO 371/128224/VY1015/98, FO to Baghdad, 20 August 1957.

103. NARG 59, Dulles memorandum for Eisenhower, 783.00/8–2057.

104. PRO, FO 371/128224/VY1015/118, J.F. Dulles to Macmillan, 22 August 1957; Memcon Department of State, 19 August 1957, *FRUS, 1955–1957*, Vol. XIII, pp. 640–1.

105. For a detailed account of US policy during the crisis, see: Lesch, *The United States and Syria, 1953–1957: The Cold War in the Middle East*, pp. 272–91 and

302–24. See also Eisenhower's account: D.D. Eisenhower, *Waging Peace* (London: Heinemann, 1966), pp. 196–204.
106. Dulles to Riyadh, 21 August, *FRUS, 1955–1957*, Vol. XIII, pp. 645–6.
107. Dulles to Tel Aviv, 21 August, *FRUS, 1955–1957*, Vol. XIII, pp. 646–7.
108. Dulles to London, 21 August, *FRUS, 1955–1957*, Vol. XIII, pp. 647–8.
109. Dulles to Beirut, 28 August 1957, *FRUS, 1955–1957*, Vol. XIII, p. 661. Eisenhower declared he was 'ready to use up his entire emergency fund in order to build up military strength around Syria'. Congressional Leaders Meeting, 27 August 1957, WDDE, Eisenhower Library.
110. NARG 59, Mallory to SS, 783.00/8–2657.
111. PRO, FO 371/128225/VY1015/155, FO to Baghdad, 6 September 1957; Miner to DoS, 3 September 1957, *FRUS, 1955–1957*, Vol. XIII, pp. 673–4.
112. Memcon Malik and Dulles, 18 September 1957, *FRUS, 1955–1957*, Vol. XIII, pp. 715–17.
113. Warren to DoS, 21 August 1957, *FRUS, 1955–1957*, Vol. XIII, pp. 642–4; NARG 59, Warren to SS, 783.00/9–2457.
114. Dulles to Ankara, 10 September 1957, *FRUS, 1955–1957*, Vol. XIII, pp. 691–3.
115. Murphy to Paris, 17 September 1957, *FRUS, 1955–1957*, Vol. XIII, pp. 707–9; Eisenhower, *Waging Peace*, p. 199.
116. PRO, FO 371/128228/VY1015/220, Stewart to Watson, 13 September 1957.
117. Circular telegram, 25 September 1957, *FRUS, 1955–1957*, Vol. XIII, pp. 715–17.
118. Memcon in White House, 7 September 1957, *FRUS, 1955–1957*, Vol. XIII, pp. 685–9.
119. NARG 59, Strong to Waggoner, 783.00/9–2057.
120. NARG 59, Strong to SS, 783.00/9–2857.
121. NARG 59, Strong to SS, 783.00/9–2757; Memcon Rountree and Alphand, 783.00/9–3057. However, Sa'udi Arabia's attitude in private was not so different from its conciliatory public policy. In talks with Dulles on 24 September Crown Prince Faysal urged the necessity of 'calm[ing] the situation down' and 'spread[ing] the spirit of calm and peace in Syria'. NARG 59, Memcon Dulles and Faisal, 783.00/9–2457. For a discussion of why neither Iraq nor Sa'udi Arabia stood by the United States, see: Lesch, *The United States and Syria, 1953–1957: The Cold War in the Middle East*, pp. 251–71 and 334–68.
122. On the UN debates, see: Lesch, *The United States and Syria, 1953–1957: The Cold War in the Middle East*, pp. 386–418.
123. PRO, FO 371/128242/VY10344/15, Dixon to FO, 16 October 1957.
124. PRO, FO 371/128242/VY10344/16, Dixon to FO, 16 October 1957
125. NARG 59, Memcon Rountree and Laboulaye, 783.00/10–1057; *FRUS, 1955–1957*, Vol. XIII, p. 720.
126. M.H. Heikal, *Nasser; The Cairo Documents*, (London: New English Library, 1972), pp. 131–2; Memcon Dulles and Lloyd, 18 October 1957, *FRUS, 1955–1957*, Vol. XIII, pp. 720–2.
127. NARG 59, Heath to SS, 783.00/10–1557.
128. Herter to Dulles, 14 October 1957, DDRS, 1985, 000357.
129. NARG 59, Lodge to SS, 682.83/11–157.
130. NARG 59, Strong to Rountree, 783.00/10–1657. Rountree replied that the hard-line had been useful in alerting 'the world ... to the extent of Soviet penetration of the Syrian Government' but agreed that the failure of 'our Arab friends ... to stand up' meant that a softer line was now appropriate. Rountree to Strong, 29 October 1957, *FRUS, 1955–1957*, Vol. XIII, pp. 735–7.

131. During November the Syrian government continued to complain of Turkish incursions and overflights. NARG 59, Strong to SS, 682.83/11-557.
132. NARG 59, Memcon Rountree and Bitar, 611.83/11-757.
133. NARG 59, US Information Agency Circular, 783.00/10-1757; Mallory to SS, 783.00/10-1857; Atherton to DoS, 783.00/11-1457; Memcon Rountree and Nuri Said, 783.00/12-557.
134. NARG 59, Strong to SS, 783.00/12-957; Strong to SS, 783.00/12-957; Strong to SS, 783.00/12-1057.
135. NARG 59, Dulles to Cairo, 783.00/12-1157; Herter to Cairo, 783.00/12-1457; Hare to SS, 783.00/12-2557; Strong to SS, 783.00/12-2357; Strong to SS, 783.00/12-3157; Strong to SS, 783.00/1-258; Yost to SS, 1-858.
136. Even the Iraqi Minister in Damascus agreed that this was the 'only effective means [of] checking [the] communists'. NARG 59, Yost to SS, 783.00/1-2258. Originally, the Ba'th had perceived the Free Officers as merely another reactionary military clique. However, by 1956 they had come to view Nasser as the best hope for Arab unity. For an account of the internal party debates which led to this change in attitude, see: J.F. Devlin, *The Ba'th Party: A History from its Origins to 1966* (Stanford University, Stanford, CA: Hoover Institution Press, 1976), pp. 80–88.
137. P. Seale, *The Struggle for Syria*, (New Haven, CT: Yale University Press, 1986), pp. 284–326; G.H. Torrey, *Syrian Politics and the Military 1945–1958* (Ohio: Ohio State University Press, 1964), pp. 347–83; K. Wheelock, *Nasser's New Egypt* (London: Steven and Sons, 1960), p. 258. As Be'eri put it, Syria's leaders could not cooperate so 'they solved the problem by "fleeing forward" to union with Egypt'. E. Be'eri, *Army Officers in Arab Politics and Society* (London: Praeger, 1970), p. 134.

6 The United Arab Republic

1. Y. Caroz, *The Arab Secret Services* (London: Corgi, 1978), p. 10.
2. E. Be'eri, *Army Officers in Arab Politics and Society* (London: Praeger, 1970), p. 135.
3. Caroz, *The Arab Secret Services*, pp. 54–6; K. Wheelock, *Nasser's New Egypt* (London: Stevens and Sons, 1960), pp. 231–2.
4. Public Records Office (hereafter PRO), Foreign Office (hereafter FO) 371/134383/VY1015/28, Scott to Rose, 19 March 1958.
5. In the UAR, Syria was known as the Northern Province, with Egypt being the Southern Province.
6. Caroz, *The Arab Secret Services*, pp. 87–8.
7. Qasim Alwan, secretary of the committee of officers which prepared Bizri's trip to Cairo in January 1958, confirmed this view. Alwan interview, 10 August 1993, Cairo. There have even been suggestions that Sarraj's over-zealousness during the Lebanese Civil War earned him a rebuke from Nasser. 'Cairo summons Col. Serraj', *Daily Telegraph*, 14 June 1958.
8. Other officers who had served him loyally were also given important postings. One such was Lieutenant Commander Muhammad Jarrah, Assistant Commander of the gendarmerie and prosecutor in the Malki, Iraqi plot and American plot trials. He was appointed Director General of Police Security – a new post which established central control of the police, gendarmerie and tribal forces. National Archives and Records Administration, Record Group 59 (hereafter NARG 59), Hart to DoS, 783.00/4-1858; Yost to SS, 786.00/3-1758.
9. Caroz, *The Arab Secret Services*, p. 63. On contacts between the CIA and

the Free Officers before the revolt, see: M. 'Abd el-Wahab Sayed-Ahmed, *Nasser and American Foreign Policy 1952–1956* (London: Laam, 1989), pp. 42–8.

10. Interview with Herman Eilts, in 1957 State Department officer in charge of Baghdad Pact affairs, subsequently Ambassador to Sa'udi Arabia and Egypt. Washington, DC, August 1992.

11. NARG 59, Yost to Secretary of State (hereafter SS), 786.00/2–1158.

12. The only significant action that appears to have been taken was cooperation between USIS and Middle Eastern radio stations in producing anti-UAR propaganda. By April there were ten clandestine stations propagandising against the UAR. *Bulletin de la Presse Syrienne*, Nos 1007 and 1045, Rubrique III. See also: Department of State (hereafter DoS) to Delegation at the Baghdad Pact Council Meeting, 25 January 1958, *Foreign Relations of the United States, 1958–1960, Vol. XIII* (Washington, DC: US Government Printing Office) (hereafter FRUS with year and volume), pp. 408–409; Berry Memorandum to Acting SS, 25 January 1958, pp. 409–11; Dulles Memorandum to Eisenhower, 8 February 1958, pp. 421–2.

13. Oral History Interview with Raymond Hare, OH–189, Eisenhower Library, p. 41.

14. NARG 59, Yost to SS, 786.00/3–658; Yost to SS, 786.00/3–758; Yost to SS, 786.00/3–858; Yost to SS, 786.00/3–1058; Ross to DoS, 786.00/3–1158; Yost to SS, 786.00/3–1258; Hart to SS, 786.00/3–3058; *Bulletin de la Presse Syrienne*, Nos. 996 and 998, Rubrique III; M.H. Heikal, *Nasser: The Cairo Documents* (London: New English Library, 1972), p. 126. Both Sarraj and Eveland claim that the United States had a hand in this plot, at least approving it. There is, however, no independent evidence for this claim. W.C. Eveland, *Ropes of Sand: America's Failure in the Middle East* (New York: W.W. Norton and Co, 1980), p. 273.

15. PRO, FO 371/134383/VY1015/25, Scott to Rose, 12 March 1958.

16. NARG 59, Yost to SS, 2–1458; Hare to SS, 786.00/2–1558; *Bulletin de la Presse Syrienne*, Nos 990 and 992, Rubrique III.

17. NARG 59, Warren to SS, 783.00/6–1858; Warren to SS, 783.00/6–2358; *Bulletin de la Presse Syrienne*, No. 1045, Rubrique III.

18. For instance, Radio Damascus accused Turkish troops of attacking the village of Buban on 28 January. *Cahiers de L'Orient Contemporarian* XXXVII (1958), p. 204. The Ilyan connection is given in: Eveland, *Ropes of Sand: America's Failure in the Middle East*, pp. 263–4. For examples of clashes on the border, see: *Middle East Journal*, Vol. 15, No. 3 (Summer 1961), pp. 323–4 and No. 4 (Autumn 1961), p. 443.

19. Subsequently Syrian courts arraigned several former officers and charged them with plotting a coup in conjunction with the SSNP and Hasan Atrash which had been scheduled for early February. 'Lebanese village shaken by bomb', *New York Herald Tribune*, 18 February 1958; *Bulletin de la Presse Syrienne*, No. 1044, Rubrique III.

20. 'Attack on Iraq aide is linked to Syrians', *New York Times*, 1 September 1958.

21. PRO, FO 371/134008/VJ1015/5, Johnston to FO, 15 January 1958; VJ1015/7, Jerusalem Consulate General to FO, 5 March 1958; NARG 59, Mallory to SS, 785.00/12–257; Wright to SS, 785.00/5–2858.

22. PRO, FO 371/134008/VJ1015/8, Johnston to FO, 22 January 1958; VJ1015/12, Johnston to FO, 5 February 1958; 134017/VJ10316/4(B), Jerusalem Consulate General to FO, 22 July 1958.

23. On the Arab Union, see: Z. Raad, *King Hussein's Foreign Diplomacy: January 1956–December 1958* (PhD Thesis, Cambridge University, 1993), Chapter 4.

24. On Hussein's reactions to the revolt, see: Raad, *King Hussein's Foreign Diplomacy: January 1956–December 1958*, pp. 197–201.

25. A. Tahir, *Iraq aux Origines du Régime Militaire* (Paris: Editions L'Harmattan, 1989), pp. 120–1.
26. PRO, FO 371/134009/VJ1015/54, Johnston to FO, 23 July 1958.
27. PRO, FO 371/134079/VJ1432/3, BBC Monitoring Report, 15 September 1958; VJ1432/4, Johnston to FO, 9 October 1958.
28. NARG 59, Mallory to SS, 785.00/7-2158.
29. PRO, FO 371/134009/VJ1015/74, Johnston to FO, 13 August 1958; 134010/VJ1015/82, Johnston to FO, 21 August 1958; VJ1015/100, Johnston to FO, 4 September 1958; 'Ahkam al-mahkamah al-'askariyah fi qadiyat tahrib al-aslihah', *Al-Difa'*, 13 August 1958.
30. PRO, FO 371/134009/VJ1015/61, Johnston to FO, 29 July 1958; 134010/VJ1015/76, Johnston to FO, 14 August 1958; NARG 59, Wright to SS, 785.00/8-458; Wright to SS, 785.00/8-558; Wright to SS, 785.00/8-1458; Wright to SS, 785.00/8-2158.
31. Amman Radio, 28 July 1958, BBC Summary of World Broadcasts (hereafter SWB) Part IV, No. 615, 31 July 1958.
32. Jerusalem Radio, 6 August 1958, SWB Part IV, No. 622, 8 August 1958.
33. NARG 59, Wright to SS, 785.00/8-1958; PRO, FO 371/134009/VJ1015/73, Johnston to FO, 11 August 1958.
34. NARG 59, Amman to DoS, 785.00/12-958. In 1960 260 political prisoners remained in Jordanian jails, most having been detained since 1957. PRO, FO 371/151117/VJ1641/1, Figg to Moberly, 20 July 1960.
35. NARG 59, Dulles to London, 785.00/7-1558.
36. Memcon Dulles and Fawzi, 14 August 1958, *FRUS, 1958–1960, Vol. XI*, pp. 469–73.
37. NARG 59, 'Causes of disaffection with Rifa'i regime', 785.00/9-358; PRO, FO 371/134009/VJ1015/74G, Johnston to FO, 12 August 1958.
38. PRO, FO 371/134094/VJ1642/2, Hooper Minute 'Internal security in Jordan', 1 August 1958.
39. P. Snow, *Hussein: A Biography* (London: Barrie and Jenkins, 1972), pp. 123–9.
40. PRO, FO 371/134010/VJ1015/120, Johnston to FO, 20 October 1958.
41. His Majesty King Hussein, *Uneasy Lies the Head* (London: Heinemann, 1962), pp. 179–85; J.Y. Lunt, *Hussein of Jordan: A Political Biography* (London: Macmillan, 1989), pp. 58–9; P. Snow, *Hussein: A Biography*, pp. 130–2.
42. PRO, FO 371/134022/VJ10389/8/File. The Jordanian complaint detailed the role of Syrian intelligence in arms smuggling and terrorism. 'S/4048, Letter dated 7 August 1958 from the representative of Jordan to the President of the Security Council', *SCOR, Supplement, 1958*, pp. 125–6.
43. NARG 59, Joint Weeka, 786B.00(W)/11-1358; *Bulletin de la Presse Syrienne*, No. 1062, Rubrique III.
44. 'Syrians force plane to land', *Daily Telegraph*, 18 February 1958; 'Syrian tax on Jordanian planes', *Egyptian Mail*, 1 March 1958; 'Syrian guns fire locust aircraft', *The Times*, 18 April 1958.
45. Additionally, it may be the case that Nasser at this stage did not want Hussein dead as this would have led to the UAR having to absorb Jordan. This would have been extremely costly and may have led to an Israeli attack on the West Bank. In August talks between Dulles and the UAR's Foreign Minister, Dr Fawzi, Dulles 'pointed out that Jordan would be a liability to whomever took it over. Dr Fawzi said that he declined the honor. It was more logical that oil-rich Iraq did so.' Memcon Dulles and Fawzi, 14 August 1958, *FRUS, 1958–1960, Vol. XI*, pp. 469–73. See also: Wheelock, *Nasser's New Egypt*, pp. 264–5.

46. PRO, FO 371/134011/VJ1015/134, Johnston to FO, 18 November 1958; VJ1015/140, Johnston to FO, 1 December 1958.

47. For the background to, and details of, the Iraqi revolution, see: M. Khadduri, *Republican Iraq* (London: Oxford University Press/Royal Institute of International Affairs, 1969), pp. 17–46; H. Batatu, *The Old Social Classes and the Revolutionary Movements of Iraq* (Princeton, NJ: Princeton University Press, 1978), pp. 764–807; U. Dann, *Iraq Under Qassem: A Political History, 1958–1963* (London: Pall Mall Press, 1969), pp. 19–32.

48. In the immediate aftermath of the revolution 'Arif had handed over to the UAR several exiles who had been working with the Iraqi monarchy against the UAR. NARG 59, Haring to DoS, 786B.00/2–1759.

49. Khadduri, *Republican Iraq*, pp. 92–8; M. Farouk-Sluglett and P. Sluglett, *Iraq since 1958: From Revolution to Dictatorship* (London: IB Tauris & Co Ltd, 1990), pp. 58–60; PRO, FO 371/140986.

50. NARG 59, Bureau of Intelligence and Research, 'Iraq: the crisis in leadership and the communist advance', Intelligence Report No. 7921, 16 January 1959.

51. NARG 59, 'Iraq: the crisis in leadership and the communist advance', Intelligence Report No. 7921, 16 January 1959.

52. Since 'substantial religious and ethnic groups, particularly the Kurds and Bedouin in the north and Shia tribes in the South, bitterly oppose absorption into the UAR, and the Army might well fragment if ordered to force this issue'. NARG 59, 'Iraq: the crisis in leadership and the communist advance', Intelligence Report No. 7921, 16 January 1959.

53. Khadduri, *Republican Iraq*, pp. 181–5; A. Nutting, *Nasser*, (London: Constable, 1972) pp. 256–62; Heikal, *Nasser: The Cairo Documents*, pp. 134–5.

54. Dann gives an account of the Rashid 'Ali plot which, he argues, was designed to lead Iraq into the UAR. Dann, *Iraq Under Qassem: A Political History, 1958–1963*, pp. 127–35. See also: PRO, FO 371/140929/EQ1017/3, Trevelyan to FO, 25 March 1959; Caroz, *The Arab Secret Services*, pp. 96–9.

55. This account of the revolt is taken from: NARG 59, Wilson to DoS, 787.00/3–1659 and Batatu, *The Old Social Classes and the Revolutionary Movements of Iraq*, pp. 866–89.

56. Mosul Radio, 9 March 1959, SWB Part IV, No. 801, 10 March 1959.

57. The UAR, naturally, denied any involvement. NARG 59, Ross to DoS, 786B.00/4–2559.

58. Farouk-Sluglett and Sluglett, *Iraq since 1958: From Revolution to Dictatorship*, pp. 66–70.

59. T. Petran, *Syria* (London: Ernest Benn Ltd, 1972), p. 132. Dann supports Petran's assessment. Dann, *Iraq Under Qassem: A Political History, 1958–1963*, pp. 164–77.

60. Nutting, *Nasser*, p. 256.

61. Batatu, *The Old Social Classes and the Revolutionary Movements of Iraq*, p. 872.

62. Mahmud al-Durrah, '"Thawrat" al-Mawsil ba'd sab' sanawat (The Mosul "revolution" after seven years)', *Arab Studies*, No. 6 (April 1966), pp. 46–59.

63. PRO, FO 371/140929/EQ1017/3, Trevelyan to FO, 25 March 1959; EQ1017/5, Trevelyan to Lloyd, 2 April 1959; Caroz, *The Arab Secret Services*, pp. 99–100.

64. NARG 59, Anschuetz to SS, 787.00/3–959.

65. NARG 59, Jernegan to SS, 787.00/3–1059.

66. The US Consul in Basra described the scene when a clerk chastised the crowd for bad-mouthing Nasser: 'the crowd fell on [him], beat him to the ground,

dropped heavy timbers across his body, gouged out his eyes with a penknife while he was still alive, and finally put a rope around his neck and dragged him through the streets ... behind a jeep'. NARG 59, Scott to DoS, 686B.87/3-1459.
67. NARG 59, Wilson to DoS, 686B.87/3-1959.
68. *Bulletin de la Presse Syrienne*, No. 1095, Rubrique III; Damascus Radio, 12 March 1959, SWB Part IV, No. 805, 14 March 1959.
69. NARG 59, Haring to DoS, 686B.87/4-2959; *Bulletin de la Presse Syrienne*, No. 1096, Rubrique III.
70. NARG 59, Glidden to Cumming, 787.00/3-1359; Reams to SS, 787.00/3-1859; *Bulletin de la Presse Syrienne*, No. 1097 and 1103, Rubrique III. This development was of course welcomed by the United States. In June Assistant Secretary of State Rountree declared he was 'greatly encouraged ... by the present UAR position on Communism' and Ambassador Hare described US relations with Nasser as a 'honeymoon'. NARG 59, Memcon Rountree and Urguplu, 686B.87/6-1959; Oral History Interview with Raymond Hare, OH-189, Eisenhower Library, pp. 26-7.
71. Iraqi forces sometimes engaged in 'hot pursuit' of these refugees, and on more than one occasion Iraqi aircraft or patrols attacked villages inside Syria. NARG 59, Joint Weeka, 786B.00(W)/3-1959; *Bulletin de la Presse Syrienne*, No. 1102, Rubrique III.
72. NARG 59, Haring to DoS, 686B.87/9-2259.
73. Saddam Husayn and his fellow would-be assassins have provided a detailed account of the operation. Iraqi News Agency, 8 and 9 October 1991, SWB, ME/1201, 12 October 1991 and ME/1202, 14 October 1991. See also: NARG 59, Jernegan to SS, 787.00/10-859; Khadduri, *Republican Iraq*, pp. 126-31; Farouk-Sluglett and Sluglett, *Iraq since 1958: From Revolution to Dictatorship*, pp. 72-3; Dann, *Iraq Under Qassem: A Political History, 1958-1963*, pp. 253-64.
74. NARG 59, Jernegan to SS, 686B.87/10-1659.
75. NARG 59, Jernegan to SS, 787.00/12-2859; PRO, FO 371/140931/EQ1017/38, Trevelyan to FO, 30 December 1959.
76. NARG 59, Anschuetz to SS, 787.00/12-2859; PRO, FO 371/140931/EQ1017/40, Trevelyan to FO, 31 December 1959.
77. Tahir, *Iraq aux Origines du Régime Militaire*, pp. 228-31.
78. Khadduri, *Republican Iraq*, p. 128 n. 35. Caroz also claims that the plotters were aided by an intelligence officer from the UAR Embassy. Caroz, *The Arab Secret Services*, pp. 100-1.
79. J.F. Devlin, *The Ba'th Party: A History from its Origins to 1966* (Stanford University, Stanford, CA: Hoover Institution Press, 1976), p. 159.
80. PRO, FO 371/134382/VY1015/35, Ankara to FO, 2 April 1958; 134384/VY1015/62, Middleton to FO, 17 June 1958.
81. P. Mansfield, *Nasser* (London: Methuen Educational Ltd, 1969), pp. 110-12; PRO, FO 371/141900/VG1017/9/G, Masan to FO, 5 August 1959.
82. PRO, FO 371/141900/VG1017/20, Canada House to FO, 3 December 1959.
83. NARG 59, Jones to DoS, 786B.00/8-59; Haring to SS, 786B.00/12-3059; Anschuetz to SS, 786B.00/12-3159; *Cahiers de L'Orient Contemporain* XLI (1959), pp. 402-3.
84. NARG 59, Meyer to Hart, 27 October 1959, 786B.00/10-2759.
85. The other functional branches were: Military Prisons, Bureau of Schedules, Supervision of Frontier Network, File Room, Interrogation Branch, Finance and Fiscal Branch, Supervision of Agents. These functional branches were in addition to the branches responsible for various sectors of the country. Centre for Lebanese Studies, Oxford (hereafter CLS), RG319, ID File, Department of the Army Intelligence Report, No. 2130391, 31 December 1959.

86. On the Kuwait incident, see; Khadduri, *Republican Iraq*, pp. 166–72.
87. One of the reasons for Nasser's split with the Ba'th in late 1959 had been the Ba'th's demands that Nasser pursue a more 'activist' and 'radical' foreign policy, in particular, making greater efforts to subvert Jordan. NARG 59, Anschuetz to SS, 786B.00/12–3059.
88. *Cahiers de L'Orient Contemporain*, XLVI (1961), p. 283; XLVII (1961), p. 399.
89. PRO, FO 371/158791/VG1016/158, Cairo to FO, 29 September 1961; VG1016/163, Clarke to Earl of Home, 1 October 1961.
90. For Nasser's perspective on the *infisal*, see: M.H. Heikal, *Ma alladhi jara fi Suriah? (What Happened in Syria?)* (Cairo: Al-Dar al-qawmiah lil-tiba'ah wa-al-nashr, n.d.).
91. A company of Egyptian paratroops did drop on Latakia airfield, but they were immediately captured. Be'eri, *Army Officers in Arab Politics and Society*, p. 144.
92. PRO, FO 371/158791/VG1016/175, Arthur to FO, 2 October 1961.

Conclusion

1. 'Campaign of terror is leading to violence', *Guardian*, 8 October 1979; 'The Secret Brothers and Syria's rising tide of violence', *Financial Times*, 19 March 1980; 'Syrians fail to crush Moslem Brotherhood', *Financial Times*, 21 October 1981; P. Seale, *Asad: The Struggle for the Middle East* (London: I.B. Tauris & Co, 1988), pp. 316–38.
2. For instance, in the mid-1970s and mid-1980s Iraqi intelligence carried out bombings and shootings in Damascus and Syria responded in kind. 'Iraq blamed for bombings', *Financial Times*, 29 December 1976; 'Bagdad reaps a religious whirlwind', *Guardian*, 1 March 1977; 'Blast in Damascus', *Guardian*, 5 July 1977; 'Assad's Bürde wird schwerer', *Frankfurter Allgemeine Zeitung*, 24 March 1986; 'Bombs in Damascus,' *Foreign Report*, 27 March 1986.

APPENDIX I

Key dates

27 September 1941	Proclamation of Syrian independence.
15 April 1946	Withdrawal of last French troops.
16 December 1948	'Azm forms cabinet.
30 March 1949	Husni al-Za'im's coup.
8 July 1949	Antun Sa'adah executed in Beirut.
14 August 1949	Sami Hinnawi's coup. Za'im and Barazi executed.
19 December 1949	Adib al-Shishakli ousts Hinnawi.
28 November 1951	Shishakli's coup against Dawilibi's government.
December 1952	Army plot uncovered; Hawrani and Ba'thists flee to Lebanon.
July 1953	Shishakli elected President.
January–February 1954	Arrest of opposition politicians; Druze uprising.
24–28 February 1954	Coup ousts Shishakli.
September 1954	Parliamentary elections.
13 January 1955	Turkish-Iraqi pact.
6 March 1955	Formation of Egypt-Syrian-Sa'udi pact.
22 April 1955	'Adnan Malki assassinated; followed by purge of SSNP.
18 August 1955	Shukri Quwatli elected President.
3 November 1956	Discovery of 'Iraqi plot' announced.
19 February 1957	Ghassan Jadid assassinated in Beirut.
April 1957	Zerqa plot in Jordan.
June 1957	Lebanese parliamentary elections.
12 August 1957	Discovery of 'American plot' announced.
1 February 1958	United Arab Republic formed.
14 July 1958	Iraqi revolution.
March 1959	Mosul revolt.
28 September 1961	Dissolution of the United Arab Republic.

APPENDIX 2

Key personalities

Politicians

'Abd al-Masih, Georges	SSNP member; President of party after Sa'adah's death; 1955 organised Malki assassination; 1956 expelled from party.
'Aflaq, Michel	Ba'th Party founder.
al-'Ajlani, Munir	Pro-Hashimite independent politician; involved in 1956 'Iraqi plot'.
Arslan, Amir 'Adil	Za'im's Foreign Minister March–June 1949.
al-'Asali, Faysal	Leader of Socialist Cooperative Party.
al-'Asali, Sabri	National Party politician; Prime Minister in 1954, 1955, 1956 and 1957.
al-Atasi, 'Adnan	Son of Hashim al-Atasi; implicated in 'Iraqi plot'.
al-Atasi, Faydi	Cousin of 'Adnan al-Atasi; Foreign Minister in 1951; implicated in 'Iraqi plot'.
al-Atasi, Hashim	President of Syria 1936, 1950–51, 1954–55.
al-Atrash, Amir Hasan	Druze notable; involved in 1956 'Iraqi plot'.
al-Atrash, Mansur	Son of Sultan Atrash; arrested by Shishakli in January 1954.
al-Atrash, Sultan Pasha	Druze leader of 1925 revolt against French; led Druze uprising against Shishakli in January 1954.
al-'Azm, Khalid	Prime Minister December 1948–March 1949; variously Prime Minister and Defence Minister during the 1950s.
Baqdash, Khalid	Syrian Communist Party leader.
al-Barazi, Husni	Pro-Iraqi politician; arrested by Shishakli November 1951.
al-Barazi, Muhsin	Za'im's Prime Minister June 1949 until execution August 1949.
Barmada, Mustafa	People's Party politician.

Barmada, Rashad	People's Party politician; Interior Minister in 1950; Defence Minister in 1954 and 1955.
Bitar, Salah al-Din	Ba'th Party founder; Foreign Minister in 1956 and 1957.
al-Dawilibi, Ma'ruf	People's Party politician; Prime Minister in November 1951, ousted by Shishakli.
Fansah, Nadhir	Husni Za'im's brother-in-law.
al-Haffar Lutfi	National Party politician.
al-Hakim, Hasan	Pro-Hashimite independent politician; Prime Minister in 1951.
al-Hawrani, Akram	ASP leader; from 1953 leader of the merged ABSP; Defence Minister in 1955, 1956 and 1957.
Ilyan, Mikhail	Pro-Iraqi National Party politician; involved in 1956 'Iraqi plot'.
Jabbara, Hasan	Finance Minister in 'Azm's 1948–49 cabinet and under Za'im.
al-Khuri, Faris	National Party politician; Prime Minister 1954.
al-Kikhia, Rushdi	People's Party politician; 1957 speaker of Chamber of Deputies.
al-Kuzbari, Ma'mun	1953 President of Chamber of Deputies; February 1954 declared himself President after Shishakli left but forced to resign. Held ministerial posts in the late 1950s.
al-Mahaiyri, 'Isam	SSNP member; 1949 head of Damascus office; 1954 Secretary-General of SSNP; imprisoned after 1955 Malki assassination.
Mardam Bey, Jamil	National Party politician; Prime Minister during 1948.
al-Qudsi, Nazim	People's Party politician; Prime Minister in 1950; President of Chamber of Deputies in 1954.
al-Quwatli, Shukri	National Party leader; President, 1943–49, 1955–58.
Sa'adah, Antun	SSNP founder; executed by Lebanese government, 8 July 1949.
Tallas, As'ad	Hinnawi's brother-in-law; pro-Iraqi politician; worked with Safa in Iraq against Shishakli 1952–54.

Army Officers

Abu Assaf, Amin	Druze officer, one of the leaders of February 1954 coup against Shishakli.
Abu Mansur, Fadlallah	Druze officer, SSNP member; involved in execution

APPENDIX 2

	of Za'im in August 1949 and arrest of Hinnawi in December 1949; in 1956 retired from army and became Defence Commissioner of SSNP.
Adham, Burhan	Close to Shishakli in 1951, left army after February 1954 coup; worked as agent for Sarraj in 'Iraqi plot'; leading officer in Deuxième Bureau under Sarraj.
al-Atasi, Faysal	One of leaders of February 1954 coup against Shishakli.
al-Bizri, 'Afif	Pro-communist; in 1957 he was President of military court trying 'Iraqi plot'; became Chief of Staff in August 1957; leader of army delegation to Cairo in January 1958.
al-Bizri, Salah	Head of Deuxième Bureau after Hinnawi's coup.
Hamdun, Mustafa	Pro-Ba'thist and pro-Hawrani. One of leaders of February 1954 coup against Shishakli; member of army delegation to Cairo in January 1958.
Hinnawi, Sami	Leader of August 1949 coup against Husni Za'im.
al-Husayni, Ibrahim	Za'im's Chief of Military Police in 1949; Director of Deuxième Bureau under Shishakli, 1949–51; Military Attaché in Rome after February 1954 coup; implicated in 1957 'American Plot'.
Jadid, Ghassan	SSNP member; in 1955 dismissed from army and became SSNP Defence Commissioner; organised SSNP militia in 'Iraqi plot'; assassinated in Beirut, February 1957.
Kallas, Bahij	Pro-Hawrani officer; backed Za'im's and Hinnawi's coups.
al-Malki, 'Adnan	Led movement in army against Shishakli in December 1952; Deputy Chief of Staff in 1955; assassinated by SSNP, April 1955.
Ma'ruf, Muhammad	Supported Hinnawi's coup in 1949; implicated in 'Iraqi plot'.
Mraywad, 'Isam	Pro-SSNP officer; involved in execution of Za'im; worked with Safa in Iraq in 1952–54 against Shishakli.
al-Nafuri, Amin	Led faction of officers in mid-1950s opposed to Ba'th and Sarraj.
Nizam al-Din, Tawfiq	Chief of Staff, June 1956 to August 1957.
Qannut, 'Abd al-Ghani	Deputy Head of Deuxième Bureau in 1950; pro-Ba'thist officer during 1950s, member of army delegation to Cairo in January 1958.
al-Rifa'i, Mahmud	Director of Deuxième Bureau in late 1949; worked with Safa in Iraq in 1952–54 against Shishakli.

Safa, Muhammad	Retired from army by Shishakli in 1952; formed 'Free Syria Government' in Iraq; jailed in Syria, June 1954; involved in 'Iraqi plot'.
al-Samarra'i, Salih	Assistant Iraqi Military Attaché in Damascus, expelled February 1954; coordinated 'Iraqi plot' from Beirut in 1956.
Sarraj, 'Abd al-Hamid	Captain in 1954; involved in anti-Shishakli coup; Attaché in Paris in 1954; appointed Director of Deuxième Bureau in February 1955; leading pro-Nasserist officer, 1955–58; Interior Minister of Northern Province of UAR; appointed Chairman of Syrian Provincial Council, September 1958; appointed Vice-President of UAR in August 1961; arrested by secessionist government in Syria, September 1961; subsequently escaped.
Selu, Fawzi	President, 1951–53.
al-Shishakli, Adib	Commander of 1st Brigade in 1949; led coup against Hinnawi, December 1949; Deputy Chief of Staff, 1949–51; President in 1953; ousted in February 1954 coup; active in exile politics in mid-1950s; assassinated in 1964.
al-Shishakli, Salah	Adib's brother; SSNP member; involved in 1956 'Iraqi plot'.
Shuqayr, Shawkat	Lebanese Druze officer; head of Za'im's *cabinet militaire*; Syrian Chief of Staff from July 1953 to July 1956.
al-Za'im, Husni	Chief of Staff, June 1948–49. Led coup in March 1949; President from June 1949; Executed in Hinnawi's coup, August 1949.

Bibliography

Primary material

Britain

PUBLIC RECORDS OFFICE, LONDON
Cabinet Papers: CAB 128
Foreign Office Papers: FO 93, FO 371, FO 800, FO 957, FO 1018

America

NATIONAL ARCHIVES, WASHINGTON, DC
Record Group 59: 611.83, 661.83, 682.83, 683A.00, 686B.87, 783.00, 783.00(W), 783.521, 783.551, 783A.00, 785.00, 786.00, 786B.00, 786B.00(W), 787.00, 890D.00, 890D.6363, 890E.00
Record Group 263: Box 113
Record Group 319: Army Intelligence Project Decimal File

NATIONAL ARCHIVES ANNEX, SUITLAND, MARYLAND
Record Group 84: Confidential File 350, Confidential File 350C, Confidential File 370

HARRY S. TRUMAN PRESIDENTIAL LIBRARY, INDEPENDENCE, MISSOURI
President's Secretary's Files: Intelligence File, National Security Council File

DWIGHT D. EISENHOWER PRESIDENTIAL LIBRARY, ABILENE, KANSAS
White House Office/NSC Staff/OCB Central Files
Office of the Special Assistant for National Security Affairs/OCB Series/Subject Subseries
Dwight D. Eisenhower White House Central Files: Confidential File
John Foster Dulles Papers: Telephone Calls Series, White House Memoranda Series
Ann Whitman Files: Dwight D. Eisenhower Diaries Series, Dulles-Herter Series, National Security Council Series
Hare, R., Oral History Interview OH-149
Yost, C., Oral History Interview OH-416

LIBRARY OF CONGRESS
Declassified Documents Reference System

OBTAINED FROM THE CIA UNDER THE FREEDOM OF INFORMATION ACT
'Syrian coup d'Etat', CIA Information Report, No. SO23547, 28 April 1949.
Special National Intelligence Estimate Number 30-3-56, 'Nasser and the Middle East situation', 31 July 1956.

Memorandum Allen Dulles to Goodpaster, 22 March 1957.
'Assessment of the political situation in Lebanon', CIA Information Report, 2 April 1958.
'The game of nations: the amorality of power politics', *Studies in Intelligence*, Vol. 14, No. 1 (Spring 1970).
'Ropes of sand: America's failure in the Middle East', *Studies in Intelligence*, Vol. 27, No. 3 (Fall 1983).

Israel

ISRAEL STATE ARCHIVES, JERUSALEM
Foreign Ministry Files

Collections of unpublished papers

CENTRE FOR LEBANESE STUDIES, OXFORD
Declassified Documents Project: RG 319, ID File

JAFET LIBRARY, AMERICAN UNIVERSITY OF BEIRUT
Middle East Files

Unpublished memoirs

Barmada, M.R., *Dhikrayat wa-ara'* (*Memoirs and opinions*)

Official documents

Department of State Bulletin, Vol. XVI, No. 403, 23 March 1947.
Department of State Bulletin, Vol. XXII, No. 570, 5 June, 1950.
US Department of State, *Syrian Support for International Terrorism: 1983–1986*, Special Report No. 157 (Washington, DC: Department of State, December 1986).
Foreign Relations of the United States, 1947, Vol. V; 1949, Vol. V; 1949, Vol. VI; 1950, Vol. V; 1951, Vol. V; 1952–1954, Vol. IX; 1955–1957, Vol. XIII; 1958–1960, Vol. XI, XIII (Washington, DC: US Government Printing Office).
The Government of Jordan, *Al-Kitab al-Urdunni al-abyad* (*The Jordanian White Book*) (Amman: n.pb., n.d.).
Inaugural Address of Harry S. Truman, 20 January 1949 (Washington, DC: Government Printing Office, 1949).
Poole, W.S., *The History of the Joint Chiefs of Staff, Volume IV, 1950–1952* (Washington, DC: Historical Research Division, Joint Secretariat, Joint Chiefs of Staff, 1979).
Resolutions Adopted by the General Assembly During its Twenty Eighth Session (Vol. I) (New York: United Nations, 1974).
Resolutions and Decisions Adopted by the General Assembly During its Thirty Fourth Session (New York: United Nations, 1980).
Security Council Official Records, Supplement 1954; Supplement 1955–1956; 823rd Meeting, 1958; Supplement 1958.
Watson, R.J., *The History of the Joint Chiefs of Staff, Volume V, 1953–1954* (Washington, DC: Historical Division, Joint Secretariat, Joint Chiefs of Staff, 1986).

Memoirs and speeches

King 'Abdallah of Jordan, *My Memoirs Completed 'Al Takmilah'*, translated by Harold W. Glidden (London: Longman, 1978).
Abu Mansur, F., *A'asir Dimashq* (*Damascus Storms*) (Beirut: n.pb., 1959).
Abu Nuwar, A., *Hin talashaat al-'arab* (*When the Arabs Wither*) (London: Dar al-saqi, 1990).
'Ajlani, M., *Difa' al-duktur Munir al-'Ajlani amam al-mahkamah al-'askariyah bi-Dimashq* (*Defence of Dr Munir al-'Ajlani Before the Military Court in Damascus*) (n.p.: n.pb., 1957).
Arslan, 'A., *Dhikrayat al-Amir 'Adil Arslan an Husni al-Za'im* (*Memoirs of Amir 'Adil Arslan about Husni al-Za'im*) (Beirut: Dar al-kitab al-jadid, 1962).
al-'Azm, K., *Mudhakkirat Khalid al-'Azm* (*Memoirs of Khalid al-'Azm*) (Beirut: Dar al-muttahida lil-nashr, 1973).
Babil, N., *Sahafa wa-siyasa* (*Journalism and Politics*) (London: Riyad al-Rayyis Books, 1987).
Bull, O., *War and Peace in the Middle East* (London: Leo Cooper, 1976).
Burns, Lieutenant General E.L.M., *Between Arab and Israeli* (London: George G. Harrap and Co Ltd, 1962).
Chamoun, C., *Crise Au Moyen-Orient* (Montrouge: Gallimard, 1963).
Copeland, M., *The Game of Nations* (London: Weidenfeld and Nicolson, 1969).
Copeland, M., *The Game Player* (London: Aurum Press, 1989).
Eden, A., *Full Circle: The Memoirs of the Rt Hon Sir Anthony Eden KG, PC, MC* (London: Cassell, 1960).
Eisenhower, D.D., *Waging Peace* (London: Heinemann, 1966).
Eveland, W.C., *Ropes of Sand: America's Failure in the Middle East* (New York: W.W. Norton and Co, 1980).
Fansah, N., *Ayyam Husni al-Za'im – 137 yawman hazzat Suria* (*Days of Husni al-Za'im – 137 Days That Shook Syria*) (Beirut: Dar al-afaq al-jadidah, 1973).
His Majesty King Hussein, *Uneasy Lies the Head* (London: Heinemann, 1962).
Hutchison, Commander E.H., USNR, *Violent Truce* (London: John Calder, 1956).
Jabrij, J., *Ma' Antun Sa'adah* (*With Antun Sa'adah*) (Beirut: n.pb., 1984).
Johnston, C., *The Brink of Jordan* (London: Hamish Hamilton, 1972).
Kirkbride, A.S., *A Crackle of Thorns* (London: John Murray, 1956).
Lloyd, S., *Suez 1956* (London: Jonathan Cape, 1978).
Macmillan, H., *Tides of Fortune, 1945–1955* (London: Macmillan, 1969).
Macmillan, H., *Riding the Storm* (New York: Harper and Row, 1971).
McGhee, G., *Envoy to the Middle World* (New York: Harper and Row, 1983).
Qaddurah, A., *Haqa'iq wa-mawaqif* (*Facts and Opinions*) (Beirut: Dar mu'assasat al-fikr, 1989).
Riad, M., *The Struggle for Peace in the Middle East* (London: Quartet Books, 1981).
Roosevelt, A., *For Lust of Knowing: Memoirs of an Intelligence Officer* (London: Weidenfeld and Nicolson, 1988).
Sa'adah, A., *Mukhtarat fi al-mas'alah al-lubnaniyah – 2 – al-ini'zaliyah 'aflasat* (*Selected Writings in the Lebanese Question – 2 – Isolationism Failed*) (Beirut: SSNP, 1976).
As Mukayil Saqaal, F., *Min dhikrayat hukumat al-Za'im Husni al-Za'im* (*From the Memoirs of the Government of General Husni al-Za'im*) (n.p.: n.pb., 1952).
Sharabi, H., *Al-Jism wa-al-ramad* (*The Body and the Ashes*) (Beirut: Dar al-tali'ah lil-tiba'ah wa-al-nashr, 1978).
Sharett, M., *Personal Diary*, Vol. II (Tel Aviv: 1978) (Hebrew).

Shuckburgh, E., *Descent to Suez* (New York: W.W. Norton and Co, 1986).
Stirling, W.F., *Safety Last* (London: Hollis and Carter, 1953).
Tlass, M., *Mir'at hayati* (*Mirror to My Life*) (Damascus: Dar al-Tlass, n.d.).

Newspapers and news agencies

L'Aube, Al-Ayam, Barada, La Bourse Egyptienne, Christian Science Monitor, Combat, Al-Difa', Egyptian Gazette, Egyptian Mail, Al-Faiha', Falastin, Frankfurter Allgemeine Zeitung, Hsinhua News Agency, L'Humanité, Jerusalem Post, Manchester Guardian, Le Monde, Neue Züricher Zeitung, New York Herald Tribune, New York Times, News Chronicle, Observer, The Observer Foreign News Service, L'Orient, Le Populaire, Sawt al-Arab, Scotsman, Le Soir, Daily Telegraph, The Times, La Tribune des Nations, Al-Wahda, Yorkshire Post

Press summaries

Bulletin de la Presse Syrienne

Theses

Amine, M., *Le Développement des partis politiques en Syrie entre 1936 et 1947* (PhD Thesis, University of Paris, 1950).
Barradah, F.K., *Saudi Arabia's Foreign Policy 1945–1984* (PhD Thesis, Aberdeen University, 1989).
Bodron, M.M., *Violence in the Syrian Social Nationalist Party* (MA Thesis, American University of Beirut, 1970).
El-Khalil, A.Y., *The Socialist Parties in Syria and Lebanon* (PhD Thesis, American University, Washington, DC, 1962).
Ghalioun, B., *Etat et luttes des classes en Syrie, 1945–1970* (PhD Thesis, University of Paris VIII, 1974).
Lesch, D.W., *The United States and Syria, 1953–1957: The Cold War in the Middle East* (PhD Thesis, Harvard University, 1990).
Maatouk, M., *A Critical Study of Antun Sa'ada and his Impact on Politics, The History of Ideas and Literature in the Middle East* (PhD Thesis, School of Oriental and African Studies, 1992).
Raad, Z., *King Hussein's Foreign Diplomacy: January 1956–December 1958* (PhD Thesis, Cambridge University, 1993).
Shihab, L.A., *The Role of the United Nations during the Lebanese Crisis of 1958* (MA Thesis, American University of Beirut, 1963).
Soysal, O., *An Analysis of the Influence of Turkey's Alignment with the West and of the Arab-Israeli Conflict upon Turkish-Israeli Relations and Turkish-Arab Relations* (PhD Thesis, Princeton University, 1983).
Stewart, J., *Aspect's of Lebanon's Reaction to the Middle East Policy of the United States (May 1950–August 1958)* (MA Thesis, American University of Beirut, 1959).

Interviews/correspondence

Private interviews were conducted with:
General Michael Sema'n (Chef d'État Majeur, Lebanese Internal Security Forces), February 1992, Beirut;
Joubran Hayek (previously editor of *Al-Bina*, SSNP newspaper), 13.2.1992, Beirut;

BIBLIOGRAPHY 231

Fu'ad Awad (leader of SSNP coup in Lebanon in 1961), 27.2.1992, Beirut;
'Abdallah Kobecsy (former official of SSNP), 27.2.1992, Beirut;
Faisal Qudsi (son of Nazim Qudsi), 24.6.1992, London;
Alfred Atherton (former US Foreign Service officer), August 1992, Washington, DC;
Herman Eilts (former US Ambassador), August 1992, Washington, DC;
Stuart Rockwell (former US Foreign Service officer), 3.8.1992, Washington, DC;
Arthur C. Close (former CIA officer), 5.8.1992, Washington, DC;
Ghaleb Kayyali (former Syrian Foreign Ministry official), 22.11.1992, Damascus;
Bourhan Kassab-Hassan (former Syrian army officer), 10.5 and 8.6.1993, Damascus;
'Abd al-Ghani Qannut (former Syrian army officer), 16.5.1993, Damascus;
'Adnan Hamdun (former Syrian army officer), 5.6.1993, Damascus;
Khalid al-Fahum (Palestine Liberation Organisation official), 8.6.1993, Damascus;
Rajah Yazija (SSNP Culture Commissioner), 30.6.1993, Beirut;
Yussuf Aschqar (SSNP President), 8.7.1993, Beirut;
Adib Qaddurah (SSNP official), 8.7.1993, Beirut;
Elias Georgi Kunayzah (SSNP official), 8.7.1993, Dayr al-Shuwayr, Lebanon;
'Abdallah Mohsin (SSNP official), 9.7.1993, Beirut;
Bachir Mousli (SSNP official), 11.7.1993, Damascus;
Naim Abd al-Haadi (member of 1956–57 Nabulsi government), 28.7.1993, Amman;
Hamad Farhan (member of 1956–57 Nabulsi government), 2.8.1993, Amman;
Ahmad Sidqi al-Dajani (Palestinian activist), 9.8.1993, Cairo;
Qasim Alwan (former Syrian army officer), 10.8.1993, Cairo.

In addition, interviews were conducted with three Syrian intellectuals with family connections to politicians and officers active in the 1950s who asked to remain anonymous. (Anonymous interviews 1, 2 and 3.)

Correspondence was exchanged with:

William M. Rountree (former US Foreign Service officer), 24.8.1992;
William Brewer (former US Foreign Service officer), 25.8.1992;
Harlan B. Clark (former US Foreign Service officer), 9.9.1992;
Deane R. Hinton (US Foreign Service officer), 27.9.1992;
Richard Bissell, Jr (former CIA officer), 22.10.1992;
Hisham Abu Jaoude (SSNP officer), 27.11.1993.

In addition, correspondence was exchanged with a former CIA officer and a former US Foreign Service officer who asked to remain anonymous. (Anonymous communications 1 and 2.)

Books

Abd-Allah, U.F., *The Islamic Struggle in Syria* (Berkeley, CA: Mizan Press, 1983).
Agwani, M.S., ed., *The Lebanese Crisis 1958* (New Delhi: Indian School of International Studies, 1965).
Ajami, F., *The Vanished Imam: Musa al-Sadr and the Shia of Lebanon* (Ithaca, NY: Cornell University Press).
Aldrich, R.J., ed., *British Intelligence, Strategy and the Cold War 1945–1951* (London: Routledge, 1992).
Ambrose, S., *Ike's Spies: Eisenhower and the Espionage Establishment* (Garden City, NY: Doubleday and Co, 1981).
Anderson, I.H., *Aramco, the United States and Saudi Arabia* (Princeton, NJ: Princeton University Press, 1981).

Andrew, C., *Secret Service: The Making of the British Intelligence Community* (London: Heinemann, 1985).
Antonious, G., *The Arab Awakening* (London: Hamish Hamilton, 1938).
al-'Ayf, B., *Al-Inqilab al-Suri: 30 adhar 1949 (The Syrian Coup: 30 March 1949)* (Damascus: Maktabat Muhammad Husayn al-Nuri, 1949).
Barakat, H., ed., *Toward a Viable Lebanon* (London: Croom Helm, 1988).
Bar-Yaacov, N., *The Israeli-Syrian Armistice* (Jerusalem: Magnes Press, 1967).
Batatu, H., *The Old Social Classes and the Revolutionary Movements of Iraq* (Princeton, NJ: Princeton University Press, 1978).
Be'eri, E., *Army Officers in Arab Politics and Society* (London: Praeger, 1970).
Berger, E., *The Covenant and the Sword* (London: Routledge & Kegan Paul Ltd, 1965).
Bhutani, S., *The United Nations and the Arab-Israeli Conflict* (New Delhi: The Academic Press, 1977).
Birdwood, Lord, *Nuri as-Said: A Study in Leadership* (London: 1959).
al-Bizri, 'A., *Al-Nasiriyah fi jumlat al-isti'mar al-hadith (Nasirism in the Body of Modern Imperialism)* (Damascus: Dar al-Sharq lil-nashr wa-al-tawzi', 1962).
Black, I. and Morris, B., *Israel's Secret Wars* (London: Hamish Hamilton, 1991).
Bloch, J. and Fitzgerald, P., *British Intelligence and Covert Action* (Dingle: Brondon, 1983).
Blum, W., *The CIA: A Forgotten History: US Global Interventions since WW2* (London: Zed Books, 1986).
Campbell, J.C., *Defense of the Middle East* (New York: Harper, 1960).
Caroz, Y., *The Arab Secret Services* (London: Corgi, 1978).
Carré, O. and Michaud, G., *Les Frères Musulmans (1928–1982)* (Paris: Éditions Gallimard/Julliard, 1983).
Cline, R.S. and Alexander, Y., *Terrorism as State-Sponsored Covert Warfare* (Fairfax, VA: Hero Books, 1986).
Cobban, H., *The Making of Modern Lebanon* (London: Hutchinson, 1985).
Dallin, D.J., *Soviet Foreign Policy After Stalin* (New York: J.B. Lippincott Co, 1961).
Van Dam, N., *The Struggle for Power in Syria* (London: Croom Helm Ltd, 1979).
Dann, U., *Iraq Under Qassem: A Political History, 1958–1963* (London: Pall Mall Press, 1969).
Deacon, R., *The Israeli Secret Service* (London: Hamish Hamilton, 1977).
Devereux, D.R., *The Formulation of British Defence Policy Towards the Middle East, 1948–56* (London: Macmillan, 1990).
Devlin, J.F., *The Ba'th Party: A History from its Origins to 1966* (Stanford University, Stanford, CA: Hoover Institution Press, 1976).
Eckstein, H., ed., *Internal War* (London: Collier-Macmillan, 1964).
Ali al-Edroos, Brigadier S., *The Hashemite Army 1908–1979* (Amman: The Publishing Committee, 1980).
Eisenberg, D., Dann, U. and Landau, E., *The Mossad* (New York: Paddington Press, 1978).
Farouk-Sluglett, M. and Sluglett, P., *Iraq since 1958: From Revolution to Dictatorship* (London: IB Tauris & Co Ltd, 1990).
Harb Farzat, M., *Al-Hayah al-hizbiyah fi Suria (Party Life in Syria)* (Damascus: Dar al-Ruad, 1955).
Freiha, A.A., *L'Armée et l'État au Liban (1945–1980)* (Paris: Librairie Générale de Droit et de Jurisprudence, 1980).
Freitag, U., *Geschichtsschreibung in Syrien 1920–1990* (Hamburg: Deutsches Orient-Institut, 1991).
Fromkin, D., *A Peace to End All Peace* (London: Andre Deutsch, 1989).

Frye, R.N., *The Near East and the Great Powers* (Cambridge, MA: Harvard University, 1951).
Gaunson, A.B., *The Anglo-French Clash in Lebanon and Syria, 1940–45* (New York: St Martin's Press, 1987).
George, A., Lall, D. and Simons, W., *The Limits of Coercive Diplomacy* (Boston, MA: Little, Brown and Co, 1971).
al-Ghadari, N., *Al-Kitab al-aswad (The Black Book)* (Damascus: n.pb., n.d.).
Glubb, J.B., *Syria, Lebanon, Jordan* (London: Thames and Hudson, 1967).
Haddad, G., *Fifty Years of Modern Syria and Lebanon* (Beirut: Dar al-Hayat, 1950).
Hahn, P.L., *The United States, Great Britain, and Egypt, 1945–1956* (Chapel Hill, NC: University of North Carolina Press, 1991).
Heikal, M.H., *Nasser: The Cairo Documents* (London: New English Library, 1972).
Heikal, M.H, *Ma alladhi jara fi Suriah? (What Happened in Syria?)* (Cairo: Al-Dar al-qawmiah lil-tiba'ah wa-al-nashr, n.d.).
Herzog, C., *The Arab-Israeli Wars* (Bath: Book Club Associates, 1982).
Heyworth-Dunne, J., *Religious and Political Trends in Modern Egypt* (Washington, DC: The author, 1950).
Hirst, D., *The Gun and the Olive Branch* (London: Faber and Faber, 1977).
Hitti, P.K., *History of Syria* (London: Macmillan, 1951).
Hopwood, D., *Syria 1945–1986: Politics and Society* (London: Unwin Hyman, 1988).
von Horn, C., *Soldiering for Peace* (London: Cassell, 1966).
Hourani, A.H., *Syria and Lebanon: A Political Essay* (London: Royal Institute of International Affairs/Oxford University Press, 1946).
Hourani, A.H., *Minorities in the Arab World* (Oxford: Oxford University Press, 1947).
Howard, H.N., *The King-Crane Commission* (Beirut: Khayats, 1963).
Hurewitz, J.C., *Diplomacy in the Near and Middle East: A Documentary Record: 1914–1956* (Princeton, NJ: D. Van Nostrand, 1956).
Ionides, M., *Divide and Lose: The Arab Revolt 1955–58* (London: Geoffrey Bles, 1960).
Johnson, J.T. and Kelsay, J., eds, *Cross, Crescent and Sword: The Justification and Limitation of War in Western and Islamic Tradition* (New York: Greenwood Press, 1991).
Johnson, M., *Class and Client in Beirut: The Sunni Muslim Community and the Lebanese State 1840–1985* (London: Ithaca Press, 1986).
Kader, H.A., *The Syrian Social Nationalist Party* (Beirut: n.pb., 1990).
Karsh, E., *The Soviet Union and Syria* (London: Royal Institute of International Affairs/Routledge, 1988).
Kedourie, E., *England and the Middle East* (London: Bowes & Bowes, 1956).
Kedourie, E., *In the Anglo-Arab Labyrinth: The McMahon-Husayn Correspondence and its Interpretations 1914–1921* (Cambridge: Cambridge University Press, 1976).
Kenny, A., *The Logic of Deterrence* (London: Firethorn Press, 1985).
Kerr, M.H., *The Arab Cold War: Gamal 'Abd Al-Nasir and his Rivals, 1958–1970* (London: Oxford University Press, 1971).
Khadduri, M., *The Law of War and Peace in Islam* (London: Luzac & Co, 1940).
Khadduri, M., *Republican Iraq* (London: Oxford University Press/Royal Institute of International Affairs, 1969).
Khadduri, M., *Arab Contemporaries* (Baltimore, MD: Johns Hopkins University Press, 1973).
Khoury, P., *Syria and the French Mandate* (London: IB Tauris & Co, 1987).

Kyle, K., *Suez* (London: Weidenfeld and Nicolson, 1991).
Lacey, R., *The Kingdom* (London: Hutchinson, 1981).
Laqueur, W.Z., *Communism and Nationalism in the Middle East* (London: Routledge & Kegan Paul, 1956).
Laqueur, W.Z., *The Soviet Union and the Middle East* (London: Routledge & Kegan Paul, 1959).
Laurens, H., *Le Grand Jeu: Orient Arabe et Rivalités Internationales* (Paris: Armand Colin, 1991).
Longrigg, S.H., *Oil in the Middle East* (London: Oxford University Press, 1954).
Longrigg, S.H., *Syria and Lebanon under the French Mandate* (London: Royal Institute of International Affairs/Oxford University Press, 1958).
Louis, W.R., *Imperialism at Bay, 1941–1945* (Oxford: Clarendon Press, 1977).
Louis, W.R., *The British Empire in the Middle East* (New York: Oxford University Press, 1984).
Louis, W.R. and Owen, R., eds, *Suez 1956: The Crisis and its Consequences* (Oxford: Clarendon Press, 1991).
Love, K., *Suez: The Twice Fought War* (London: Longman, 1969).
Lucas, W.S., *Divided We Stand: Britain, The US and The Suez Crisis* (London: Hodder & Stoughton, 1991).
Lunt, J., *Hussein of Jordan: A Political Biography* (London: Macmillan, 1989).
Mansfield, P., *Nasser's Egypt* (Harmondsworth: Penguin, 1965).
Mansfield, P., *Nasser* (London: Methuen Educational Ltd, 1969).
Mansfield, P., *The Ottoman Empire and its Successors* (London: Macmillan, 1973).
Mardam Bey, S., *Syria's Quest for Independence 1939–1945* (Reading, MA: Ithaca Press, 1994).
Marlowe, J., *Perfidious Albion: The Origins of Anglo-French Rivalry in the Levant* (London: Elek Books, 1971).
Melman, Y. and Raviv, D., *The Imperfect Spies* (London: Sidgwick & Jackson, 1989).
Miller, R.C., *Dag Hammarskjöld and Crisis Diplomacy* (Washington, DC: Oceana, 1961).
Monroe, E., *Britain's Moment in the Middle East 1914–1956* (London: Chatto & Windus, 1963).
Morris, B., *Israel's Border Wars, 1949–1956* (Oxford: Clarendon Press, 1993).
Murphy, J.F., *State Support of International Terrorism: Legal, Political, and Economic Dimensions* (London: Mansell Publishing & Westview Press, 1989).
Musa, S., *A'lam min al-Urdunn (Outstanding Personalities from Jordan)* (Amman: Dar al-sha'b, 1986).
Nutting, A., *No End of a Lesson: The Story of Suez* (London: Constable, 1967).
Nutting, A., *Nasser* (London: Constable, 1972).
Omissi, D., *Air Power and Colonial Control* (Manchester: Manchester University Press, 1990).
Osmanczyk, E.J., *The Encylopedia of the United Nations and International Relations* (New York: Taylor and Francis, 1990).
Painter, D.S., *Oil and the American Century* (Baltimore, MD: Johns Hopkins Press, 1986).
Payne, R., *Mossad: Israel's Most Secret Service* (London: Bantam Press, 1990).
Perthes, V., *Staat und Gesellschaft in Syrien: 1970–1989* (Hamburg: Deutsches Orient-Institut, 1990).
Petran, T., *Syria* (London: Ernest Benn Ltd, 1972).
St John Philby, H., *Sa'udi Arabia* (London: Ernest Benn Ltd, 1955).
Picard, E., *Liban: Etat de Discorde* (Mesnil Sur l'Estree: Flammarion, 1988).

Picard, E., *Espaces de Reference et Espace d'Intervention du Mouvement Rectificatif au Pouvoir en Syrie 1970–1982* (Paris: n.pb., n.d.).
Pipes, D., *Greater Syria: The History of an Ambition* (Oxford: Oxford University Press, 1990).
Prados, J., *Presidents' Secret Wars* (New York: William Morrow and Co., 1986).
Qubain, F.I., *Crisis in Lebanon* (Washington, DC: Middle East Institute, 1961).
Ra'anan, U., *The USSR Arms the Third World* (Cambridge, MA: MIT Press, 1969).
Rabbath, E., *La Formation Historique du Liban Politique et Constitutionnel* (Beirut: Librarie Orientale, 1986).
Rabinovich, I., *The Road Not Taken: Early Arab-Israeli Negotiations* (Oxford: Oxford University Press, 1991).
Randal, J., *The Tragedy of Lebanon: Christian Warlords, Israeli Adventurers and American Bunglers* (London: Chatto and Windus, 1983).
Raymond, A., ed., *La Syrie d'aujourd'hui* (Paris: Centre d'études et de recherches sur l'Orient arabe contemporain, 1980).
Rengger, N.J., *Treaties and Alliances of the World* (Harlow: Longman, 1990).
Richelson, J.T., *Foreign Intelligence Organizations* (Cambridge, MA: Ballinger Publishing Co, 1988).
Richelson, J.T., *The U.S. Intelligence Community* (Cambridge, MA: Ballinger Publishing Co, 1989).
Roberts, D., *The Ba'th and the Creation of Modern Syria* (London: Croom Helm, 1987).
Rubin, B., *The Great Powers in the Middle East, 1941–1947* (London: Frank Cass, 1980).
Salibi, K.S., *The Modern History of Lebanon* (London: Weidenfeld and Nicolson, 1965).
Salibi, K.S., *Crossroads to Civil War: Lebanon 1958–1976* (London: Ithaca Press, 1976).
'Abd el-Wahab Sayed-Ahmed, M., *Nasser and American Foreign Policy 1952–1956* (London: Laam, 1989).
Schmid, A., ed., *Political Terrorism: A New Guide to Actors, Authors, Concepts, Data Bases, Theories, & Literature* (Amsterdam: Transaction Books, 1988).
Seale, P., *The Struggle for Syria* (New Haven, CT: Yale University Press, 1986).
Seale, P., *Asad: The Struggle for the Middle East* (London: IB Tauris & Co, 1988).
Seurat, M., *L'État de Barbarie* (Paris: Editions du Seuil, 1989).
Shlaim, A., *Collusion Across the Jordan* (Oxford: Clarendon Press, 1988).
Shulsky, A.N., *Silent Warfare: Understanding the World of Intelligence* (Washington, DC: Brasseys, 1991).
Shwadran, B., *Jordan: A State of Tension* (New York: Council for Middle Eastern Affairs Press, 1959).
Shwadran, B., *The Middle East, Oil and the Great Powers* (New York: Council for Middle Eastern Affairs, 1959).
Sinai, A. and Pollack, A., eds, *The Hashemite Kingdom of Jordan and the West Bank* (New York: American Academic Association for Peace in the Middle East, 1977).
Snow, P., *Hussein: A Biography* (London: Barrie and Jenkins, 1972).
Syrian Social Nationalist Party Information Bureau, *Antoun Sa'adah: Leadership and Testimony* (n.p.: n.d.).
Tahir, A., *Iraq aux Origines du Régime Militaire* (Paris: Editions L'Harmattan, 1989).
Tibawi, A.L., *A Modern History of Syria* (London: Macmillan, 1969).
Torrey, G.H., *Syrian Politics and the Military 1945–1958* (Ohio: Ohio State University Press, 1964).

Treverton, G.F., *Covert Action: The Limits of Intervention in the Postwar World* (New York: Basic Books Inc, 1987).
Troeller, G., *The Birth of Saudi Arabia* (London: Frank Cass, 1976).
Vatikiotis, P.J., *Politics and the Military in Jordan* (London: Frank Cass, 1967).
Vatikiotis, P.J., *Conflict in the Middle East* (London: George Allen & Unwin Ltd, 1971).
Walzer, M., *Just and Unjust Wars* (Harmondsworth: Penguin Books, 1980).
Wheelock, K., *Nasser's New Egypt* (London: Stevens and Sons, 1960).
Wilkinson, P., *Political Terrorism* (London: Macmillan, 1974).
Wilkinson, P., *Terrorism and the Liberal State* (London: Macmillan, 1977).
Yamak, L.Z., *The Syrian Social Nationalist Party: An Ideological Analysis*, Harvard Middle Eastern Monographs XIV (Cambridge, MA: Center for Middle Eastern Affairs, Harvard University, 1966).
Zeine, Z.N., *The Struggle for Arab Independence* (Beirut: Khayats, 1960).

Monographs

Jenkins, B.M., *International Terrorism: A New Kind of Warfare* (RAND Corporation P-5261, 1974).
el-Khazen, F., *The Communal Pact of National Identities* (Oxford: Centre for Lebanese Studies, 1991).
The Principles and Aims of the Syrian Social Nationalist Party (Beirut: SSNP, 1949).
Wilkinson, P., *Terrorist Targets and Tactics: New Risks to World Order*, Conflict Studies No. 236 (London: Research Institute for the Study of Conflict and Terrorism, 1990).

Articles

al-Asad, H., 'Hafiz al-Asad: Terrorism and the anti-Syria campaign', *Journal of Palestine Studies*, Vol. XV, No. 4 (Summer 1986).
Ball, S., 'Bomber bases and British strategy in the Middle East, 1945–1949', *Journal of Strategic Studies*, Vol. 14, No. 4 (December 1991).
Blechmann, B., 'The impact of Israel's reprisals on behaviour of the bordering Arab nations', *Journal of Conflict Resolution*, Vol. XVI, No. 2 (June 1972).
Carleton, A., 'The Syrian coups d'état of 1949', *Middle East Journal*, Vol. 4, No.1 (1950).
Coady, C.A.J., 'The morality of terrorism', *Philosophy*, No. 60 (1985).
'Document sur les origines de la Ligue des États Arabes', *Orient*, 4e année, 2e trimestre, numéro 14 (1960).
Dovey, H.O., 'Security in Syria, 1941–45', *Intelligence and National Security*, Vol. 6, No. 2 (April 1991).
al-Durrah, M., '"Thawrat" al-Mawsil ba'd sab' sanawat (The Mosul "revolution" after seven years)', *Arab Studies*, No. 6 (April 1966).
Eilts, H.F., 'Ropes of sand: America's failure in the Middle East', *Middle East Journal*, Vol. 38, No. 2 (Spring 1984).
'Elections in the Lebanese Republic', *World Today*, Vol. 13, No. 6 (June 1957).
Gorst, A. and Lucas, W.S., 'The other collusion: Operation Straggle and Anglo-American intervention in Syria, 1955–56', *Intelligence and National Security*, Vol. 4, No. 3 (1989).
Gray, J.W.D., 'Abdin against the Wafd', *Middle East Forum*, Vol. XXXVIII, No. 2 (February 1962).

Hottinger, A., 'Zu'ama and parties in the Lebanese crisis of 1958', *Middle East Journal*, Vol. 15, No. 2 (Spring 1961).
Hourani, C.A., 'The Arab League in perspective', *Middle East Journal*, Vol. 1, No. 2 (April 1947).
Kaylani, N.M., 'The rise of the Syrian Ba'th, 1940–1958: political success, party failure', *International Journal of Middle East Studies*, Vol. 3, No. 1 (1972).
Khouri, F.J., 'Friction and conflict on the Israeli-Syrian front', *Middle East Journal*, Vol. 17, Nos 1 & 2 (1963).
Kirk, G., 'Cross currents within the Arab League: the Greater Syria plan', *World Today*, Vol. IV, No. 1 (January 1948).
Little, D., 'Cold War and covert action: the United States and Syria 1945–1958', *The Middle East Journal*, Vol. 44, No. 1 (1990).
Malik, C., 'The Near East: the search for truth', *Foreign Affairs*, Vol. 30, No. 2 (January 1952).
Manley, M.L., 'The Syrian constitution of 1953', *Middle East Journal*, Vol. 7, No. 4 (Autumn 1953).
Pipes, D., 'Terrorism: the Syrian connection', *The National Interest* (Spring 1989).
Pipes, D., 'Dealing with Middle Eastern conspiracy theories', *Orbis*, Vol. 36, No. 1 (Winter 1992).
Pritchett, D.T., 'The Syrian strategy on terrorism, 1971–1977', *Conflict Quarterly* (Summer 1988).
Rastier, J., 'A la recherche de socialism Syrien', *Orient*, 1re année, 4e trimestre, numéro 4 (1957).
Rondot, P., 'Tendances particularistes et tendances unitaires en Syrie', *Orient*, 2e année, 1er trimestre, numéro 5 (1958).
Roucek, J.S., 'Syria: a lesson in geopolitics', *Current History* (April 1952).
Salibi, K.S., 'Lebanon since the crisis of 1958', *World Today*, Vol. 17, No. 1 (January 1961).
Salibi, K.S., 'The Lebanese crisis in perspective', *World Today*, Vol. 14, No. 9 (September 1961).
Sanjian, A.K., 'The Sanjak of Alexandretta (Hatay): its impact on Turkish-Syrian relations (1939–1956)', *Middle East Journal*, Vol. 10, No. 4 (Autumn 1956).
Sayigh, Y., 'Reconstructing the paradox: the Arab Nationalist Movement, armed struggle and Palestine, 1951–1966', *Middle East Journal*, Vol. 45, No. 4 (Autumn 1991).
Schiff, Z., 'The dispute on the Syrian-Israeli border', *New Outlook* (February 1967).
Shlaim, A., 'Husni Za'im and the plan to resettle Palestinian refugees in Syria', *Journal of Palestine Studies*, Vol. XV, No. 4 (Summer 1986).
Weir, J., Bloch, J. and Fitzgerald, P., 'Sun sets over other empire', *The Middle East* (October 1981).

Index

'Abdallah ibn Husayn, King of Transjordan, 17, 23-4, 27-8, 31, 52, 55; relations with Shishakli, 64, 66; and Greater Syria plot, 67-9; assassination of, 78
'Abd al-Masih, Georges, 99-102
'Abd al-Nasser, Gamal, 19, 101, 104, 107, 112-5, 123; bid for leadership of Arab world, 91-2, 95; relations with USSR, 110, 136; and SSNP, 126; and King Sa'ud, 137; conflict with Qasim, 145, 153-6, 158; US attitude to, 147; assassination attempt on, 148; attitude to Iraqi revolt, 150; and Jordan, 135, 151, 153; and formation of UAR, 143-4; and Syria, 158-9; *see also* Egypt, United Arab Republic
'Abd al-Rahim, Yunis, 98-9, 101
'Abd ul-Ilah, Regent of Iraq, 12, 27, 55, 69; subversion of UAR by, 148; murder of, 149
Abu Assaf, Amin, 50, 88, 105
Abu Mansur, Fadlallah, 50-2, 127
Abu Nuwar, 'Ali, 132-3, 162
Acheson, Dean, 41, 56, 62, 72, 77
Adham, Burhan, 89, 120, 123, 136, 155
'Aflaq, Michel, 10, 59, 82, 84
al-Ahmad, Sulayman, 97
al-'Ajlani, 'Adil, 119
al-'Ajlani, Munir, 67, 69, 119, 162
Alabi, Bahjat, 70
Alexandretta, 8, 37-9
Algeria, 3
Alpha, Plan, 112-14
al-Amari, Subhi, 119
American plot (1957), 136-40 *passim*, 162; CIA role, 138-9; involvement of Ibrahim Husayni in, 139; involvement of Adib al-Shishakli in, 139; discovery of, 139-40

al-Amin, 'Abd al-Moutalib, 86-7
Amir, 'Abd al-Hakim, 158-9
Amir, 'Abd al-Kadir, 70-1
Anderson, Robert, 114
Anglo-Iranian Oil Company (AIOC), 18-9, 33, 41
Anglo-Persian Oil Company, *see* Anglo-Iranian Oil Company
Arab-American Oil Company (ARAMCO), 18, 108
Arab-Ba'th Socialist Party (ABSP), 91, 93-4, 97-8, 104-6, 131, 136-7; and campaign against Shishakli, 83-4; and Malki assassination, 102; bombing of office, 126; and formation of UAR, 142-4; in Iraq, 154-5, 157; in UAR, 158; *see also* Ba'th Party, Arab Socialist Party
Arab League, 23, 27, 63, 65, 96, 142; formation of, 13
Arab Legion, 16, 27, 33, 67, 131
Arab Liberation Movement (ALM), 81, 93, 117
Arab National Movement (ANM), 70
Arab Socialist Party (ASP), 10, 62, 75, 81-2; *see also* Arab-Ba'th Socialist Party
Arab Suicide Redemption Phalange, 69-70, 72; and Deuxième Bureau, 71-2; *see also* Kata'ib al-Fida' al-'Arabi
al-Ard, Midhat Shaydah, 70
al-Ard, Nasha't Shaykh, 70
'Arif, 'Abd al-Salam, 153
armistice talks, Rhodes, 25, 27, 38-41
Arslan, 'Adil, 29, 35, 39
al-Asad, Hafiz, 98
al-'Asali, Faysal, 66
al-'Asali, Sabri, 99, 105, 124, 143-4; and formation of National Party, 9; leadership of National Party by,

INDEX

55–6; imprisonment by Shishakli, 84; becomes Prime Minister, 92–3, 97, 116–17, 125
Aswan Dam, 115
al-Atasi, 'Adnan, 84, 95, 120
al-Atasi, Faydi, 76
al-Atasi, Faysal, 88
al-Atasi, Hashim, 76, 78, 96–7, 105, 120; becomes Prime Minister, 55; becomes President, 58, 66, 92; and campaign against Shishakli, 83–4, 87–90, and Hinnawi coup, 176 n16
Atoms for Peace, 116
al-Atrash, Hamad, 51
al-Atrash, Hasan, 27, 52, 84, 120–1, 123
al-Atrash, Mansur, 85
al-Atrash, Muhammad, 88
al-Atrash, Sultan Pasha, 83, 85–6
Attlee, Clement, 15
Awadallah, Tu'mah, 93
al-Ayubi, 'Ali Jawdat, 142
al-'Azm, Khalid, 26, 30; as Prime Minister, 24, 33, 36, 39–40, 43, 63–5, 75; as Foreign Minister, 97; as leader of leftist current in Syria, 104, 124–6; as presidential candidate, 105–6; as Defence Minister, 136; visits Moscow, 137; and formation of UAR, 142–4
Azzam Pasha, 27

Baghdad Pact, 20, 92, 96–7, 100, 148; formation of, 94; American support for, 115; Jordan and, 131
Baghdad Radio, 154
al-Banna, Hasan, 11
Bannud, Anwar, 62–3, 66, 68, 96
Baqdash, Khalid, 10, 37, 144
al-Barazi, Husni, 29, 95, 105, 122
al-Barazi, Muhsin, 30–1, 43–4, 47, 49, 50, 72; execution of, 50–1, 58, 83, 164
Barudi, Fakri, 181 n132
Barmada, Mustafa, 9
Barmada, Rashad, 109
Bashayan, Foreign Minister of Turkey, 107, 120
Ba'th Party, 4–5, 10, 24, 62, 75, 81–3; see also Arab-Ba'th Socialist Party
Bayar, Celal, 128
Ben Gurion, David, 39, 113

Bevin, Ernest, 31, 57
Bitar, Salah al-Din, 10, 82, 84, 138, 143, 158
al-Bizri, 'Afif, 140, 143–4
al-Bizri, Salah, 60, 63, 72
Bourse Egyptienne, La, 54
Brazil, 45
British Council, 150
Broadmead, Philip Mainwaring, 25, 31–2
Bulgaria, 142
Buraimi Oasis, 115
Burrows, Bernard, 31

Carleton, Alfred, 26
Caroz, Yakov, 145
Cassin, Vernon, 139
Central Intelligence Agency (CIA), 2, 22, 165, 168; and Za'im, 39–42, 44; and propaganda, 96; involvement in Iraqi Plot, 111–13, 116, 118, 120; covert action in Syria, 127–8; and Lebanon, 129; involvement in American plot, 138–9; and Nasser, 147; see also Allen Dulles
Chamoun, Camille, 45–6, 49, 126, 128–9, 131
Chehab, Farid, 48
Chehab, Fu'ad, 109, 128–9
Christian Science Monitor, 52
Churchill, Winston, 18
Close, Arthur, 139–40
Cold War, 2, 11–12, 62, 92
Combat, 30, 52
Communist Party, of Syria, 10–11, 37–9, 41–2, 59–60, 62, 91, 136, 165; opposition to Western defence plans, 75; involvement in campaign against Shishakli, 84; attacks on by SSNP, 126–7; and formation of UAR, 143–4; attacks on by Nasser, 156; of Jordan, 135; of Iraq, 153–4, 156; of Lebanon, 157; see also Partisans of Peace
conspiracy theories, 1–2, 22, 35, 167–8; and Za'im coup, 25–6, 59
Copeland, Miles, 36–8, 42–4, 150
covert action, 1, 3, 5, 22, 26; see also American plot, CIA, Iraqi plot, SIS, SDECE, intelligence agencies and under individual country headings

Daghistani, Ghazi, 119–20
Daghistani, Talib, 105
al-Dahi, Guéhad, 70–1
Dandash, tribe, 47–9, 109
Dayri, Akram, 201 n32
al-Dawilibi, Ma'ruf, 64, 76–7, 78, 83, 93
al-Dawilibi, Mustafa, 83
Dayan, Moshe, 86
Department of General Security (Syria), 140
al-Dessuki, Adib, 134
Deuxième Bureau, 7, 12, 57, 63, 66, 83, 91, 98; and Israeli spy, 46; and communists, 60; and Kallas-'Ajlani plot, 67–9; and Arab Suicide Redemption Phalange, 71–2; strengthened by Shishakli, 78–9; and interrogation, 81; and overthrow of Shishakli, 85, 88; and propaganda, 105, 110; and battle with SSNP, 108–9, 126–8; Internal Affairs section of, 123; subversion of Lebanon by, 128–31; Palestinian unit of, 130; subversion of Jordan by, 134; Soviet aid to, 137; and CIA, 139; extension of domestic influence, 140; reorganisation of during the UAR, 146, 159; *see also* American plot, covert action, intelligence agencies, Iraqi plot
Druze, Jabal, *see* Jabal Druze
Dubussy, 'Abd al-Mun'im, 98–100
Dulles, Allen, 113–14, 118, 122, 138; attitude to Nasser, 147
Dulles, John Foster, 79–80, 113–6, 122, 138, 140–3, 165; attitude to Nasser, 147; attitude to Jordan, 151

Eddé, Emile, 45
Eden, Anthony, 113–4
Egypt, 13, 16, 25, 31, 43, 55–6; relations with Za'im, 26–30, 39, 41; relations with Shishakli, 61–3, 83; and Arab Suicide Redemption Phalange, 71–2; relations with Britain, 74; relations with Syria, 93, 106, 117; opposition to Baghdad Pact, 96–7; Soviet arms deal, 110; radio propaganda by, 87, 131; subversion of Lebanon by, 129, 131; subversion of Jordan by, 131, 133, 135, 149–50; subversion of Sa'udi Arabia by, 133; arms supplies to Syria, 137; relations with Iraq, 153; intelligence services, 145, 147, 159; Directorate of Military Intelligence, 128, 145–6; Directorate of General Investigations, 146; Directorate of General Intelligence, 146; *see also* radio stations
Egypt-Syria-Sa'udi Pact (ESS), 97, 106, 129
Eisenhower Doctrine, 125, 136; and Lebanon, 125, 128; and Jordan, 125; and Iraq, 125; and Sa'udi Arabia, 125
Eisenhower, Dwight D., 79, 114–16, 122, 125, 165; *see also* Eisenhower Doctrine
elections, to Syrian parliament (1947), 23; for Syrian presidency (1948), 24; Syrian referendum (1949), 29–30, 47; to Syrian parliament (1949), 57–8; Syrian plebiscite (1953), 82; to Syrian parliament (1953), 82; to Syrian parliament (1954), 93–4, 161; to Syrian presidency (1955), 103, 105, 108, 161, 164; to Lebanese parliament (1957), 128–30, 137, 161; Syrian by-elections (1957), 136; to Syrian parliament (planned for 1958), 143
Eveland, Wilbur Crane, 112, 120, 150

al-Fadil, Muhammad, 119
al-Faiha', 86
Fansah, Nadhir, 50, 95–6, 105, 111, 161
Faruq, King of Egypt, 28, 30, 52, 71; and Antun Sa'adah, 49–50
Faysal II, King of Iraq, 12, 59; murder of, 149
Faysal ibn Abdulaziz, Crown Prince and King of Saudi Arabia, 148
Faysal ibn Husayn, King of Syria and Iraq, 7–8, 12
Fedayeen, 131
Fertile Crescent, 9, 12–13, 19, 54, 104; British attitude to, 31–2, 34; loss of interest in, 77
France, 8, 25, 31, 123; as mandatory power, 8–9, 12; interests in Middle East, 19, 92; arms supply to Syria, 19; relations with Britain, 19; and

INDEX

Za'im, 24, 40, 44; financial agreement with Syria, 24–5; and Shishakli, 60, 84, 90; covert action in Syria, 56, 94, 96, 103; opposition to Syrian leftists, 137; *see also* Service de Documentation Extérieure et de Contre-Espionage
Franc-Tireur, 52
Free Iraqis Organisation, 157

Game of Nations, The, 42
Game Player, The, 42
al-Gaylani, Rashid 'Ali, 70, 154
Gemayel, Pierre, 46; *see also* Kata'ib
gendarmerie, in Syria, 65, 76, 79, 93
General Command of the Free Syria Forces, 83–4
al-Ghazzi, Sa'id, 93, 107, 116–17
Glubb, John Bagot, 32, 90, 113
Great Britain, 5, 8–9, 13, 25, 62–3; interests in Middle East, 15–18, 73–4, 92, 95, 104; relations with France, 19; and Za'im, 30–1, 40, 44; and Hinnawi, 52–3, 55; and Shishakli, 77, 86; relations with Syria, 107–8, 110, 112–14, 123; relations with Jordan, 131–3, 151–2; attitude to UAR, 147; and covert action/intelligence, 5; *see also* Secret Intelligence Service, Iraqi plot
Greater Syria, 10, 12, 19, 30–2, British attitude to, 34; and King 'Abdallah, 23, 27, 55–6, 64, 66–7; Greater Syria plot, 62, 64, 68; loss of interest in, 77–8; conspiracy leading to Republic of, 133
Gromyko, Andrei, 142

Habash, Georges, 70
al-Haffar, Lutfi, 9, 105, 116
al-Hakim, 'Adnan, 46; *see also* Najjada
al-Hakim, Hasan, 66–8, 75–6, 83, 95, 108
al-Hakim, Husayn, 119
al-Hakim, Nuri, 68
Hamdun, 'Adnan, 102
Hamdun, Mustafa, 88, 93, 117, 158
Al-Hamishmar, 85
Hammad, Jamal, 93
Hare, Raymond, 144, 147
Harmar, V. D'Oyly, 31–2
Hashim, Ibrahim, 133

Hatay, *see* Alexandretta
al-Hawrani, Akram, 10, 52, 59, 69, 76, 97, 136; involvement in overthrow of Shishakli, 81–4, 88; influence in parliament, 94; support for union with Egypt, 117; leader of leftist current in Syria, 124–5; concern at communist influence, 142–3; resignation of, 158
Heikal, Muhammad, 49
Henderson, Loy, 141
Herut party, 85
Hiddi, Husayn, 89
al-Hindi, Hani, 70–1
al-Hindi, Muhammad, 28
al-Hinnawi, Sami, 22, 30, 58–60, 62–3, 83, 97; coup (1949), 50–4, 119, 162, 164; assassination of, 72
Hiyari, 'Ali, 132–3
Homsi, Edmond, 95
Houstoun-Boswell, William Evelyn, 27, 32, 34
Hrant, Colonel, 50
al-Hubbi, Sa'id, 68, 96, 105
L'Humanité, 59
Husayn, Sharif, 7, 13
al-Husayni, Hajj Amin, 28
al-Husayni, Ibrahim, 82, 84, 95, 122; and Sa'adah affair, 48, 50; as head of Deuxième Bureau, 63, 66, 68–9, 72; and American plot, 139–40; and Turkey, 142
al-Husayni, 'Isam, 203 n72
Hussein, King of Jordan, 85, 113, 125, 131, 134–5; and Zerqa incident, 132–3; assassination attempt, 133; and Arab Union, 149; and UAR, 150–1; and MiG incident, 152; *see also* Jordan

Ibrahim, Shaykh Asad, 148
Ilyan, Mikhail, 117, 119, 127–8, 148
intelligence (and security) agencies, 2, 160; of Syria, 4, 6, 42, 48, 125–6, 145, 163; of Syria, under UAR, 146, 154, 158–9; of Syria, activities in Lebanon, 129–31, 136; of Syria, activities in Jordan, 131–3, 135–6, 149–50; of Syria, activities in Iraq, 154–5; of Egypt, 28, 67, 72; of Jordan, 133; *see also* American plot, CIA, covert action, Department of

General Security, Deuxième Bureau, Gendarmerie, Iraqi plot, military intelligence, Mossad, SIS, SDECE, Special Bureau, Sûreté Générale, and under individual country headings
Intelligence services, *see* intelligence agencies
Iran, 2, 20, 139
Iraq, 5, 13, 16, 39, 55; relations with Syria, 97, 104–5, 111, 114; relations with Za'im, 27–9, 33; relations with Shishakli, 59–60, 64, 77; sponsorship of covert action against Shishakli, 63, 83, 85–7, 90; revolts of Rashid 'Ali al-Gaylani, 70, 154; encouragement of Syrian unionists, 93, 107–8; intelligence service of, 107–8, 119, 121; relations with Jordan, 132; and US aid, 141; and opposition to Syrian leftists, 141; attitude to UAR, 147; relations with UAR, 148, 153–5; and Arab Union, 149; revolution in (1958), 145, 149, 151; *see also* Iraqi plot, Qasim, Mosul revolt
Iraqi plot, 111–24, 126–7, 140, 164; and Operation Straggle, 112–13, 118, 122; British role in, 112–3, 116, 118, 121; American role in, 113–14, 116–8, 120–2; Iraqi role in, 114, 118–22; SSNP role in 114, 120–3; Turkey and, 121–2; propaganda in, 121
Iraq Petroleum Company (IPC), 18, 78, 107, 111, 186 n240; sabotage of pipeline, 123–4, 138
Islamic Socialist Front, 11, 75
Israel, 29, 37, 64, 73, 141, 165; Demilitarised Zones with Syria, 14; border clashes with Syria, 14–5, 75, 91–2, 106, 110; and SSNP, 49; relations with Syria, 5, 19, 39–41, 85–6; intelligence service of, 2; invasion of Sinai by, 122; reprisal raids by, 131; relations with Jordan, 132; *see also* Mossad
Israeli Defence Forces (IDF), 14, 110

Jabal Druze, 8, 23, 51; role in overthrow of Shishakli, 85–6, 89; role in Iraqi plot, 121, 123

Jabara, Hasan, 33, 41
Jabr, Salih, 16
Jadid, Fu'ad, 99
Jadid, Ghassan, 77, 94, 97, 99–100, 120–1; assassination of, 127
al-Jamali, Fadhil, 54, 84, 86–7, 105, 108
Jamayzah incident, 46–7
Jarrah, Muhammad, 216 n8
Jeton, Frank, 139–40
al-Jihad, 149
Johnston, Charles, 133–4
Johnston, Eric, 80
Jordan, 5, 12–13, 17, 25, 28, 55; and Greater Syria plot, 62, 64, 68; relations with Shishakli, 83, 85; relations with Syria, 126, 141; relations with Britain, 132; relations with USA, 113, 116, 132, 141; Zerqa incident, 132; attitude to UAR, 147; relations with UAR, 145, 159; and Arab Union, 149; subversion of by UAR, 145–6, 149, 150–1; security services of, 150–2; *see also* King Hussein
Jordan Development Board, 150
Juma', Sami, 191 n63, 203 n72
Junblatt, Kamal, 130, 145

Kabbara, Sami, 119, 122
al-Kallas, Bahij, 67–9, 162, 176 n16
Karam, 'Assaf, 48
Karamah, 'Abd al-Hamid, 46, 49
Karamah, Rashid, 109
Kassab-Hassan, Bourhan, 102
Kata'ib, 46–7
Kata'ib al-Fida' al-'Arabi, 190 n45; *see also* Arab Suicide Redemption Phalange
Kayyali, Ghaleb, 127
Keeley, Minister, 36, 40, 43–4
Khalil, Hasan, 128
Khan, Umar Tamir, 88
Khruschev, Nikita, 142, 157
al-Khuri, Bechara, 45–6, 129, 183 n169
al-Khuri, Faris, 9, 96–7
Khuri, Sami, 99
Kikhia, Rushdi, 9, 60, 63, 77, 83–4, 105
Kirkbride, Alec, 29, 68, 78
Kobecsy, 'Abdallah, 100
Kurds, 43
Kuwait, 159

INDEX

Kuzbari, Ma'mun, 89–90

Latakia, 8; Egyptian troop landings at, 142, 221 n91
Lavon, Pinchas, 86
Lebanon, 5, 10, 12–13, 25, 28; relations with Za'im, 41, 45; security services of, 39, 45–8, 128–30; and Sa'adah affair, 44; National Pact, 45; economic agreements with Syria, 50, 65; relations with Shishakli, 83; Western aid to, 116; subversion of by Syria, 128–31, 145–6; elections in (1957), 128–30; relations with UAR, 147
Lloyd, Selwyn, 113–14, 118, 131, 134, 136, 141

Mack, Ambassador, 32
Macmillan, Harold, 141
Madfai, Jamil, 83
al-Mahaiyri, 'Isam, 47, 100, 108
Mahdawi, President of Iraqi court (1959), 156
al-Majali, Hazza, 85
Makhluf, Badi', 98–101
Malik, Charles, 100, 109, 128, 131, 134, 141
al-Malki, 'Adnan, 51, 82, 89, 93, 97; assassination of, 92, 98–101, 103, 105, 109, 120, 164
Malki, Kamal, 88
Mapam party, 85
Mardam, Jamil, 9, 23–6, 37–9, 55
Maruf, Muhammad, 97, 119–20, 127
McNeil, Hector, 23
McGhee, George, 37, 73, 75
Meade, Stephen, 36–7, 41–4, 46
Menderes, Prime Minister of Turkey, 113, 137–8, 141
Middle East Airlines, 152
Middle East Command (MEC), 73–4, 76
Middle East Defence Organisation (MEDO), 79, 95
Middle East Journal, 112
Middle East Pipeline Ltd (MEPL), 24, 31, 33–4, 41, 53, 186 n240; establishment of, 18
Military Intelligence, 140; see also Egypt
al-Mir, Juliette, 99

Molloy, Robert, 140
Monde, Le, 52–3
Moose, James, 79
Morocco, 77
Mossad, 145
Mosul Revolt (1959), 154–6, 162
Mraywad, 'Isam, 50–1, 83, 90
Muslim Brotherhood, 11, 24, 64, 81, 91, 134

Nabulsi, Sulayman, 131–4
Nafuri, Colonel, 117, 144
al-Nahhas, Mustafa, 13
Nahlawi, 'Abd al-Karim, 159
Nahmah, Muhammad, 127
Najjada party, 46
al-Nas, 105
Nasir, Muhammad, 65–6, 68, 70, 72, 88
Nasir, Sharif, 135
National Bloc, 8–9
National Pact, in Syria (1953), 82, 84
National Party, 29, 58, 91–2, 97, 106, 125, 144; formation of, 9; in government, 23; advocates union with Iraq, 55–6; and Shishakli, 62, 64, 66, 81; rivalry within, 117
National Security Council (NSC), 79, 127
Near East Development Corporation (NEDC), 18
Neguib, President, 80, 86, 95, 147
Neue Züricher Zeitung, 53
al-Nimr, 'Abd al-Halim, 132
Nizam al-Din, Tawfiq, 117, 136, 140
Nuri Pasha, see Nuri al-Sa'id
North Atlantic Treaty Organisation (NATO), 106, 136–7, 141

oil industry, 18; see also Arab-American Oil Company, Iraq Petroleum Company, Middle East Pipeline Ltd, Near East Development Corporation, Tapline
Operations Coordinating Board (OCB), 104, 114, 116
Ottomans, the, 7–8

Palestine, 12–14
Palestine Conflict (1948), 23–4, 26; see also Rhodes armistice talks
Parti Populaire Syrien, see Syrian Social Nationalist Party

Partisans of Peace, 154, 156; *see also* Communist Party
People's Party, 24, 29, 56, 62–3, 76, 91–2, 106, 125; formation of, 9; orchestrates disturbances, 24; in government, 55, 65–6; and Shishakli, 81, 83;
Phalange, *see Kata'ib*
Point IV aid, 74–5
PPS, *see* Syrian Social Nationalist Party
Pravda, 30
propaganda, 3, 136, 161; by Britain, 65, 112; by USSR, 30; in Iraqi plot, 121; British and American cooperation regarding, 115, 143; by Syria, 134, 159; by Egypt, 134; by USA, 142; by Jordan, 143, 151; by UAR, 150, 154, 157–8; *see also* radio stations

Qannut, 'Abd al-Ghani, 66
Qasim, 'Abd al-Karim, 145, 155; conflict with Nasser, 153–8; claim on Kuwait, 159
al-Qudsi, Nazim, 59, 77, 105; and formation of People's Party, 9; as Foreign Minister, 55–6; as Prime Minister, 66–7, 69–70, 72, 75
al-Quwatli, Shukri, 8–9, 23–7, 37, 58, 96, 116; as President, 40, 43, 45, 106–7, 136; in Egypt, 55–6; and Shishakli, 63, 69– 71; and USSR, 110, 118, 122; and Zerqa incident, 133; struggle against communists, 144

radio stations, 161; in Aleppo, 88–9; in Amman, 134, 151; in Baghdad, 154; in Cairo, 87, 116, 135; in Damascus, 28, 90, 134–5; in Israel, 30, 67, 85–6; in Jordan, 151; in Moscow, 36, 116; in Mosul, 154–5; in UAR, 154; Jordanian People's Radio, 150; *see also* propaganda, *Sharq al-Adna Ra'i al-'Am*, 105
Rashid, Nazir, 132
Raslan, Jawwad, 88, 117
al-Rawi, 'Abd al-Jalil, 95, 117
Riad, Mahmud, 102, 117
Rifa'i, Mahmud, 60, 72, 83, 90, 97
Rifa'i, Nur al-Din, 48
Rifa'i, Samir, 133, 141, 151

al-Rikabi, Fu'ad, 157
al-Rimawi, 'Abdallah, 131
Robertson, Brian, 75
Roosevelt, Archie, 127
Roosevelt, Franklin D., 18
Roosevelt, Kermit, 139
Rountree, William, 142–3
Royal Air Force (RAF), 132
Russia, *see* Union of Soviet Socialist Republics
Ruwayha, Amin, 70–1

Sa'adah, Antun, 10, 12, 44–9 *passim*, 162; execution of, 48, 50
Sa'adah affair, 22, 44–7, 49, 164
Sadat, Anwar, 86
Safa, Muhammad, 83–6, 90, 93, 97, 119, 162
Safadi, Akram, 130
Sa'id, Jalal, 119
al-Sa'id, Nuri, 12–3, 27, 29, 32, 34, 96, 111; and Hinnawi coup, 69; 54–5; and Shishakli, 77; as Defence Minister, 83; opposition to Syrian leftists, 107–8, 113, 119, 141, 143; and Jordan, 132; murder of, 149
Salam, Sa'ib, 128, 30
al-Samarra'i, Salih Mahdi, 87, 120, 123, 127, 144
Sarraj, 'Abd al-Hamid, 97, 105, 117, 125–6, 136, 163; takes over Deuxième Bureau, 98; as Military Attaché in Paris, 93; and SSNP, 102–3, 110, 144; and Iraqi Plot, 123; and Jordan, 132; and American plot, 139–40; power struggle with Bizri, 143–4; during UAR, 146, 158–9; and Sa'udi plot, 148–9; and Qasim, 154–5, 157–8; attitude to USA, 199 n206
Sa'ud, Ibn, King of Sa'udi Arabia, 23, 27, 30, 70–1
Sa'ud, King, of Sa'udi Arabia, 92, 115, 129, 137, 141–3; and Sa'udi Plot, 148
Sa'udi Arabia, 23, 161–2; and Za'im, 26–30; and Shishakli, 59– 64, 83, 90; and Arab Suicide Redemption Phalange, 70–2; opposition to Syro-Iraqi union, 93, 106, 108; opposition to Baghdad Pact, 96–7; relations with Syria, 113, 115,

117–8; relations with Jordan, 132; aid to Syrian factions, 137, 141; US aid to, 141; and Turkish crisis, 142; and UAR, 147, 159; and Sa'udi plot, 148–9
Secret Intelligence Service (SIS), 3, 111, 113, 116, 118, 168; *see also* Iraqi Plot
security services, *see* intelligence agencies
Selu, Fawzi, 76, 79, 83
Serov, General, 140
Service de Documentation Extérieure et de Contre-Espionage (SDECE), 3, 36; *see also* France
Sha'lan, Fawwaz, 70
Shammar tribe, 154
al-Shanqiti, Muhammad Amin, 67–8
al-Sharabati, Ahmad, 24, 70–1
Sharabi, Hisham, 99–100
Sharett, Moshe, 85–6
Sharq al-Adna radio station, 47
Sh'ath, Izzat, 127
Shawi, Iskander, 99, 101
Shawkat, Mahmud, 94–5, 105
Shawwaf, 'Abd al-Wahab, 154–6, 162
Shehadi, 'Abd al-Haq, 89
al-Shishakli, Adib, 48, 62–3, 65, 75, 93, 161–2; 1949 coup by, 22, 58–61; 1951 coup by, 73, 76–85, 162; overthrow of (1954), 87–91; involvement in Iraqi plot, 111, 119–20; involvement in American plot, 139; attitude to Israel, 173 n37; assassination of, 199 n205
al-Shishakli, Salah, 119
Shuqayr, Shawkat, 68, 92–4, 96–100, 104–6, 110–11; and Za'im, 35; and Shishakli, 89–90; resignation of, 117
al-Siba'i, Mustafa, 11
Sixth Fleet, 132
Socialist Cooperative Party, 66
Soviet Union, *see* Union of Soviet Socialist Republics
Special Bureau, of Syrian intelligence, 146
Srur, Hayil, 123
Stalin, Josef, 19–20
Stirling, Colonel W.F., 57, 69–72
Stone, Howard, 139–40
Straggle, Operation, *see* Iraqi plot
Strang, William, 32, 34

Strong, Robert, 136, 142–4
Sudan, 16, 74
Suez Crisis, 5, 19, 112, 122–3, 125, 131, 138
al-Sulh, Rashid, 47
al-Sulh, Riyad, 29, 35, 44–9, 101, 108
al-Sulh, Sami, 128–9
Sûreté Générale, in Syria, 38–9, 48, 60, 78–9
Syrian Social Nationalist Party (SSNP), 5, 62, 91, 94, 108, 125, 162, 168; formation of, 10; and Sa'adah affair, 44–50; and execution of Za'im, 51–2; and Shishakli, 81–2; and Malki assassination, 97–103; involvement in Iraqi plot, 114, 119–23; covert battle with Deuxième Bureau, 109–110, 126–8, 149; cooperation with Jordan, 134; Turkish attitude to, 137; cooperation with USA, 138; overture from Sarraj, 144

Tabbarah, Captain, 46
Talal bin 'Abdallah, King of Jordan, 78
Talhuni, Bahjut, 132–3
Tallas, As'ad, 51, 54–5, 58–9, 83, 105
Tapline, 32, 36–41, 59–60, 99, 161, 186 n240; establishment of, 18; and 'Azm's government, 24, 30, 39–40
Taqi al-Din, Sa'id, 103, 119–20
Tawfiq, Husayn, 69–70
terrorism, 1–6, 162, 166–7; state-sponsored, 3, 5; state-supported, 3; in Syria, 69–72; between Deuxième Bureau and SSNP, 126–8; by Syria, 129–30, 133; by Egypt, 133; by UAR, 145, 150; *see also* Covert action, Deuxième Bureau, intelligence agencies, SSNP, under individual country headings
Thabit, Ayad Sa'id, 157
Tlass, Mustafa, 98, 102
Transjordan, *see* Jordan
Tripartite Declaration, 64, 78, 80
Troupes Spéciales, 8, 36
Truman, Harry S., 16–7, 37–8, 54, 74
Turkey, 7–8, 16, 29, 37–9; relations with Syria, 95, 97, 114, 121–2; relations with Lebanon, 128; opposition to Syrian regime, 137–8, 141–2; military pressure on Syria,

142–3, 148; attitude to UAR; *see also* Alexandretta, Syrian Social Nationalist Party

United Arab Republic (UAR), 4, 126, 145; formation of 143–4; effect inside Syria, 145–6, 158; foreign attitudes to, 147–8; subversive activites of, 149; relations with Jordan, 150–3; relations with Iraq, 154–7; break up of, 159; *see also* covert action, intelligence agencies, Mosul Revolt, Terrorism, and under individual country headings

United Nations (UN), 11–2, 38, 152

United Nations General Assembly, 142

United Nations Relief and Works Agency (UNRWA), 69, 80, 150

United Nations Security Council, 122

United Nations Truce Supervision Organisation (UNTSO), 14

United States of America (USA)/US/America, 4, 16–17, 25; interests in Middle East, 17, 73–4, 79, 92, 95, 104–5; covert action by, 5, 125; relations with Syria, 106, 108, 110–11; relations with Za'im, 30, 36–7, 38–44; and SSNP, 49, 100; and Shishakli, 59–60, 77, 80, 62–3, 72, 75–6; propaganda by, 96; opposition to Syrian leftists, 136, 138, 140–1; relations with Jordan, 132, 151; attitude to UAR, 147; *see also* Central Intelligence Agency, covert action, American plot

United States Information Service (USIS), 99, 130, 135, 142, 150, 161

Union of Soviet Socialist Republics (USSR)/Soviet Union/Soviets, 11, 29, 38, 62; interests in Middle East, 19–20, 92; propaganda by, 30, 52, 96; arms deal with Egypt, 110; arms deal with Syria, 110–11, 136–7, 164; relations with Syria, 65, 104, 114–15; influence in Syria, 138, 142; aid to Syrian intelligence, 137, 140; relations with Jordan, 132; relations with Iraq, 145;

al-Ustuwani, Ibrahim, 87

Wahhab, Shakib, 123
Wappen, Operation, 214 n93; *see also* American plot
White, Dick, 113

Yafi, 'Abdallah, 128, 130
Yemen, 13
Yorkshire Post, 53
Young, George, 116

al-Za'im, Husni, 11, 22, 45, 55, 58, 72, 78; coup by (1949), 25–7, 32, 162, 165; relations with Arab states, 28–30, 46; relations with France, 35–6; relations with Britain, 33–5; relations with USA, 36–9; relations with Turkey, 39; relations with Israel, 39; and SSNP, 44–50; execution of, 50–1, 71, 83, 164

Zein, Queen, 134
Ziub, Aziz, 127
Zouain, Simone, 109–10

www.ingramcontent.com/pod-product-compliance
Lightning Source LLC
Chambersburg PA
CBHW061439300426
44114CB00014B/1745